# Dollars Deficits & Trade

*A Cato Institute book*

# Dollars Deficits & Trade

edited by

**James A. Dorn**

and

**William A. Niskanen**

Springer-Science+Business Media, B.V

Distributors

for the United States and Canada: Kluwer Academic Publishers, 101
Philip Drive, Assinippi Park, Norwell, MA, 02061, USA

for all other countries: Kluwer Academic Publishers Group,
Distribution Centre, P.O. Box 322, 3300 AH Dordrecht, The
Netherlands

**Library of Congress Cataloging-in-Publication Data**

Dollars, deficits & trade / edited by James A. Dorn and William
A. Niskanen.
p. cm.
"Many of the essays ... were initially presented at the Cato
Institute's Sixth Annual Monetary Conference held in
Washington, D.C., February 25-26, 1988"—Pref.
"A Cato Institute book."
ISBN 978-94-017-1290-3 ISBN 978-94-017-1288-0 (eBook)
DOI 10.1007/978-94-017-1288-0
1. Monetary policy—Congresses. 2. Balance of trade—
Congresses. 3. Foreign exchange—Congresses. I. Dorn, James
A. II. Niskanen, William A., 1933- . III. Monetary Conference
(Cato Institute) (6th : 1988 : Washington, D.C.) IV. Title: Dollars,
deficits, and trade.
HG230.3.D65 1989
332.4—dc20 89-37481
CIP



*Cover design: Kent Lytle*

# CONTENTS

# Editors' Preface

The essays in this volume are timely and provocative. They address the key issues of the changing world economy and consider the implications of the erosion of the rule of law that has occurred both domestically and internationally to an increasing degree over the past half century.

The debates over the role of the dollar in the international economy, the future shape of the international monetary system and the exchange rate regime, the significance of the U.S. twin deficits, and the rise of nontariff barriers to world trade deserve serious attention. At the bottom of these debates lie differing conceptions of economic policy and the role of government in a free society. Adam Smith's vision of a limited democracy operating to protect persons and property has been increasingly replaced by a vision of a paternalistic state that is designed to protect special interests at the expense of the larger society. Many of the contributors to this volume point to the lack of long-run rules designed to promote sound money, fiscal integrity, and open markets as the fundamental flaw of modern democratic governments. Although the authors disagree on the specific rules to adopt, the consensus is that a constitutional perspective is needed to ensure a stable world order. Moreover, since such a perspective must be developed at home before it can spread among nations, the search for optimal international policy coordination is generally seen as misguided.

Many of the essays in this volume were initially presented at the Cato Institute's Sixth Annual Monetary Conference held in Washington, D.C., February 25–26, 1988. Grants from the Chicago Mercantile Exchange, the John M. Olin Foundation, and Sears, Roebuck & Co. supported the conference and are gratefully acknowledged. A major grant from the Lynde and Harry Bradley Foundation both supported the conference and greatly contributed to the preparation of this book, for which we are especially grateful. The editors also wish to thank Edward H. Crane for his encouragement throughout the many stages in this endeavor and Barbara Hart for the excellent job she did in copyediting and proofreading many of the essays. Finally, Jim Dorn gratefully acknowledges research support from Towson State University in the form of a sabbatical that facilitated the completion of this volume.

# Dollars Deficits & Trade

# 1

# INTRODUCTION

## THE CHANGING WORLD ECONOMY*

*James A. Dorn*

Where an open communication is preserved among nations, it is impossible but the domestic industry of every one must receive an increase from the improvements of the others. . . . Nature, by giving a diversity of geniuses, climates, and soils, to different nations, has secured their mutual intercourse and commerce, as long as they all remain industrious and civilized.

—David Hume[1]

## Key Issues in the World Economy

The world economy has undergone significant changes since the collapse of Bretton Woods in August 1971. We are now living in a pure fiat money world, a world in which the purchasing power of national currencies depends primarily on the discretion of central bankers and ultimately on the politicians they serve. Other characteristics of the post–Bretton Woods landscape include floating exchange rates for the dollar and other key currencies; wide swings in the foreign exchange value of the dollar; persistent U.S. budget and trade deficits; growing economic interdependence among nations due in part to the information revolution and the globalization of financial markets; and a rebirth of protectionist policies, especially in the form of nontariff barriers that distort the international price system.

The lack of any anchor for the dollar under the current international monetary system, or "nonsystem" as it is sometimes called, places heavy responsibility on the Federal Reserve to preserve the value of the dollar. Credible U.S. monetary policy, prudent fiscal policy, and

---

*This introduction is an enlarged and revised version of Dorn (1988).

The author is Editor of the *Cato Journal* and Professor of Economics at Towson State University. He is also a Research Fellow of the Institute for Humane Studies at George Mason University.

[1]Hume ([1777] 1985, pp. 328–29).

a firm commitment to open markets are essential to international economic stability. The volatility and unpredictibility of both the domestic and foreign exchange value of the dollar are due in large part to the failure of U.S. policymakers to adhere to a long-run goal of price stability, to limit government spending and borrowing, and to abolish trade restrictions. While it is true that inflation has been reduced significantly since the early 1980s, there is still much uncertainty about the future price level in the absence of any constitutional limit on the monetary powers of government. Likewise, the large and persistent federal budget deficits and the rapid increase in federal debt appear to be built-in features of a political system characterized by virtually unlimited democracy and a redistributive state driven by "rent seekers" who cry out for protectionist measures in the name of the public good.

Yet, the fact remains that insofar as nations have maintained "open communication" (especially by maintaining open markets) and have remained "industrious and civilized" (especially by lowering marginal tax rates to encourage individuals to work, save, and invest, and by adhering to a rule of law protecting rights of persons and property), they have prospered. The rapid growth of Japan and the Pacific Rim countries, and the respectable growth of the United States, Great Britain, and Europe during the 1980s resulted in large part from following the Humean recipe.

The future holds great potential for continued growth of the world economy, but the extent to which this potential is realized will depend on the success of the United States and other major democratic governments in strengthening their commitment to sound money, limited government, and freer markets. The ideal of Adam Smith ([1776] 1937, p. 651)—namely, a "system of natural liberty" wherein "every man, as long as he does not violate the laws of justice, is left perfectly free to pursue his own interest his own way, and to bring both his industry and capital into competition with those of any other man, or order of men"—remains a useful blueprint for generating a stable world order.

The abandonment of the international monetary system based on the Bretton Woods agreement and the substitution of a system of managed floating for "fixed but adjustable" exchange rates paved the way for national economies to independently pursue their own monetary policies. Major industrial democracies, therefore, could choose to insulate their economies from the monetary disturbances previously transmitted under a fixed exchange regime. In practice, however, monetary independence proved difficult because of the policymakers' incentive to politicize the system of floating exchange rates. Nevertheless, until 1985, the United States largely refrained from interfering with the foreign exchange value of the dollar and focused more on domestic targets than on rigging the exchange rate to achieve external balance.

With the possibility of increased monetary independence under floating, the integration of world financial markets, the growing importance of international trade as a component of the U.S. economy, and the corresponding importance of the foreign exchange market, it is essential to reconsider the framework for domestic monetary policy and the relation between domestic stability and exchange rate stability.

These and other key issues in the world economy are the focus of the present volume. By considering the role of the dollar, the shape of the international monetary system, the future of floating rates, the risks associated with alternative exchange rate regimes, the transmission of real and monetary shocks under fixed and floating rates, the seriousness of and the relation between the U.S. budget and trade deficits, and the role of policy coordination, the contributors to this volume help separate real from false problems and help design the framework for a more stable world economy. Moreover, by comparing the current international monetary arrangements to alternatives such as a gold standard, a commodity-basket standard, a single world fiat money geared to stabilize a broad-based price index of internationally traded goods, and a free-market currency, insights are gained that may permit the evolution of a sounder international monetary system.

The essays in this volume also consider questions about the inflationary bias of national fiat money regimes; the risk of foreign exchange controls, capital controls, and trade barriers under pegged exchange rates; the ability of floating rates to insulate a national economy against monetary and real shocks from abroad; and the ability of the European Monetary System (EMS) to achieve exchange rate stability, financial stability, and increased trade. Many questions remain, but the breadth of the papers and the many interesting questions they address make this a useful volume for those interested in the key issues facing the world economy today.

## The Dollar and Domestic Monetary Policy

The dollar's purchasing power depends largely on the course of domestic monetary policy. If money growth consistently outpaces the growth of real output, inflation will result. Short-run changes in the demand for money can alter the relation between money and prices, but historical evidence of the long-run relation is too strong to ignore. The framework within which domestic monetary policy is conducted is therefore of great importance for the future value of money. The conduct of domestic monetary policy is also critical for the foreign exchange value of the dollar under floating rates and for the smoothness of the adjustment process during which the foreign exchange value of the dollar is moving toward a new equilibrium exchange rate. In the absence of a predictable purchasing power for the dollar, its foreign exchange value will also be less predictable. The pursuit of stable money, therefore, will spill over onto the foreign exchange market under floating rates, so that increasing domestic price-level stability will tend to foster exchange rate stability.[2] The papers by *Manuel H. Johnson*, *Leland B. Yeager*, and *Allan H. Meltzer* in Part I consider these and related issues.

*A Framework for Monetary Policy*

In the opening paper, Johnson points to the importance of central-bank credibility in a fiat money regime and argues that in establishing a framework for monetary policy it is essential to clearly state the long-run goals of monetary policy and how they can be achieved. For Johnson, a primary goal is to achieve price-level stability. This goal is important because, in addition to competitive markets, price-level predictability is a necessary ingredient for a rational price system.

In Johnson's opinion, the volatile nature of monetary velocity in the 1980s has made it necessary for the Fed to shift from monetary aggregates to alternative indicators for conducting monetary policy. These indicators "should be accurately measurable and readily available," "should respond to changes in Federal Reserve policy," and "should be reliably related to the ultimate goals of monetary policy." Johnson therefore suggests looking to financial markets to help guide monetary policy. He recommends that the Fed rely on the yield curve, the foreign exchange value of the dollar, and selected broad-based commodity price indices in formulating monetary policy. Changes in these indicators, he believes, would provide the Fed with clues as to whether monetary policy is overly restrictive or overly expansive. Thus, Johnson expects that when these indicators are used jointly they should help the Fed avoid serious policy errors and maintain long-run price stability.

[2]The foreign exchange value of the dollar under floating, of course, also depends on the monetary policies of foreign central banks.

*Domestic Stability versus Exchange Rate Stability*

If a choice has to be made between domestic stability and exchange rate stability, Yeager favors the former. Abandoning floating exchange rates would not solve the fundamental problem confronting every national economy, namely, the absurdity of a fiat money system in which the future purchasing power of money is unknown. Without solving this problem, it makes little sense, in Yeager's opinion, to focus on exchange rate stability. However, if national currencies can be reformed to achieve sound money, then floating exchange rates will be less volatile. Yeager therefore calls for fundamental monetary reform.

In reforming the monetary regime, Yeager would "give defined values to currencies," preferably in terms of a commodity basket rather than in terms of gold. If there were a credible commitment to maintain the long-run purchasing power of the monetary unit in terms of a representative basket of commodities, Yeager believes the well-known problem of lags associated with a price-level rule would be minimized. He also thinks that the use of monetary aggregates and policy indicators, such as those advocated by Johnson, would help avoid prolonged monetary disequilibrium and restore price-level stability without serious lags.

Moving from a government fiat money standard to a governmentally managed commodity-basket standard no doubt would provide a more stable anchor for the price level, but Yeager goes on to argue for the complete privatization of money. Once government fiat money is abolished, a new private unit of account could be defined in terms of a broadly selected bundle of commodities with a given total value. If the standard bundle were representative of a large enough number of goods and services, a relatively high degree of price stability could be achieved. Indeed, Yeager argues that the new monetary unit would be "endowed practically by definition with a stable purchasing power."

Under the monetary scheme Yeager envisions, private bank notes and deposits would serve as circulating media, and private suppliers would respond to changes in the demand for money without altering the stable unit of account. Any deviation of the price level from that associated with the defined value of the unit of account would quickly be corrected by arbitrage. With the maintenance of monetary equilibrium and price stability, Yeager predicts that the private money arrangement would avoid the high costs of inflation and recession that have hampered government fiat money regimes.[3] Moreover, once

[3]For an elaboration of the private money and payments system, see Greenfield and Yeager (1983).

governments could no longer abuse and politicize national currencies, the foreign exchange value of the dollar would itself become more stable.

### *Monetary Stability and Monetary Reform*

Meltzer adopts a rules-based approach to monetary reform, arguing that the variability of price levels and exchange rates that has characterized domestic and international monetary policy over the past 20 years can be mitigated by disciplining national monetary authorities. To do so, he would have the United States, West Germany, and Japan adhere to a simple monetary rule. Each of these countries would be required to limit the growth of their monetary base to the "difference between the moving average of past real output growth and past growth in base velocity." Meltzer argues that strict adherence to this rule would achieve price stability and promote exchange rate stability in a regime of floating exchange rates.

Meltzer supports his theoretical case for a monetary rule and a continuation of floating rates by showing that (1) uncertainty—as measured by the variability of prices and output—has not increased, in general, under floating exchange rates, and (2) those countries that have adopted rules for achieving internal and external stability—mainly West Germany and Denmark—have actually reduced uncertainty. The failure of discretionary monetary policy and economic forecasting convinces Meltzer that stubborn reliance on either discretionary monetary authority or monetary rules tied to economic forecasting will not perform as well as his forecast-invariant monetary rule. A major advantage of his proposal is that it reduces uncertainty by relying on *domestic* policy action rather than on the need for international policy coordination as currently practiced.

## International Monetary Reform

The papers by *Jacob A. Frenkel* and *Morris Goldstein*, *Richard N. Cooper*, and *Ronald I. McKinnon* in Part II survey the current terrain of the international monetary system and consider how it might be improved.

### *Developments and Prospects*

In their wide-ranging paper, Frenkel and Goldstein review recent developments in the world economy and the key issues that must be addressed in any meaningful discussion of international monetary reform. Recent developments include the large U.S. current account deficits, increased official intervention in the foreign exchange markets, a substantial fall in the foreign exchange value of the dollar since 1985, and an increased recourse to policy coordination in international economic affairs.

Frenkel and Goldstein associate four basic issues with these developments: (1) whether fiscal policy can be disciplined by the choice of the exchange rate regime; (2) the extent to which monetary independence is reduced by moving away from floating exchange rates and the costs involved; (3) the best means for determining equilibrium exchange rates; and (4) the characteristics of a sound international monetary order.

In discussing the relation between fiscal policy and the exchange rate regime, the authors find little evidence that the choice of the regime significantly influences the size of the budget deficit.[4] The authors imply that a better understanding of how to discipline the fiscal authorities is necessary *before* considering any reform of the exchange rate regime.

On the question of monetary independence, Frenkel and Goldstein note that the relevant issue is the cost in terms of alternative policy options forgone when moving to fixed exchange rates. The question that policymakers will have to address is whether the cost of sacrificing monetary independence is worth the benefit of achieving more stable exchange rates.[5]

With respect to whether the government or the market is better able to determine equilibrium exchange rates, the authors are skeptical that official intervention is likely to hit upon the market-clearing exchange rate. The proclivity of governments to err in determining equilibrium exchange rates makes official estimates subject to frequent revision. Official intervention typically adds "noise" to foreign exchange markets and provides opportunities for destabilizing speculation. In comparison, competitive foreign exchange markets use existing information about myriad forces affecting exchange rates. This information, in turn, enables individuals to adjust their plans in a rapid and consistent fashion without incurring the costs of government intervention. Even so, there seems to be an unending stream of official advice and arguments for greater intervention in the hope that governments may still be able to outguess the foreign exchange market. The problem is that by interfering with the free-market pro-

[4]Niskanen (1988, p. 177), for example, reports that no predictable relation has been found between exchange rates and budget deficits from either time-series or cross-country studies.

[5]For a useful discussion of this tradeoff, or what has become known as the "Doctrine of Alternative Stability," see Yeager (1976, pp. 651–53).

cess, official intervention makes the foreign exchange market less, not more, efficient as a mechanism for disseminating relevant information and coordinating individual plans.[6]

In considering the international monetary system, the authors address the question of whether a smoothly operating system requires rules, leaders, and explicit anchors. They note that although the current floating rate regime has no well-defined rules like the gold standard and no dominant leader like the United States in the Bretton Woods system, it does embody an implicit contract and anchor. Notably, each country is expected to institute sound monetary and fiscal policies and thereby generate greater exchange rate stability under floating than would occur in the absence of such domestic policy coordination. But this coordination is decentralized and each government must maintain responsibility for disciplining its own monetary and fiscal policies for the international monetary system to become more stable. For this and other reasons, the authors reject the so-called crisis-management approach to international monetary reform and prefer instead to view reform as "a constitutional change" requiring a "long-term perspective." Any changes in the current system, therefore, should receive close scrutiny before they are implemented.

*An International Fiat Money*

Richard Cooper provides a careful survey of various commodity-reserve proposals and examines the performance of the gold standard. On the basis of his observations, he rejects the commodity-based approach to international monetary reform in favor of an international fiat money. By instituting a single monetary unit for the major industrial democracies, Cooper hopes to circumvent the problem of exchange rate uncertainty. The backbone of his proposal is to establish an International Central Bank (ICB) that would be instructed to achieve price-level stability and maintain the purchasing power of the international fiat money.

The question that arises with respect to Cooper's proposal is whether the ICB has any incentive to consistently follow a price-level rule and maintain a long-run noninflationary growth of the world money supply. The long experience of the Federal Reserve and other central banks operating under national fiat money regimes certainly does not warrant much optimism in this regard. Nevertheless, even if the ICB were merely to "muddle through" without any specific operating

[6]F. A. Hayek's argument about the market as a mechanism for using the decentralized knowledge that is available only to individuals "on the spot" is as relevant for the foreign exchange market as it is for other markets (see Hayek 1945).

rule, Cooper still thinks his international fiat money would be superior to the present system and other alternatives—though he clearly prefers the ICB to be bound by a price rule.

Lawrence H. White and Paul Craig Roberts question Cooper's enthusiasm for an international fiat money. They argue that handing over monetary policy to a group of world central bankers may simply make the world economy more, not less, unstable by further politicizing money. For this reason, White (like Yeager) prefers to abandon government fiat money altogether and ultimately privatize money.[7]

### *An International Gold Standard without Gold*

An alternative proposal is presented by McKinnon who favors returning to a fixed exchange rate regime but abandoning gold as an anchor for national price levels. As a substitute for gold, he would have the monetary authorities of the leading industrial democracies jointly manage their respective monetary bases (fiat monies) in order to stabilize a price index of internationally traded commodities. He believes that his "international gold standard without gold" will ensure exchange rate stability but avoid the bouts of inflation and deflation that characterized the historical gold standard.

McKinnon's scheme, however, raises the same question as Cooper's, namely, whether any *government* fiat money can avoid being politicized over the long run. It also raises two additional issues: whether the monetary authorities will succumb to controls over trade and capital when facing a balance-of-payments problem under a fixed exchange rate regime, and whether (as Robert E. Keleher mentions in his comment) the exchange rate itself will be used as a policy tool so that the stability inherent in fixed rates becomes more rhetoric than reality.

## Exchange Rate Regimes: Rules and Consequences

The papers by *Thomas D. Willett, Martin J. Bailey* and *George S. Tavlas, Michael D. Bordo* and *Anna J. Schwartz, Michele Fratianni,* and *Gottfried Haberler* in Part III provide a detailed investigation of the nature of alternative exchange rate regimes. In doing so, they offer a broad perspective of the arguments for and against floating.

[7]In his comment, White makes an important distinction between proposals for governmentally directed commodity standards, as discussed in Cooper's paper, and proposals for denationalizing money. The latter are characterized by commodity standards that emerge and operate via voluntary choice—in the absence of any monetary authority or monopoly central bank.

*Key Exchange Rate Regimes: A Constitutional Perspective*

In his perceptive paper, Willett provides an overview of key exchange rate regimes from a constitutional perspective. He does not attempt to review the extensive theoretical literature on alternative exchange rate regimes. Rather, his objective is to offer a conceptual framework for analyzing exchange rate regimes in terms of whether they are constrained or unconstrained, and whether the constraints are imposed at the domestic or international level. From his viewpoint, the most fundamental issue in analyzing the consequences of alternative exchange rate systems is whether national monetary and fiscal policies are disciplined by effective rules that lend stability to both the domestic economy and exchange rates.

Willett cautions against "the severe danger of analyzing exchange rate issues in isolation." Political factors and economic factors are both obviously important in evaluating alternative exchange rate regimes. One must ask how constrained and unconstrained domestic monetary and fiscal policies will affect different exchange rate regimes and how the choice of regime will subsequently influence domestic policy choices.

Three key issues come to mind when looking through Willett's constitutional political economy window: (1) What is the best way to discipline domestic monetary and fiscal policy—by international policy coordination or by national constitutional limitations on the economic powers of government? (2) Which of these two approaches is more likely to be politically feasible, and how can the new set of rules be implemented and maintained? (3) Within the set of feasible alternatives, which is most likely to generate long-run economic stability?

Given the proclivity of all governments to abuse their power, moving political authority to an international body may create more problems than it solves. Moreover, national governments are unlikely to give up their sovereign powers to an international organization. Considerations of simplicity and enforceability, therefore, may require turning to internal constraints to limit the monetary, spending, and borrowing powers of national governments. If successful, the greater domestic stability will also ensure greater exchange rate stability under floating, argues Willett.

For Willett, then, there is a strong case for focusing on "fundamental institutional reforms to help promote long-run economic and financial stability, including exchange rate stability." In his view, the key industrial democracies should *first* get their own financial houses in order by constraining monetary and fiscal authorities before looking for a more stable exchange rate regime. Floating exchange rates may place some pressure on national governments to correct inappropriate monetary and fiscal policies by openly disclosing policy errors in the foreign exchange markets. This indirect discipline, however, is insufficient in Willett's view and must be supplemented by domestic measures designed to bring about greater financial stability.

### *U.S. Trade and Investment under Floating Rates*

The effect of floating exchange rates on international trade and investment is an important issue. The post–Bretton Woods system of managed floating has been characterized by wide swings in nominal and real exchange rates. Opponents of floating argue that the greater variability of exchange rates under floating, as compared to fixed rates, reduces the volume of trade and investment. Bailey and Tavlas investigate this issue in detail and find that neither theory nor evidence can definitely support any significant effect of floating exchange rates on trade or investment.

In the theoretical section of their paper, the authors offer important insights into the determinants of exchange rate variability (both short-run volatility and long-run misalignment) and the consequences for trade and investment. The unpredictable nature of many of the factors that account for exchange rate movements helps explain the variability of exchange rates—and the greater the unpredictability, the more volatile a floating regime will be. The question that Bailey and Tavlas seek to answer is, "To the extent that the size and variance of movements in exchange rates have been unpredictable, have they also been harmful?" The results of their study imply that the post-1973 floating rate regime has not had any serious effects on U.S. trade or direct investment.

Once we allow for the politicization of exchange rates under a Bretton Woods–type system and the possibility of trade and capital controls, the risk normally associated with freely determined exchange rates appears less problematic.[8] And once it is recognized that exchange

[8]For a fuller discussion of the impact of alternative exchange rate regimes on trade and investment, see Yeager (1976, chap. 13).

All exchange rate regimes entail risk and uncertainty of one kind or another. The contention that floating has led to greater variability of prices and output than under the Bretton Woods system of pegged rates, for example, cannot be supported from existing data (see *Economic Report* 1989, p. 118). Moreover, Niskanen (1988, p. 180) makes the important point that "a move toward a more stable exchange rate system [engineered by government controls], as with domestic price or interest rate controls, would reduce uncertainty about exchange rates only by increasing uncertainty about government policy—at best a Faustian bargain."

rates are asset prices, which change rapidly to reflect actual or expected changes in real and monetary forces, the variability of flexible exchange rates will depend in part on the policy environment. Sound monetary and fiscal policies, the protection of property rights, a commitment to open markets, and the enforcement of an international rule of law will all help reduce the variability of exchange rates by lowering institutional uncertainty and increasing predictability. These and other considerations lead Bailey and Tavlas to the conclusion that, in theory, it is difficult to determine the precise impact of exchange rate variability on trade and investment.

In the absence of either hard theoretical support or empirical evidence that, on net, floating exchange rates harm trade and investment relative to fixed rates (or, more correctly, relative to the fixed but adjustable rate system that characterized the Bretton Woods system), one will have to incorporate considerations of constitutional political economy (as suggested by Willett) when choosing among alternative exchange rate regimes.

*Transmission of Real and Monetary Disturbances under Fixed and Floating Rates*

Michael Bordo and Anna Schwartz examine the various channels through which real and monetary disturbances are transmitted under fixed and floating exchange rates. In their analysis, they further distinguish between exchange rate regimes operating in an open and closed world economy. With these distinctions in mind, Michael Darby (in his comment on the authors' paper) recommends a four-way classification of exchange rate regimes: "fixed open," "fixed closed," "floating open," and "floating closed." Bordo and Schwartz consider the transmission of real and monetary disturbances for each of these regimes in theory and practice.

The traditional approach to analyzing real and monetary disturbances under fixed open and floating open exchange regimes is contrasted with the Keynesian approach to transmission in a closed world economy. The latter approach was devised to help explain the interwar years while the traditional approach applied to the pre-1914 gold standard. The Keynesian model was further developed to apply to the post-1973 floating rate system.

For a system of fixed exchange rates in an open world economy, the traditional approach to transmission relied on the balance-of-payments adjustment mechanism. Monetary and real disturbances in one country spread to other countries linked to the gold standard. Balance-of-payments disequilibria were corrected by the Humean price-specie-flow mechanism, by direct changes in expenditures and incomes, and by arbitrage and capital flows. Thus, the adjustment process under the gold standard required sacrificing autonomy over domestic stability in order to maintain balance in international payments. In an open world economy with floating rates, the transmission of real and monetary disturbances is mitigated by having the foreign exchange market absorb most of the shocks, as reflected in movements in the foreign exchange rate. Thus, domestic stability can be pursued with monetary and fiscal policy while external balance is brought about through adjustments in the exchange rate.

Unlike the traditional approach in which the theory of transmission is fairly clear-cut, the Keynesian approach to transmission in a closed world economy has generated a host of ever more complex models. Indeed, as Bordo and Schwartz note, the growing complexity of these models has made it difficult, in theory, to predict the outcome of the international transmission process.

After a close examination of the traditional and Keynesian approaches to transmission, the authors consider the policy implications of the two approaches with regard to the role of government intervention. The traditional approach, of course, sees no role for intervention in either the fixed rate regime or the floating rate regime. The purpose of the gold standard is to discipline national governments, while under floating rates domestic policy is largely insulated from balance-of-payments considerations. Under the Keynesian approach, however, it is taken for granted that government will play a role in the transmission process.

Within the Keynesian framework, arguments based on negative externalities and game theory imply that a more efficient adjustment to monetary and real shocks under fixed rates is possible with policy coordination. Similar arguments have been used by Keynesians to justify intervention in a regime of floating rates. But as Bordo and Schwartz emphasize, such arguments really miss the mark since "intervention under floating rates shifts adjustment away from the exchange rate back to the real economy, abandoning the benefits of floating." Moreover, with respect to policy coordination in general, the authors correctly note, "If there are negative spillover effects, the likely reason is that domestic policies from which they originate are misguided."

In sum, Bordo and Schwartz's reaction to the Keynesian proposal for intervention via policy coordination as an efficient means to better the international monetary system is that such a proposal "is visionary." In theory, it is possible to generate beneficial outcomes from policy coordination. But in practice, argue Bordo and Schwartz, such an approach is likely to fail because its theoretical framework ignores "the vested interest of politicians in safeguarding their home country sovereignty."

From a historical perspective, the authors point out that during the classical gold standard prior to 1914, national governments largely adhered to the "rules of the game" and maintained convertibility. The fixed open model was therefore appropriate. However, after 1914, with the demise of classical liberal attitudes, intervention became commonplace. The interventionist attitude was evident under the gold exchange standard of the interwar period, as well as during the Bretton Woods system, and it has clearly been the case under floating since 1973.

In examining the historical record, Bordo and Schwartz provide empirical evidence supporting the traditional approach to the transmission of monetary and real disturbances. They recognize that under the gold standard, business cycles were frequently transmitted from one country to another. And they draw on balance-of-payments adjustments during the U.S. greenback episode (1862–78) to provide evidence supporting the traditional approach under open floating. As predicted, during the period in which the dollar floated, the U.S. economy was insulated from monetary and real shocks originating abroad. Further evidence of the transmission of business cycles under fixed exchange rates is found in the interwar experience with the gold exchange standard and under the Bretton Woods system. However, since the U.S. dollar floated in 1973, the authors find no clear evidence bearing on the transmission process. They venture that the interdependence that has been found to exist under the present system is not necessarily at odds with the traditional theory, since that theory applies to a freely floating exchange regime rather than to managed floating. In fact, they argue that "much of the interdependence may be a consequence of policy management and U.S. policy instability."

An important lesson that Bordo and Schwarz draw from their study of the transmission of real and monetary disturbances under alternative exchange regimes is that "a stable international order is achievable with a floating rate system that provides independence to pursue stable domestic policies consistent with that preference. For international economic stability, policy coordination is neither necessary nor attainable." The question still remains, however, about how best to discipline domestic policymakers to achieve the stability that is *theoretically* achievable.

*The European Monetary System: An Appraisal*

Michele Fratianni argues that the EMS (initiated in 1979) has not been the failure many had predicted, nor has it been an unqualified success. On the positive side, the EMS has reduced exchange rate volatility under an adjustable peg system and has used the credibility of the Bundesbank to discipline the French and Italian central banks. The EMS has also provided for greater European financial integration and lessened the extent of exchange controls by France and Italy. As a result, the French franc and Italian lira have both appreciated in real terms against the Deutsche mark and other EMS currencies. However, on the negative side, Fratianni points to the decline in trade within the EMS and to the fact that the reduction in inflation in France and Italy, while notable, has not been as significant as the disinflation experienced by non-EMS countries that have followed their own independent monetary policies under floating rates.

In Fratianni's view, the main benefit of the EMS has been in using the reputation of the Bundesbank to lower the costs of disinflation in Italy and France, both of which have comparatively weak central banks. Insofar as the leadership role is more evenly distributed within the EMS, Fratianni warns that without enhanced reputations for the Italian and French central banks, democratization would defeat the very purpose of the EMS, namely, to establish a "zone of monetary stability."

In his comment, Alan Walters is less sanguine about the benefits of the EMS, noting that the United Kingdom has made considerable progress against inflation and unemployment in the absence of EMS membership. More specifically, he believes that the EMS has politicized the exchange rate regime and made European financial stability largely dependent on German hegemony. He also sees the increased protectionism in Europe flowing in part from the EMS. As such, he holds that European monetary intergration would be better served by an alternative institutional arrangement.

*The Case for Floating*

Haberler asks, "Should floating continue?" To answer this question, he compares the current system of "loosely managed floating" to proposals for a Bretton Woods–type system with fixed but adjustable exchange rates—such as the commonly proposed system of target zones. He argues that any system based on "stable but adjustable exchange rates" would have collapsed during the 1980s. One major advantage of floating is that it avoids the destabilizing speculation associated with a Bretton Woods–type arrangement. Furthermore, floating avoids the need for international policy coordination and the problem of trying to predict equilibrium exchange rates. "The fact is," writes Haberler, "that we, economists as well as ministers of finance and central bankers, do not know what the equilibrium rates are."

From his review of the strengths and weaknesses of the present system relative to those systems that are likely to emerge through the process of international negotiation, Haberler concludes that "the present international monetary system does not require a radical change and that floating should continue." He reaches this conclusion because of the inclination of nations to control international trade and impose capital controls, and because of the inflexibility of wages and prices, which would generate considerable unemployment under a fixed rated system. Haberler also points to the price-level risk inherent in a modern gold standard under which the world price level would depend largely on Soviet and South African gold production. Thus, under current conditions, Haberler sees a comparative advantage in staying with floating rates.[9]

## The Political Economy of Deficits and Trade

The growing volume of international trade and the corresponding increase in economic interdependence are characteristics of the world economy today. Yet national interests continue to prevail as special interests try to use the redistributive state to secure economic advantages for themselves at the expense of the larger society. Budget policy and international trade policy have both become so politicized that it is difficult for the nonspecialist to distinguish fact from fiction when listening to arguments for or against increased government spending and trade restrictions.

Are budget deficits and trade deficits detrimental to a citizen's economic well-being? What, if any, is the relation between the budget and trade deficits? Are the budget and trade deficits only symptoms of more deep-seated problems that are being ignored by policymakers and the media? What is the significance of the deterioration in the U.S. net international investment position, as officially reported? These and other issues are addressed by *William A. Niskanen, A. James Meigs, Paul Heyne,* and *Michael Ulan* and *William G. Dewald* in Part IV.

### *U.S. Budget Policy and the Trade Deficit*

The relation between the U.S. budget deficit and the trade deficit is an uneasy one at best, argues Niskanen. In his view, there is insufficient evidence to support the hypothesis of a direct link between

[9]For a detailed treatment of the case for floating, see Melamed (1988).

the two deficits. The past several years have witnessed high levels of both deficits. Economists have tried to explain these twin deficits by relying on an accounting identity and the so-called Feldstein chain linking increased trade deficits to increased budget deficits. But as Niskanen illustrates, the observed parallel movements in the two deficits prove nothing, since both the budget and trade deficits may be responding to outside forces. Moreover, on the basis of available evidence, Niskanen warns that our theoretical understanding of the relation between the budget and trade deficits, while useful, is not sufficient to establish a firm basis for positing a statistically significant direct relation between changes in the budget deficit and changes in the trade deficit.

The trade or foreign balance (exports minus imports) is identical to the difference between private saving and investment plus the government balance (the difference between government taxes and expenditures). This accounting identity implies that an increase in the government deficit will lead to an equal change in the trade deficit, if other things are constant. Niskanen, however, finds no compelling evidence to support this postulated relation. It appears that for the postwar era, changes in U.S. saving and investment largely offset changes in the government balance, so that the foreign balance was not significantly affected. Niskanen therefore argues that the rise in the U.S. trade deficit during the 1980s cannot be explained by the rise in federal government deficits.

Finding no satisfactory evidence to support a positive relation between the government and trade deficits, implicit in the accounting identity, Niskanen next considers the "Feldstein chain" as a "plausible hypothesis." Under this approach, economists have argued that "real budget deficits increase real interest rates, which increase the real exchange rate, which increases the real trade deficit." Although Niskanen finds this line of argument reasonable, he cannot find any strong evidence to support each link in the Feldstein chain. As a result, he cautions against placing much weight on the argument as a whole.

In light of the inconclusive evidence for a stable positive relation between the budget and trade deficits, Niskanen approaches the twin deficit issue from a different angle. He notes that the twin deficits really point to a single problem: "The increase in private and government consumption, financed in part by borrowing abroad, will not provide a stream of returns to finance the increased debt." The solution is to reduce the rate of private and government consumption relative to the growth of real output. Niskanen emphasizes that politicians must confront this issue head on and stop focusing their attention on the trade deficit, which is not the real problem.[10]

The present situation in which total U.S. debt is growing faster than real output is not sustainable, argues Niskanen. To face this problem squarely requires turning from the trade deficit to the federal budget deficit. In this respect, Niskanen recommends cutting the budget deficit in a way that is least harmful to continued economic growth, regardless of the impact on the trade deficit. His preference is to restrain government spending in the areas of defense, health care, and agriculture rather than to increase taxes. In his view, the main priority of U.S. policymakers should be to restore fiscal soundness and reduce the growth of total debt, rather than to sacrifice domestic stability for foreign balance.

*Substituting False for Real Problems*

For Meigs the twin deficits point to more serious problems that are often ignored in the heat of the debate over the budget and trade deficits. The continued growth of government spending, which draws resources away from the private sector, and the use of the trade deficit to motivate protectionist legislation are the real problems, according to Meigs. By focusing attention on the twin deficits as evils in and of themselves, the nation may lose sight of these real problems. In his paper, Meigs thoroughly explores the implications of substituting the false problems associated with the twin deficits for the real problems of excessive government spending and protectionism.

Meigs takes a public choice approach to analyzing the persistence of government growth and the rise in U.S. protectionism. The logic is simple: Public officials gain by conferring large benefits on special interest groups with political clout while spreading the costs over the general public or pushing the costs into the future by borrowing. In principle, Meigs prefers a balanced budget, but only if the balance is brought about by reducing the size of government. He strongly opposes tax increases because he believes that they would simply be used to create new spending programs and allow government to continue on its high-growth path while discouraging individual initiative. The present budget deficit, according to Meigs, places a constraint on further increases in government spending, and in this sense is to be preferred over higher taxes. Furthermore, Meigs does not see that the budget deficit has been harmful to economic growth

[10]Niskanen remarks that the trade deficit has become a problem mainly because it has been used as a straw man by special interest groups seeking to protect their products and jobs from foreign competition, which many Americans have come to see as "unfair."

or that it has led to inflation and high interest rates. Yet, Meigs does not address the issue of whether the deficit imposes an ethical cost on a free society by sanctioning the taking of property from future generations without their consent in order to finance current government expenditures. This ethical issue is at the heart of the proposed constitutional amendment to balance the federal budget, a proposal Meigs would undoubtedly support.[11]

With respect to trying to cure the trade deficit by protectionist measures or by intervening in the foreign exchange market, Meigs explains that these so-called cures would only make matters worse. Like Jan Tumlir, Meigs emphasizes the danger that nontariff trade restraints pose for the international price system and how quantity restrictions impede the efficient allocation of resources among nations. Introducing such "noise" into the international price system necessarily reduces the wealth of nations.

There is no moral dilemma inherent in the trade deficit as long as it reflects the voluntary actions of private individuals. If foreigners wish to sell more goods and services to Americans than they buy and invest the difference in the United States, why should such privately motivated actions harm the U.S. economy? Meigs shows that they do not and, in the process, dispels many of the myths behind the protectionist mentality. The fact is that during most of the 1980s U.S. output and employment both increased at healthy rates even though the current account deficit reached record levels—which lends support to Meigs's contention that the trade deficit is largely a false problem.[12]

The reversal in 1985 of the Reagan administration's initial decision to refrain from intervening in the foreign exchange market and the increased willingness of the United States since then to intervene concerns Meigs. Foreign exchange intervention is detrimental in the long run because it increases uncertainty and masks real changes in relative prices, contends Meigs. Trade patterns will therefore be distorted away from what real market forces would otherwise have dictated. And insofar as monetary policy is held hostage to exchange rate policy, the attainment of both domestic stability and exchange rate stability (in the sense of lower variability of floating rates) will elude policymakers.

Real progress in resolving the critical issues underlying the twin deficits will be made only by reducing the growth of government

[11]On the ethical issue behind the budget deficit, see Niskanen (1988, pp. 112–13).

[12]Although U.S. imports increased from 1982 to 1987 by over 65 percent, employment rose by 13 percent and real output increased by more than 21 percent (*Economic Report* 1989, p. 166).

spending, instituting a more neutral tax system, maintaining a sound monetary policy to achieve long-run price stability, protecting private property, keeping markets open to competition, and enacting a balanced budget amendment. For Meigs these are the steps that must be taken to cure the cancer that is slowly eroding our economic and personal liberties; superficial concerns with the twin deficits will not carry the day.

*Do Trade Deficits Matter?*

In his iconoclastic article, Heyne contends that there is a misplaced emphasis on the trade deficit and that the very notion "ought to be abandoned" for the sake of clear thinking. As a matter of fact, a nation's balance of payments must always balance, since every transaction is two-sided and double-entry bookkeeping ensures overall balance. An imbalance or disequilibrium in a nation's international transactions, therefore, is a conceptual or analytical distinction arrived at by *omitting* certain transactions. A merchandise trade deficit, for example, omits services, while a balance-of-payments deficit omits certain "compensating" transactions. However, the line between ordinary transactions and compensating transactions is itself largely arbitrary and, as Heyne notes, not consistent with economic rationality.

The ambiguity surrounding the concept of a trade deficit has served special interest groups seeking protectionist policies and arguing that the United States has lost its competitiveness. Accordingly, Heyne points out that "all concepts of a trade deficit harbor concealed concerns and disguised political judgments." Since its inception, the concept of a trade deficit has been an instrument for special interests to exert political pressure for wrongheaded policies that have undermined the rule of law. As such, the notion of a trade deficit generates more heat than light, argues Heyne. By abandoning this antiquated concept—and the mercantilist attitude it engenders—Heyne hopes to address economic problems more forthrightly instead of under the guise of a deficit in the balance of trade.

*The U.S. Net International Investment Position*

Ulan and Dewald argue that the U.S. net international investment position (NIIP) is "misstated and misunderstood." For year-end 1987, the Bureau of Economic Analysis (BEA) reported a U.S. NIIP of *minus* $368 billion, and this figure is typically used to indicate that the United States is now a "net debtor." Nevertheless, this figure and its interpretation both miss the mark, according to Ulan and Dewald. First, the official estimate is incorrectly calculated using the book value rather than the market value of U.S. net direct foreign investment. Second, the U.S. NIIP—defined as the official U.S. gold stock plus U.S. holdings of foreign assets less foreign holdings of U.S. assets—includes both debt and equity, as well as international reserves. Consequently, the U.S. NIIP is not identical with "net debt," even though the two are used interchangeably by the BEA.

When Ulan and Dewald recalculate U.S. net direct foreign investment using market values, they find that the official estimates have substantially exaggerated the deterioration in the U.S. NIIP during the 1980s. Using their revaluation methods, the authors find that the U.S. NIIP was $400 billion to $600 billion higher at year-end 1987 than indicated by the BEA estimates.

Since annual changes in the NIIP reflect the condition of the current account balance, official figures that overstate the deterioration in the U.S. NIIP during the 1980s also overstate the size of U.S. current account deficits. When the NIIP is adjusted for changes in market values and for inflation, Ulan and Dewald find that both the nominal and real current account deficits were significantly *lower* than the official estimates. The authors also find that U.S. wealth has continued to increase during the 1980s, though at a slower rate, and that changes in the NIIP—measured either by official figures or revalued figures—continue to be a relatively small fraction of overall U.S. wealth or its increase.

What the Ulan-Dewald study suggests, then, is that the concern expressed in certain quarters over official BEA figures showing a deterioration of the U.S. NIIP and the persistence of large current account deficits is overstated. Draconian measures to stem foreign investment or to restrict imports would make the United States worse off by depriving consumers of foreign goods and investment resources, both of which have increased our standard of living during the 1980s.

Ulan and Dewald's study is valuable in that it lays the foundation for a more rational approach to policymaking and helps to undermine the alarmist attitude currently surrounding the twin deficits. Moreover, their analysis further illustrates Heyne's point about the dangers inherent in the very use of balance-of-payment statistics and the incentive to use the current account deficit (or in this case the deterioration in the NIIP) to politicize the international economic order.

## Toward a Stable International Order

The central issue raised in Part V is whether a stable world order is best achieved via a spontaneous market order resting on a rule of law and a smoothly functioning international price system or via a more centrally directed economic order resting on international economic coordination. Fundamentally, the choice is between two policy perspectives: (1) a classical liberal or constitutional perspective in which democratic government is limited to the protection of property rights, the maintenance of sound money, the practice of fiscal responsibility, and the preservation of free markets; and (2) a modern liberal or welfare state perspective in which democratic government becomes virtually unlimited in its ability to redistribute income and wealth for the alleged "public interest." In their paper, *Joachim Scheide* and *Stefan Sinn* examine the arguments for international policy coordination and find them lacking, while *Jan Tumlir* shows the danger the modern redistributive state poses to the international price system.

*The Failure of International Policy Coordination*

Scheide and Sinn examine the case for international coordination of monetary and fiscal policies to achieve greater economic stability. Models based on game theory have been used to make a case for international policy coordination, but the authors find these models suspect because of their unrealistic assumptions. The game-theoretic approach to international coordination assumes that, in the absence of coordination, policymakers do not change their behavior in light of new information and are therefore incapable of learning. Scheide and Sinn show that this nonrationality assumption in a noncooperative setting is inconsistent with observed behavior and, therefore, cannot serve as the basis for a cooperative game. Hence, the supposed gains from international coordination are largely illusory.

The authors also criticize the assumption that the number of policy targets exceeds the available instruments, so that policy coordination is seen as necessary to bridge the gap between targets and instruments. Scheide and Sinn note that if external targets such as a balance on current account or a specific foreign exchange rate are viewed as inappropriate policy objectives, then there is no mismatch; the domestic authorities can adopt rules to achieve price-level stability and fiscal soundness *without* international policy coordination. In fact, international policy coordination involves the risk of further politicizing monetary and fiscal policy and increasing inflationary expectations, thereby increasing private transactions costs. Another argument against international policy coordination is that government officials do not have sufficient information to fine-tune the world economy, and in trying to do so they ignore the function of the international price system and act to destabilize the world economic order (a point also brought out in Tumlir's chapter).

Scheide and Sinn find little empirical support for international policy coordination, thus adding weight to their theoretical case against such coordination. The "locomotive strategy," often used to exemplify successful coordination, increased worldwide inflation in the late 1970s and led to a recession. The EMS, meanwhile, was not as successful in reducing inflation in member countries as were non-EMS, OECD countries that disciplined their monetary and fiscal authorities.

The very weakness of the case for international policy coordination points to the comparative advantage of a decentralized approach to world economic order. As an alternative to myopic international policy coordination, therefore, the authors suggest a rules-based approach to coordination in which each country adopts specific rules to achieve monetary and fiscal stability. Arguments from rationality and competition suggest that such an approach would allow policymakers to learn from each other and that over time only the best policy rules would survive.

*Economic Policy and World Order*

According to Tumlir, a stable international economic order requires that national governments adhere to credible monetary and trade policies to ensure price stability, currency convertibility, and open markets. Within this policy framework, an international price system can operate to transmit relevant economic information across national boundaries and allow for a more efficient allocation of resources. The present danger, in Tumlir's view, is that national governments have eroded the world price system by veering from sound monetary and trade policies. The erratic behavior of money, prices, and interest rates during the 1970s and 1980s has been compounded by interventions on the "real side" of the international economy, argues Tumlir. In particular, the increased use of nontariff barriers to international trade has impaired the world price system and added to the instability of real exchange rates.

Seeking to address the problems confronting the world economy, national governments have opted for a negotiations approach to trade liberalization. Tumlir, however, criticizes this approach for its failure to recognize the underlying issue, namely, the lack of a set of rules constraining the opportunities of governments to cause monetary instability and to interfere with markets and prices. According to Tumlir, the negotiations approach to achieving world economic order is bound to fail because it places too much emphasis on international agreement, ignores the self-interest of politicians, and is not bound by clear-cut principles that would benefit all nations. Instead of producing greater stability, the negotiations approach, in Tumlir's view, is more likely to lead to international organizations that act as redistributive agents for member nations. The consequent attenuation of property rights can serve only to increase uncertainty and lower the world's wealth.

With respect to the debt crisis, Tumlir calls for "macroeconomic tightening and microeconomic liberalization," both for debtor and creditor nations. To achieve this goal, however, requires a change of perspective—from seeing government as responsible for all aspects of economic life to seeing government as a rulemaker and rule enforcer in an economic system where individuals retain a high degree of freedom and responsibility. For Tumlir, the "threat to democratic constitutions" stems from the difficulty of replacing the modern concept of the redistributive state with the older liberal conception of the minimal state. Thus, although at first glance trade restrictions appear as devices to protect special interest groups, Tumlir emphasizes that ultimately such restrictions "protect a particular conception of economic policy, of the government's role in the economy, and a particular form of politics, all of which are at variance with constitutional prescriptions."

*Restoring the Constitutional Perspective*

Government failure, not market failure, appears to be the basic source of international economic disorder.[13] Without changing this fundamental flaw by constitutional reform at the national level, there is little reason to be optimistic about the success of international policy coordination or global approches to reform.

In considering the path toward greater international economic order, the presumption should be in favor of freedom rather than additional government controls or what Roland Vaubel (1986, p. 53) has called "naive internationalism," that is, an internationalism that "welcomes international agreements for their own sake—regardless of what is being agreed upon." In Vaubel's opinion, this type of international policy coordination is dangerous because there is "a systematic built-in tendency toward collusion at the expense of the citizens." Moreover, there is the possibility that such an approach to international organization "crowds out unambiguously desirable forms of international cooperation: agreements to remove non-market obstacles to market interdependence in the field of international trade and capital movements."

[13]According to Tumlir (1985, p. 71), "An economist contemplating the present state of the mixed economics of the West cannot escape the impression that, while market failure is occasionally discernable, government failure is glaring and massive."

The move to floating, in Haberler's judgment, has been "a great victory of economic freedom over controls" (Haberler 1986, p. 8). Yet, it would be even more so if governments would discontinue their attempts to subject market exchange rates to their own policy preferences. In an open market the exchange rate is an important indicator of the state of nature *and* the state of political economy. As Josef Molsberger (1978, p. 26) has so aptly put it:

> The rate of exchange is only the seismograph that registers the earthquake. . . . The earthquake did not by any means begin on March 19, 1973, with the beginning of floating, but since that time the seismograph has been working. And now everyone can see what had been hidden before: the discouraging fact that the countries of the Western world do not agree on fundamental questions of economic policy, above all on the question of the stabilization of the domestic value of money.

Masking exchange rates by official intervention or outright control can serve only to slow the necessary adjustments process. The current volatility of the foreign exchange value of the dollar reflects fundamental policy imbalances, which will not be corrected by more rigid exchange rates. In the words of Milton Friedman (1962, p. 69): "Instability of exchange rates is a symptom of instability in the underlying economic structure. Elimination of this symptom by administrative freezing of exchange rates cures none of the underlying difficulties and only makes adjustment to them more painful."

The signaling function of floating exchange rates is important because it can point to the need for corrective policy actions.[14] Signaling itself, however, does not indicate the precise measures needed. For establishing these measures, a careful analysis is necessary based on the long-run, constitutional perspective taken by many of the contributors to the present volume. By taking such a perspective and tracing out the implications of alternative monetary and exchange rate regimes, including a free-market money regime, the contributors to this volume aim at the core problems now confronting the world economy.

Much work remains to be done in getting the message of economic liberalism across to an entrenched Congress whose ears are attuned mostly to special interest groups rather than to economic logic and the general consumer. Perhaps the best we can hope for is that each country look to its own state of economic and constitutional disorder and slowly attempt to restore what F. A. Hayek (1960) has called the

[14]The recent *Economic Report* (1989, p. 106) stated: "Although flexible exchange rates exhibit substantial short-run variability, they provide efficient and timely signals to markets and governments when actions and policies go awry."

"constitution of liberty." To do so, however, also requires that individuals begin to acquire what James Buchanan (1977, p. 298) has referred to as a "constitutional attitude," that is, "an appreciation and understanding of the difference between choosing basic rules and acting within those rules."

In the process of restoring a constitutional perspective, it will be useful to recall the policy advice of Adam Smith ([1776] 1937, p. xliii), whose vision helped pave the way for economic freedom and prosperity:

> Little else is requisite to carry a state to the highest degree of opulence from the lowest barbarism, but peace, easy taxes, and a tolerable administration of justice; all the rest being brought about by the natural course of things. All governments which thwart this natural course, which force things into another channel or which endeavour to arrest the progress of society at a particular point, are unnatural, and to support themselves are obliged to be oppressive and tyrannical.

The challenge facing the United States and other countries is to revive the Smithian constitutional perspective and then to maintain it for a more stable international order.

## References

Buchanan, James M. *Freedom in Constitutional Contract: Perspectives of a Political Economist.* College Station: Texas A & M University Press, 1977.

Dorn, James A. "Dollars, Deficits, and Trade." Introduction. *Cato Journal* 8 (Fall 1988): 229–51.

*Economic Report of the President.* Washington, D.C.: Government Printing Office, January 1989.

Friedman, Milton. *Capitalism and Freedom* Chicago: University of Chicago Press, 1962.

Greenfield, Robert L., and Yeager, Leland B. "A Laissez-Faire Approach to Monetary Stability." *Journal of Money, Credit, and Banking* 15 (August 1983): 302–15.

Haberler, Gottfried. "The International Monetary System." *The AEI Economist* (July 1986): 1–8.

Hayek, Friedrich A. "The Use of Knowledge in Society." *American Economic Review* 35 (September 1945): 519–30.

Hayek, Friedrich A. *The Constitution of Liberty.* Chicago: University of Chicago Press, 1960.

Hume, David. "Of the Jealousy of Trade." 1777. In Hume, *Essays: Moral, Political, and Literary,* pp. 327–31. 2d ed. 1889. Reprint. Edited by Eugene F. Miller. Indianapolis: Liberty Classics, 1985.

Melamed, Leo, ed. *The Merits of Flexible Exchange Rates: An Anthology.* Fairfax, Va.: George Mason University Press, 1988.

Molsberger, Josef. "How Floating Exchange Rates Are Working: A European View." In *Exchange Rate Flexibility,* pp. 25–45. Edited by Jacob S. Dreyer,

Gottfried Haberler, and Thomas D. Willett, Washington, D.C.: American Enterprise Institute, 1978.
Niskanen, William A. *Reaganomics: An Insider's Account of the Policies and the People*. New York: Oxford University Press, 1988.
Smith, Adam. *The Wealth of Nations*. 1776. Reprint. Edited by Edwin Cannan. New York: The Modern Library, Random House, 1937.
Tumlir, Jan. *Protectionism: Trade Policy in Democratic Societies*. Washington, D.C.: American Enterprise Institute, 1985.
Vaubel, Roland. "A Public Choice Approach to International Organization." *Public Choice* 51 (1986): 39–57.
Yeager, Leland B. *International Monetary Relations: Theory, History, and Policy*. 2d ed. New York: Harper & Row, 1976.

# Part I

# The Dollar and Domestic Monetary Policy

# 2

# CURRENT PERSPECTIVES ON MONETARY POLICY*

*Manuel H. Johnson*

Rather than discuss the specifics of the Federal Reserve's current concerns and goals for policy, I wish to discuss the more fundamental long-term goals of monetary policy and how we can proceed to reach these goals—particularly under current domestic and international monetary arrangements. Clarifying the goals of policy is especially important in our current monetary environment in which essentially every currency in the world is directly, or indirectly, on a pure fiat standard.[1] In such circumstances, the credibility of the world's monetary authorities is of utmost importance.

## Appropriate Goals of Monetary Policy

Despite all of our problems, we have learned a great deal about the appropriate goals of monetary policy in recent years. We know, for example, that under fiat arrangements, price stability is an achievable goal and should be a principal objective of monetary policy. A policy that fosters steadiness and predictability in the general price level is essential for genuine noninflationary economic growth.

We have also learned that sharp unanticipated changes in monetary policy can be disruptive to the economy. Accordingly, the pursuit of price stability should also seek to minimize such short-term disruptions to economic activity.

Among monetary experts, there probably is little disagreement on these policy goals. However, there is currently a good deal of disagreement on how to best achieve these objectives.

---

*Reprinted from *Cato Journal* 8 (Fall 1988): 253–60.

The author is Vice Chairman of the Board of Governors of the Federal Reserve System. This paper is based on a luncheon address Governor Johnson gave at the Cato Institute's Sixth Annual Monetary Conference, Washington, D.C., February 25, 1988.

[1]See, for example, Friedman and Schwartz (1986, p. 38).

## The Conduct of Monetary Policy

### *Deterioration in the Performance of Monetary Aggregates*

Until a few years ago, there was a growing consensus among monetary economists that the best way to conduct policy was to target monetary aggregates as an intermediate objective. It appeared that the quantity of money was a superior target for the Fed to use in order to achieve price stability and to promote stable economic activity.

Unfortunately, in recent years it has become evident that the relationship between the monetary aggregates and income has become less predictable. Various measures of the velocity of money, for example, have experienced large deviations from trend during the 1980s. Indeed, over this period the velocity decline for most monetary aggregates has been unprecedented in the postwar era. And, as yet, this decline is not fully understood. Consequently, future movements in velocity remain uncertain.

There are several factors that have contributed to this deterioration in performance of the monetary aggregates. While it is probably premature to draw any definite conclusions, it appears that the interaction of deregulation, disinflation, and sizable movements in interest rates have worked to alter the behavior of money supply measures. Due to these factors, money growth is much more sensitive to changes in interest rates and opportunity costs than was previously the case. Since this increased sensitivity works to lessen the predictability of the relationship between money and GNP, these aggregates become less reliable as policy targets.

Admittedly, it is probably too early to conclude that the monetary aggregates will not be useful in the future as policy indicators or targets. But even if stable, predictable velocity reemerges, it will take an extended period before enough confidence and credibility can be mustered so that money supply measures can be used as the sole intermediate target of policy.

### *Alternative Indicators for Implementing Monetary Policy*

Given this (at least temporary) deterioration in the performance of the monetary aggregates, what alternative indicators are available for implementing policy? Policymakers, after all, necessarily will use some guides in executing policy. What properties or characteristics should such indicators possess?

First, useful indicators should be accurately measurable and readily available. Second, they should respond to changes in Federal Reserve policy actions. And third, they should be reliably related to the ultimate goals of monetary policy. A corollary to these guidelines is that monetary policy can only reliably influence nominal but not real variables. It is well known, for example, that attempts to target variables such as unemployment, or real growth, can lead to procyclical, destabilizing movements in general prices.

Given these guidelines, there has been some interest recently in the use of nominal prices of certain financial instruments traded in auction markets. Such interest has not been to use these prices as policy targets but rather as indicators or informational supplements to policy. Preliminary research suggests that these variables may satisfy the above-cited criteria for policy indicators. More specifically, information contained in the term structure of interest rates (yield curve), the foreign exchange market, and certain broad indices of commodity prices has proven useful in the formulation of monetary policy.

Other things equal, all of these indicators should provide signals as to when monetary policy becomes expansionary (easy) or restrictive (tight). This is particularly the case when these indicators are examined together or in conjunction with one another. For example, should one observe the simultaneous occurrence of steepening yield curve, increasing commodity prices, and a depreciating dollar, then it may be inferred that monetary policy most likely has been expansionary.

However, this approach certainly is not foolproof and when such indicators are followed in isolation they can sometimes prove to be misleading. These indicators can be volatile and are sometimes determined or influenced by factors other than monetary policy. Also, they are not always independent from each other and can be affected by expectations of policy change.

Despite these caveats, preliminary evidence is promising enough to suggest that these indicators may prove useful in the formulation of policy. In particular, each of these indicators can provide useful information. When used cautiously and in conjunction with one another so as to piece together a consistent intepretation of overall policy, they can often provide valuable insights into the policymaking process. And being nominal variables, if they are used in a strategy to foster price stability, they will work to prevent any major monetary policy mistakes. If nothing else, they provide useful information that should not be ignored.

The use of market-determined prices as policy indicators (or informational supplements) is an appealing strategy for several reasons. First, the data measuring these variables are readily available, literally by the minute. These market prices provide observable, timely, and more accurate information than is provided by other sources. There are no problems with revisions, seasonal adjustment procedures, or shift adjustment corrections that plague quantity or volume data. Moreover, the strategy does not rely on unobservable variables such as real interest rates that depend on accurate measurements of future price expectations.

Second, the strategy is premised on the notion that market prices encompass the knowledge and expectations of a large number of buyers and sellers. And while it is true that individual market participants may be irrational, this is not likely to be the case for the market as a whole. Therefore, financial auction market prices reflect the consensus about the current and expected future values of financial instruments. As such, these prices serve as communicators of changing knowledge of market conditions.

Third, since there is evidence that the broader price measures such as the CPI or GNP deflator are slow to reflect new information, changes in monetary policy should be reflected in financial auction market prices well before they affect the broader price measures. Thus, there is reason to believe these prices may give advance warning of impending change for important concerns such as inflation.

It is worth noting that monitoring financial markets in conjunction with one another to piece together a consistent interpretation is not novel. During the period when England had gone off the gold standard in the early 19th century, for example, classical monetary writers monitored such indicators to assess central bank policy. There is a passage in the famous Bullion Report published in 1810 in which this is clearly documented. Because financial innovations had occurred and accurate and timely monetary statistics were not available at the time, these monetary analysts argued that the central bank should use financial market prices as guides to policy.

In the following brief discussion I cannot possibly provide a detailed analysis of all the research and evidence pertaining to the yield curve, the foreign exchange rate, or commodity prices. Nor can I provide any simple, foolproof prescription on how these indicators should be interpreted. Suffice it to say that there are some difficulties associated with each of the indicators as separate forecasting tools. But when examined together, they often yield valuable insights in evaluating the stance of monetary policy and particularly in assessing movements in expectations of inflation.

With this in mind, I will provide a rough sketch of how each of these market prices may provide useful insights into policy. Each indicator makes a contribution to this approach, but these indicators are not intended to be used as explicit targets for policy.

## The Yield Curve

With respect to money and bond markets, empirical evidence suggests that expansionary monetary policy is often reflected in a more positively sloped yield curve whereas a yield curve that becomes inverted (negatively sloped) often reflects a restrictive policy stance.[2] Inverted yield curves, for example, have preceded most recessions in the postwar era. Indeed, the results of one recent study indicated that the spread between the Fed funds rate and the long bond rate outperformed three other variables as an indicator of the impact of the monetary policy on future real economic activity.[3]

Most analysts do believe that there is useful information reflected in the yield curve. And there are theoretical reasons and evidence to suggest that this spread reflects expectations of future yields as determined in part by expectations of future inflation. These observations imply, of course, that it is not the level of interest rates but the change in the spread that may serve as a useful indicator of the posture of monetary policy.

But one cannot perfectly predict the effects that a change in policy will have on the yield curve; hence this indicator should not serve as a target of policy. The yield curve is affected by a number of other factors such as changes in Treasury funding policy, altered risk premiums, and tax policy, as well as changes in liquidity preference.

Consequently, while the yield curve may provide useful information about monetary policy, it must be interpreted with caution and reservation. The yield curve is certainly not an infallible indicator.[4] However, when it is analyzed in conjunction with other market prices, the yield curve can be interpreted with more confidence and can make an important contribution to policymaking.

[2]The yield curve referred to in this paper is the spread between the Federal funds rate and the 30-year Treasury bond rate. It is important for the arguments made herein that the funds rate be used as the appropriate short-term rate since it is this rate that Fed monetary policy most directly influences.

[3]See Laurent (1988).

[4]While useful in assessing the thrust of monetary policy, the spread between the Fed funds rate and the long-term bond rate does not necessarily tell us anything about changes in inflationary expectations.

## Commodity Prices

There is also some empirical evidence to suggest that broad indices of commodity prices respond to changes in monetary policy and tend to lead changes in broader measures of inflation. Governor Angell's research project, indicating that commodity prices lead turning points in the CPI, is interesting in this regard (see Angell 1987). Of course, there remain questions as to exactly which commodities and weights should be employed in such a broad index. Research is currently under way at the Federal Reserve to investigate these questions and examine these relationships.

It is true that the reliability as well as the quantitative importance of these empirical relationships have not been firmly established. And little evidence exists that indicates the Fed can accurately control such indices. Moreover, commodity prices are volatile and are influenced by a number of factors not related to monetary policy. Accordingly, commodity prices are more valuable as an indicator for monetary policy than as an explicit policy target.

## The Foreign Exchange Value of the Dollar

It has long been recognized that the foreign exchange value of the dollar can also provide useful information for monetary policymakers. The exchange rate often indicates the stance of U.S. monetary policy relative to that in other countries. As such, the exchange rate offers a gauge of relative monetary expansion or contraction.

For example, if the dollar is depreciating while the yield curve is steepening and commodity prices are rising, policy is likely expansionary and perhaps overly so. On the other hand, if the dollar is depreciating while commodity prices and the yield curve are stable, the dollar may reflect restrictive foreign monetary policy or other external factors.[5] Moreover, if the dollar was declining and the yield curve was steepening but commodity prices remained stable, this could reflect an outflow of foreign funds from the U.S. bond market for reasons other than inflationary expectations.

Monitoring exchange rate movements to supplement other indicators, of course, is not foolproof. The exchange markets are volatile and intervention can (at least temporarily) distort signals from this market. Moreover a great deal of information about foreign economic performance and policy is required to properly assess this market.

[5]In assessing movements in commodity prices and the dollar, it should be mentioned that commodity prices denominated in foreign currencies or special-drawing rights (SDRs) should also be monitored in order to assess whether commodity price movements reflect world inflation or exchange-rate-related domestic price movement.

It should also be pointed out that exercises in international coordination of monetary policy—which necessarily implies a move to more stable exchange rates—tend to lessen the information content of foreign exchange rates. While stable exchange rates are desirable, stability removes information from this market. After all, it is (theoretically) possible to have either rapid inflation or rapid deflation with stable exchange rates.

Accordingly, information provided by commodity prices and yield curves may assume more importance in analyzing inflationary expectations should coordination be used to stabilize exchange rates.

## Additional Considerations

It could be argued that since the Federal Reserve will be watching the markets and market participants will be watching the Fed, there is a simultaneity problem with the approach I have suggested. Accordingly, there is a risk that market price volatility will increase and that market prices and the Fed funds rate will spiral up and down together.

Concerns that this strategy will bring about increased volatility or instability are ill-founded for several reasons. First, some economic or fundamental event has to initiate market price movement; such events must either cause the Fed to act or the markets to anticipate Fed action. Anticipations do not change for no reason.

An example serves to illustrate that this strategy will not foster unstable or volatile market conditions. Indeed, such a strategy may work to stabilize such prices. Suppose, for example, that commodity prices and long-term interest rates started to increase while the dollar began to depreciate. It might be anticipated that the Fed would tighten policy. This anticipation may or may not lead to higher long-term rates. But anticipations of Fed tightening would not lead to higher commodity prices or a lower dollar. If anything, such anticipations would work to dampen both increases in commodity prices and further dollar depreciation. And such anticipations certainly would not lead to an upward spiral in long-term rates. In fact, long-term rates would continue to rise until the Fed had tightened policy enough to reduce or reverse the initial economic pressures that led to higher commodity prices and a weakened dollar in the first place. Just because the Fed moves the Fed funds rate in one direction does not mean that long-term rates will always move in the same direction. There are many cases where a funds rate movement in one direction has elicited movements in long-term rates in the opposite direction.

In short, such a strategy may work to stabilize rather than to destabilize these markets. Moreover, if the Federal Reserve has garnered a good deal of credibility, there should not be important movements in commodity prices, the dollar, or long-term rates due to changes in price expectations.

The timing of any potential Fed responses to these indicators is also a relevant concern. Clearly, the Fed will wait for a certain amount of time for confirming evidence regarding market price movements before responding to signals from these indicators even when all three are pointing in the same direction. The volatility of these prices, the fact that expectations can affect these markets, and the fact that these markets are not independent, all suggest the appropriateness of allowing for a reasonable period of time to observe trends. After all, the lapse of a certain amount of time may allow overreactions or false expectations of policy action to unwind. On the other hand, the Fed does not want to delay too long or it will forgo the advantages of using such price data. Certainly the magnitudes of the price movements will also alter the response time.

## Conclusion

In spite of several caveats and in the absence of reliable alternative indicators, financial auction markets can provide useful information to the process of monetary policy formulation. I believe the strategy outlined here provides a framework for focusing monetary policy on the conditions for price stability. And price stability is a goal that should direct our attention to these markets.

## References

Angell, Wayne D. "A Commodity Price Guide to Monetary Aggregate Targeting." Paper presented for the Lehrman Institute, 10 December 1987.

Friedman, Milton, and Schwartz, Anna J. "Has Government Any Role in Money?" *Journal of Monetary Economics* 17 (January 1986): 37–62.

Laurent, Robert D. "An Interest Rate Based Indicator of Monetary Policy." Federal Reserve Bank of Chicago *Economic Perspectives* 12 (January/February 1988).

# 3

# Domestic Stability Versus Exchange Rate Stability*

*Leland B. Yeager*

## Purchasing Powers and Exchange Rates

In accepting the title assigned for this paper, I do not mean to agree that the two stabilities *necessarily* conflict. Often, to be sure, they do. Countries that clung to the fixed gold parities of their currencies in the early 1930s, including France and other members of the European gold bloc until 1936, suffered worse contagion of the world depression than if they had let their currencies depreciate. Other countries mitigated the contagion by accepting relatively early depreciation, as Great Britain and the Sterling Area countries did in 1931 and as Spain did around the same time.

Experience with the Bretton Woods system of fixed exchange rates after World War II provides many examples of countries suffering imported inflation in consequence of attempts to maintain fixed rates despite bullish speculation on their currencies. The upward floats of the German mark in September 1969 and May 1971, of the Swiss franc in January 1973, and of the Singapore dollar in June 1973, to mention just a few cases, were attempts, belated attempts, to ward off the further import of inflation. The worldwide spurt of monetary inflation in the early 1970s, followed in due course by accelerated price inflation, traces largely to attempts to keep dozens of currencies from rising against the U.S. dollar. This last-ditch defense of the Bretton Woods system finally collapsed early in 1973. The world economy would have fared better in the 1970s and afterwards (I could so argue) if policymakers had voluntarily abandoned the Bretton Woods system years earlier, before the worst damage had been done.

None of this is to say that floating exchange rates guarantee domestic monetary stability. A floating rate can soften the domestic impact

*Reprinted from *Cato Journal*, 8 (Fall 1988): 261–77.

The author is the Ludwig von Mises Distinguished Professor of Economics at Auburn University.

of monetary instability originating abroad, but no economist known to me ever argued that floating rates would provide insulation against all foreign disturbances. None ever argued that they would make sound monetary institutions and policies unnecessary. My own chief argument for abandoning the Bretton Woods system was that doing so would largely relieve national monetary authorities—or the more responsible among them—of balance-of-payments problems and other international complications and allow them to concentrate more nearly fully on achieving stability for their own countries. I did not hail the collapse of Bretton Woods when it actually occurred, for I regretted the particular way it came about and recognized that it represented no intellectual conversion on the part of policymakers.

Neither exchange rate stability nor purchasing power stability guarantees the other (for example, a domestically stable currency would fluctuate against unstable foreign currencies). The two stabilities could be compatible, however: Rates could be fairly stable among currencies of dependably stable purchasing powers.

## Volatile and Misaligned Exchange Rates

Today's world exhibits both types of *in*stability. It is most conspicuous in exchange rates. Bilateral rates have fluctuated 10 and 20 percent over weeks and months and sometimes several percent from day to day or even within days. Over hours, days, months, and perhaps even years, gross capital transactions—transactions to reshuffle asset portfolios, including speculative transactions—have far overshadowed trade in goods and services. The *daily* volume of foreign exchange trading in the United States, Britain, and Japan alone is estimated to total nearly $200 billion (*Wall Street Journal*, 28 December 1987, p. 24).

One apparent source of rate volatility is "noise" (cf. Black 1986). High-technology communications and data processing bring facts and figures and rumors to the attention of traders more frequently and in more discrete bits than in the past, causing frequent shifts in noise-oriented trading decisions. The special role of the U.S. dollar as the predominant transactions, vehicle, reserve, and intervention currency places it in a particularly conspicuous and vulnerable position. Participants in sensitive markets must eagerly watch each day's economic and political news and must not only form their own interpretations but must also wonder what other people's interpretations are likely to be. No wonder quasi-speculative capital movements, and exchange rates in consequence, are as volatile as they are.

Official market intervention, though ideally smoothing exchange rate movements, contributes to the noise. It is an unsettled issue whether intervention, together with news and rumors of its being started, altered, or suspended, has made exchange rates more or less volatile on the whole than they otherwise would have been. (My 1976, chapter 14, discusses how intervention might increase volatility and surveys episodes in which it apparently did.) For several years I have been collecting stories from the *Wall Street Journal* and other financial publications purporting to explain hour-to-hour, day-to-day, and week-to-week jumps in exchange rates. Remarkably often the stories point to changes in intervention and to rumors and supposed clues about it, including statements and offhand remarks of government officials. I wonder how the foreign exchange market would have behaved without such disturbances.

Floating rates have exhibited not only short-run volatility but also medium-run misalignments, resulting—critics plausibly allege—in distorted patterns of trade and production and in wasteful shifts of resources between domestic industries and export and import-competing industries. Only in a tautological, pollyannistic sense can one say that the exchange rate of the dollar has been "right" all along, even at its trough of mid-1980, its peak of early 1985, and its current depressed level.

## Superficial Advice

It is superficial to conclude that we should have kept exchange rates fixed 15 years ago and that we should fix them again now. Prodigious efforts to keep them fixed simply collapsed. But if those efforts had somehow prevailed a while longer, what even more immense foreign-exchange crises would have destroyed the system in the face of the even more unstable "fundamentals" of the 1970s and 1980s, including the oil situation and swollen national budget deficits! (One can plausibly argue, however, that even OPEC's predation was largely triggered by worldwide inflation tracing, in turn, to last-ditch defense of the Bretton Woods system.) More recently, even efforts to peg exchange rates loosely within fuzzy and unannounced ranges—the Louvre accord of February 1987—collapsed later that year. What is the point of saying that something should have been done or should now be done if in fact it could not and cannot be done?

It is superficial to argue against floating exchange rates by deploring the apparent consequences—first of the strengthening and then of the weakening of the U.S. dollar in the 1980s. A legitimate comparison between floating and fixed exchange rates must refer to otherwise similar circumstances—if, indeed, circumstances could have been kept otherwise similar. It is illegitimate to compare actual experience with a situation lacking the circumstances (such as those of the U.S. government budget) that made the dollar swing as widely as it in fact did. If we want to consider how things would have worked out with the dollar prevented from rising to its peak of early 1985, for example, we must specify how its appreciation would have been prevented. Monetary expansion, accomplished either by unsterilized exchange market intervention or by Federal Reserve policy, would have inflated prices of domestic goods relative to prices of internationally traded goods—would have lowered the latter prices relatively—and so would have affected resource allocation and the country's trade balance in a way similar to what in fact occurred. Preventing dollar-strengthening capital inflows, conceivably by direct controls, would have relieved domestic producers of internationally traded goods from some adversity; but it would have allowed interest rates to rise and government deficit spending to crowd out some interest-sensitive investment activity, including housing. (See, in part, Gradison 1986 and Frankel 1985.)

## Where Lies the Absurdity?

It seems absurd to let so pervasively influential a price as a country's exchange rate jump around in response to investors' and speculators' changeable whims about their asset holdings. It seems absurd that changes in and expectations and rumors about monetary and fiscal policies, trade policies, and market interventions should be allowed to exert such quick, magnified, and pervasive effects. But we should be clear about just *what* is absurd. It is not the free flexibility of exchange rates (they are not *freely* flexible anyway). It is not the free-market determination of prices on the exchange markets.

The absurdity consists, rather, in what those prices are the prices *of*. They are the prices of national fiat moneys expressed in each other, each lacking any defined value. The purchasing power of each national money depends on confrontation between a restricted quantity of it and the demand for holdings of it. At bottom, the unit of account in the United States is whatever value supply and demand fleetingly accord to a scruffy piece of paper, the dollar bill. The value of each money thus depends on conjectures about the good intentions of the government issuing it and about its ability to carry through on its good intentions. These conjectures are subject to sharp change, quite understandably.

It is an absurd system in which people cannot count on money's future purchasing power. Money's value simply emerges as the by-product of the monetary authorities' doing whatever seems best to them month by month and day by day. It is an absurd system in which the Federal Reserve gets badgered daily with diverse unsolicited advice in *Business Week* and the *Wall Street Journal* by such people as Alan Blinder, Paul Craig Roberts, Irving Kristol, Milton Friedman, and miscellaneous editorial writers.

Given this fundamental absurdity, it is irrelevant to propose mere changes in the details of how governments manipulate exchange rates. (The proposal for "target zones," it seems to me, is hardly more than a superficially attractive combination of words, words calling for all of the advantages and none of the disadvantages of both floating and fixed exchange rates.)

A fundamental solution would give defined values to currencies. A meaningful definition of a currency's value must consist of something more than a specified rate of exchange against one or more foreign currencies, each of which continues to lack a defined value. The most familiar and plausible kind of meaningful definition would run in terms of one or more commodities.

## Commodity Money

Should gold be the single defining commodity? I agree with those who say that the world should never have gone off the gold standard, which means that the nations should never have blundered into World War I. I fervently wish we could repeal World War I and all its many evil consequences, but I do not see how. Restoring the special historical circumstances under which the gold standard appeared to flourish (but only for a very few decades) would have to include restoring certain attitudes that seemed more prevalent in public affairs before 1914 than now. Those attitudes favored limitations on government activity and restraint on seeking special advantage through the instrumentality of government. Without a return to liberal attitudes and self-restraints, a restored gold standard would not work well and would hardly endure. After all, the gold standard is simply a particular set of rules for monetary institutions and policy; and these rules are no more inherently self-enforcing than any other set of monetary rules. Even today, before we have gone back to a supposed gold standard, there is reason to suspect that what some of its supporters are advocating is not a real but a pseudo gold standard, to echo a distinction made by Milton Friedman (1961).

The durability of a particular set of monetary rules will depend in large part on its performance characteristics, and those of the gold standard are far from ideal. (I waive discussing the difficulties of a *transition* back to gold; uncoordinated steps by individual countries would surely work badly.) A unit of account defined as the value of a quantity of a single commodity like gold is preposterous in the same general way as, though perhaps in lesser degree than, a unit coinciding with a unit of a fiat medium of exchange like the dollar bill. Like fiat money, gold has an unstable value in relation to other goods and services. The stock of gold is historically given and cannot rapidly accommodate changes in demand. The demand for it, under a gold standard, arises primarily from its use as coins and, especially, as a reserve and redemption medium for other forms of money; it is largely a monetary demand rather than a purely industrial or consumption demand. That demand shifts with changes in money-holding and reserve-holding practices, with the availability of near-moneys, and with other financial innovations.

The value of gold-based money is thus conventional or artificial only in lesser degree than the value of fiat money. The effective size of a gold-defined unit of value, like that of the fiat dollar bill, is defined poorly and is maintained only precariously. It is changeable in a way just not true of other units, like the meter or kilogram.

When, furthermore, the supply-and-demand situation calls for a change in the value of the money unit (that is, in the general price level) and if the supply of money is not cleverly manipulated to accommodate the demand for it, then monetary disequilibrium persists, bringing macroeconomic pains (Yeager 1986). In particular, prices and wages are not and cannot be flexible enough in the downward direction quickly to correct an excess of the demand for money holdings over their supply. And even if they were flexible enough, the associated rise in the real value of outstanding debts would cause trouble. A catch-22 plagues a system exposed to emergence of excess demand for or excess supply of money: It is damned both if prices *are* flexible enough and if they are *not* flexible enough to correct monetary imbalance quickly.

## Money of Stable Purchasing Power

These considerations recommend seeking a system that would maintain balance between the demand for and supply of money at a stable general price level. The old issue of money of stable purchasing power is ripe for reconsideration. A tentative judgment in its favor would have to be thrown out if no satisfactory way of *imple-*

*menting* it turns out to be available. Before considering implementation, though, I want to review arguments for and against regarding a stable unit as an ideal.

Money whose value is under no pressure either to rise and fall is money whose actual quantity is in balance with the quantity demanded. By that very token, the economy employing it escapes the pains of monetary disequilibrium. Why monetary disequilibrium can be so painful and its avoidance so important hinges on certain distinctive characterictics of money, notably that it, among all goods, lacks a market of its own and a single price of its own on which the pressures of supply-demand imbalance can come to a focus and work effectively to maintain or restore equilibrium. The importance of this point is far out of line with how briefly it can be stated. (Admittedly, statement is not explanation; again, see my 1986 discussion.)

A more familiar line of argument for stable money—which can be challenged, as I recognize below—draws analogies between the unit of account and units of weights and measures. A seriously unstable unit impairs the meeting of minds between borrowers and lenders and other transactors. Economic calculation and the coordination of economic activities are at stake; for the unit of account is used pervasively in proposing the terms of transactions, in assessing costs and benefits, and in business and personal planning. Imagine the difficulty of constructing and equipping a house if the foot varied capriciously in size. The absurdity of unstable money is like letting the length of the meter fluctuate according to supply and demand in the market for meter sticks. A stable unit, in contrast, provides a sound basis for economic calculation and contracting.

## Objections to the Goal of Price-Level Stability

One objection to seeking a stable unit of account rejects the analogy between such a unit and units of weight and length and other physical magnitudes. The kilogram and meter are widely applicable across time and space, and any redefinitions made are mere refinements (e.g., definitions of the meter as one ten-millionth of the distance between the equator and the north pole, then as 1,650,763.73 wavelengths of the radiation of krypton 86, and currently as 1/299,792,458 of the distance that light travels in one second). The definition of a unit of value in terms of a price index or basket of commodities, however, must concern itself with the quality characteristics of each commodity, the terms of its delivery satisfying the rules of specified commodity exchanges, and other such technicalities. If changes in supply and demand conditions affecting commodities in the bundle defining the unit of value should require respecification of that bundle, it might be more difficult to keep the new and old values exactly equal at the time of redefinition than in the case of redefinition of the meter. The definition of the unit of value has a subjective aspect, furthermore, that is absent in the definition of physical units.

All this may be true, but it amounts to mere quibbles. Of course analogies between physical units and a value unit are just that, analogies, and not exact correspondences. So what? People do regard the unit of account—the money unit, under our existing system—as the unit for measuring values. They so use it every day. They so use it in trying to quantify prospective costs and benefits of purchases and sales and other activities and in forming and carrying out plans. Its use plays a vital role in coordinating the activities of different persons. People do not care about the dollar size or gold-unit size of a particular price, income, debt, or accounting magnitude except as it indicates value in relation to a much wider set of goods and services. A unit of greatly variable purchasing power subverts people's calculations and degrades the information supposedly conveyed by prices and accounting. If we take seriously the burgeoning literature on various subtle damages wrought by inflation, we should appreciate the importance of a stable unit.

Admittedly, the choice of a particular price index or bundle of goods and services for defining the unit is bound to be somewhat arbitrary, but we should not exaggerate the difficulty. What sorts of goods and services to consider, and even criteria for weighting them, should command a broad consensus. A real distinction holds between unmistakable change in the value of money as shown by *any* reasonable indicator and, on the other hand, genuine doubt about any trend in its purchasing power as some prices hold steady, others rise, and still others fall under pressures specific to their own markets. Maintenance of such doubt would count as achievement of a stable unit and would reflect avoidance of any severe monetary disequilibrium.

Another objection to maintaining a stable unit is the argument against price-fixing. Prices, even including the value of the money unit, should be determined on free markets rather than determined by authority. Freely flexible prices and wages have functions to perform. (Anderson 1929 loosely alludes to such an argument, as does Rothbard 1985, p. 6.) Yes, but this is properly an argument for free-market determination of individual prices and wages, not against appropriate specification of the unit of account. Adopting a stable unit would aid, not impair, the working of markets. (I sympathize with advocates of the gold standard when they are criticized for supposedly advocating price-fixing. The critics should recognize the difference between fixing some ordinary price and adopting a quantity of gold as the unit of account. Consider an analogy: Offering a specific definition of a unit of length, the meter, is not properly open to criticism of the sort that would be justified against governmental decrees about the length of trouser legs and the dimensions of rooms in houses. Instead of being criticized for recommending a defined monetary unit, gold-standard advocates might better be criticized for the particular definition they recommend.)

Still another line of argument insists that cheapening of real costs of production through the rise of productivity ought to show up in declining prices (and conversely for a deterioration in productivity). David Davidson expounded such arguments with the aid of examples. A policy of stabilizing the price level would deprive a creditor of any share of the gains from a general rise in productivity, while someone who had borrowed for productive purposes would unfairly keep the entire gain for himself. Or consider two owners of farm land, only one of whom had leveraged his holding by debt. A general rise in the output of land would tend to depress the prices of its products and so not unambiguously press the money value of the land itself either up or down. A monetary policy of stabilizing the product price level, however, would raise the land's money value; and the leveraging landowner would gain differentially, which also seemed unfair to Davidson. Presumably money should be stabilized, if at all, in terms not of products but of labor and other factors of production. (Davidson 1906. Davidson and Knut Wicksell debated such issues over many years in the pages of *Ekonomisk Tidskrift*. I have not yet had access to the issues after 1908; but Uhr [1960] 1962, pp. 270–305, summarizes the debate.)

Admittedly, one may think up cases and propound ethical judgments according to which the holder of a nominal claim should share, through a change in the price level, in the gain or loss caused by a rise or fall in productivity. It is hard to see, however, how detailed conditions, varying from case to case, can be taken into account by monetary institutions and policy. It is unreasonable to burden the monetary system with the task of preserving justice between debtors and creditors and between other groups of the population in the face of multifarious changes in productivity and other conditions. No single institution can do that.

A monetary system should do what it can reasonably be expected to do, and other institutions should undertake tasks more suitable for them. Savers need not restrict themselves to buying interest-bearing securities of fixed nominal value; they can diversify. They can try to take account of prospective changes in productivity by investing in equities. Likewise, would-be borrowers need not borrow only in nominal terms; they can sell stock or obtain loans with equity participations. A sound monetary system with a stable money unit can help provide such opportunities by facilitating the development of financial intermediation. In and by itself, a monetary system cannot solve all sorts of problems.

George Selgin (in personal correspondence) supposes the technological cheapening of some particular good whose price figures significantly in the general price level. As a matter of arithmetic, the price level then falls (unless monetary institutions or policy resist this spontaneous tendency). The cheapened good is not and has not been in excess supply, for its producers have cut its price, painlessly, in line with its reduced cost. The technological advance presumably raises the output of the affected good or of other goods into whose production factors have been released. Thus the real volume of transactions to be lubricated increases, and so does the associated demand for real cash balances. That increased demand is more or less accommodated automatically, however, through money's rise in purchasing power over the cheapened good. The arithmetical decline of prices on average must not be seen as evidence of monetary disequilibrium being corrected, perhaps sluggishly. Monetary expansion to resist this price decline would have "injection effects," probably including the distortion of interest rates, and so would itself be a source of disturbance to market equilibrium.

Such effects were apparently the reason why F. A. Hayek, in early publications, was skeptical about price-level stabilization. Keeping prices constant following an increase in productivity requires banks to expand money and credit by lowering their interest rates. The loan rate that might keep prices from falling is likely to initiate a cumulative and unhealthy investment boom, and the increase in the loan rate that might stop it is likely to reverse it into a downturn, which would require an interest-rate cut before the downturn gains momentum. Hence, an interest-rate policy to stabilize the price level would entail rises and falls around the original or normal level of prices. These oscillations might spawn a growing collection of unfinished and abandoned capital processes, and the waste involved might even overshadow the initial rise in productivity. (Hayek [1931/1935] 1967, Lecture IV; see also the discussion by Uhr [1960] 1962, p. 283.)

Such arguments seem to take it for granted that pursuing a money unit of stable general purchasing power means manipulating the quantity of a fiat money, or of what would be a fiat money except only for the price-level rule. Whether this supposition about how the policy would be implemented is necessarily valid will be examined later in this paper.

Of course a particular good affected by a technological advance tends to fall in price relative to other goods and services and so to fall in price as expressed in a unit of stable general purchasing power. If the index or bundle defining the pricing unit happens to include the affected good, then its price still falls. (It is legitimate to use the terms "price index" and "bundle" almost interchangeably here, for a price index involves a bundle whose total price is being compared over time.) The individual prices of the bundle's other components rise, however, in such a way that the price of the bundle as a whole remains unchanged. This is a straightforward implication of how the unit is specified. The appropriateness of such a specification is what is at issue.

What are the alternatives? Defining the unit as an amount of some single commodity exposes the whole range of goods and services to price inflation if that commodity, say gold under the gold standard, happens to be the one affected by technological advance. That possibility is one of the reasons for defining the unit by a broad bundle in which no single commodity carries a heavy weight.

In reality, all sorts of micro changes are continually occurring, raising the real or relative prices of some goods and lowering those of others. In such a context, it is hard to see what kind of monetary environment is preferable to the one provided by a unit of stable general purchasing power. Selgin's counterexample, like those of Davidson mentioned earlier, seems tacitly to presuppose a fiat money managed in some ideally clever way so as best to suit each particular constellation of circumstances as it arises and is perfectly and instantly diagnosed. But such an instruction to the monetary authorities cannot be operational. It would provide a poor basis for the orientation of expectations and for confident calculations by market participants.

Sometimes it is said that while influences on the price level coming from the side of money should be avoided, influences from the side of goods should be allowed their full natural scope. General changes in productivity, as distinguished from changes affecting only a particular good, enter into this argument. A gentle downtrend in prices would be the natural consequence of generally rising productivity.

I wonder whether such ideas do not rest on some underlying money illusion, some unarticulated belief that money has a value of its own, a value in a profoundly true sense, distinct from its purchasing power as mirrored in the price level. (Davidson 1906 and Anderson [1917] 1922, especially p. 57, did try to distinguish, though not in a way intelligible to me, between the value of money and its purchasing power, the reciprocal of the price level.) On such a notion, situations may arise in which money remains stable in value while goods in general are becoming dearer or cheaper in real terms, and both their individual prices and their average price level should be allowed to reflect these real changes.

Well, rising productivity cheapens some goods relative to others (notably, consumer goods relative to human effort), but it can hardly cheapen goods and services in general relative to goods and services in general. It seems reasonable to expect each good's price to express its value relative to others, which is what pricing in a unit of stable general purchasing power does. The money-side/goods-side distinction does not bear much weight, for growth over time in the physical quantities of goods and services to be traded operates as much on the money side as on the goods side. It leads people to raise their demands for holdings of money, which exerts a deflationary effect, unless the supply of nominal money is somehow made to keep pace with the growing demand for it.

## Money in Adversity

Something more needs to be said about the case of an adverse supply shock, one like or worse than the international oil shock of 1973–74. Prices directly affected rise, and keeping the average level steady means pressing other prices down. Because many of those other prices exhibit downward stickiness, the necessary deflationary process will depress production and employment as well. Far from indicating an excess supply of money, the initial price rise shrinks the money supply in real terms, and a contraction of the nominal money supply in addition would aggravate the deflationary damage to the economy.

Considerations like these have led Robert Hall to recommend a quasi-automatic policy aiming at a stable price level only as a long-run target, while tolerating strictly temporary deviations from the target level. (See Hall 1986 and my comment that follows there.)

If a major calamity or a great war should require distributing the adversity or burden widely throughout the population, an inflationary tax on cash balances and on nominal incomes can hardly be ruled out a priori as one of the means to be employed. (Apparently Wicksell, toward the end of his life, modified his call for price-level stabilization to allow for some such cases of extreme scarcity of goods; see Uhr [1960] 1962, pp. 300–305.)

A country's monetary institutions, like its other institutions, cannot be constructed with guaranteed robustness in the face of external calamities. Institutions should serve the relatively normal conditions in which they have a good chance of surviving and flourishing. It can even be argued that stable money provides a better basis for government borrowing and money issue in rare emergencies than money that commanded little confidence in the first place. (One argument made by advocates of the gold standard in Russia during discussions in the late 19th century about reforming the country's floating paper currency was that a gold standard would provide a sound starting point, a standard to go *off of*, in some future war.)

## Implementation

Some objections to the goal of money of stable purchasing power are really objections to more or less tacitly assumed *methods of implementing* the policy. Critics (e.g., Anderson 1929) often assume that efforts to stabilize the price level would work only through money and credit manipulation by the Federal Reserve. "Austrian" economists worry about "injection effects" or "Cantillon effects" of expanding the money supply to keep the price level from sagging in a technologically advancing and otherwise growing economy. New money impinges first at particular points in the economy, where it distorts the price signals that guide resource allocation. In particular—so goes one familiar story—injection of new money is likely to lower interest rates below the real, natural, or equilibrium rate and so lead business investors to embark on capital-construction projects that will eventually turn out to have been unwise. This is supposedly what happened in the United States in the 1920s: Although monetary expansion was not extreme enough to cause actual price inflation, it prevented what would otherwise have been a healthy decline in prices; and through interest-rate distortions in particular, it set the economy up for the Great Depression that followed (Rothbard 1975).

Three things, it seems to me, are unsatisfactory about this line of objection. First, it relies on a dubious business cycle theory (Yeager 1986, pp. 378–82). Second, it does not demonstrate the quantitative importance of the effects alluded to, nor does it demonstrate the harm done by fairly steady, mild monetary expansion even if that expansion did serve as a marginally significant way of making the savings of the economy available for investment purposes. Third, it unwarrantedly presupposes that new money is put into the economy in particular ways that lower interest rates and skew resources into business investment.

If inserting new money in the assumed channels did have real and quantitatively important effects of the asserted kind, those particular channels might be avoided. For example, newly created money could serve as a supplement to government tax revenues, perhaps ideally to finance tax reductions.

Prominent arguments against price-level stabilization center around lags. Lags are likely to occur between incipient monetary disequilibriums and their reflection in the price index on which the central bank may be targeting. Lags occur between index movements and the adoption and impact of corrective policy actions. By the time these actions take effect, they may no longer be appropriate. Thus, attempts to heed a price-index rule might turn out more destabilizing than stabilizing.

This difficulty would presumably bedevil a policy of large, sharp changes, not a steady policy. Policymakers might further circumvent the problem of lags by watching sensitive commodity prices, growth rates of monetary aggregates, industrial production, and possibly even interest rates and exchange rates and other early indicators of monetary disequilibrium pressing on the target price level and by promptly countering such pressure. The rule imposed on the monetary authorities should insist that any such early indicators of disequilibrium serve that purpose only and not be erected into goals rivaling the price-level target. Perhaps, too, the salaries of the money managers might be calculated so as to penalize departures from the target level of the specified price index.

Their instructions might be reinforced by saddling the monetary authorities with an obligation to *do* something at the initiative of private parties. They might be required to maintain two-way convertibility between dollars and whatever quantity of gold would command a physically specified basket of goods and services. This (changeable) quantity would be calculated, perhaps every day, from the actual market prices of gold and of the specified goods and services. The system would be a commodity-basket standard rather than a gold standard; and something other than gold, perhaps specified securities, might more conveniently serve as the redemption medium. (This suggestion is inspired by, but is not the same as, Irving Fisher's 1920 proposal for a "compensated dollar.") Even more so than a gold standard, this system would deprive the monetary authorities of any substantial discretion. It would seem to circumvent the problem of lags. It would also circumvent the supposed problem of injection effects; for instead of being injected and withdrawn through the loan market, money would be injected and withdrawn at numerous points in the economy almost automatically as arbitrageurs acted to profit by, and thus nip in the bud, discrepancies between money's actual and defined values.

Standard worries about lags envision a central bank managing a fiat money with its ordinary policy weapons, notably open-market operations. The supposed problems of lags and injection effects and, perhaps more important, the danger of governmental abuse of money might better be overcome by the more radical reform of privatization. Having been abolished, government money could no longer serve as unit of account.

The government might designate a new unit and promote its general voluntary adoption by using it in its own accounting, taxation, contracting, wage payments, and other operations. The new unit would be defined as the total value of a bundle of suitably chosen goods and services. If the standard bundle were rather comprehensive, the general level of prices expressed in the unit so defined would be approximately stable. Thus endowed practically by definition with a stable purchasing power, the unit of account would no longer fluctuate capriciously according to changing demand for and supply of the medium of exchange.

The issue of notes and checkable deposits would be left to private banks (which might well also offer checking privileges against equity mutual funds). The quantity of these media of exchange would accommodate itself to the demand for them at the price level corresponding to the definition of the unit of account; imbalances, showing up in incipient movements of the price level and in the spread between interest rates on deposits and on banks' earning assets, would trigger corrective arbitrage. This automatic maintenance of equilibrium between demand for and supply of media of exchange at a stable price level would prevent price inflation and major recessions.

It is unlikely that the privately issued notes and deposits would be directly redeemable in the actual goods and services defining the unit of account, for that practice would be too awkward for all concerned. Instead, their issuers, disciplined by competitive pressures, would stand ready to redeem them in convenient redemption property (gold or, more probably, agreed securities) in amounts having the same total value in bundle-defined units of account, at actual market prices of the day or hour, as the denominations of the notes and deposits to be redeemed. Most redemptions would probably take place at clearinghouses, where banks acquiring notes issued by or checks drawn on other banks would routinely present them for settlement against their own obligations presented by others. Net balances at the clearinghouse would be settled by transfers of the agreed redemption medium. The necessary calculations and operations would be carried out every business day by professionals, and the ordinary person would no more need to understand what determined the purchasing power of the unit of account than he needs to understand what determines the purchasing power of the dollar nowadays. (The proposed system is described in Greenfield and Yeager 1983. Further published and unpublished articles provide clarifications and answer objections. The present paper hardly offers scope to make a convincing case for the system. It can only emphasize that alternatives are available which circumvent several of the most prominent objections to seeking *government* money of stable purchasing power.)

## Conclusion

Situations can arise in which exchange rate stability and domestic monetary stability are incompatible objectives. Then, it seems to me, the case is persuasive for giving priority to domestic stability. Domestic and exchange rate *in*stability can easily go together, as current experience all too clearly shows. The current volatility of exchange rates is hardly puzzling, given the undefined character of the national monetary units among which the foreign exchange market determines relative prices. A reform must occur first and fundamentally on the national level. Achieving stable money along private-enterprise lines is eminently feasible as a matter of economics. Although such a reform is outside the range of immediate political feasibility, that fact should not discourage our considering it. The force of ideas can eventually change what is politically feasible. By providing a sharp contrast with our existing unsatisfactory system, furthermore, far-out reform ideas can help us perceive and evaluate existing features that we might otherwise take so much for granted as not even to recognize them.

As long as national currencies remain distinct fiat units, absurd units whose management comes under the shifting influences of government irresponsibility and political pressures, there just are no such things as long-run or medium-run or "fundamental" equilibrium exchange rates between them. Actual rates necessarily are short-run market-clearing rates pushed around by fleeting pressures. Barring reform of the currencies themselves, attempts to manipulate exchange rates will do more harm than good. The misalignments and volatility we observe nowadays may be disillusioning, yet nothing is clearly preferable to letting exchange rates continue to float until we undertake fundamental monetary reform.

## References

Anderson, Benjamin M., Jr. "Commodity Price Stabilization: A False Goal of Central Bank Policy." *Chase Economic Bulletin* 9 (8 May 1929): 3–24.

Anderson, Benjamin M., Jr. *The Value of Money*. 1917. Reprint. New York: Macmillan, 1922.
Black, Fischer. "Noise." *Journal of Finance* 41 (July 1986): 529–43.
Davidson, David. "Något om begreppet 'penningens värde.' " *Ekonomisk Tidskrift* 8 (1906): 460–68.
Fisher, Irving. *Stabilizing the Dollar*. New York: Macmillan, 1920.
Frankel, Jeffrey A. *Six Possible Meanings of "Overvaluation": The 1981–85 Dollar*. Essays in International Finance no. 159. Princeton: International Finance Section, Princeton University, December 1985.
Friedman, Milton. "Real and Pseudo Gold Standards." *Journal of Law and Economics* 4 (October 1961): 66–79.
Gradison, Bill. "Thinking Twice about Monetary Reform." *AEI Economist* (January 1986): 1–3.
Greenfield, Robert L., and Yeager, Leland B. "A Laissez-Faire Approach to Monetary Stability." *Journal of Money, Credit, and Banking* 15 (August 1983): 302–15.
Hall, Robert E. "Optimal Monetary Institutions and Policy." In *Alternative Monetary Regimes*, pp. 224–39. Edited by Colin D. Campbell and William R. Dougan. Baltimore: Johns Hopkins University Press, 1986. (Followed by comments by Leland B. Yeager and Michael R. Darby.)
Hayek, Friedrich A. *Prices and Production*. London: 1931, 2d ed. 1935. Reprint. New York: Kelley, 1967.
Rothbard, Murray N. *America's Great Depression*. 3d ed. Kansas City: Sheed and Ward, 1975.
Rothbard, Murray N. "The Case for a Genuine Gold Dollar." In *The Gold Standard: An Austrian Perspective*, pp. 1–17. Edited by Llewellyn H. Rockwell, Jr. Lexington, Mass.: Lexington Books, 1985.
Uhr, Carl G. *Economic Doctrines of Knut Wicksell*. 1960. 2d printing. Berkeley and Los Angeles: University of California Press, 1962.
Yeager, Leland B. *International Monetary Relations*. 2d ed. New York: Harper and Row, 1976.
Yeager, Leland B. "The Significance of Monetary Disequilibrium." *Cato Journal* 6 (Fall 1986): 369–99.

# COMMENT

# IS MANAGED MONEY THE ROOT OF ALL EVIL?*

*Ben W. Crain*

## The Conventional Approach to the Stability Question

A conventional paper on "domestic stability versus exchange rate stability" would highlight some familiar current topics: the Louvre Accord and dollar stabilization; calls for strengthening or abandoning international monetary coordination; proposals to establish target zones or commodity price indicators.

The paper might begin by asking whether monetary policy can hit two targets—one by creating the right amount of money, another by altering the composition of assets that the central bank purchases in the process of creating money. It would probably conclude that, except for short periods, monetary policy is really limited to one instrument, one target.

Then it would ask how that target should be chosen. For some countries, an exchange rate target might be the best way to attain "domestic" stability, which I take to mean price stability. Indeed, for large portions of the world economy a fixed exchange rate system would surely be optimal, if it could ensure stability for the system as a whole.

This discussion would open the door to a consideration of proposals to establish an explicit system for exchange rate management, and to an appreciation of the difficulties in doing so. In particular, it would address the problem of determining who sets policy for the system as a whole. The logic of one instrument, one target implies that N-1 countries must devote their one instrument to pegging exchange rates, while the Nth country is free to determine monetary growth for the system as a whole. Monetary coordination then becomes the political art of obfuscating any explicit, clear-cut assignment of these

*Reprinted from *Cato Journal* 8 (Fall 1988): 297–84.

The author is Staff Director of the Subcommittee on Domestic Monetary Policy of the House Banking Committee.

powers and responsibilities among sovereign nations, while somehow holding the system together in practice.

## Yeager's Approach

Leland Yeager virtually dismisses this whole complex of questions, because they all presume that money is issued and managed by governments. Managed money, he argues, is the fundamental cause of instability. He wants to dethrone managed money, not improve, ever so marginally, the way it is managed.

Nonetheless, he does offer a brief assessment of the behavior of exchange rates between managed moneys. He supports the determination of prices—including exchange rates—in competitive markets. But he accepts the charge that floating rates have been the *proximate* cause of much mischief: There has been persistent serious misalignment; real resources have been misallocated and wasted; speculation has been destabilizing.

There is, however, no way to rid managed money of these ills. Cat-and-mouse intervention to scare speculators has probably enhanced, not dampened, exchange rate volatility. More formal intervention commitments only buy time, solving nothing, as demonstrated by the collapse of the Bretton Woods system.

Yeager usefully reminds us that the dollar became overvalued under the nominally "fixed" regime of Bretton Woods. The "prodigious" efforts made to sustain that regime had to fail because they could not accommodate any of the avenues by which real exchange rates could adjust to relieve dollar overvaluation. Germany would not accept substantial inflation and we would not accept substantial deflation. The expanding scope for capital flows among major currencies eventually forced the hand of policymakers, who chose to sacrifice exchange rate stability rather than abandon or compromise their preferred versions of "domestic stability."

Consider the dollar overvaluation of 1982–85. Yeager insists, and rightly so, on asking how a fixed exchange rate regime would have prevented dollar appreciation. Would we have acquiesced in the continuation, probably even the acceleration, of double-digit inflation? I doubt it, since inflation was a major factor in the unseating of an incumbent president. Would we have run an entirely different fiscal policy, never enacted tax changes, or never increased defense spending? I doubt it, since a popular president was elected with a very specific mandate on those issues. Could a commitment to fixed rates—a largely irrelevant abstraction to most Americans—exert enough "discipline" on our political system to have blocked major changes desired by most Americans? Of course not.

Whether or not those changes were wise is not the point. Their proponents won the right to implement those changes as clearly and cleanly as any major policy changes can be legitimated in our democratic system. The flexibility of exchange rates served us quite well, for it permitted those policy changes to be tested in practice—indeed, it made the implementation of those changes relatively easy, since dollar appreciation accommodated a huge capital inflow and allowed the widening gap between domestic savings and investment to be closed.

Flexible exchange rates did exactly what you would want them to do: They gave us good running room to try new policies, and they cleanly transmitted the consequences of those policies into market and political pressures for corrective adjustments. Flaws in the original policies, or in the ensuing correctives, can hardly be blamed on flexible exchange rates.

Bretton Woods collapsed because Germany insisted on reclaiming monetary sovereignty. I see no reason to think that, in the foreseeable future, the United States, Germany, or Japan will or should sacrifice any substantial degree of sovereignty just to preserve nominal exchange rate stability. Thus, I concur completely with Yeager when he asks, in reference to the rate-pegging effort under the Louvre accord, "What is the point of saying that something should have been done or should now be done if in fact it could not and cannot be done?"

## Monetary Stability and Disequilibrium

Now let me turn to the real topic or Yeager's paper, his attack on managed money. He wants to abolish money, as conventionally understood. He certainly wants to abolish monetary policy. Why? Because he sees no satisfactory way to manage money.

He does write that "if the supply of money is not cleverly manipulated to accommodate the demand for it, then monetary disequilibrium persists, bringing macroeconomic pains." That statement implies that the supply of money could, in principle, be manipulated with sufficient skill to preclude monetary disequilibrium. But Yeager does not really believe that it can be. Since he urges the abolition of government money as the only route to guaranteed price stability, he necessarily rejects all common approaches to the management of money, including gold standards, commodity price indexes, and monetarist rules.

Purely discretionary money management is characterized as absurd and preposterous. Manipulating money to stabilize the price of gold, or a commodity price index, is judged to be only somewhat less absurd. Yeager laments the demise of the gold standard, while recognizing that we lack the "liberal attitudes and self-restraints" necessary for it to work relatively well and to endure. But even if we could rekindle those attitudes and self-restraints, a gold standard would be far from ideal.

A monetarist rule likewise fails to preserve monetary equilibrium. Monetarism itself insists that any such rule will be suboptimal. It promises only a degree of average long-run stability better than discretionary management could realistically deliver.

## Assessing Yeager's Attack on Managed Money

Yeager's attack on managed money has at least one important virtue. It undermines the conventional dichotomy between rules and discretion in the conduct of monetary policy. That dichotomy typically posits a sharp distinction between unbound discretion to create and exploit monetary disequilibrium, and a rigid commitment to manage money according to some rule or "objective" standard. But that distinction is not as hard and fast as it is typically depicted.

The most rigid gold or commodity standard is a rule for money management. A gold standard, Yeager writes, "is simply a particular set of rules for monetary institutions and policy; and these rules are no more inherently self-enforcing than any other set of monetary rules." Any set of rules can be sustained only if the rules perform satisfactorily, and the performance characteristics of the gold standard "are far from ideal." A broader commodity standard might perform better, but would still fall well short of sustained monetary equilibrium. No one, I would add, should doubt that, in a modern democracy, the first serious failure of any rule or standard to sustain modest growth would spell its quick demise. (A similar failure of discretion does not, however, spell the demise of discretion. It simply induces a discretionary shift in the direction of policy.)

Yeager's treatment of discretion, rules, and standards as variations on the common principle of managed money is well taken, but his attack on managed money is overdrawn and misdirected.

I cannot accept his characterizing as *absurd* a system in which people cannot count on money's future purchasing power. Long-term price stability is a major objective of paramount importance. But the problem should not be cast in such absolute terms. Taken literally, his characterization implies democracy itself is absurd, since any system, any structure, and any set of policies— including Yeager's own private money alternative—lie at the mercy of future democratic majorities. In practice the politics of "guaranteeing" stable prices would quickly be transformed into the politics of guaranteeing full employment and other noble objectives, with disastrous consequences all around.

One should not, therefore, take Yeager's hyperbole literally. But the question remains: Has the actual performance of managed money been so miserable that one is driven to his radical alternative? I think not. The expectation of tolerable price stability in Germany and Japan is pretty solid. It is less so in the United States, but there is no inherent reason we cannot equal German or Japanese price performance. Indeed, at the moment, the Fed enjoys considerable prestige, having won a major victory for discretion over the past few years.

Let me quote two recent witnesses before the House Banking Committee on that point. Robert Hall (1987), whom Yeager cites as a source of inspiration for his plan to overthrow managed money, testified that "the Fed's performance in the 1980s has been sufficiently successful as to cast doubt on the desirability of an autopilot . . . current monetary policy is on the right track." He notes, moreover, that the commodity bundle that most closely tracked inflation as of 1981 completely collapsed, as a reliable indicator, in the ensuing years. He argues, instead, for a nominal income target, which would certainly require considerable discretion in money management.

Another witness, William Poole (1987), noting that higher money growth has offset declining velocity, stated, "I thought . . . that higher money growth ran the risk of reigniting inflation. But Paul Volcker called it right at the time."

Yeager recognizes that his radical alternative is "politically unrealistic." It is unrealistic not just because it could not be enacted under present conditions; that would be a trivial criticism of his proposals. Institutional revolutions of the magnitude he champions depend on major crises that completely undermine the credibility of the current regime. Such crises would, however, most likely push policy toward price controls and greater regulation of credit and financial markets— not toward laissez-faire money. It is not in the nature of democratic governments to respond to crises by abandoning their field of activity. Surely, then, the optimal strategy is to try to avert such crises by improving money management, however modestly, instead of defining the perfect, but unattainable, alternative to managed money.

## References

Hall, Robert. Testimony before the Subcommittee on Domestic Monetary Policy of the Committee on Banking, Finance, and Urban Affairs, House of Representatives, 17 November 1987.

Poole, William. Testimony before the Subcommittee on Domestic Monetary Policy of the Committee on Banking, Finance, and Urban Affairs, House of Representatives, 10 June 1987.

# 4

# On Monetary Stability and Monetary Reform*

*Allan H. Meltzer*

Some of the most important questions that can be asked of economists concern stability. How do we achieve greater stability? How big are the instabilities now, and how many of them are caused, or magnified, by current policy arrangements? Do fluctuating exchange rates augment or buffer shocks arising elsewhere, or are fluctuating exchange rates an independent source of disturbance? Can monetary reforms, domestic or international, increase stability without fiscal reforms, greater stability of trade policy and perhaps, either changes in political systems or fewer opportunities for politicians to influence economic events?

Alas, like most big questions, these questions (and others that might be asked) are much easier to pose than to answer. It is not difficult to develop optimal policies for a world in which all prices are flexible, information is costless, policymakers relentlessly pursue the public interest, and we all agree on the arguments and parameters of a social objective function. The abstract world of economic theory is useful. We rely on it to guide our thinking and to increase knowledge and understanding. Unfortunately, economic analysis has not offered, and probably cannot now offer, more than conditional answers to many of the questions. Some of the answers depend on empirical estimates, while others depend on more comprehensive models than we have yet developed or on a combination of the two—more comprehensive models and more data analysis.

---

*This paper was originally presented as the keynote address at the Third International Conference of the Institute for Monetary and Economic Studies at the Bank of Japan, June 3, 1987. The conference proceedings were published by the University of Tokyo Press. The present paper, with minor revisions by the editors, is reprinted by permission of the Bank of Japan.

The author is the John M. Olin Professor of Political Economy and Public Policy at Carnegie Mellon University. He is indebted to Eduard Bomhoff, Herbert Buscher, Manfred J.M. Neumann, and Saranna Robinson for supplying some of the data used in this paper.

To answer questions such as these, we need to specify a criterion or objective. I propose to use measures of variability—unanticipated variability—to compare alternative policy arrangements. I take as the proper objective of economic policy reduction of risk and uncertainty to the minimum level inherent in nature and trading arrangments. Risk and uncertainty are assumed to increase with unanticipated variability.

Critics of fluctuating exchange rates implicitly use variability as a criterion when they decry the variability of exchange rates. Unfortunately, the critics typically err in their use of the criterion by emphasizing the variability of real or nominal exchange rates. Variability of either nominal or real exchange rates is not evidence that an economy experiences excessive risk or bears an excess burden. The benefits of relative price changes are known to often exceed the costs. Despite greater variability of real exchange rates, or even as a result of such variability, fluctuating exchange rates may permit a country to reach an optimum.

To measure variability, I use the variance of unanticipated changes in output and the general price level. These measures are relevant for decisions to hold domestic or foreign assets or to hold money or real capital, so they affect the rate of interest, the intertemporal allocation of resources and the size of the capital stock. Excessive variability of output and prices contributes to the variability of returns, thereby raising the required rate of return on private investment above the minimum rate of return that society could reach.

Since past efforts to determine analytically whether fixed or flexible exchange rates are Pareto superior have been inconclusive, I have taken an empirical approach. In the following section, I restate some of the main arguments for fixed and fluctuating exchange rates and discuss the importance of variability. Both exchange rate systems can be operated under an inflexible rule, under a flexible rule, or with different degrees of discretion. Variability and uncertainty are affected by the choice between a rule and discretionary action. On this issue also, I present some evidence. The evidence suggests that discretionary action is likely to increase variability and uncertainty.

The empirical findings suggest that uncertainty can be reduced by developing rules for monetary policy. I propose a rule to increase domestic price stability while reducing exchange rate variability. A conclusion summarizes principal findings.

## Fixed Versus Fluctuating Exchange Rates

Fixed exchange rates require the government to relinquish control of money and fix a relative price. Fluctuating exchange rates typically require a government monopoly to control the stock of money. Generally, economic theory supports neither price fixing nor monopoly. For these reasons alone conclusions from theoretical work about the proper exchange regime can at most be qualified and conditional. Small, open economies are said to benefit more from fixing than from floating, but not much has been done to establish a dividing line. The small open economy model helps to explain why Holland, Belgium, and Luxembourg choose to peg their exchange rate to the Deutsche mark or why many countries in Central America peg to the dollar. The model has much less to say about the optimal choice of regime in the United Kingdom, the European Monetary System (EMS), Japan, and the United States. It does not explain why Britain, the United States, and Japan have fluctuating rates while Germany, France, and Italy have adjustable, pegged rates within the bloc of countries known as the EMS and have fluctuating rates outside the bloc. The model has little to say about the risk of relative price changes, or about the comparative cost of changing exchange rates instead of changing income and price levels, or about the risk of sudden policy changes.

In a comprehensive system of fixed exchange rates, some means of determining the growth of world reserves must be agreed upon. This is the n-country problem, a standard problem of price determination involving the choice of a numeraire to set, in this case, the world price level. In practice, this is a difficult problem involving comparison of the costs of holding commodities, the gains from seigniorage, the cost to the public of forgoing domestic concerns to maintain international price stability, and some thorny political issues. Formal analysis of several of these issues has not produced firm conclusions. We must rely on less than fully formal analyses.

A useful, starting point for discussion of exchange rate systems is Milton Friedman's "The Case for Flexible Exchange Rates" (Friedman 1953). Friedman considers a world in which changes in trade and payments occur continuously in response to unanticipated real and nominal changes. Adjustment to these shocks requires changes in relative prices and changes in the relative demands for assets denominated in different currencies. Friedman, and much subsequent analysis, considers four ways of adjusting, of which two are most relevant here. Countries can allow exchange rates to clear the market, or they can hold exchange rates fixed and wait until prices and money wages adjust. Where the adjustment of some relative prices and real wages is sluggish, as in most modern economies, fixed exchange rates necessarily introduce changes in the demand for labor and in unemployment as part of the adjustment process.

Flexible exchange rates do not avoid all changes in domestic unemployment when major trading partners experience changes in technology or change policy. But, flexible exchange rates avoid some changes in internal prices and incomes. The clearest, but not the only, example is the adjustment to an anticipated foreign inflation. The perceived costs of an inflation, anticipated as to occurrence but uncertain in magnitude and timing, became so large in the 1970s that many central bankers and governments changed their views about the relative costs of fixed and fluctuating rate systems. Flexible exchange rates can also increase stability if prices or money wages adjust slowly and if there are frequent changes in relative rates of productivity growth at home and abroad.

To a considerable extent, the case in favor of fluctuating exchange rates rests on the greater stability of prices and output that can be achieved at times by allowing exchange rates to adjust prices relative to production costs and foreign prices. An added advantage, claimed for fluctuating rates, is that fewer resources are invested in holding commodity reserves or foreign exchange, so more saving is available for investment in physical capital. As far as I know, the latter argument has not been challenged; the greater resource cost of fixed rate systems is generally accepted.[1]

Against the benefits claimed for fluctuating exchange rates, proponents of fixed, or fixed but adjustable rates, offer three main arguments. First is the claim that fluctuating exchange rates increase the instability of output. The main evidence of increased instability is usually the greater variability of real exchange rates. Second, fluctuating rates are said to reduce trade. The reason given is that exporters and importers face increased uncertainty about prices of traded goods, or they must pay the cost of hedging against uncertainty. Third, fluctuating exchange rates are said to cause greater variability of prices and inflation. The argument is that fluctuating exchange rates work by changing prices of foreign goods relative to prices of domestic goods and by changing product prices relative to costs of production. These changes in relative prices affect the price level and, particularly in countries with money wages indexed to the price level, they trigger price adjustment and inflation.

The claims and counterclaims are well known by now. Advocates of fluctuating rates point out that price and output variability are caused by shocks and policies. Advocates of fixed rates respond that

[1]Some possible exceptions are papers that claim that price stability can be achieved using commodity money systems without holding commodities. McCallum (1985) finds these arguments invalid.

fluctuating exchange rates amplify the responses in two ways. First, they claim that there is destabilizing speculation under fluctuating exchange rates. Second, they argue that fluctuating rates free countries from the discipline of a fixed rate system, so they pursue more expansive monetary policies and experience more inflation.

Support for these last conjectures is, at best, weak. There is not much evidence of a relation between the exchange rate regime and the rate of inflation. Inflation was a principal reason for ending the fixed exchange rate regime, and disinflation has been carried out in many countries under fluctuating exchange rates. Countries have learned to use crawling pegs and adjustable pegs to reconcile differences in inflation with fixed real exchange rates. If alternating periods of inflation and disinflation are a greater problem under one type of regime than under the other, much of the cost arises from variability and uncertainty. The issue is, again, one of relative uncertainty.

Mussa's (1986) comprehensive study of the variability of ex post real exchange rates shows that the short-term variability of bilateral exchange rates is higher under fluctuating rates, often substantially higher. His finding is that the more rapid adjustment of nominal exchange rates, under a fluctuating rate regime, is not matched by a corresponding increase in the speed of price adjustment. Mussa notes, however, that his findings have no clear welfare implications. Nominal exchange rate changes have real effects, but these effects are the result of the slow, gradual adjustment of prices. He notes that his work does not show that fluctuating exchange rates increase the social cost of the monetary system relative to a system in which exchange rates are fixed permanently or relative to a system with discrete changes in currency parities. Exchange rate data cannot resolve the issue. We want to know whether uncertainty about variables such as output and the price level is increased or reduced, whether there are efficiency losses such as might occur if trade were more restricted under one system than another, or whether there is some evidence of an excess burden.

Studies of the effects of exchange rate variability on trade and capital movements have not produced evidence of a reliable effect. Surveys by Farrell (1983) and by the IMF (1984) report that the evidence is weak or inconclusive. If there is an effect of variability on trade, it has been hard to detect reliably. Farrell notes that many of the studies that have been done fail to distinguish between anticipated and unanticipated changes or between persistent and transitory changes, thereby increasing the difficulty of interpreting the empirical work.

One reason for the absence of demonstrable effects on trade may be that relevant measures of variability have not increased markedly. There is a tendency in discussions of fluctuating rates to jump from the finding of increased variability of real exchange rates to the conclusion that uncertainty has increased. An alternative interpretation is that the variability of real exchange rates reduces the response of prices and output to changes in the environment.

## Rules, Discretion, and Forecast Accuracy

Models incorporating rational expectations show that every policy is a choice of rule; the only purely discretionary policy is haphazard or random action. Complete discretion is dominated by systematic policy that permits people to learn and to anticipate future actions. Proponents of discretion typically do not favor random or haphazard policies; they favor authority to deviate from a rule or to change the rule when, or if, available information suggests to the policymaker that it is desirable to do so. As always, there are type 1 and type 2 errors; discretionary action may increase or decrease variability and uncertainty. Kydland and Prescott (1977) show that, in general, deviations from a rule reduce welfare.

Empirical comparisons of rules and discretion are difficult to make. There are many different rules to compare to the history of discretionary changes in rules or departures from rules. Further, a change from the discretionary action we have experienced to a rule would affect expectations and structural parameters, so it is difficult to design experiments that sharply discriminate between the history of discretionary action and behavior that would occur under a particular rule.

If the information available to the policymaker is more reliable than the information available to the public, public agencies may have some advantage in forecasting the future and when making discretionary changes based on such forecasts. Some of the information may be obtained from other governments under conditions that prevent release. Meltzer (1987) summarizes some quarterly and annual inflation forecasts and real output growth by the Federal Reserve and by private forecasters. There is some evidence from work by Lombra and Moran (1983) that the Federal Reserve made smaller errors in quarterly forecasts during 1970–73, but the advantage is small and is not found for annual forecasts.

A notable finding of the comparison of forecast errors is the low accuracy of the forecasts made by each of the forecasters. Forecast errors for output growth are so large relative to quarterly changes that it is not possible for any forecaster, on average, to distinguish reliably between a boom and a recession either in the current quarter or a year in advance. Forecasts included in the study are made using all or most of the techniques commonly in use, including judgment, econometric modeling, and time series analysis. The errors from the best forecasts using each method, and from most forecasters, are sufficiently close on average to suggest that the remaining errors are close to the minimum we are likely to achieve with current techniques and models. Remaining errors may be random variation caused by unanticipated real shocks, changes in expectations, and perceived or actual changes in foreign countries.

The information on forecast accuracy and on the value of forecasts in Meltzer (1987) comes from the United States, so it may not be general. Table 1 shows root mean square forecast errors for forecasts of real or nominal GNP (or GDP) growth by governmental and private forecasters in different countries. The first two rows summarize results reported in Meltzer (1987). For comparison, row 3 shows that quarterly forecasts for the United States over a longer period have somewhat lower errors than the forecasts for more recent years. The median value of the root mean square error is about equal to the average annual rate of growth, however, so it remains true that, on average, forecasters cannot distinguish between a boom and a recession in the current quarter.

Annual forecast errors for Holland and Germany show a decline in the variability of forecast errors for output under the current system of pre-announced monetary growth, adjustable pegged rates within the EMS, and fluctuating rates against other major currencies.[2] For Germany, forecasts are relatively accurate. The root mean square error is less than one-half the average growth rate for the period 1978–86. It remains true, however, that policymakers who rely on forecasts to determine the time for discretionary changes will mistake booms and recessions. For this reason alone discretionary action based on forecasts is likely to increase variability.

Smyth (1983) studied the accuracy of OECD forecasts for seven countries—the United States, Japan, Germany, France, the United Kingdom, Italy, and Canada—for the years 1968–79. He found no correlation between the errors and the year of the forecast, suggesting that forecast accuracy has not improved significantly but did not worsen after major currencies adopted the fluctuating rate system. Zarnowitz (1986) reports a similar result.

[2]Data for seven additional German forecasters are available, but I have not computed the root mean square errors for each forecaster.

*TABLE 1*

ROOT MEAN SQUARE ERRORS OF FORECAST
(ANNUAL RATES IN PERCENT)

| | Current Quarter | | Year or Four Quarters Ahead | |
|---|---|---|---|---|
| Real GNP Growth | Value or Range | Median | Value or Range | Mean (M) or Median (Md) |
| U.S. 1980/2–1985/1[a] | 3.1–4.4 | 3.8 | 2.2–3.4 | 2.7 (Md) |
| U.S. Federal Reserve 1970–73[b] | 2.1 | n.a.[h] | 3.5 | n.a. |
| U.S. 1970/4–1983/4[c] | 2.8–3.6 | 3.0 | — | — |
| German Council of Economic Experts 1969–86[d] | | | 1.9 | n.a. |
| German Council of Economic Experts 1978–86[d] | | | 0.7 | n.a. |
| Dutch Central Economic Plan 1953–85[d] | | | 3.2 | n.a. |
| Dutch Central Plan 1975–85[e] | | | 2.0 | n.a. |
| OECD 1968–79[f] | | | 1.4–4.4 | 2.3(M) |
| Naive OECD 1968–79 (Random Walk)[f] | | | 2.8–4.5 | 3.8(M) |
| Nominal GNP Growth | | | | |
| U.S. Federal Reserve 1967–82[g] | | 5.5 | 5.7 | n.a. |
| U.S. Federal Reserve 1973–82[g] | | 6.1 | 6.2 | n.a. |
| U.S. 1970/4–1983/4[c] | 3.5–4.3 | 3.8 | | |

[a]Twelve econometric and judgmental forecasts from McNees (1986).
[b]From Lombra and Moran (1983).
[c]From Zarnowitz (1986), four forecasters.
[d]Supplied by Herbert Buscher; see Neumann and Buscher (1985). Forecasts are for one year ahead.
[e]Central Economic Plan, various years for one year ahead.
[f]Smyth (1983); seven country root mean square error.
[g]Federal Reserve "green" books.
[h]n.a., not applicable; single forecaster.

Smyth reports the results of several tests. He used Theil's decomposition to show that most of the errors for output growth and inflation are random. He also compared the accuracy of forecasts to a naive model, the latter a random walk using preliminary data for the preceding year to forecast real output. Table 1 shows the comparison. The OECD forecast for each country is more accurate than the random walk but, Smyth notes, all of the improvement is in 1974–76, following the first round of oil price increases. Information about the oil shock was available to private individuals as well as to public bodies, so the mechanical procedure probably overstates the error that people would have made. The results for other years suggest that any private information available to the OECD could not be translated into greater forecast accuracy.[3]

Several economists have proposed that central banks adjust monetary policy to correspond to forecasts of nominal GNP growth and, recently, some have urged coordinated adjustments in other countries. Many of the proposals for international policy coordination, target zones, or stabilization of world money growth or exchange rates depend on forecasts of nominal GNP growth. Table 1 presents some evidence on the quality of these forecasts.

The Federal Reserve's record of forecasting nominal GNP growth four quarters ahead has a root mean square error (RMSE) approximately equal to 60 percent of average nominal growth of GNP under both fixed (1967–72) and fluctuating (1973–82) exchange rates. The relative size of these errors makes it appear unlikely that discretionary policy action based on forecasts of GNP, or efforts to coordinate policy based on forecasts of GNP growth, are likely to reduce variability and uncertainty.[4] For comparison, I have included forecast errors for the current quarter made by private forecasters and by the Federal Reserve. The Federal Reserve forecasts are less accurate than private forecasts, suggesting that any information available to the staff and not made public did not improve forecast accuracy during the period considered.

An additional problem with Federal Reserve forecasts is that they are biased. Mean absolute errors four quarters ahead and for the current quarter are 5.4 percent and 5.2 percent, respectively; mean errors are very similar. A plausible reason is that the Federal Reserve

[3]Comparison of the root mean square error (RMSE) of forecast to the average growth rate for 1968–79 shows that the ratio of RMSE to average growth ranges from 0.35 (France) to 0.95 (United Kingdom). The mean for the seven countries is 0.78. An alternative measure of the value of forecast is the ratio of RMSE to the standard deviation of real growth. These ratios range from 0.57 (United States) to 1.03 (Japan). The results again suggest that, on average, forecasts cannot distinguish reliably between booms and recessions.

[4]The forecasts are made in January for the current quarter and four quarters ahead. Forecasts are revised periodically so other periods may show more or less accuracy.

consistently underestimated inflation during these years. This systematic error may have occurred because of unwillingness to recognize the inflationary consequences of past policies or may be the result of adaptive forecasts that adjust slowly to new information. Whatever the reason for the bias may be, the presence of persistent bias, lower accuracy than private forecasters, and large errors relative to the mean rate of change give little support to proposals for nominal GNP targeting, policy coordination, target zones, or other discretionary actions based on forecasts of this kind. If the aim of policy is to reduce rather than augment variability and uncertainty, discretionary action based on forecasts or rules that rely on forecasts is unlikely to achieve that goal.

Table 2 shows measures of forecast accuracy for inflation. The root mean square errors are smaller than for real growth, reflecting the lower variability of inflation rates. The errors are broadly similar to those reported in Meltzer (1987) for the United States, and generally between 1 percent and 2 percent at annual rates. The OECD root mean square forecast error for each of the seven countries is less than the average rate of price change; the ratio of RMSE to average rate of change is 0.2 to 0.6. Naive forecasts, based on a random walk, are less accurate for six of the seven countries. This suggests that inflation forecasts may be more useful to private and public decisionmakers than forecasts of real growth. It is less clear that inflation forecasts can be used to reduce the variability of the price level.

The data in Tables 1 and 2 support some preliminary conclusions about fluctuating exchange rates and about discretionary policy action. First, the shift to fluctuating exchange rates has not been followed by lower forecast accuracy. Forecast errors for rates of change of prices and output are a relevant measure of uncertainty faced by decisionmakers. These data suggest that the change in monetary regime has not increased uncertainty. Second, the size of forecast errors for growth and inflation, particulary the former, is large relative to the average change. Discretionary actions conditioned on forecasts are more likely to increase variability and uncertainty than to reduce uncertainty to the minimum inherent in nature and trading practices.[5]

## Variability under Fixed and Fluctuating Exchange Rates

In earlier work, using quarterly data for the years from the 1960s to the 1980s, I compared the variability of unanticipated changes in

[5]Smyth (1983) also studied the accuracy of trade balance forecasts. These were least accurate, a possible warning to those setting or coordinating policies to reduce the U.S. trade deficit.

*TABLE 2*

ROOT MEAN SQUARE ERRORS OF FORECAST FOR INFLATION (ANNUAL RATES IN PERCENT)*

| | Current Quarter | | Year or Four Quarters Ahead | |
|---|---|---|---|---|
| | Value or Range | Median | Value or Range | Mean (M) or Median (Md) |
| U.S. 1980/2–1985/2[a] | 1.4–2.2 | 1.6 | 1.1–3.3 | 1.6(Md) |
| U.S. Federal Reserve 1970–73[b] | 1.4 | n.a. | 3.4 | n.a. |
| U.S. 1970/4–1983/4[c] | 2.0–2.6 | 2.2 | | |
| U.S. 1980/2—1985/1[c] | 1.4–2.0 | 1.8 | | |
| German Council of Economic Experts 1969–86[d] | | | 1.4 | n.a |
| German Council of Economic Experts 1978–86[d] | | | 0.7 | n.a. |
| Dutch Central Economic Plan 1953–85[e] | | | 1.1 | n.a. |
| Dutch Central Economic Plan 1975–85[e] | | | 0.5 | n.a. |
| OECD 1968–79[f] | | | 1.2–4.6 | 3.0(M) |
| OECD 1968–79 (Random Walk)[f] | | | 2.2–7.3 | 4.3(M) |

*Footnotes are given in Table 1.

prices, output, money, velocity, and exchange rates under fixed and fluctuating rates for five countries—Canada, Germany, Japan, the United Kingdom, and the United States. Meltzer (1985, 1986a) reports these findings and the interrelation among current and lagged values of unanticipated changes in these variables. The results suggest that some countries were able to reduce the variability of unanticipated changes in prices or output, or both, during the fluctuating exchange rate period. Further, I found little relation between unanticipated changes in nominal exchange rates and unanticipated changes in prices and output. Exchange rate variability did not appear to be a main source of uncertainty about (or unanticipated changes in) prices and output.

The quarterly data used in previous work may give excessive weight to short-term movements. One reason is that organized futures and forward markets are more active for short- than for long-term maturities. These markets can be used to reduce the cost of variability. It seems useful to extend the analysis to see whether annual data give different results.

To compute measures of variability and uncertainty under fixed and fluctuating exchange rates, I again use the multi-state Kalman filter, discussed by Bomhoff (1983) and Kool (1983), to compute forecast errors for real output (GNP or GDP) and the price level.[6] The forecasts, like those reported in Tables 1 and 2, use only information available at the time of the forecast and are based on annual data for 1950 to 1985. Fluctuating exchange rates begin in 1973.

Countries differ in size and in choice of monetary regime. Two countries, Germany and Denmark, are members of the European Monetary System. They have fixed, but adjustable, exchange rates within the group and fluctuating rates against other major countries. The remaining four countries have fluctuating exchange rates, but they differ in the degree to which they have intervened to affect the exchange rate. The six countries were subject to similar shocks such as the oil shocks of the 1970s and the relatively large devaluation and subsequent revaluation of the dollar from 1978 to 1984. Each country has an independent fiscal policy and differs in product mix, in technology, and in other ways that may affect variability.

The multi-state Kalman filter computes the univariate forecast error for each year from past values and subdivides the error into transitory and permanent changes in level and permanent changes in growth rate. The statistical model used for these computations treats each of the errors as independent. Let $\epsilon$, $\gamma$, and $\rho$ be respectively the transitory error in level, the permanent error in level, and the permanent error in the growth rate. These errors are given by

$$X_t = \overline{X}_t + \epsilon_t$$
$$\overline{X}_t = \overline{X}_{t-1} + \hat{X}_t + \gamma_t$$
$$\hat{X}_t = \hat{X}_{t-1} + \rho_t$$

where $X_t$, $\overline{X}_t$, and $\hat{X}_t$ are the level, permanent or expected level, and permanent or expected growth rate of $X$.

The statistical model cannot assign causality to the change in exchange rate regime as a reason for the reduction or increase in forecast error. Reduced, or increased, variability can occur for reasons unrelated to the change in monetary arrangements. The forecast errors can be used, however, to reject the hypothesis that the change from fixed to fluctuating exchange rates increased excess burdens as

[6]See, also, Meltzer (1985, 1986a) for a discussion of the procedure.

measured by the variability of unanticipated changes in prices and output.

Table 3 shows the root mean square errors of forecasts under fixed and fluctuating exchange rate regimes. The errors are computed for levels of real income and prices and for rates of growth of output and for rates of price change. The errors for the levels are the sum

$$\sqrt{V(\epsilon) + V(\gamma) + V(\rho)}$$

where $V$ is the variance of the error. The errors for growth and inflation omit $V(\epsilon)$, the variance of the transitory error in the levels of output and prices.

Many of the errors lie in the neighborhood of 2 percent, not very different from the forecast errors reported in Tables 1 and 2 but higher than the best forecasts in some countries. The errors in the earlier tables are for forecasts of growth and inflation, but most shocks are durable, so $\epsilon$ is generally small, and the two sets of errors are often identical at the level of accuracy reported in Table 3.[7]

*TABLE 3*

ROOT MEAN SQUARE ERRORS 1950–85
(ANNUAL RATE IN PERCENT)

| | | Real Income | Growth | Price Level | Inflation |
|---|---|---|---|---|---|
| Denmark | 1952–72 | 2.5 | 2.3 | 2.4 | 2.3 |
| | 1973–85 | 1.9 | 1.9 | 1.3 | 1.5 |
| Germany | 1952–72 | 2.3 | 2.1 | 1.8 | 1.7 |
| | 1973–85 | 1.8 | 1.7 | 0.7 | 0.4 |
| Japan | 1952–72 | 1.9 | 1.8 | 1.9 | 1.8 |
| | 1973–85 | 1.8 | 1.8 | 2.6 | 2.6 |
| Sweden | 1952–72 | 1.7 | 1.6 | 2.5 | 2.4 |
| | 1973–85 | 1.8 | 1.8 | 1.5 | 1.5 |
| United Kingdom | 1952–72 | 1.6 | 1.5 | 1.7 | 1.6 |
| | 1973–85 | 2.1 | 2.1 | 4.1 | 4.1 |
| United States | 1952–72 | 1.3 | 1.2 | 2.8 | 2.6 |
| | 1973–85 | 2.3 | 2.3 | 1.4 | 1.4 |

[7]The errors are from univariate models, so in principle efficiency can be increased. Meltzer (1985, 1986a) estimates vector autoregressions (VAR) using unanticipated changes to money, output, and prices in part to measure the efficiency loss from the univariate model. The reduction in forecast errors is often small. Since the VARs use data for the entire sample period to compute the error in each period, they overstate the reduction in forecast error that would be achieved in practice.

Comparison of the fixed and fluctuating exchange rate periods provides no support for the claim that fluctuating exchange rates increased variability and uncertainty. Only one of the six countries, the United Kingdom, shows increases in uncertainty for both prices and output. Two countries, Denmark and Germany, show reductions in all measures, with relatively large reductions in price level (or inflation) uncertainty during the fluctuating exchange rate period. Despite the oil shocks of the 1970s, price level and inflation uncertainty declined in four of the six countries under fluctuating exchange rates.

The reduction in uncertainty for Germany is highly suggestive. Germany has preannounced rules for money growth and exchange rates. The exchange rate rule is an adjustable peg against currencies in the European Monetary System and fluctuating rates against other currencies. To provide information about its policy and about expected inflation, the central bank announces targets for central bank money, a measure very similar to the monetary base. While the targets are not always achieved, the record suggests that the government and the central bank are constrained by the targets. The Bundesbank, unlike the Federal Reserve, does not systematically exceed its money growth target. Money growth is generally within the target range.

The two rules appear to have increased stability relative to other countries and relative to the fixed exchange rate regime. The Bundesbank raised the credibility of its announced disinflationary policy by holding money growth to a preannounced disinflationary path through the late 1970s and the 1980s. Deviations from the path, for example to support the dollar in 1978, induce a smaller flight from money if the public believes the deviations are transitory. Further, the government has been willing to revalue the mark rather than import inflation from the countries in the EMS with more inflationary policies.

Denmark, and other countries in the EMS, can pursue independent monetary policies, if they choose to do so. Since they bear most of the cost of such policies under the adjustable exchange rate system, they have an incentive to follow stabilizing policies. Denmark appears to have reduced variability and uncertainty relative to its experience under the Bretton Woods agreement. These data suggest that, despite the oil shocks of the 1970s and the variability of real exchange rates for the dollar, Denmark was able to reduce uncertainty by the choice of policy, in this case, membership in the EMS.

The United States is the only country showing a relatively large increase in uncertainty about output and its rate of growth. Inspection of the detail shows that much of the increase is the result of a substantial increase in the forecast error for the permanent growth rate of output. A plausible explanation of the increased uncertainty about output and its rates of growth, relative to the past and relative to other countries in Table 3, is the frequent change in the thrust of U.S. monetary and fiscal policies in the past decade. Frequent policy changes make the current and maintained rates of growth difficult to forecast, leading to frequent changes in the expected return to capital invested in the United States. These, in turn, cause changes in the demand for U.S. assets and in real exchange rates.

Japan shows no reduction in output uncertainty and increased price uncertainty following the shift to fluctuating exchange rates. This is misleading. Removing one large error for prices and output changes the results. For output, the forecast error made at the time of the 1974 oil shock is more than five times the mean absolute error. For prices, the forecast error for 1975, when the Bank of Japan changed to a policy of monetary targets and disinflation, is more than four times the mean absolute error.

Table 4 compares the size of errors in forecasts of output for Japan and the United States in different periods by type of error. The table shows that the errors for the fixed exchange rate period are not affected by starting the period in 1950. Mean errors are not much different if 1960–72 is used instead.

For Japan, the three computed values of the mean absolute errors for 1973–85 decline, but for the United States all three increase following the adoption of fluctuating exchange rates. Omitting the year with the largest forecast error substantially reduces the mean absolute error for output (and prices) in Japan and the RMSE for Japan. Thus, omitting 1974, reconciles the annual results for Japan with the results reported using quarterly data in Meltzer (1985). For the United States, the largest error occurs in 1984. Omitting this year

*TABLE 4*

MEAN ABSOLUTE ERRORS FOR OUTPUT IN JAPAN AND THE UNITED STATES (ANNUAL RATE IN PERCENT)

| | Japan | | | United States | | |
|---|---|---|---|---|---|---|
| | $\epsilon$ | $\gamma$ | $\rho$ | $\epsilon$ | $\gamma$ | $\rho$ |
| 1950–72 | 0.5 | 1.0 | 1.2 | 0.3 | 0.6 | 0.7 |
| 1960–72 | 0.5 | 1.1 | 1.4 | 0.2 | 0.6 | 0.7 |
| 1973–85 | 0.1 | 0.6 | 0.9 | 0.3 | 1.0 | 1.7 |
| 1973–85[a] | 0.1 | 0.3 | 0.2 | 0.3 | 0.9 | 1.7 |

[a]Omitting year with largest error: 1974 for Japan, 1984 for the United States.

slightly reduces the mean absolute error but does not alter the direction of change or the conclusion that output uncertainty increased in the United States under fluctuating rates. Since increases are not observed for other countries, we can reject the hypothesis that the increased output uncertainty is a consequence of the fluctuating exchange rate system.

A plausible, but not fully tested, hypothesis is that the increased variability and uncertainty in the United States is the result of more frequent changes in U.S. policy than in the policies of Germany, Japan, or Sweden. Under the fixed exchange rate regime, these countries absorbed many of the shocks emanating from the United States. Under fluctuating rates, they can avoid some of the shocks. During the 1970s and 1980s, several countries adopted and sought to implement medium- or long-term strategies for economic policy. The United States repeatedly changed the direction of tax, defense, energy, and monetary policies in response to changes in economic activity and popular sentiment. It should not be surprising, given the inaccuracy of forecasts, that frequent policy changes can create an excess burden, raising social costs and increasing the real rate of interest by imposing a risk premium. Mascaro and Meltzer (1983) find evidence that this occurred in the 1980s.

Two main conclusions emerge from these comparisons. First, as already noted, there is no evidence that a system of fluctuating exchange rates necessarily increases uncertainty. Second, in the United Kingdom and the United States uncertainty about output or the price level is higher than in earlier periods. To the extent that the variability in the United States and the United Kingdom affect other countries, uncertainty in these countries also is not at the minimum inherent in nature and trading arrangements.

## A Rule to Reduce Variability

In *A Tract on Monetary Reform*, Keynes (1923) considered two types of rules—rules for domestic price or internal stability and rules for exchange rate or external stability. He favored internal price stability but there, and in his later work, he recognized the advantages of reducing both internal and external instability. He recognized also that each country operating alone must sacrifice either internal or external stability unless some country adopts a credible rule of achieving price stability.

Countries operating together can individually achieve internal price stability (or reduce instability) and collectively reduce instability of the exchange rate. Keynes's argument recognizes that stability is a public good and that there are costs of providing stability. One of his main arguments against the classical gold standard is that under this standard the social cost of exchange rate stability is higher than can be achieved by alternative arrangements. Throughout his life he proposed alternatives. The Bretton Woods agreement was Keynes's last effort to solve the problem of internal and external stability.

In practice, countries have achieved neither price nor exchange rate stability in the postwar period. Excess burdens, measured by the variability of unanticipated changes in prices and output, appear to be lower than during the interwar period or under the classical gold standard.[8] As noted in the preceding section, however, variability can be reduced further by an appropriate rule.

Policy rules differ on many dimensions. McCallum (1984) makes the useful distinction between activist and discretionary rules.[9] An activist policy rule permits the policymaker to respond to events in the economy, or in other economies. The responses follow a rule; they are predictable by private individuals. Hence the changes do not increase the unanticipated component in output and prices. Since all changes are made in accordance with a rule, they are nondiscretionary.

A second characteristic distinguishes activist rules that rely on forecasts of future values from rules that make policy action conditional on observed values. The data summarized in Tables 1 and 2 give no reason to believe that a rulemaking action conditional on forecasts reduces uncertainty. Policies based on forecasts appear to be a less effective means of reducing variability and uncertainty than (some) rules that constrain policy action to a more predictable path.

A rule to achieve price stability must choose between the stability of the actual or anticipated price level.[10] Permanent productivity changes, and other permanent changes in the level of output, affect the price level. A rule that calls for stability of the actual price level requires the policymaker to reverse all changes in the price level. A rule that maintains stability of the anticipated price level allows the actual price level to adjust as part of the process by which the economy adjusts real values to unanticipated supply shocks. Once adjustment is complete, real values are the same under either rule. Differences arise during the adjustment, however. To maintain stability of actual prices, the policymaker must know the proper amount by

[8]Meltzer (1986b) compares the different regimes from 1890 to 1980 for the United States. Additional computations for other countries generally support this conclusion.

[9]Dornbusch and Fischer (1978, chap. 10) make a similar distinction.

[10]If the optimal rate of inflation is non-zero, the rule should distinguish between actual and anticipated inflation.

which to change money and other nominal values, so he must know structural parameters including the size of the real wealth effect, the magnitude of the productivity shock, and the price elasticity of aggregate supply. The public must have confidence that the policymaker knows these magnitudes. Such confidence would be misplaced. We simply do not know, and after several decades of empirical work in macroeconomics, we should not expect to learn these values with enough precision to improve on market adjustment of the price level to one-time shocks.

Further, there is no reason why current owners of nominally denominated assets should not share in the gains and losses resulting from changes in productivity or supply shocks. One of the main benefits of price stability is that stability of anticipated prices reduces uncertainty faced by transactors, thereby lowering the risk of long-term investment. This is, of course, the argument stressed by proponents of the classical gold standard. Another main benefit is that individuals who save for retirement (or for the distant future) have less reason for concern about the form in which assets are held and less reason to fear that the real value of accumulated saving will be altered by unanticipated inflation. Stability of the anticipated price level reduces these risks.

The rule I propose is activist, but nondiscretionary. No use is made of forecasts when setting policy variables. The rule recognizes that, within a period relevant for policy, the trend growth of output is not a fixed value but varies stochastically. The rule has two parts.

The first achieves stability of the anticipated domestic price level by setting the current growth rate of the monetary base ($b_t$) equal to the difference between a moving average of the growth rate of domestic output ($\bar{y}$) and a moving average of the rate of growth of base velocity ($\bar{v}$). Since forecasts cannot distinguish, on average, between booms and recessions, the rule adjusts $b_t$ in response to the most recent past values of $\bar{y}$ and $\bar{v}$ that are known reliably. Formally, the rule sets

$$b_t = \bar{y}_{t-1} - \bar{v}_{t-1}.$$

The second part of the rule reduces variability of exchange rates. This requires major trading countries—the United States, Germany, Japan, and perhaps the United Kingdom—to adopt the same rule for stability of the anticipated domestic price level. The rate of growth of the monetary base would differ with the experience of each country and would change over time. Anticipated and actual exchange rates would be subject to change with changes in relative productivity growth, rates of growth of intermediation, differences in rates of saving, in expected returns to capital, in labor-leisure choice or other real changes. Prices would continue to fluctuate, but anticipated domestic price levels would be constant in all countries that follow the rule, so the rule eliminates this source of short-term instability in real and nominal exchange rates and of long-term changes in nominal exchange rates. The remaining changes in real exchange rates facilitate the efficient allocation of resources in response to changes in tastes and technology at home and abroad.

To complete the rule, we have to choose the period over which moving averages of output and base velocity are computed. In the past, I have suggested a three-year moving average. In practice, a longer or shorter period may provide more stability. Empirical studies can help to determine the length of the period used to compute the moving averages.

Smaller countries could choose to import enhanced price and exchange rate stability by fixing their exchange rate to a basket of the currencies of major countries or to one of those currencies. They would not be required to do so. There are no international exchange rate agreements under the rule. Each country would choose its own course. If all countries—large and small—choose independent policies, or make frequent discretionary changes, uncertainty will not be at a minimum. Everyone must accept greater variability of exchange rates, if large countries fail to supply stability.

The proposed rule has some additional advantages:

- Costs of monitoring are relatively low. The public can observe, and the central bank can control, the monetary base with very little error. Departures from the rule can be observed quickly, so the principal effect of deviations from the rule is on the exchange rate and not on aggregate real demand.
- The rule does not adjust to short-term, transitory changes in level, but it adjusts fully to permanent changes in growth rates of output and intermediation (or other changes in the growth rate of velocity) within the term chosen for the moving averages.
- The rule is adaptive and modestly counter-cyclical, particularly if recessions last for several quarters. If there is an unanticipated decline in real growth, the moving average rate of output growth falls but not as much as the growth rate of current output. Hence growth of the monetary base declines much less than the growth of output in recessions and rises less than the growth of output in expansions.
- The rule reflects the difficulties of forecasting and uses certain knowledge about quantitative magnitudes.

## Conclusion

Through most of the postwar period, the international financial system has been based on the dollar. The dollar served as the principal reserve currency, or store of value, and as the principal standard for deferred payments. For a time the dollar standard provided exchange rate stability with relatively low inflation in major trading countries, although formal devaluation or revaluations of the mark, the French franc, the pound, and other currencies occurred from time to time.

The period of relative stability ended with the inflation of the 1960s. For the past 20 years, domestic and international monetary policy has provided neither price nor exchange rate stability. As measured by the variability of unanticipated changes in prices and output, however, uncertainty has not increased and in some cases has decreased. Computations for Germany, Denmark, and Japan suggest that uncertainty can be reduced further if countries adopt a common monetary rule for internal and external stability.

Neither discursive argumentation nor formal analysis has resolved major issues about the relative costs and benefits of fixed and fluctuating exchange rates for individual countries. Comparisons of policy rules and discretionary action have been advanced by the development of dynamic models with rational expectations, but many countries have not agreed on the type of rule or even accepted the principle that a rule or a medium-term strategy increases welfare.

On the other hand, some countries—notably Germany and Japan—have been reluctant to deviate from their policy rules or to alter their policies. They have remained committed to price stability, or low inflation, in the face of substantial changes in nominal and real exchange rates and exhortations from other countries. Those urging discretionary changes in the monetary policy of these countries often rely on forecasts. Others emphasize the value of stability and the advantage of rules.

To advance the discussion of policy rules and discretionary action and of fixed and fluctuating exchange rates beyond the point at which they are usually left, I have introduced two types of data. One shows the forecasting record of private and public bodies. The other uses the variability of annual forecast errors in prices and output as measures of uncertainty under fixed and fluctuating exchange rates for several countries.

The forecasting record gives little reason to believe that variability and uncertainty would be reduced by discretionary action based on forecasts or by policy rules conditioned on forecasts.[11] Whether based on econometric models, statistical models, judgment, or some combination of these methods, forecasts are so wide of the mark that, on average, they cannot distinguish reliably between booms and recessions in the current quarter or a year ahead. Further, comparison of Federal Reserve and OECD forecasts and of private forecasts shows that public agencies have not been able to use confidential information to improve forecast accuracy. Federal Reserve forecasts of nominal GNP growth have been less accurate and show substantial bias, while errors by private forecasters appear to be unbiased.

The data suggest that the shift from fixed to fluctuating exchange rates was not followed by a general rise in uncertainty about prices and output, as is often suggested in policy discussions. In some countries both measures of uncertainty are lower under fluctuating than under fixed exchange rates. Of the six countries studied, only one shows an increase in both price and output uncertainty under fluctuating exchange rates.

Two lessons can be drawn from this experience. First, fluctuating exchange rates do not of necessity increase uncertainty for private decisionmakers.[12] Second, the two countries that adopted rules for internal and external stability—Germany and Denmark—reduced uncertainty absolutely and relative to other countries studied.

On the basis of these findings, I propose a rule to increase price and exchange rate stability that does not require agreements to take coordinated policy action. The rule is simple to follow and easy to monitor. Each major country—Germany, Japan, the United States, and perhaps the United Kingdom—achieves price stability on average by setting the rate of growth of the monetary base equal to the difference between the moving average of past real output growth and past growth in base velocity. If each country adopts a compatible rule, the rule reduces variability of exchange rates arising from differences in expected rates of inflation.

The rule may not be optimal. We know little about the structure of optimal rules. Meanwhile, we have reason to believe that uncertainty can be reduced, if we have the wisdom and the will to adopt more stable policies and a common rule.

[11]In a recent paper, Zarnowitz (1986) finds that forecast accuracy has not improved since the 1950s and that forecasts are less accurate for recession than for expansions.

[12]I have not attempted to reconcile the reduced variability of unanticipated changes in prices and output with the increased variability of ex post real exchange rates. Financial markets may effectively buffer the real economy from these shocks. Whether this occurs and whether the result approaches optimality remains open.

## References

Bomhoff, Eduard. *Monetary Uncertainty*. Amsterdam: North-Holland, 1983.

Dornbusch, Rudiger, and Fischer, Stanley. *Macroeconomics*. New York: McGraw-Hill, 1978.

Farrell, Victoria, with DeRosa, Dean A. and McCown, T. Ashby. "Effects of Exchange Rate Variability on International Trade and Other Economic Variables: A Review of the Literature." Board of Governors of the Federal Reserve System *Staff Studies* 130 (December 1983): 1-21.

Friedman, Milton "The Case for Flexible Exchange Rates." In Friedman, *Essays in Positive Economics*, pp. 157–203. Chicago: University of Chicago Press, 1953.

Friedman, Milton. *Exchange Rate Variability and World Trade*. Washington, D.C.: International Monetary Fund, 1984.

Keynes, John Maynard. *A Tract on Monetary Reform*. Vol. 4. *The Collected Writings of John Maynard Keynes*. 1923. Reprint. London: Macmillan and St. Martin's Press for The Royal Economic Society, 1971.

Kool, Clemens J.M. "Forecasts with Multi-State Kalman Filters." In Eduard Bomhoff, *Monetary Uncertainty*, app. 1. Amsterdam: North-Holland, 1983.

Kydland, Finn E., and Prescott, Edward C. "Rules Rather than Discretion: The Inconsistency of Optimal Plans." *Journal of Political Economy* 85 (1977): 473–92.

Lombra, Raymond, and Moran, Michael. "Policy Advice and Policymaking at the Federal Reserve." *Carnegie-Rochester Conference Series on Public Policy* 13 (1980): 9–68. Reprinted in *Theory, Policy and Institutions*, pp. 385–444. Edited by Karl Brunner and Allan H. Meltzer. Amsterdam: North-Holland, 1983.

Mascaro, Angelo, and Meltzer, Allan H. "Long- and Short-Term Interest Rates in an Uncertain World." *Journal of Monetary Economics* 12 (November 1983): 485–518.

McCallum, Bennett T. "Monetary Rules in the Light of Recent Experience." *American Economic Review* 74 (May 1984): 388–96.

McCallum, Bennett T. "The 'New Monetary Economics,' Fiscal Issues and Unemployment," *Carnegie-Rochester Conference Series on Public Policy* 23 (Autumn 1985): 13–45.

McNees, S. K. "The Accuracy of Forecasting Techniques." Federal Reserve Bank of Boston *New England Economic Review* (March/April 1986): 20–31.

Meltzer, Allan H. "Variability of Prices, Output and Money under Fixed and Fluctuating Exchange Rates: An Empirical Study of Monetary Regimes in Japan and the United States." *Bank of Japan Monetary and Economic Studies* 3 (December 1985): 1–46.

Meltzer, Allan H. "Size, Persistence and Interrelation of Nominal and Real Shocks." *Journal of Monetary Economics* (January 1986a): 161–94.

Meltzer, Allan H. "Some Evidence on the Comparative Uncertainty Experienced under Different Monetary Regimes." In *Alternative Monetary Regimes*, pp. 122–53. Edited by Colin D. Campbell and William R. Dougan. Baltimore: Johns Hopkins University Press, 1986b.

Meltzer, Allan H. "Limits of Short-Run Stabilization Policy" *Economic Inquiry* 25 (January 1987): 1–13.

Mussa, Michael. "Nominal Exchange Rate Regimes and the Behavior of Real Exchange Rates: Evidence and Implications." *Carnegie-Rochester Conference Series on Public Policy* 25 (Autumn 1986): 117–213.

Neumann, Manfred J. M., and Buscher, Herbert S. "Wirtschaftsprognosen im Vergleich: Eine Untersuchung anhand von Rationalitätstests." *IFO-Studien* 31 (1985): 183–201. (Berlin: Dunker and Humblot.)

Smyth, David J. "Short-run Macroeconomic Forecasting: The OECD Performance." *Journal of Forecasting* 2 (January 1983): 37–49.

Zarnowitz, Victor. "The Record and Improvability of Economic Forecasting." *Economic Forecasts* 3 (December 1986): 22–30.

# Part II

# International Monetary Reform

# 5

# THE INTERNATIONAL MONETARY SYSTEM: DEVELOPMENTS AND PROSPECTS*

*Jacob A. Frenkel and Morris Goldstein*

## Introduction

This paper addresses several fundamental issues raised by recent developments in the world economy and considers their implications for the design and functioning of the international monetary system. We do not make any proposals. Our purpose instead is to identify factors that merit attention in any serious examination of the system.

First, some background. Over the past several years, the international economic landscape in the industrial world has been dominated by the following key developments. To begin with, there have been unprecedented current account imbalances for the three largest economies. In 1987, the United States recorded a current account deficit of $154 billion, while Japan and the Federal Republic of Germany registered surpluses of $87 billion and $45 billion, respectively (see Table 1). A primary objective of policy has been to reduce these external imbalances while still maintaining satisfactory growth of the world economy. The contribution that fiscal policy should make to reducing absorption relative to output in the United States, and to increasing it in surplus countries, has become an integral—and often a contentious—element in the policy dialogue. Suffice it to say that the adjustment of fiscal positions has proven to be a difficult process, with firm evidence of a narrowing of earlier divergencies apparent only within the last year or so (see Table 2).

Heavy official intervention in exchange markets (especially during 1987) and episodes of coordinated adjustments in interest rates—both undertaken in an effort to foster more stability in key-currency

---

*Reprinted from *Cato Journal* 8 (Fall 1988): 285–306.

The authors are, respectively, Economic Counsellor and Director of Research, and Deputy Director of Research at the International Monetary Fund. The views expressed are the authors' alone and do not necessarily represent the view of the International Monetary Fund.

*TABLE 1*

MAJOR INDUSTRIAL COUNTRIES: BALANCE OF PAYMENTS ON CURRENT ACCOUNT, 1980–87

| | 1980 | 1981 | 1982 | 1983 | 1984 | 1985 | 1986 | 1987 |
|---|---|---|---|---|---|---|---|---|
| Balance on Current Account[a] | | | | | | | | |
| (In billions of U.S. dollars) | | | | | | | | |
| United States | 1.87 | 6.89 | −8.68 | −46.26 | −107.08 | −115.11 | −138.83 | −153.97 |
| Japan | −10.75 | 4.77 | 6.85 | 20.80 | 35.00 | 49.17 | 85.84 | 87.02 |
| Fed. Rep. of Germany | −13.85 | −3.57 | 5.12 | 5.32 | 9.85 | 16.58 | 39.31 | 45.01 |
| (In Percent of GNP) | | | | | | | | |
| United States | 0.07 | 0.23 | −0.27 | −1.36 | −2.84 | −2.87 | −3.27 | −3.40 |
| Japan | −1.01 | 0.41 | 0.63 | 1.76 | 2.78 | 3.67 | 4.34 | 3.64 |
| Fed. Rep. of Germany | −1.69 | −0.52 | 0.78 | 0.81 | 1.58 | 2.62 | 4.37 | 4.00 |

[a]Including official transfers.

*TABLE 2*

MAJOR INDUSTRIAL COUNTRIES: GENERAL GOVERNMENT FISCAL BALANCES AND IMPULSES, 1980–87

| | 1980 | 1981 | 1982 | 1983 | 1984 | 1985 | 1986 | 1987 |
|---|---|---|---|---|---|---|---|---|
| Fiscal Balance[a] | | | | | | | | |
| (In billions of U.S. dollars) | | | | | | | | |
| United States | −34.50 | −29.60 | −110.80 | −128.60 | −105.02 | −131.80 | −144.40 | −104.87 |
| Japan | −46.94 | −44.86 | −39.15 | −43.23 | −26.25 | −11.02 | −21.91 | −8.74 |
| Fed. Rep. of Germany | −23.68 | −25.17 | −21.65 | −16.60 | −11.87 | −7.23 | −10.87 | −19.06 |
| (In Percent of GNP) | | | | | | | | |
| United States | −1.26 | −0.97 | −3.50 | −3.78 | −2.78 | −3.28 | −3.41 | −2.32 |
| Japan | −4.41 | −3.84 | −3.60 | −3.66 | −2.09 | −0.82 | −1.11 | −0.37 |
| Fed. Rep. of Germany | −2.89 | −3.67 | −3.29 | −2.52 | −1.90 | −1.14 | −1.21 | −1.69 |
| Fiscal Impulse[b] | | | | | | | | |
| (In percent of GNP) | | | | | | | | |
| United States | 0.65 | −0.50 | 0.55 | 0.57 | 0.60 | 0.72 | 0.16 | −0.84 |
| Japan | −0.40 | −0.78 | −0.52 | −0.19 | −1.22 | −0.94 | −0.20 | −0.70 |
| Fed. Rep. of Germany | −0.19 | −0.51 | −1.87 | −0.42 | −0.55 | −0.86 | 0.25 | 0.17 |

[a]Data are on a national income accounts basis; + surplus, − deficit.
[b]+ expansionary, − contractionary.

exchange rates—have been a second prominent feature of the landscape (see Figure 1). These efforts, in combination with the monetary response to the global stock market crash of October 19, 1987, and with plans for a liberalization of capital controls in the European Monetary System (EMS) by 1992, have once again put the spotlight on an old question: How successful can monetary policy be when it is asked to wear two hats, one for internal and the other for external balance?

Another distinguishing characteristic of the last several years has been the sizable decline in both the nominal and real value of the U.S. dollar. By now, all of the 1980–85 real appreciation of the dollar (on an effective basis) has been reversed (see Figure 2). The central question has been "Do you think the dollar decline has gone far enough?" On a number of occasions (e.g., the Louvre Accord, February 22, 1987; the September 1987 meetings of the Interim Committee; and the G-7 statement of December 22, 1987), officials have supplied their own answer—by offering a concerted view on the consistency of the existing pattern of exchange rates with "fundamentals." Moreover, interest continues to be expressed in some reform proposals—including a system of target zones—that hinge on knowledge of equilibrium exchange rates.

Last but not least, the period since the Plaza Agreement (September 22, 1985) has witnessed a strengthening of international economic policy coordination among the major countries. Coordination agreements have featured both country-specific policy commitments and official pronouncements on the pattern of exchange rates, but have not specified rules, anchors, or a center-country for the exchange rate system. Debate continues on whether the present coordination process is merely an intermediate stage on the way to a more far-reaching, rule-based reform of the system, or whether it is instead a durable, workable compromise between what some regard as the excesses of decentralized floating and the straitjacket of fixed rates.

So much for the landscape. How does it relate to prospects for the international monetary system? We would say "quite a lot." Indeed, much of the controversy over reform of the system can be traced back to different views about the capabilities and limitations of more managed exchange rate regimes to deal with just the sort of policy problems outlined above. In our view, four central issues merit particular attention in the current climate:

- Can the exchange rate regime do much to help discipline fiscal policy?
- What are the extent and costs of reduced monetary independence under greater fixity of exchange rates?

*FIGURE 1*

**THE DOLLAR AND REAL INTEREST RATES (Q1 1980–Q3 1988)**

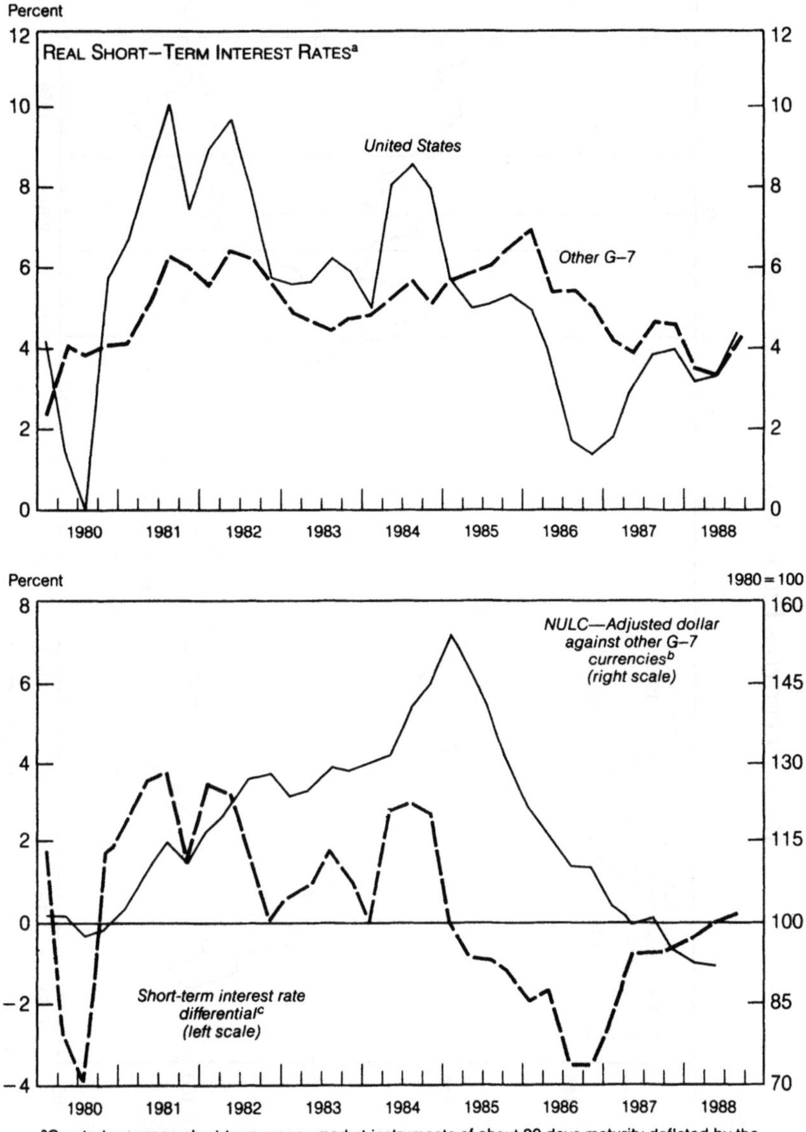


[a]Quarterly average short-term money market instruments of about 90 days maturity deflated by the private domestic demand deflator. Other G-7 interest rate is a weighted average of individual rates. Weights are defined in note b.

[b]The NULC adjusted dollar is a weighted average index of the exchange value of the dollar against the currencies of the other G-7 countries, where nominal exchange rates are multiplied by the relative normalized unit labor costs in manufacturing. Weights are proportional to each country's share of world trade in manufactures during 1980.

[c]U.S. real short-term interest rate minus other G-7 real short-term interest rate.

*FIGURE 2*

REAL EFFECTIVE EXCHANGE RATES, 1980–88[a]

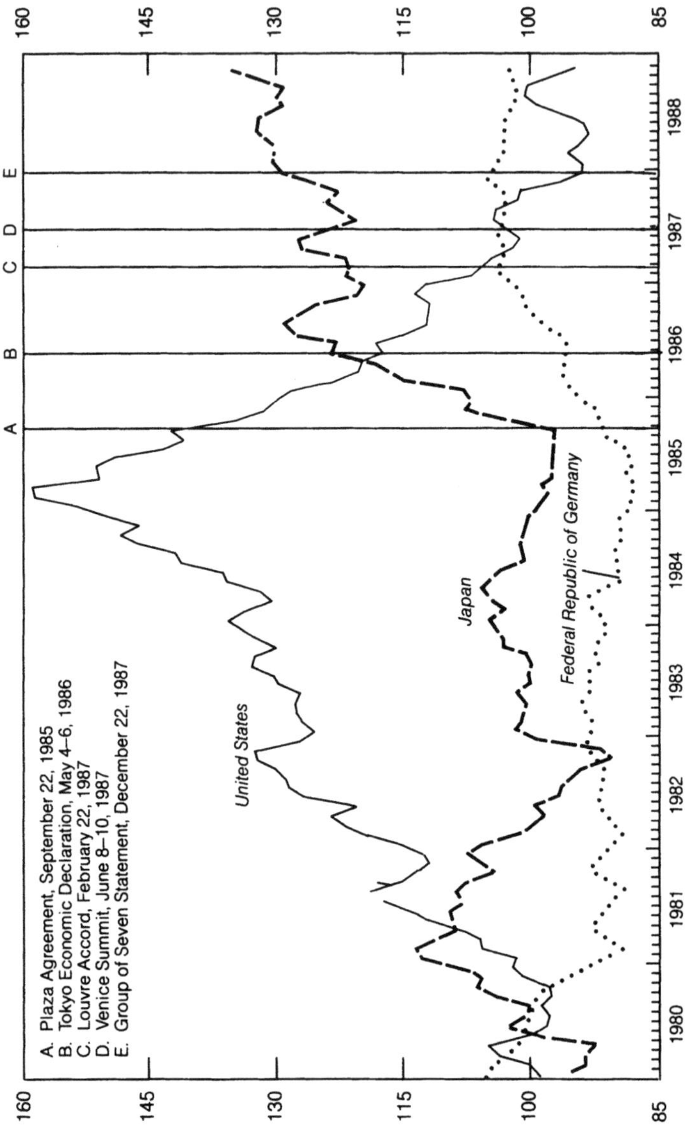


[a]Real effective exchange rates based on normalized unit labor costs in manufacturing.

- How can the equilibrium exchange rate best be determined?
- Does a well-functioning international monetary system require a clearly defined set of rules, an acknowledged leader, and an explicit anchor?

We will examine each of these issues in turn.

## Fiscal Policy and the Exchange Rate Regime

The proposition that the commitment to defend the parity provides economic agents with increased discipline to avoid inflationary policies is one of the oldest and most durable arguments for fixed rates. Yet close scrutiny of the typical focus of the discipline hypothesis suggests that it could be akin to Hamlet without the Prince of Denmark. In what follows, we elaborate on this point.

The traditional province of the discipline hypothesis is monetary policy. Under the well-known Mundell-Fleming model, monetary policy is completely ineffective for a small country with fixed exchange rates in a world of high capital mobility. This is merely one application of the dictum that policymakers who seek to achieve simultaneously fixed rates, open capital markets, and an independent monetary policy will be frustrated. The best they can do is to achieve any two of the three objectives. Thus, once the choice is made for fixed rates and open capital markets, monetary policy is effectively disciplined. The exchange rate could be devalued to give monetary policy a longer leash, but this approach is ruled out by the assumption that devaluation would bring with it heavy political costs.[1]

More recently, the domain of the discipline argument has been extended to wage policy. The basic idea here is that if exchange rate adjustments do not completely offset inflation differentials, then the resultant real appreciation for high-inflation countries will deter exports, real output, and employment, thereby acting as a disincentive to excessive wage settlements.[2] An interesting and unresolved question is how long it will take to convince workers of the downward slope of the labor-demand schedule, especially if wage developments are dominated by insiders with jobs rather than by outsiders without them.

Surprisingly enough, disciplinary effects on fiscal policy have been relatively neglected. And this neglect is despite the role often attrib-

[1]The issue of whether the consequences of a more expansionary monetary policy will be as visible under a fixed rate as under flexible rates is discussed in Frenkel and Goldstein (1986).

[2]See Giavazzi and Giovannini (1988).

uted to lax fiscal policy (particularly in the United States) in both the breakdown of Bretton Woods and the large—many would say "excessive"—real appreciation of the dollar during the 1980–85 period. It is, therefore, worth asking if and how alternative exchange rate regimes might influence fiscal policy.

First, consider fixed rates. With high capital mobility, a fiscal expansion will yield an incipient, positive, interest rate differential; a capital inflow; and a balance-of-payments surplus—not a deficit. Hence, exchange rate fixity helps to finance—and by no means to discipline—irresponsible fiscal policy. As suggested in the recent literature on "speculative attacks,"[3] only if and when the markets expect fiscal deficits to be monetized will they force the authorities to choose between fiscal policy adjustment and devaluation. The better the reputation of the monetary authorities, the longer in coming will be the discipline of markets. In this connection, it is worth observing that whereas the EMS has produced significant convergence of monetary policy, convergence of fiscal policies has not taken place.[4]

Second, consider the outcome under target zones. Suppose the zones are to be defended by monetary policy. In that case, a fiscal expansion that puts appreciating pressure on the exchange rate will produce a loosening of monetary policy to keep the rate from leaving the zone. Again, the exchange rate regime will have exacerbated—not disciplined—the basic cause of the problem. Only if the threatened departure of the exchange rate from the zone initiates a review of the whole range of policies, and if that (multilateral) review tilts the balance of power in the domestic debate toward fiscal responsibility, will the target zones discipline fiscal policy. This missing link between exchange rate movements and fiscal policy under target zones is being increasingly recognized. We should note that whereas first-generation target zone proposals spoke mainly of monetary policy, second-generation proposals have added a specific rule to rein in fiscal policy (contrast Williamson 1985 with Williamson and Miller 1987).

What about floating rates? With high capital mobility, one would again expect fiscal expansion to prompt appreciation of the real exchange rate. Pressures for reversal are then likely to come from the beleaguered traded goods sector, as it looks for ways to turn around its decline in competitiveness. The trouble here is that there is also the protectionist alternative to fiscal discipline, which, if adopted,

[3]See Flood and Garber (1980) for a model of such speculative attacks.

[4]See Holtham et al. (1987).

would again follow one inappropriate policy with another. The recent U.S. experience is suggestive of the difficulties associated with forging a dominant constituency for fiscal reform, and of the perseverance necessary to combat measures for quick-fix protectionist alternatives.

Finally, consider the influences operating on fiscal policy in a regime of managed floating with international economic policy coordination. One immediate advantage is that the potential for a perverse monetary policy response is reduced since specific fiscal policy commitments can be specified directly as part of a negotiated policy package. That is, one avoids the intermediate link between the exchange rate signal and the policy response. But this regime too is not entirely without pitfalls. For one thing, the kind of specific, quantitative policy commitments that lend themselves to reliable monitoring may be perceived as intruding too much on national sovereignty. For another, there is no explicit mechanism for sharing the fiscal adjustment across participants. Also, there is the problem of implementation of fiscal policy agreements when the responsibility for implementation lies with different branches of government in different countries.[5]

The bottom line of all this is that if proposals for modification or reform of the exchange rate system are truly to lead to more disciplined macroeconomic policies, more attention has to be given to how the exchange rate regime will have an impact on fiscal policy behavior. To some observers, the answer is that fiscal reform must precede reform of the exchange rate system. To others, the answer may be that better fiscal discipline requires mechanisms outside of the exchange rate system, such as Gramm-Rudman legislation. And to still others, the answer may be that the multilateral give-and-take encouraged by policy coordination or a system of target zones is a necessary, if not sufficient, tool for achieving greater fiscal responsibility. One thing is clear: It will be hard to know how to shape the evolution of the exchange rate system without knowing beforehand how to better discipline fiscal policy.

## Monetary Policy Independence

As suggested earlier, a strong message from the theoretical literature is that a more fixed exchange rate regime requires keeping more of an "eye" on the exchange rate in the conduct of domestic monetary policy. What is much more controversial is what such a reduced independence of monetary policy would cost.

[5]See Feldstein (1987).

Concern about reduced monetary independence is often strongest in countries with either relatively low or relatively high inflation rates. In the former, there is a worry about repetition of the latter days of Bretton Woods when disequilibrium exchange rates, heavy exchange market intervention, and massive capital flows combined to wrestle control of the money supply away from the authorities. In their view, a similar occurrence would jeopardize both their price-stability objectives and their hard-won, anti-inflationary reputations. For the high-inflation countries, there is a concern that less monetary independence could handicap the battle against the cyclical component of high unemployment. In addition, high-inflation countries often suffer from weak fiscal systems with relatively heavy reliance on the inflation tax.[6] In this regard, they worry that a lower inflation rate will reduce their revenue from seignorage, run up against tax evasion in seeking to compensate for it by raising other taxes, and, hence, complicate what are already difficult fiscal problems.

More generally, there is a concern that greater stability of exchange rates would be purchased at the cost of both greater instability of other prices in the economy—including interest rates and prices of nontraded goods—and of a diminished capacity to use monetary policy to pursue other objectives of policy. For example, a large hike in interest rates taken to protect a weak currency could disrupt stock market prices. Similarly, a firm commitment to defend a given exchange rate pattern might limit the freedom of maneuver of monetary authorities in combating a weakness of certain financial institutions.

Some would say that exchange market intervention offers a solution to the "two-hat" problem by introducing an additional policy instrument to handle the exchange rate. We note that this line of argument should refer exclusively to sterilized intervention because nonsterilized intervention is best regarded as monetary policy by another name. Yet the available empirical evidence on sterilized intervention is not very encouraging to those who favor highly managed rates. In brief, the Jurgensen Report (1983) concluded that sterilized intervention is not likely to have a powerful effect on the level of the exchange rate over the medium to long run. Thus, while intervention may be helpful in smoothing short-run volatility and in providing the market with a "signal" about the future course of policies,[7] it is not by itself likely to deliver monetary policy from having to serve two masters.

[6]See Frenkel (1975) and Dornbusch (1988).
[7]See Mussa (1981).

Another possible way out of the box would be controls on international capital flows. This is indeed the route sometimes taken in the past by some members of the EMS, as evidenced by the widening of interest differentials (adjusted for differences in tax treatment) between onshore and offshore financial instruments (denominated in the same currency) during periods of exchange rate crisis.[8] No one asserts that capital controls are costless. The argument instead is that such controls are less costly to the real side of the economy than alternative policy options. In fact, James Tobin's (1980) "sand-in-the-wheels" proposal for an international round-tripping tax on all capital flows employs just this rationale.

In our view, the case for capital controls is a weak one on at least five counts.

First, the benefits from liberalization of capital controls appear to be substantial, including higher real returns to savers, smaller spreads between borrowing and lending rates, a lower cost of capital to firms, better hedging possibilities against a variety of risks, and a more efficient allocation of investment.[9]

Second, capital controls themselves induce changes in financial structure and rent-seeking activities that make it difficult to subsequently reverse them; yet the longer they stay in place, the more serious the distortions associated with them.

Third, there is no effective way to separate a priori productive from nonproductive capital flows. Also, the costs of an inappropriate classification could be large. In this connection, if some speculators are deterred from seeing through the "J-curve," exchange market stability could be adversely affected—a result directly opposite to the original rationale for controls.

Fourth, since controls are seldom negotiated on a multilateral basis, they can poison the atmosphere for advances in coordination and cooperation in other areas; in particular, controls on capital flows run counter to the development of an outward-looking policy strategy.

Fifth, round-tripping taxes are neither practical nor desirable. To work, such taxes need to be applied universally; yet an incentive always exists for some country not to impose the tax and thereby to capture much of other countries' business (i.e., their effectiveness will be diminished by "regulatory arbitrage").[10] Also, they would require a country that wishes to attract a capital inflow to raise interest

[8]See Giavazzi and Giovannini (1988).

[9]See Folkerts-Landau and Mathieson (1987).

[10]See Levich (1987).

rates even more, to offset the effect of the tax, thereby possibly increasing the variability of interest rates.

Yet another tack would be to assign fiscal policy to internal balance so that monetary policy can concentrate more on the exchange rate. Such an argument, however, faces two immediate problems. One is that fiscal policy is considerably less flexible than monetary policy in almost all industrial countries. We can contrast, for example, the frequency in the United States of meetings of the Federal Open Market Committee with the frequency of budget submissions to Congress. The other problem is that fiscal policy is not oriented to short-run stabilization goals in most industrial countries; it is instead guided by other considerations (e.g., reducing the share of government in Gross Domestic Product, reducing the burden of taxation, and so on) that often become objectives in themselves. For these reasons, it is hard to think of fiscal policy as a close substitute for monetary policy.

Thus far, we have outlined some of the costs and trade-offs that might be associated with less independent monetary policy. There is, however, another side of the issue that sees both the loss and consequences of monetary independence under greater exchange rate fixity as much less serious. Advocates of this position make the following points.

First, the independence of monetary policy disappears once the exchange rate is transformed from a policy instrument to a policy target. Experience suggests that few countries are able to treat the exchange rate with "benign neglect" once it moves by a large amount.[11]

Second, increased independence of monetary policy is not synonymous with increased effectiveness. The true constraint on the latter is not the exchange rate regime but instead the openness of national economies, particularly high international capital mobility. With floating rates, exchange rates respond rapidly to perceived changes in monetary policy; nominal wages and prices adjust rapidly to changes in exchange rates; and the invariance of real wages to exchange rate changes limits the effects of monetary policy on real output and employment.[12] In the end, the real choice is between accepting reasonable constraints beforehand or having them imposed at higher cost later by markets.[13]

[11]See Goldstein (1980).

[12]For an elaboration of these considerations, see Frenkel and Mussa (1981) and Frenkel (1983).

[13]See Duisenberg (1988).

Third, the inflexibility of fiscal policy is an asset—not a liability—in a world of inflation-prone authorities. Growth and price stability will be best served when fiscal policy is put on a steady, medium-term course. If there is an unusual situation that is widely recognized as calling for a shorter-term adjustment of fiscal policy, it can be accomplished (witness recent temporary departures from the medium-term path of fiscal consolidation in Japan and in the Federal Republic of Germany).

To sum up, the real issue is not whether monetary policy is capable of restoring more stability to exchange rates. Surely it can. It is instead what one has to give up in terms of other objectives to get it. To some observers, that shadow price is too high and they would, therefore, prefer to live with a "natural" degree of exchange rate stability—much in the way that one accepts a "natural" rate of unemployment. To others, the exchange rate regime cannot take away what is no longer there in any case, namely, the ability of monetary policy to influence real output and employment in the long run under conditions of high capital mobility. Again, the view that prevails in the end will have a lot to do with the structure of any modification or reform of the exchange rate system.

## Identifying Equilibrium Exchange Rates

As highlighted in our earlier snapshot of key developments in the world economy, the 1980s have been marked by large swings in major currency exchange rates. One popular position has been that these currency swings have been subject to large and persistent misalignments, where by "misalignment" one means a departure of the actual (real) exchange rate from its equilibrium level. One implication of this view is that the exchange rate is too important a relative price to be left entirely to the market and, therefore, that officials should guide the market by supplying it with their own concerted view of the equilibrium rate. An opposing position is that the very concept of an equilibrium exchange rate different from the market rate is so riddled with conceptual and empirical problems as to render it operationally vacuous.[14]

The case that the equilibrium exchange rate may differ from the rate generated by the free operation of the marketplace rests on a number of arguments.

The first is that the equilibrium rate should reflect the sustainability of policies.[15] For example, if the market exchange rate reflects an

[14]See Haberler (1987)

[15]See Frenkel (1987).

unsustainable budget deficit, then this rate may not be considered as an equilibrium even though it clears demand and supply in the market.

A second rationale for rejecting the market rate as an equilibrium rate is that it may imply undesirable values for certain objectives of policy, such as unemployment, growth, or the degree of restriction in goods and capital markets. Ragnar Nurkse (1945), for example, defined the equilibrium rate as the rate that would produce equilibrium in the balance of payments, without wholesale unemployment, undue restrictions on trade, or special incentives to incoming or outcoming capital.

The existence of market imperfections represents another possible reason for eschewing the market's verdict, this time on second-best considerations. Specifically, the existence of imperfect labor mobility is sometimes put forward as a reason for concluding that the market rate is too "noisy,"[16] and that exchange rate stability shares certain "public good" attributes.[17] The recent literature on "speculative bubbles" can also be seen as antagonistic to the market-rate-is-the-right-rate position by demonstrating that models of profitable destabilizing speculation can exist.

On the empirical side, there is likewise by now a large body of empirical work that suggests there have been periods over the past 15 years when the market's evaluation of the equilibrium rate was considerably different from the sustainable rate (Krugman 1985), or when it was difficult ex post to explain actual rate movements in terms of "fundamentals" (Buiter and Miller 1983).

Finally, even if one did want to look to the market for the equilibrium rate, opponents of floating rates point out the market rate is distorted by a variety of official interventions that render it a far cry from a "clean float." Since there are many ways to skin a cat and since it is hard to envisage a prohibition on all such interventions, the market rate is, in their view, of limited use. Still, it takes an estimate to beat an estimate. That is, if the market's view is rejected, then authorities need to supply their own estimate of the equilibrium rate. What then are the leading approaches?[18]

Perhaps the most long-lived is the purchasing power parity approach. This can be expected to generate reasonable estimates if one can

[16]For an empirical attempt to judge whether actual exchange rates are too noisy in terms of departures from fundamentals generated by a monetary model of exchange rate determination, see West (1987).

[17]See Frenkel, Goldstein, and Masson (1988).

[18]See Goldstein (1984) and Frenkel and Goldstein (1986) for more comprehensive discussions of alternative methods for estimating the equilibrium exchange rate.

identify an equilibrium base period and if all shocks between the base and current periods are monetary in origin. But when there are real shocks, one normally wants a departure from PPP. The following are just some of the real factors that call for a change in real exchange rates: trend intercountry differences in labor productivity (not just in tradables relative to nontradables à la Balassa [1964] but in tradables as well);[19] permanent changes in the terms of trade; and shifts from net creditor to net debtor positions. In this sense, it can be hazardous to assume that the equilibrium exchange rate is constant over time.

A second approach is to resort to structural models of exchange rate determination to produce estimates of the exchange rate consistent with "fundamentals." The fly in the ointment here, aside from measurement problems for some of the right-hand side variables, is that these models—be they of the monetary or portfolio balance variety—have been shown to possess poor out-of-sample forecasting properties.[20] But why then should markets trust these models as reliable indicators of equilibrium rates?

Yet a third approach is to use an econometric trade model to solve for the level of the exchange rate that—given anticipated real output and inflation paths over the next 18 months or so, and given any relative price effects still "in the pipe"—will produce a current account equal to "normal capital flows." This way is often referred to as the underlying balance approach. The main sticking point with this approach, aside from the wide range of estimates of trade elasticities,[21] is the need to estimate "normal capital flows." Given the instability of perceived investment opportunities across countries and over time, it is hard to say if, for example, the United States should be regarded as a net capital exporter or a net capital importer, and if the latter, whether normal inflows are $10 billion or $100 billion.

All of this suggests—at least to us—that estimates of equilibrium exchange rates could be subject to rather substantial margins of error, and that official estimates of equilibrium rates should be allowed to change over time in response to changes in real economic conditions. Those who favor a modification or reform of the exchange rate system, therefore, need to ponder two questions: Are official estimates of the

[19]See Marston (1986) for an empirical analysis of trend differences in labor productivity in tradables as between the United States and Japan, and for evidence on the drawbacks of measures of competitiveness that rely on broad price indices such as the CPI. On the broader issues concerning the limitations of the PPP approach, see Frenkel and Mussa (1980) and Frenkel (1981).

[20]See Meese and Rogoff (1983).

[21]See Goldstein and Khan (1985) for a survey of trade elasticities.

equilibrium exchange rate likely to be better on average than the market's estimate, and would a moving official estimate of the equilibrium exchange rate with a relatively wide band be helpful as an anchor for medium-term expectations about exchange rates? If both these questions can be answered in the affirmative, then the recent evolution of the system toward more "management" and more "fixity" of exchange rates is likely to continue. If not, then strong reliance on the market to determine the right exchange rate, like democracy, may be the worst system—except for all the others.

## Leaders, Rules, and Anchors

The strengthening of international economic policy coordination that began in earnest at the Plaza in September 1985 represents, as noted above, a move in the direction of more cooperative management of the system. Yet some might describe present arrangements as a "nonsystem" because relative to, say, Bretton Woods or the EMS, there is a less formal structure, no acknowledged leader, and no explicit anchor. It is, therefore, of interest to consider whether such factors are likely to influence the effectiveness of an exchange rate system.

A convenient way of characterizing the Bretton Woods system is as an "implicit contract" between the leading country, or hegemon, and the satellite countries.[22] The leader accepted the obligation to conduct its macroeconomic policies in a prudent, stable way—perhaps best summarized by a steady, low rate of inflation. This obligation was also reinforced by the leader's commitment to peg some nominal price—in this case, the price of gold. Since there were only N-1 separate exchange rates among N currencies, the leader was passive about its exchange rate. The satellite countries were committed to peg their exchange rates within agreed margins to the leader. As a reaction to the competitive depreciations of the 1930s, all exchange rate adjustments were placed under international supervision and were to be undertaken under conditions of "fundamental disequilibrium." As a consequence of their exchange rate obligations, the satellites gave up independence in their monetary policies but received the assurance that they had hitched their wagons to an engine that would stay on the tracks. Under this implicit contract, both sides can be said to be "disciplined" by their obligations, and both share any efficiency gains associated with moving closer to an international money.

[22]See Frenkel and Goldstein (1988).

With the benefit of hindsight, it is apparent that such implicit contracts can come under strain from a number of directions (in addition to Triffin's [1960] well-known "confidence problem"). One such strain is a breakdown of discipline by the leader so that the satellites come to see it as exporting inflation rather than stability. The satellites are then likely to sever their links with the leader and to seek stability through other mechanisms, including money-supply targeting and regional exchange rate arrangements with a more stable leader. A second strain is a change in underlying conditions that calls for a change in the real exchange rate between the leader and some of the satellites to restore external balance. If that equilibrating change in the real exchange rate is blocked by too much rigidity of nominal exchange rates (in surplus satellite countries), then the leader is apt to abandon its commitment to be passive about the exchange rate.

The EMS, like Bretton Woods, places exchange rate adjustments under common supervision. It also has clear rules about the intervention obligations of members. While there is no formal leader, many observers regard the Federal Republic of Germany (and its Bundesbank) as the de facto or acknowledged leader.[23] In this sense, it might be regarded as a system with informal hegemony. The implicit contract is similar in many ways to that under Bretton Woods. Germany follows macroeconomic policies that "export" price stability and anti-inflationary credibility to the others. It is noteworthy that while there have been 11 realignments within the EMS, none of them has resulted in a revaluation relative to the Deutsche mark, thus leaving Germany's reputation as an exporter of stability intact. Other EMS members are often described as "tying their hands" on domestic monetary policy. Exchange rate realignments may not always provide full compensation for past inflation differentials. In this way, the resulting real appreciation for high-inflation countries can act as a disincentive to inflation, while low-inflation countries receive a gain in competitiveness that provides some compensation for their export of anti-inflationary credibility. Monetary policy in Germany is typically regarded as the anchor.

While there clearly have been periods when large countries have exerted a stabilizing influence on the system, it would, in our view, be erroneous to conclude that hegemony is a necessary characteristic of a well-functioning international monetary system. For one thing, Eichengreen's (1987) careful study of alleged hegemonic systems, including the gold standard, reveals that the amount of coordination needed for smooth functioning was substantial. A case in point is the

[23]See Giavazzi and Giovannini (1986).

coordinated action in the EMS when Germany and the Netherlands lowered their interest rates, while France raised its rate during the autumn of 1987. Also, the appearance of hegemony can sometimes result as much from common objectives as from asymmetries in economic size or reputation among countries. Again, the EMS serves as a fascinating laboratory. In the early 1980s, disinflation was the top priority in virtually all EMS countries. Since Germany had the best reputation for price stability, there was a commonality of interests in trying to converge to the German inflation rate. Now, however, some observers (for example, Dornbusch 1988) argue that given both the progress already made on the inflation front and the high unemployment rates prevailing in some EMS (and potential EMS) countries, it is time to give greater weight to objectives other than inflation. To some, such a decision would inevitably result in a more symmetric EMS. Indeed, these observers (e.g., Holtham et al. 1987) view the proposals on the EMS put forward to the EC Monetary Committee last fall by Minister Balladur of France as prefacing such a development of the EMS.

The system of floating rates that replaced Bretton Woods in 1973 could be said to have its own implicit contract. This contract suggested that each country should adopt sound and stable macroeconomic policies at the national level, with the expectation that stability of exchange markets would emerge as a useful by-product. In the event, some major countries did not adopt sound and stable policies at the national level, spillovers or externalities associated with these poor policies were significant (including protectionist pressures), and exchange rates displayed considerable volatility. In this decentralized system, there was no acknowledged leader. National macroeconomic policies served as anchors. The fact that intervention practices were sometimes different and uncoordinated led some (McKinnon 1984) to argue that an upward rise was imparted to the world money supply.

The perceived inadequacies of the decentralized floating rate system were, not surprisingly, the impetus for the move to stronger international economic policy coordination. The rationale behind the coordination process—and we think it can be regarded only as an evolving process—is that you need a mechanism to internalize the externalities of policy actions by the larger countries.[24] Specifically, multilateral surveillance is employed to see that the international spillovers—both good and bad—of each country's policies—including the feedback of these spillovers to the country itself—are

[24]See Frenkel, Goldstein, and Masson (1988).

taken into account in the final, multilateral policy bargain. In some cases, countries may also be able to use "peer pressure" to help them take policy actions that are unpopular domestically but which are beneficial to them in the long run.[25]

Although successive coordination agreements share several common elements (policy commitments, a concerted view on exchange rate developments, and pledges for closer cooperation on exchange market intervention), there are no explicit rules that apply across agreements. This flexibility carries both advantages and disadvantages. On the one hand, the agreements can cover a broad range of policies (including structural as well as macroeconomic policies), they can be quite country-specific and quantitative, and they can be custom-tailored to the most pressing problems of the day. On the other hand, without rules there are higher negotiation and recontracting costs.

Countries' monetary and fiscal policies serve as anchors in this system. Recently, however, U.S. Treasury Secretary Baker and U.K. Chancellor Lawson suggested the possible use of a commodity-price basket indicator as an early warning signal of future aggregate price developments. The use of this indicator might provide some assurance that stabilization of exchange markets does not come at the expense of either global inflation or deflation.

Another recent and noteworthy innovation in the coordination exercise is the consideration of aggregate indicators for the G-7 countries as a group. Their rationale is straightforward: Even when members of the coordination group reach agreements that are viewed as mutually beneficial, care still needs to be taken to ensure that such policy packages have satisfactory implications for those not at the table. This rationale is particularly relevant in the case of the G-7 countries since the spillover effects of their policies on the rest of the world are known to be large. Aggregate indicators, covering such variables as G-7 growth rates, G-7 interest rates, the G-7 current account, and the G-7 real exchange rate are simply an analytical vehicle for getting a better handle on these spillovers. In this connection, it is well to remember that there is a debt problem as well as a problem of improving the functioning of the international monetary system, and measures introduced to alleviate one will inevitably affect the other.

## Conclusion

It follows from the preceding remarks that we do not view reform of the international monetary system as an instrument of crisis man-

[25]See Haberler (1987) for a different view on peer pressure.

agement. Instead, we see it as akin to a constitutional change that should be governed by a long-term perspective. In keeping with that orientation, there is much to be gained by subjecting all proposals for modification of the system to careful scrutiny and study so that their full implications—both positive and negative—can be fully understood.

## References

Balassa, Bela. "The Purchasing Power Parity Doctrine: A Reappraisal." *Journal of Political Economy* 72 (1964): 584–96.

Buiter, Willem, and Miller, Marcus. "Changing the Rules: Economic Consequences of the Thatcher Regime." *Brookings Papers on Economic Activity* (1983): 305–79.

Dornbusch, Rudiger. "Money and Finance in European Integration." In *Money and Finance in European Integration*, pp. 9–22. Geneva, Switzerland: FITA, 1988.

Duisenberg, W. F. "Toward European Exchange Rate Stability." European Free Trade Association, Geneva, January 1988.

Eichengreen, Barry. "Hegemonic Stability Theories of the International Monetary System." Discussion Paper no. 193, Centre for Economic Policy Research, London, September 1987.

Feldstein, Martin. "Rethinking International Economic Coordination." Lecture on the Occasion of the Fiftieth Anniversary of Nuffield College, Oxford, 23 October 1987.

Flood, Robert, and Garber, Peter. "Market Fundamentals vs. Price Level Bubbles: The First Tests." *Journal of Political Economy* 88 (August 1980): 745–70.

Folkerts-Landau, David, and Mathieson, Donald. "The Process of Innovation, Institutional Changes, and Regulatory Response in International Financial Markets." Paper presented to AEI Conference on Restructuring Financial Markets, Washington, D.C., November 1987.

Frenkel, Jacob A. "Reflections on European Monetary Integration." *Weltwirtschaftliches Archiv* 111 (1975): 216–21.

Frenkel, Jacob A. "The Collapse of Purchasing Power Parities in the 1970s." *European Economic Review* 16 (May 1981): 145–65.

Frenkel, Jacob A. "Monetary Policy: Domestic Targets and International Constraints." *American Economic Review* 73 (May 1983): 48–53.

Frenkel, Jacob A. "The International Monetary System: Should It Be Reformed?" *American Economic Review* 77 (May 1987): 205–10.

Frenkel, Jacob A., and Goldstein, Morris. "A Guide to Target Zones." International Monetary Fund *Staff Papers* 33 (December 1986): 633–70.

Frenkel, Jacob A., and Goldstein, Morris. "The Evolution of the International Monetary System and the Choice Between Fixed and Flexible Exchange Rates." *Informacion Comercial Espanola* 657 (May 1988): 13–26.

Frenkel, Jacob A.; Goldstein, Morris; and Masson, Paul. "International Coordination of Economic Policies: Scope, Methods, and Effects." In *Economic*

*Policy Coordination*, pp. 149–92. Edited by Wilfried Guth. Washington, D.C.: IMF/HWWA, 1988.

Frenkel, Jacob A., and Mussa, Michael. "The Efficiency of Foreign Exchange Markets and Measures of Turbulence." *American Economic Review* 70 (May 1980): 374–81.

Frenkel, Jacob A., and Mussa, Michael. "Monetary and Fiscal Policies in an Open Economy." *American Economic Review* 71 (May 1981): 253–58.

Giavazzi, Francesco, and Giovannini, Alberto. "The EMS and the Dollar." *Economic Policy* (April 1986): 455–73.

Giavazzi, Francesco, and Giovannini, Alberto. "Interpreting the European Disinflation: The Role of the Exchange Rate Regime." *Informacion Comercial Espanola* 657 (May 1988): 83–113.

Goldstein, Morris. *Have Flexible Exchange Rates Handicapped Macroeconomic Policy?* Special Papers in International Economics, no. 14. Princeton, N.J.: Princeton University Press, June 1980.

Goldstein, Morris. *The Exchange Rate System: Lessons of the Past and Options for the Future.* IMF Occasional Paper no. 30. Washington, D.C.: International Monetary Fund, July 1984.

Goldstein, Morris, and Khan, Mohsin. "Income and Price Effects in Foreign Trade." In *Handbook of International Economics*,pp. 1041–1105. Edited by Ronald Jones and Peter Kenen. Amsterdam, North-Holland: 1985.

Haberler, Gottfried. "Recent Developments in Historical Perspective." *Aussenwirtschaft* 4 (1987): 373–85.

Holtham, Gerald; Keating, Giles; and Spencer, Peter. *EMS: Advance or Face Retreat.* London: Credit Suisse First Boston Ltd., 1987.

Jurgensen, Philippe. *Report of the Working Group on Exchange Market Intervention.* Washington, D.C.: U.S. Treasury, 1983.

Krugman, Paul. "Is the Strong Dollar Sustainable?" Federal Reserve Bank of Kansas City, *The U.S. Dollar—Recent Developments, Outlook, and Policy Options* (1985): 103–32.

Levich, Richard. "Economic Consequences of Innovations in International Financial Markets." New York University Business School, New York, N.Y., July 1987.

Marston, Richard. "Real Exchange Rates and Productivity Growth in the United States and Japan." NBER Working Paper no. 1922, Cambridge, Mass., May 1986.

McKinnon, Ronald. *An International Standard for Monetary Stabilization.* Policy Analysis in International Economics no. 8, Institute for International Economics, Washington, D.C., 1984.

Meese, Richard, and Rogoff, Kenneth. "Empirical Exchange Rate Models of the Seventies: Do They Fit Out of Sample?" *Journal of International Economics* 19 (February 1983) 3–24.

Mussa, Michael. *The Role of Official Intervention.* Occasional Paper no. 6, Group of Thirty, 1981.

Nurkse, Ragnar. "Conditions of International Monetary Equilibrium." *Essays in International Finance*, no. 4. Princeton, N.J.: Princeton University Press, 1945.

Tobin, James. "A Proposal for International Monetary Reform." Cowles Foundation Paper no. 495, Cowles Foundation for Research in Economics, Yale University Press, 1980.

Triffin, Robert. *Gold and the Dollar Crisis: The Future of Convertibility*. New Haven, Conn.: Yale University Press, 1960.

West, K. D. "A Standard Monetary Model and the Variability of the Deutschmark–Dollar Exchange Rate." *Journal of International Economics* 23 (August 1987): 57–76.

Williamson, John. *The Exchange Rate System*. 2d ed. Policy Analyses in International Economics, no. 5. Washington, D.C.: Institute for International Economics, 1985.

Williamson, John, and Miller, Marcus H. *Targets and Indicators: A Blueprint for the International Coordination of Economic Policy*. Policy Analyses in International Economics, no. 22, Institute for International Economics, Washington, D.C., September 1987.

# 6

# Toward an International Commodity Standard?*

*Richard N. Cooper*

Determination of the basis for a national currency is one of the foremost attributes of national sovereignty. At irregular intervals over the past half century, countries have been urged to link their currencies by more or less rigid formulae to a variety of commodity baskets, with contents varying from one (gold) to several dozen commodities, and even beyond to an index of prices of goods and services, with varying intermediate combinations. Usually the stated aim is to ensure stability of the real value of money or, what is not the same, to reduce uncertainty in the real value of money. These objectives are typically assumed to be sufficient unto themselves, but sometimes they are justified as reducing uncertainty for business and household decisions that involve allocation of resources over time, and thereby as contributing to national well-being.

This paper will discuss the desirability of basing an international monetary system, which encompasses the formal rules and conventional practices governing payments among residents of different nations, on a basket of commodities. To anticipate the conclusion, the paper finds that such a move, while technically workable (though difficult), would not have much to recommend it. The paper offers an alternative suggestion for improving the international monetary system: a common currency among the industrialized democracies, with a common, jointly agreed monetary policy, which might well be targeted on some measure of price stability.

But as background it will be helpful first to review briefly the various suggestions that have been made over the years to tie a given national currency to commodities, that is, to tie money to the real economy so as to "anchor" the price level in some way.

---

*Reprinted from *Cato Journal* 8 (Fall 1988): 315–38.

The author is the Maurits C. Boas Professor of International Economics and the acting Director of the Center for International Affairs at Harvard University.

## National Commodity-Based Monetary Systems

### *Commodity Money*

The most straightforward way to link a national currency to the real side of the economy is to have a commodity *be* the currency or, closely related, to require the money-issuing authority to buy and sell the currency for the commodity at a fixed price (perhaps with a mint charge between the buying and selling price), as was done under the metallic standards (usually based on gold or silver, occasionally copper) of bygone times. But unless the commodity in question is an unusual one, which is representative of the whole collection of goods and services in which producers and consumers have an interest, this procedure will lead both to fluctuations over time in the growth of the money supply and to fluctuations in the general price level measured in terms of currency and of the monetized commodity. These fluctuations are simply a manifestation of changes in the commodity terms of trade, for any commodity in terms of others, that will occur in any economy undergoing continual changes in technology and in the level and composition of final demand. If $P$ is an index of money prices of a broad and relevant collection of goods and services, $P_G$ is the money price of the monetary commodity (e.g., dollars per ounce of silver), and $T$ is an index of the terms of trade between the monetized commodity and the other goods and services, then

$$P = P_G \times T \qquad (1)$$

A commodity standard fixes $P_G$ by law or convention, but that is not sufficient to ensure the stability of $P$, the widely accepted objective, so long as $T$ is not also fixed. However, $T$ will vary in response to variations in the supply and demand for the monetized commodity relative to other goods and services. If $P_G$ is fixed, $P$ will vary with $T$. Moreover, not only will $P$ be variable, but it will also be unpredictable except insofar as future movements in $T$ can be predicted with confidence. More will be said below about the stability and the predictability of $P$ under the historical gold standard.

### *Commodity-Convertible Money*

The foregoing problem can be mitigated by enlarging the contents of the monetized commodity basket. Alfred Marshall (1926) suggested a century ago that a basket comprising fixed weights of gold and silver, with the price between them free to vary, would offer a more stable monetary medium (measured in $T$ or $P$) than would gold or silver alone. Francis Edgeworth dubbed it a symmetallic standard (to differentiate from a bimetallic standard) based on gold and silver at a fixed price, which ran the risk under Gresham's Law of evolving into a monometallic standard as one or the other became more valuable as a commodity than as money. (Isaac Newton had undervalued newly reminted silver coins relative to gold in 1717, and thus inadvertantly put Britain on the gold standard as silver was exported; a similar development occurred in the United States in 1834 when legislation designed to correct an undervaluation of gold in terms of silver overdid it by altering the mint ratio from 16:1 to 15:1, and full-bodied silver ceased to circulate as money.)

A logical extension of Marshall's symmetallism would be to enlarge the basket of commodities, fixed in quantities, in which money is defined and against which it is issued. Such a proposal was put forward by Benjamin Graham (1937) in the 1930s.[1]

Graham proposed that the dollar be defined in terms of a fixed-weight basket of 23 commodities and that the Federal Reserve issue notes against warehouse receipts for the basket thus defined. He selected his commodities on the strength both of their economic importance and their storability; the commodities included the standard list, varying from coal to wood pulp. Graham was motivated in large measure by antidepression considerations; his idea was first advanced in 1933. He felt that support for commodity prices in times of economic slack would help stabilize overall economic activity. By the same token, sale of the commodity basket (demonetization) would limit inflationary pressure in booms, both by supplying commodities out of stocks and by contracting the money supply. In effect his scheme would provide perfectly elastic demand for the commodities (taken as a group, their individual relative prices were free to vary) in the monetary unit in times of depressed economic activity, and it would provide perfectly elastic supply (so long as physical stocks lasted) in times of boom.

Graham envisioned that his scheme should supplement the then-existing monetary system. His unrelated namesake Frank D. Graham (1942) carried the proposal further. He would have included a much longer (but unspecified) list of commodities in his basket, and he would have required all future money growth to be based solely on purchases of warehouse receipts for these commodities, in the stipulated proportion. This proposal would have tied money growth directly to production of the monetized commodities, in this respect much like a metallic gold standard but with an enlarged basket.

Stabilizing the price level of a basket of storable commodities will stabilize the general price level only if the terms of trade between

[1]The next few paragraphs draw heavily on Cooper (1982, pp. 38–43).

the monetized commodities and other goods and services are unchanging over time, an improbable event. Broadening the basket from a single commodity may help, but the problem in equation (1) remains: fixing $P_G$ will not in general stabilize $P$. For instance, over the period 1947–86 the price index for crude materials, which includes all the items in Graham's list plus some, increased by 177 percent. Prices of finished manufactured goods rose by 291 percent over the same period, and prices of services in the consumer price index rose by 684 percent. Reducing the price increase of crude materials to zero would not have avoided inflation in a broader index.

Apart from this problem and from the fact that real resources are tied up in warehoused monetary commodities (proponents have placed the annual costs at 3 to 4 percent of the outstanding value), it is unclear why there has not been more enthusiasm for commodity-reserve proposals. While they could not stabilize the general price level, these proposals might make its movements more predictable insofar as prices of finished goods and services have a reasonably stable relationship to commodity prices. (More on this subject will be presented below.) Yet these proposals have found little interest beyond intellectuals. I suspect that conservatives really want gold for reasons of history and sentiment, whereas nonconservatives prefer managed fiat money.[2] Also, the schemes are too complicated to appeal to a wider public.

*The Tabular Standard*

In the mid-1960s Albert Hart, Nicholas Kaldor, and Jan Tinbergen revived the idea of commodity-reserve currency in an explicitly international context; their proposal is discussed below. But first, it is worth mentioning the "tabular" standard, described by W. Stanley Jevons in 1875, advocated by Irving Fisher in 1920, and revived by

[2]It is of interest, though, that F. A. Hayek (1943) viewed commodity money favorably. John Maynard Keynes and Milton Friedman both opposed it. Keynes, though highly supportive of stabilization schemes for individual commodities, opposed a commodity-reserve currency on the grounds that it would have the same disadvantages as a gold standard in failing to persuade organized labor to keep its demands for money wages in line with the increase in efficiency wages (that is, productivity). He considered the risk of excessive money wage demands as one of the major obstacles to maintenance of a full employment economy. See his 1943 letter to Benjamin Graham, reprinted as an appendix to B. Graham in Yeager (1962, pp. 215–17).

Friedman (1953) opposed a commodity-reserve currency on the grounds that a full commodity-reserve currency, lacking the mystique and historical legitimacy of gold, would in time become financially burdensome because of the real costs associated with it. This problem in turn would lead to discretionary policy, which he also opposed. In Friedman's view, therefore, a commodity-reserve currency is dominated both by a gold standard, with its mystique, and by a properly managed fiat money, which he favors.

Robert Hall in 1982. This standard is the logical extension of the commodity-money idea to the entire basket of goods and services, in the context of a national currency. The price level associated with this basket is regarded as the most relevant price level for purposes of stabilization.

Writing during the gold standard period, Fisher (1920) proposed that the definition of the dollar in terms of gold should be indexed to the cost of living. In this way not only contracts written in nominal terms but currency itself in effect would be indexed so as to stabilize their real value over time, except during the intervals between adjustments.[3] If, for instance, the cost-of-living index fell, the number of grains of gold that defined the dollar as a unit of account would be reduced by a corresponding amount. For purposes of settling debts, the real value of the dollar would be preserved, since more gold would be required to settle a given dollar debt. The reverse adjustment would take place if the relevant price index rose. In terms of equation (1), $P_G$ would be adjusted exactly to compensate for movements in $T$, thus stabilizing $P$ over time.

This scheme amounts to the full indexation of all contracts, including gold convertible paper money, against changes in the value of gold, with gold remaining the formal basis of the dollar. Fisher would also have adjusted the gold money supply in parallel, with adjustments in the gold value of the dollar. If the price level fell, for instance, the dollar price of gold would be raised, and gold would flow into the Treasury (against the issuance of gold certificates) from private holdings, from abroad, and eventually from new production. The reverse would occur if the price level rose. Fisher would have reinforced this natural influence by issuing new gold certificates against the capital gains on existing Treasury stocks of gold, or by retiring gold certificates in the event of rising prices.

Robert Hall (1982) has revived the idea of a tabular standard (without endorsing it), but he suggests substituting for gold a fixed-weight basket of four commodities (ammonium nitrate, copper, aluminum, and plywood—ANCAP for short) whose index tracked well the U.S. consumer price index over 30 years. The dollar would be defined in terms of the ANCAP basket, and the basket would be legal tender in settlement of debts. Bank notes could be issued freely and would be fully redeemable in ANCAPs. When the consumer price index rose, the dollar would be redefined to contain more ANCAPs. In this way,

[3]Fisher (1920, p. 142) suggested an adjustment every two months, with a 2 percent brassage fee to prevent gold speculation at the expense of the Treasury immediately before each adjustment.

dollar contracts with deferred payment would involve repayment that was constant in terms of purchasing power, as measured by the consumer price index. Unlike Fisher or the Grahams, Hall would not require or even permit the government to engage in purchases or sales of the commodities composing ANCAP. The government would simply define the dollar in terms of ANCAPs and endow them with the attribute of legal tender, so that debts could be settled in ANCAPs or paper claims on them. Private arbitrage, which would involve some physical storage of the commodities in the ANCAP basket, would be relied upon to ensure that a paper dollar or dollar-demand account remained equal in value to the current ANCAP definition of the dollar.

*Price-Level Target*

Storage costs could be avoided by dropping the intermediary commodities (gold in Fisher's proposal, the ANCAP basket in Hall's) and simply gearing monetary action to a target price level. If the price level rose above the target, the monetary authorities would take steps to reduce some definition of the money supply (relative to trend), or to raise interest rates; and the reverse if the price level fell below its target. The action could be governed by formula. Since this approach would not involve the direct purchase and sale of commodities, however, the linkage between changes in monetary policy and prices would be an indirect one, which would be mediated by the full economy and by the responsiveness of the public to, say, additions or subtractions from some measure of the money supply. How close and how reliable the linkage is between money and prices is a deeply controversial question. We have known for years, moreover, that when there are response lags in the system, maintaining steadiness in one variable (the price level) by controlling another variable (the money supply or short-term interest rates) in the face of diverse and not directly observable shocks is not an easy task. Indeed if improperly formulated, even well-intended policy actions may lead to less, rather than greater, stability (Phillips 1954).

Futhermore, if the response lags themselves are unknown and variable, simple formula-based control will be suboptimal and might even be destabilizing. Proponents of discretionary control of monetary policy, aimed at a well-defined target such as stability in some measure of the price level, rest their case on this observation. They presuppose that the complex and not fully articulated "feeling" of the monetary authorities in a variety of circumstances will yield superior results to a formula-based response. This presupposition continues to be a source of controversy for it entails comparing discretionary responses, which will always be suboptimal (ex post) except by sheer luck, with a formula-based response, which can always be made optimal (ex post) with sufficient imagination. Such a comparison, however, is irrelevant in examining regimes with respect to future disturbances and responses.

If a price level is to be targeted, a *specific* measure of the price level must be chosen. What should it be? The consumer price index is the obvious choice, but that choice involves certain problems when considered in the context of an international monetary system (discussed below). Moreover, in an open economy the consumer price index contains imported items; it thus may be strongly and directly influenced by prices of imported goods, a problem that is less acute for value-added deflators.[4] The appropriate choice requires careful consideration of exactly what ultimate objectives are to be served by price-level stability.

Even the notion of price-level stability, on any particular measure, requires more careful specification if it is to be targeted. Do we mean by stability *constancy* over time (i.e., an expectation of return to a particular level)? Or do we mean that it should not change from where it is now (i.e., a zero expected rate of change)? These definitions are not the same, and they have quite different implications for policy if the price level is altered by some unforeseen event or is unexpectedly altered by a foreseen event. Should bygones be bygones, or should the price level be forced back to its earlier level? Finally, when we talk about the desirability of stability in the price level, that goal may really represent a loose way of expressing a desire for predictability in the price level. Most of the costs economists have attributed to price-level "instability" really arise from unpredictable movement rather than from predictable movement. Again, a more precise statement of ultimate objectives is required to sort out these various possibilities.

Once this necessity is acknowledged and active manipulation of monetary policy is countenanced, whether by formula or discretion, the question naturally arises whether stability of some measure of the price level is, or should be, the sole economic objective of society and, if not, whether monetary policy should be directed solely toward that objective rather than, say, to reducing unemployment, to increasing home ownership, or to fostering investment in plant and equipment.[5]

[4]Although the problem is less acute for value-added deflators, it is not entirely absent insofar as some domestically produced goods are in close competition with foreign-produced goods.

[5]See Hall (1986) for a proposal for formula-based use of monetary policy to achieve both price stability and employment stability.

Since stability of the price level is manifestly not society's only economic objective, the case for directing monetary policy solely toward that objective must rest on one or another of several possible assumptions:

- Price stability is a necessary condition for the attainment of other objectives, so there is no real conflict or "trade-off" among objectives.[6]
- Monetary actions cannot influence any other objectives. This view, often adopted in the formal theorizing of professional economists, is clearly erroneous in the short run. Moreover, it is unlikely to be true in the long run for any given definition of money (Tobin and Buiter 1976).
- Monetary actions have a comparative advantage in influencing the price level, and other instruments are better suited to the pursuit of other objectives. This proposition has some validity but runs up against William Brainard's (1967) observation that optimal policy formulation in an uncertain world would require that all objectives influence the choice of all policy instruments.
- While monetary actions might usefully help to attain other objectives, attempts to use them for this purpose and disagreements over which objectives should be emphasized are likely to reflect inconstancy of purpose and may lead to instability in real activity and in the price level, or even to neglect of the latter objective. This observation, while possibly valid, takes economists out of their role as economic analysts and prescribers of economically optimal policies and into the realm of political and social analysis. That is fair enough, but consistency requires that a similar perspective be taken on other proposed policy regimes as well, and on the political prospects for their survival in the form proposed under the impact of the serious disturbances and social strains.

## An International Commodity-Based Monetary System

The world has more than 160 distinct national monies. The collection of national choices concerning the basis for these monies deter-

[6]See, for example, the congressional testimony of Alan Greenspan (1987) during which he argued: The mandate for economic policy in the United States and elsewhere should be to maintain the maximum growth in real income and output that is feasible over the long run. A *necessary condition* for accomplishing that important objective is a stable price level, the responsibility for which has traditionally been assigned in large part to the central bank, in our case to the Federal Reserve [emphasis added].

mines the character of the international monetary regime. The regime may (but need not) involve formal and explicit undertakings by national authorities with regard to their monetary relationships with other countries. Likewise, the regime may (but need not) involve formal multilateral agreement on the main features of the international monetary system. Two key observations concerning the relationship between national monetary bases and the international regime are in order.

First, if two or more countries choose the same national standard linked to the same basket of goods and services (e.g., gold), by so doing they also fix the exchange rate between their national monies, which to that extent determines the international standard as well. A special case involves the choice by one country to peg its currency to the currency of another country. It thereby indirectly chooses the same standard as the other country, whatever it may be.

Second, if two or more countries choose different standards (i.e., a different basket) as bases for their currencies, then inevitably the exchange rate between those currencies will have to be altered from time to time, if not continuously. In particular, this proposition is true even if the countries choose the same principle, such as stabilizing the national consumer price index. A corollary is that if a country chooses to peg its currency to that of another country, it will not, in general, stabilize its national price level except by coincidence. The reason has to do with the presence of nontradable goods and services, combined with the proposition that over time there is likely to be an upward drift in the price of (mostly nontradable) services ($P_N$) with respect to the price of (generally tradable) goods ($P_T$). This drift will occur at a rate that will vary from country to country, depending largely on the differences in per capita income and in growth rates.

The secular rise in $P_N/P_T$ occurs in part from a slower growth in productivity in services than in tradable goods and in part because we have much greater difficulty in measuring productivity growth in services than in goods, which leads to a tendency to overstate price increases in services. Indeed, for a number of services the national statistical authorities identify outputs with inputs (e.g., an hour of a physician's time) so that by assumption there can be no increase in measured productivity. Under these circumstances, the secular upward drift in $P_N/P_T$ will be a positive function of the national growth in productivity, which will be especially rapid in low-income, rapidly growing countries such as Japan in the 1950s or South Korea in the 1980s.

When we speak of a national price level, we usually mean a weighted average of $P_N$ and $P_T$ in which the weights must be adjusted from time to time, generally giving more weight over time (at least for high-income countries) to the service component of consumption. If $P = a(t)P_N + (a - 1)P_T$ is targeted for constancy in each of two countries that differ in per capita income, a secular decline in ($P_T$) will be required in both countries, but more sharply in the poor than in the rich country. That decline in turn will require a secular appreciation of the currency of the poor country, provided tradable goods in the two countries are in close competition. Alternatively, if the exchange rate is fixed between the two currencies, $P$ will increase more rapidly in the poor but growing country than in the rich one, as experience has generally confirmed.[7]

The alteration in exchange rates need not take place continuously, but failure to do so will generate a transitory misallocation of resources—toward tradable goods in the low-income, growing countries and away from tradable goods in the high-income countries. Moreover, discrete changes in exchange rates, or the prospect of them, provoke substantial international movements of speculative capital, unless prevented by exchange controls. So these characteristics also affect the international monetary regime by pushing it toward floating exchange rates or at least toward managed flexibility, whether by formula or not. The general point is that national consumer price levels and exchange rates cannot both be stabilized over time; one or the other must sooner or later be given up. The strains become less severe, however, as the ratio of tradables to nontradables in national output grows (a function of trade barriers and of transport and communication costs) and as the dispersion among nations in per capita income declines.

If nations choose to target their exchange rates (i.e., to fix their currencies to other currencies), that action will anchor individual currencies, but it will not anchor the international monetary system as a whole. That anchoring can be accomplished in one of two ways:

- The first is by a collective agreement to some common target such as the price of tradables ($e\ P_T$, where $e$ is each country's exchange rate fixed to a numeraire currency), to some average

[7]During the 1950s when the Japanese currency was fixed at 360 yen per dollar, the consumer price index in Japan grew at 4 percent per annum compared with 2.1 percent in the United States, even while Japanese tradable goods were becoming more competitive relative to American goods. This general phenomenon has been emphasized by Balassa (1964) and shows up in a different way in Kravis et al. (1982), who show that real purchasing power in poor countries is far higher than is suggested by per capita income converted at official exchange rates.

of national consumer price indices, or to some other common basket.

- The second is by an implicit agreement that the country whose currency is used as an anchor by others will target some basket of goods and services. If the basket is its consumer price index and if $P_N/P_T$ rises over time, the money price of tradables will fall both in the anchor country and in all countries whose currencies are tied to it. The consumer price index will also fall in those countries where the upward drift of $P_N/P_T$ is slower than in the anchor country.[8]

## International Monetary Standards as Proposed

There has been much less systematic discussion of the international monetary standard than of national standards. Historically, the international standard has simply been the result of national standards. There have, however, been several exceptions to this generalization.

### *The Genoa Conference of 1922*

The Genoa conference was called after World War I to deal explicitly with the international standard and to address concretely the shortage of monetary gold that would emerge as countries resumed convertibility of their currencies into gold—as it was taken for granted they would. Exchange rates among currencies were floating at the time, but that arrangement was viewed as unsatisfactory and therefore a temporary condition. The problem was that national price levels had greatly increased since 1914 and could not be supported by the available gold; yet a monetary contraction sufficient to restore convertibility was seen as requiring a substantial and prolonged depression in economic activity.

The proposed solution was to economize on monetary gold in two ways: (1) to call in gold from circulation, which would be held by central banks (largely an accomplished fact outside the United States), and (2) to encourage central banks to hold in their reserves "bills of exchange" drawn on foreign financial centers in partial substitution for gold reserves. Thus a multiple reserve currency system was formally sanctioned, along with exchange rates fixed by gold convertibility. Under a simple monetarist model, the world price level could then ultimately be determined by the world's monetary gold stock,

[8]This statement abstracts from a number of factors, such as changes in product mix or in barriers to trade, that would permit changes in the price levels of tradable goods to diverge from country to country, even at unchanged exchange rates.

plus the willingness of central banks to hold in their reserves financial claims in other currencies. Without specifying the latter component quantitatively, however, the price level would be strictly indeterminant. At the time, the problem was assumed to be that central banks would hold too little foreign exchange reserves, not too much, and that the gold holdings of the countries whose currencies were held (combined with a commitment to gold convertibility) would limit the expansion of foreign exchange holdings—and thus also of domestic currencies and the price level. The significance of the Genoa Conference lies mainly in its attempt to view the international monetary system as a whole.

*Bretton Woods*

During World War II, British and American authorities negotiated a plan for the international monetary system whose purpose was to foster trade and growth and to avoid a repetition of the economic disasters of the interwar period. The regime that emerged was structurally similar to the regime envisaged at Genoa: fixed exchange rates determined by a gold parity for each currency, convertibility into gold or into a currency that was convertible into gold (the U.S. dollar), and the holding of foreign exchange as international reserves. There were two important additions: The regimen of the system was not to prevent the pursuit of national employment policies; and if the combination of commitments and policies became irreconcilable, a country could, with international permission, change the parity of its currency (i.e., devalue or revalue against gold and other currencies).

In practice, after some postwar adjustments, major currencies rarely changed their parities, and the U.S. dollar came to play a much greater role in reserves than had originally been envisioned. Gold provided a de jure anchor for the system, except for a somewhat mysterious provision for a "uniform change in par values" (i.e., a change in the price of gold). In fact, the system relied for its anchor on the prudence of U.S. economic policies, influenced in part by conversion of dollars into gold.

The world economy grew much more rapidly in the 1950s and 1960s than anyone dared anticipate in the late 1940s, and the demand for reserves grew with it. The reserves were supplied in part from the large U.S. gold stock but in larger part by a build up of dollar balances. This development led to the dilemma posed by Robert Triffin (1960): If dollar balances continue to grow, the gold-convertibility of the dollar would cease to be credible; if they did not, the growth in world trade might be constrained by insufficient internationally acceptable monetary medium.

The dilemma was resolved in 1968 by the decision to create a new international fiat money, the SDR—now defined as a fixed-weight basket of the five leading currencies. The International Monetary Fund was to create the SDR at not less than five-year intervals with the aim "to meet the long-term global need, as and when it arises, to supplement existing reserve assets in such manner as will promote the attainment of [IMF] purposes and will avoid economic stagnation and deflation as well as excess demand and inflation in the world" (IMF Article XVIII(1a)). In 1976 it was agreed that IMF members should strive to make the SDR "the principal reserve asset in the international monetary system" (IMF Article XXII). In principle, the SDR could be issued to satisfy the secular growth for international reserves, subject to the general guideline of avoiding both inflation and economic stagnation. Thus was introduced a fully discretionary monetary system at the international level, which, in fact, mirrored the practice at the national level in virtually all countries with the exceptions of Liberia and Panama (which use U.S. dollars), the CFA franc zones of west and equatorial Africa, and a few British colonies that still use fully backed currency boards for local issue. In fact, there have been only two decisions to allocate SDRs over a 20-year period, totaling 21 billion SDRs, or $29 billion at current exchange rates (a sum that accounts for less than 5 percent of existing official foreign exchange reserves and even less if officially held gold is included in reserves).

In short, neither national monetary systems nor the international monetary system is anchored to the world of goods and services, except by the prudence of monetary authorities. In addition the present international monetary system is extremely permissive with regard to exchange rates, requiring only that nations notify the IMF of their exchange arrangements and that these arrangements conform with the objectives of fostering "orderly economic growth with reasonable price stability" and of promoting economic and financial stability. Member nations are enjoined to "avoid manipulating exchange rates or the international system in order to prevent effective balance of payments adjustment or to gain an unfair competitive advantage over other members" (IMF Article VIII(1)), and those nations cannot introduce discriminatory exchange rate practices.

### *An International Commodity-Reserve Currency*

When discussion of the Triffin dilemma was in full swing, Hart, Kaldor, and Tinbergen (1964) proposed that the dilemma be resolved by creation of an international commodity-reserve currency (ICRC), which is an international version of the Graham proposal. The proposal was updated in a post-SDR context by Hart (1976). He suggests that the goods in question should be both standardized and storable, and he offers an illustrative list (reproduced in Table 1) of 31 commodities that might make up the basket. Hart suggests that annual storage and turnover costs on the commodities selected should not exceed 5 percent. He would leave some operational flexibility for the final list of goods to be included in the ICRC, and their weights, which would be necessary if the initial accumulation period is to have a fixed time period of, for example, five years.

The IMF would purchase the basket of commodities, aiming at an amount equal to, say, 25 percent of world trade in these commodities, and would issue SDRs in exchange.[9] The SDRs so issued would be the principal source of new international reserves. Increases in monetary gold and in foreign exchange reserves would not be allowed once the scheme was in full swing, although Hart would permit the IMF to engage in open-market operations in SDRs to provide some monetary flexibility beyond purchases of the commodity basket.

The commodity basket would be bought or sold as a unit, by telegraphic instruction to the different markets and storage areas in which the various goods were physically held around the world. To cover costs and to gain a bit of seigniorage, the IMF would have a 10 percent buy-sell spread on its purchases and sales of the basket. The gross costs of managing the scheme would involve storage costs plus

*TABLE 1*

STANDARDIZED AND STORABLE COMMODITIES FOR POSSIBLE INCLUSION IN AN INTERNATIONAL COMMODITY-RESERVE CURRENCY

| | | |
|---|---|---|
| Wheat | Pork bellies, frozen | Cotton |
| Maize | Orange juice, frozen | Wool |
| Rice | Butter | Jute |
| Soybeans | Lard | Hard fibers |
| Oats | Milk, dried | Silk |
| Linseed | | Rubber |
| Peanuts | Copper | |
| Sugar | Lead | Plywood |
| Coffee | Zinc | Lumber |
| Tea | Tin | Woodpulp |
| Cocoa | Silver | Newsprint |

SOURCE: Hart (1976, p. 6).

[9]Hart (1966) suggested 75 percent of world trade in the listed commodities. No explanation is given for the lower figure suggested in 1976.

interest plus the costs of turnover, since some of the commodities deteriorate physically over time and would have to be changed occasionally. Hart reckons annual storage costs for most of the commodities at 1 percent or less of their value, although for wheat and maize it approaches 6 to 7 percent. It is noteworthy that the interest costs, from a social point of view, might be negligible if the stocks are acquired mainly in times of economic slack when the future opportunity cost of producing now is low, a point that Hart fails to mention. He does note that net social cost would be lower than gross cost to the extent that the existence of public storage of these commodities permits some reduction in private stocks and to the extent that his scheme headed off various proposals for export-restricting commodity schemes that were under discussion at UNCTAD in the mid-1970s.

Hart makes the interesting suggestion that the IMF might occasionally substitute future contracts for physical holdings of individual commodities in the basket, thereby releasing those commodities into the market under conditions of an emergency.

Under this conception of an international currency, individual nations would be free to set national monetary standards as they chose and to allow their currencies to float against one another and against the SDR. But individual countries would be permitted to peg their currencies to the SDR. In all likelihood many would do so, just as today many peg their currencies to some other currency or to a basket of currencies.

In sum, this proposal involves an international unit of account and the creation of an international money that is anchored in a basket of economically significant commodities. The unit of account would over time maintain a stable value in those commodities through purchase or sales of the basket within a margin of plus or minus 5 percent. The omission of oil and coal from the basket is noteworthy: They were both included in Graham's list in 1937. Moreover, this scheme obviously would not stabilize a more general price level if there is secular drift between the average prices of the ICRC commodities and other prices. The problem of a secular increase in prices of services, as we measure them, has already been discussed.

The question of whether there is secular drift in the prices of primary products relative to the price of manufactured goods has long been debated. The view of David Ricardo, revived in the 1970s by the Club of Rome, is that the price of manufactured goods must decline secularly relative to the price of primary products in a world of growing population and income. This decline is the result of the increase in rents on agricultural land and on resources in limited supply. Under these circumstances, stabilizing the value of the monetary unit in terms of primary products would result in a secular decline in the price of manufactured goods, although that decline would perhaps be offset in whole or in part by the rise in the measured price of services.

In the early 1950s, Raul Prebisch took the opposite view, widely held in many developing countries, that there is a secular rise in the price of manufactured goods relative to that of primary products. If the monetary unit is stabilized in terms of the prices of primary products and if the Prebisch view is correct, the ICRC scheme will generate secular inflation. In fact, the historical evidence is ambiguous on very long-term movements in the ratio of primary product to manufactured prices (Spraos 1980). There do seem to be swings in one direction or the other for periods of a decade or longer, such as the swings that took place under the gold standard, but those swings are less pronounced than for gold alone.

## International Monetary Systems in Practice

### *The Gold Standard*

The pre-World War I gold standard does not fall into the category of carefully worked out international monetary systems. It was a historical consequence of national choices, strongly influenced by the political, military, and economic successes of Britain, plus the historical accident of Britain's being on the gold standard. It was, moreover, a period of great economic tension and considerable instability both in prices and in output (Cooper 1982).

An idealized version of the gold standard was, to be sure, a self-correcting mechanism that could both stabilize the world price level and generate the right amount of international liquidity. For a single country with an insufficient monetary base to support its desired activities, the national price level would fall, a trade surplus would develop, gold would flow into the country from the rest of the world, and this process would continue until price level equality was restored with sufficient additions to gold money to support the higher desired economic activity. This mechanism was described by David Hume clearly and concisely in 1752.

For the world monetary system, inadequate gold would lead to a decline in the world price level, thus increasing the real value of money and satisfying the need for money in that way. But a longer-term adjustment would also be set in motion. With gold more valuable in real terms, gold production could be expected to increase, and the total supply of money in physical terms would thus be augmented. This process would ensure long-run stability of the price level, provided technological improvements in ore extraction and new discoveries could be assumed to offset exactly the gradual exhaustion of known gold supplies and to thwart the emergence of Ricardian rents, which otherwise would require a trend decline in the general level of prices measured in gold money so long as the economy was growing.

Unhappily, this idealized version was not readily observable in reality. The lags in the adjustment process were so long that large swings in prices could be observed as a result of periodic surpluses or shortages of gold relative to commodities. Table 2 records the changes in wholesale prices that occurred during a century under the gold standard (roughly parallel movements in all four countries listed) by amounts between 30 and 70 percent. This experience is certainly not a record of stability.

It is conceivable that, despite these long swells, economic agents expected an eventual return to a "normal" price level. Certainly a striking feature of the 19th century is that there were long periods of price decline as well as long periods of inflation.

If the relevant public expected the long-term price level to be stable, long-term interest rates should be *negatively* correlated with the price level. High price levels would give rise to expectations of a subsequent fall in prices, which should lower nominal long-term interest rates, and vice versa for a lower-than-normal price level. In fact, long-term nominal interest rates were *positively* correlated with prices—rising as the price level rose, falling as it fell. This phenomenon was dubbed the Gibson Paradox by Keynes (1930) and was already a puzzle to analysts in the 1920s.

The movements in long-term interest rates are more easily interpreted by assuming that the relevant public expected the contemporary price level to remain unchanged regardless of where it is

*TABLE 2*

WHOLESALE PRICE CHANGES UNDER THE GOLD STANDARD

| Years | United States | United Kingdom | Germany | France |
|---|---|---|---|---|
| | | (Percentage Change) | | |
| 1816–1849 | −45 | −41 | −29 | −33 |
| 1849–1873 | 67 | 51 | 70 | 30 |
| 1873–1896 | −53 | −45 | −40 | −45 |
| 1896–1913 | 56 | 39 | 45 | 45 |

SOURCE: Cooper (1982, p. 9).

relative to past levels, perhaps adjusted slightly for recent changes. That is, if prices have fallen recently, the public expected them to fall a bit more and then remain unchanged.

But if this was the public's expectation—and it fits best the relationship between the price level and long-term interest rates—they were constantly fooled. We now know that, at least for a 20-year holding period (this was the maturity of many bonds), ex post real interest rates varied much more sharply than did nominal interest rates, and both series were positively correlated with the price level. This is not a record of intertemporal constancy in contract values.

It is conceivable too that short-term predictability was quite high despite long-term swells in prices, despite apparently erroneous expectations about the real value of long-term contracts, and despite the high variability both of short-term prices and of short-term interest rates. Lawrence Summers (1983) has shown, however, that short-term nominal interest rates did not, in fact, adjust well to compensate for short-term fluctuations in the price level. More recently, Allan Meltzer (1986) has shown that quarterly prediction errors (on a simple forecasting model relying only on past data of each series) were much higher in the gold standard era both for prices and for real output than they were in the 1950–80 period. Table 3 records the forecast errors for quarterly forecasts of U.S. GNP and the prices for each of six monetary periods as characterized by Meltzer. (He distinguishes between a gold standard with and without a Federal Reserve System, and he separates the period of fixed long-term interest rates during

*TABLE 3*

VARIANCE OF QUARTERLY FORECAST ERRORS (TIMES 1,000) FOR THE UNITED STATES

| | Nominal GNP | Price Level | Real GNP |
|---|---|---|---|
| Gold Standard | | | |
| 1890(1)–1914(4) | 2.98 | .25 | 2.83 |
| 1915(1)–1931(3) | 1.80 | .60 | 1.41 |
| No Clear Standard | | | |
| 1931(4)–1941(4) | 5.64 | .24 | 4.02 |
| 1942(1)–1951(1) | .67 | .60 | .78 |
| Bretton Woods, 1951(2)–1971(3) | .13 | .02 | .11 |
| Fluctuating Rates, 1971(4)–1980(4) | .13 | .02 | .14 |

NOTE: Quarterly forecasts are made using a Kalman filter with respect to expected level and expected rate of change on past data for each series.
SOURCE: Meltzer (1986, p. 141).

the 1940s. He does not exclude the two world wars.) A comparison of the first two rows with the last two rows shows a *dramatic* improvement in quarterly predictability on moving from the gold standard to either the managed monetary system under Bretton Woods or the period of fluctuating exchange rates since the early 1970s. The forecast errors decline relative to price and output variability as well as in absolute terms, and they decline sharply on expectations with respect to level and rate change of the variables as well as with respect to general background noise (Meltzer 1986, pp. 141–44). It is likely, furthermore, that an extension of Meltzer's analysis through 1981–87 would show, by these standards, a marked superiority of the Bretton Woods system over the full period of fluctuating exchange rates. Of course, we could not be sure that the difference was attributable to the change in international monetary arrangements.

In sum, the historical gold standard did not perform very well—indeed it was a source of consternation and controversy to those who lived through it—except with respect to fixing exchange rates among currencies.

*The Present Non-standard*

The present mixed arrangement of fixed and fluctuating exchange rates also does not reflect a considered collective judgment on what the international monetary system should be. Rather, present arrangements are a jumble reflecting national choices and evasion of choices. They are not "anchored" in anything, neither a commodity basket nor even (except for the United States) the prudence of U.S. macroeconomic policy. This lack of an anchor is a source of uneasiness. Neither national price levels nor the SDR-denominated price level are determined in the "logic" of the arrangements, although they are determinant at every moment of time. The lack of a clear anchor may suggest that there is no foundation for long-term expectations about the price level, although, as we have seen, such expectations were not very accurate under the historical gold standard either.

There are two further problems with present international monetary arrangements. The first concerns unsettled expectations about the future value of real exchange rates among major currencies, over the horizon of one to five years that is appropriate for investment and production decisions. It is noteworthy that price levels moved substantially under the gold standard but that in different countries price indexes moved roughly in parallel with one another, suggesting that there may not have been significant variations in national competitiveness arising from the monetary side of national economies. This aspect of the gold standard deserves a closer examination.

If they are to be subjected to economic disturbances, most businesses, especially in manufacturing, place a high value on their competitors being subjected to the same disturbances so they are not put at a competitive disadvantage. The problem with present arrangements involving flexible exchange rates is that the arrangement provides no such assurance in industries operating in a world market. On the contrary, for reasons that are remote from a firm's activity and that often originate in the arcane world of finance, the firm can suddenly find itself facing much stiffer competition (or much less, but that is rarely a cause of concern) as the result of the movement of an exchange rate.

This uneven source of uncertainty will have several consequences that are adverse to the efficient allocation of resources. First, businesses, at the national level, will attempt to blunt the source of supposedly unequal competition by urging an increase in trade barriers of various kinds. This response was manifest in the United States in 1983–86. It will slow import liberalization in Japan in the late 1980s, and I expect it to become more pronounced in Europe as trade surpluses decline there.

Second, investment will be reduced in the tradable sector as a result of the greater uncertainty arising from fluctuations in real exchange rates—an uncertainty of a more compelling type for investors than uncertainty about the general price level over the period of their investments. The latter influences profitability, but the likelihood that unanticipated changes in the price level will cause bankruptcy is much lower than the likelihood that unanticipated changes in the exchange rate will cause bankruptcy. It is perhaps not a complete coincidence that investment rates in manufacturing have dropped sharply in all major industrial countries since the advent of flexible exchange rates, although there are other explanatory factors as well, most notably the two oil price increases and the associated sharp recessions in economic activity.

Third, firms will adjust their investment behavior to hedge against the offending uncertainty. Since they cannot hedge their future commitments to production through financial markets, they will do so by investing abroad, across currency zones, even if that means giving up some of the advantages of cost and scale associated with exporting from their home bases or some other lowest cost location. One possible consequence, since some of this diversification takes place through takeovers and buyouts, is a greater world concentration in certain industries, leading to a reduction in worldwide competition.

So on all these counts, a regime that reduced uncertainty about real exchange rates without increasing costs elsewhere would be an improvement over the present arrangements.

The second problem with current monetary arrangements is that the most important official international reserve continues to be the U.S. dollar, despite a general commitment to make the SDR the principal reserve asset. The dollar is supplemented by holdings of other currencies, most notably the German mark and the Japanese yen. In practice, dollars are likely to provide most of the growth in reserves over the next decade, although the share held in other currencies may grow somewhat. Reserves are necessary and are thought to be necessary, because the exchange rates of almost all countries are either fixed to something or are subject to managed floating. We have a mixed and permissive system rather than a floating rate system. Moreover, as many countries have now discovered, access to the international capital market is not ensured at all times, especially when a country is seen to be in some external economic difficulty (i.e., just when it needs foreign funds most badly). So monetary authorities feel they need owned reserves, and they will want those reserves to grow, on average, over time.

Sometimes countries acquire reserves as the lesser of evils, as a result of exchange market intervention to keep their currencies from appreciating too rapidly or too far. But once acquired, the higher level of reserves sets a new expectation: While some decline may be tolerated and even welcome, a decline toward the former level more often than not provokes restrictive action to halt the drop. A rachet is thus introduced into implicit reserve targets.

Over the coming decades the relative importance of the United States in the world economy is likely to decline—not because the U.S. economy is performing badly, but because others are performing well. Europe and Japan are also likely to experience relative declines as well, and for the same reasons: low population growth rates and productivity that advances only as rapidly as new technology permits. Other countries have more rapid population growth, and they can continue to introduce existing technology from abroad. Of course, poor economic policies or political turmoil may retard their growth, but on balance the U.S. share of gross world product is likely to decline over time.

The combination of reduced relative U.S. economic importance with growing use of the dollar as an international reserve will sooner or later put serious strains on U.S. monetary policy. In a certain sense, it implies more external "discipline" on the United States. But this discipline will not necessarily conduce toward greater economic or monetary stability, so as to provide a firm anchor for the system. Rather, the Federal Reserve will find itself more frequently having to respond to international financial pressures, whether they are rational in the larger scheme of things or not, and these pressures may sometimes cause less rather than more stability in monetary affairs. Yet the proper role of a monetary system, national or international, is to provide a stable expectational environment for the wealth-producing sectors of the economy and for the public generally.

## An International Fiat Money

The exceptional importance of real exchange rate uncertainty suggests that a system should be introduced that can reduce it. Several proposals to accomplish this objective have been made, ranging from target exchange rate zones that would limit exchange rate movements around a calculated equilibrium real exchange rate (Williamson 1985) to close coordination of monetary policy among the three largest countries with a view both to stabilizing their exchange rates and controlling their collective monetary growth (McKinnon 1984).

But to eliminate exchange rate uncertainty definitively—and sharply reduce real exchange rate uncertainty—requires a single currency. For the international monetary system, this objective could be effectively achieved with much greater prospect of negotiability by first introducing the single currency to the large industrialized democracies of Europe, North America, and Japan. A single money requires a single monetary policy. The constitution of the new International Central Bank (ICB), as we may call it, could be modeled on the Federal Reserve System, with changes appropriate to the circumstance that participants would be nations rather than regions within a nation. Representatives of national central banks, whether or not under control of sitting governments, could make up the Board of Governors with votes weighted by the relative size of national economies. Or finance ministries could be directly represented. Or there could be nationally selected independent appointees with the number of appointees apportioned by economic size. Whatever its exact constitution, the key point is that monetary policy would be a collective decision; no single government could determine the outcome.

The ICB's powers would be similar to those of central banks today, with a discount window for distress lending and open market operations to influence the monetary base. Governments would share the seigniorage resulting from the issue of central bank money. But no government could finance budget deficits at the ICB beyond its share of the seigniorage; it would have to go to the financial market for that.

Other democratic countries could formally join the system, and any nonmember could choose to fix its exchange rate vis-à-vis the international kroner,[10] which would permit many of the advantages of fixed exchange rates without the formal commitments.

What principles should guide the actions of the ICB? It would face much the same choices that nations face today, although it could not fix the exchange rate, because there would be no plausible currency to which to fix it. The earlier discussion about various national standards becomes relevant, including the various disadvantages of a commodity-based standard. Nonetheless the ICB needs some guidelines. The standard could be, as Keynes (1930, p. 391) suggested, a tabular standard based on an index of wholesale prices of 62 internationally traded commodities with an implied secular inflation in consumer prices, which Keynes recognized and welcomed. Or it could be a target based on a weighted average of the consumer price indices in the participating countries with an implied secular decline in commodity prices. Or the standard could be a defined price level but modified in response to movements in unemployment away from some target level, as Hall (1986) has suggested. Or the ICB could even fail to agree on a sharply defined target and muddle through as the Federal Reserve does now. That would not be intellectually satisfying, but Meltzer's findings suggest that we could be much worse off under many alternatives.

## References

Balassa, Bela. "The Purchasing-Power Parity Doctrine: A Reappraisal." *Journal of Political Economy* 72 (December 1964): 584–96.

Brainard, William C. "Uncertainty and the Effectiveness of Economic Policy." *American Economic Review*, 57 (May 1967): 411–25.

Cooper, Richard N. "The Gold Standard: Historical Facts and Future Prospects." *Brookings Papers in Economic Activity* (1982, no. 1): 1–45.

Fisher, Irving. *Stabilizing the Dollar*. New York: Macmillan, 1920.

Friedman, Milton. "Commodity-Reserve Currency." In *Essays in Positive Economics*, pp. 204–50. University of Chicago Press, 1953.

Graham, Benjamin. *Storage and Stability*. New York: McGraw-Hill, 1937.

Graham, Frank D. *Social Goals and Economic Institutions*. Princeton, N.J.: Princeton University Press, 1942.

[10]It does not matter what the new currency is called. In view of the widespread use around the world of the U.S. dollar, "dollar" would be a natural designation, but that designation might be politically offensive to some. So it could be called the thaler, or the kroner, or the franc. *The Economist* (9 January 1988, p. 9) has suggested the "phoenix."

Greenspan, Alan. Testimony before several subcommittees of the House Committee on Banking, Finance, and Urban Affairs, 18 December 1987.

Hall, Robert E. "Explorations in the Gold Standard and Related Policies for Stabilizing the Dollar." In *Inflation: Causes and Effects*, pp. 111–22. Edited by Robert E. Hall. Chicago: University of Chicago Press, 1982.

Hall, Robert E. "Optimal Monetary Institutions and Policy." In *Alternative Monetary Regimes*, pp. 244–39. Edited by Colin D. Campbell and William R. Dougan. Baltimore: Johns Hopkins University Press, 1986.

Hart, Albert G. "The Case for and against an International Commodity Reserve Currency." *Oxford Economic Papers* 18 (July 1966): 237–41.

Hart, Albert G. "The Case as of 1976 for International Commodity-Reserve Currency." *Weltwirtschaftliches Archiv* 112 (1976): 1–32.

Hart, Albert G.; Kaldor, Nicholas; and Tinbergen, Jan. "The Case for an International Commodity Reserve Currency," In Kaldor, *Essays on Economic Policy*, vol. 2, pp. 131–77. New York: Norton, 1964.

Hayek, F. A. "A Commodity Reserve Currency." *Economic Journal* 53 (June–September 1943): 176–84.

Jevons, W. Stanley. *Money and the Mechanism of Exchange*. London: D. Appleton, 1875.

Keynes, J. M. *A Treatise on Money*, vol. 2. New York: Macmillan, 1930.

Kravis, Irving; Heston, Alan; and Summers, Robert. *World Product and Income: International Comparisons of Real Gross Product*. Baltimore: Johns Hopkins University Press, 1982.

Marshall, Alfred. *Official Papers by Alfred Marshall*. New York: Macmillan, 1926.

McKinnon, Ronald I. *An International Standard for Monetary Stabilization*. Washington, D.C.: Institute for International Economics, March 1984.

Meltzer, Allan H. "Some Evidence on the Comparative Uncertainty Experienced under Different Monetary Regimes." In *Alternative Monetary Regimes*, pp. 122–53. Edited by Colin D. Campbell and William R. Dougan. Baltimore: Johns Hopkins University Press, 1986.

Phillips, A. W. "Stabilization Policy in a Closed Economy." *Economic Journal* 64 (1954): 290–353.

Spraos, John. "Statistical Debate on the Net Barter Terms of Trade." *Economic Journal* 90 (March 1980):109–25.

Summers, Lawrence H. "The Non-Adjustment of Nominal Interest Rates: A Study of the Fisher Effect." In *Symposium in Honor of Arthur Okun*, pp. 201–44. Edited by James Tobin. Washington, D.C.: Brookings Institution, 1983.

Tobin, James, and Buiter, Willem. "Long-Run Effects of Fiscal and Monetary Policy on Aggregate Demand." In *Monetarism*, pp. 273–309. Edited by J. L. Stein. Amsterdam: North-Holland, 1976.

Triffin, Robert. *Gold and the Dollar Crisis*. New Haven: Yale University Press, 1960.

Williamson, John. *The Exchange Rate System*, 2d ed. Washington, D.C.: Institute for International Economics, June 1985.

Yeager, Leland B., ed. *In Search of a Monetary Constitution*. Cambridge: Harvard University Press, 1962.

# COMMENT

# TOWARD AN INTERNATIONAL FIAT STANDARD?*

*Lawrence H. White*

Richard Cooper's paper evokes in me a certain nostalgia. It is somehow reassuring to find that the ideological outlook at Harvard has not changed appreciably since my days as an undergraduate economics major. Though Cooper has joined Harvard's economics faculty since I graduated, it is evident from his paper that he shares what I remember as a parochial and rather wishful view of the beneficence of government institutions.

In one respect, though, his paper shows that the outlook at Harvard is perhaps not as parochial now. Cooper cites Allan Meltzer, whose name I certainly never heard in any Harvard classroom. Even more remarkably, the paper cites Meltzer (1986) favorably. The occasion for this outreach is revealing. Cooper finds Meltzer's work useful because they agree on one thing: that a commodity money system is inferior to a fiat money system run the right way. Of course, Cooper and Meltzer have very different ideas about what is "the right way" to run a fiat money system. But monetary politics can make for strange bedfellows. We have here a question of politics because both want a political system to supply the economy with its basic money.

Meltzer, like many other monetarists, wants base money supplied by a national monetary authority, albeit an authority bound by a strict money growth rule, with cleanly floating exchange rates among industrial nations. Cooper, like at least a few other Keynesians, wants a world central bank that is either managed to stabilize some price index or empowered to engage in activist counter-cyclical policy. The most important question is not which of these two political money-supply systems is better, but whether we would not be better off with a nonpolitical, market-based monetary system.

The idea of a nonpolitical monetary system, unfortunately, nowhere intrudes into Cooper's paper. (In fact he suggests that any monetary

*Reprinted from *Cato Journal* 8 (Fall 1988): 339–46.

The author is Associate Professor of Economics at the University of Georgia.

system not consciously designed and collectively installed is per se unsatisfactory.) This omission is understandable, of course; denationalization of money is not yet within the realm of the politically realistic. It will no doubt be as absent from the agenda of the next Democratic administration as it was from the last one, in which Cooper occupied a position of importance.

## Commodity Standards and Free Market Money

Cooper's first sentence reminds us of how deep-rooted political control is over money: "Determination of the basis for a national currency is one of the foremost attributes of national sovereignty." This statement is certainly true, but it is not a necessary truth. It is instead a sad reflection of the pervasiveness of state intervention in our daily lives that the currency we carry in our wallets, and more importantly the ultimate medium of settlement in our payments system, is today nothing but a token of state sovereignty.

It need not be so. Determining the basis for currency could be left to the market. Once it was: Commodity money evolved long before nation-states discovered the profits to themselves in (1) monopolizing the mints, (2) monopolizing the issue of commodity-redeemable paper currency, and (3) finally terminating the commodity standard by abrogating the central bank's obligation to redeem its currency. Thus a commodity standard (particularly a gold or silver specie standard, but perhaps even a nongovernmental commodity basket standard) can be viewed in a way quite distinct from what one finds in Cooper's paper. He characterizes single-commodity and multi-commodity standards as a set of "rigid formulae," which are urged on national governments by would-be reformers, for linking national currencies to arbitrary commodity baskets. Instead, a commodity standard may be viewed as the naturally evolved market (or nonpolitical) arrangement for supplying money.[1]

To have a single-commodity standard, contrary to Cooper's account, is not characteristically "to require the money-issuing authority to buy and sell the currency for the commodity at a fixed price." There simply need not be any monopoly currency-issuing authority.[2] Paper currency (banknotes) can instead be supplied by a plurality of competing banks. Redeemability of paper currency for the money commodity at a prearranged rate is then not an imposed requirement, but simply a natural part of the contract freely made between a bank and the holders of its banknotes.

[1]See Selgin and White (1987).

[2]A point made by McCulloch (1986).

I cannot go into more detail here about (1) how such a "free banking" system has worked historically or would work under modern conditions; (2) whether a free banking system would tend, or should be nudged (as Leland Yeager has suggested), to evolve beyond a single-commodity standard with direct redeemability to a multi-commodity standard with only indirect redeemability; (3) the reasons for believing that political money supply regimes are radically flawed; or (4) why the intellectual case for government provision of money, on the grounds that it is a "natural monopoly" or "public good," is an empty box. I refer the reader to other works on these topics.[3]

The point I want to emphasize is that, from the perspective of denationalization, a free-market commodity standard is quite unlike the contrived, government-run, commodity-basket proposals to which Cooper devotes most of his paper. The most forceful argument for a gold standard, in my view, is not that it would best guide the monetary authorities, but that it would allow us to do without monetary authorities. Even among gold advocates who do not go that far, the case for gold is generally the case for a nonpolitical, self-regulating monetary order, free of covert inflationary finance (thus they speak of "honest money") and free of central-bank-generated monetary instability (thus "stable money").

When Cooper writes that gold advocates "really want gold for reasons of history and sentiment," he shows little understanding of the case for gold. The history of gold is relevant because, to some extent, it shows us how a monetary system evolves and how it can operate in the absence of state intervention—not because what is traditional is per se better than what is new. Perhaps he assumes that the case must be built on history and sentiment because it is not built on optimal control theory. Indeed, a better system can always be designed for hitting any specific nominal goal one likes, such as a price index target.

As Cooper argues, a commodity standard is not sufficient to ensure the stability of any particular price index. As I have indicated, however, there is at least one other important reason for preferring gold: the desire to have a basic money that is outside the hands of governments and is not subjugated to whatever goal authorities decide to pursue. Why should the monetary system be hitched by force of law to any centrally planned goal? I am not against price stability, mind

[3]Regarding (1), see White (1984a) and Selgin (1988); for (2), see Greenfield and Yeager (1983, 1986), Yeager (1985), and White (1984b, 1986); for (3), the two major reasons are the possibilities of monetary policy being turned toward seignorage maximization or toward creation of unintentional or intentional (political) business cycles (see Willett 1988); and for (4), see Vaubel (1984).

you. (As central bank goals go, it is far from the worst.) I just believe that everyday transactors are smart enough, and the market selection process is responsive enough, that the monetary standard and payment media they converge on in a free-market setting will embody as much purchasing-power stability as they feel is worth having, given the cost of enchancing it.

## Monetary Policy Rules

Cooper asks why monetary policy should be exclusively concerned with stability of the price level (or more generally, with producing whatever path for the price level). Once we take a national government-run fiat money regime for granted, this is an important question. Cooper ponders several possible answers to why the price level should be the central bank's sole concern. Oddly, he does not address the strongest case for precommitting monetary policy toward a single objective of zero inflation rather than toward some combination of low inflation and something else (low unemployment, for example): namely, the case made by Kydland and Prescott (1977) and by Barro and Gordon (1983). These authors show that a discretionary policy authority in a "natural rate" world, which is known by the public to face the temptation of exploiting the short-run Phillips Curve, is driven to produce pointlessly high inflation. A natural rate world is one in which unemployment can be reduced (or the real interest rate reduced, or any other supposedly beneficial real effect produced) by monetary policy only when the policy fools the public, inflating faster than they expected. Monetary shocks can disturb the real economy but cannot improve its results. Cooper apparently doubts that we live in such a world, though it is not clear why he doubts it. Surely the possible "Tobin effect" of inflation on capital accumulation, even overlooking the weakness of its empirical support, provides no grounds for a monetary policy targeted on real variables.

The discretionary monetary authority in Kydland and Prescott's example is driven to create high inflation, because the authority knows that the public expects high inflation and that to create low inflation, with its negative monetary surprise, would increase unemployment. The public rationally expects high inflation because it knows the authority is tempted to notch up the inflation rate whenever the employment gain from surprise inflation is worth it. This is known in the literature as the "time inconsistency" problem with discretionary monetary policy. Cooper cites Brainard (1967) as an argument for having all objectives influence the choice of all policy instruments, but the whole optimal-control approach to monetary policy represented by that advice has yet to be rehabilitated from the time-inconsistency critique.

As mentioned earlier, Cooper favorably cites Meltzer (1986), a work claiming to show that greater macroeconomic uncertainty was experienced under the historical classical gold standard than has been experienced under the postwar Bretton Woods international monetary system and the floating-rate system. Meltzer's evidence, however, has problems that we ought to note. Most importantly, the older time series Meltzer uses were not collected in the postwar manner. They were constructed after the fact and, because of limitations on readily available data, were constructed in a way that very likely exaggerates their cyclical volatility. A much narrower basket of commodities was available for the construction of price indices, for instance. Christina Romer (1986) has shown that the unemployment and GNP series similarly exaggerate cyclical variability. Thus the poor showing of the gold standard in Meltzer's tests may be simply a figment of the data.

## The Proposal for an International Political Fiat Money

Finally, we have the punch line of the paper: a reiteration of the call Cooper (1984) made earlier for an international fiat money issued by an international central bank. Forthrightly facing the fact that any genuine fixity of exchange rates between independent national fiat monies is absurd and unworkable (the fixity of a currency's exchange rate cannot be sustained unless the national monetary authority gives up its independence), Cooper opts for fixity through an international fiat money. One must respect him for being radical (or "utopian") enough to take his ideals (fiat money and fixed exchange rates) to their limit and not to shirk from the sweeping institutional change that would be necessary to implement his vision, namely the formation of an International Central Bank among the leading Western industrial powers.

I am broadly sympathetic to the goal of a unified world monetary system, because I think such a system would be the natural child of unhampered international commerce and cross-border banking. If not for the barriers thrown up by the scourge of monetary nationalism, we would have a unified international monetary system. But it is not a goal that justifies any and all means.

An international central bank issuing fiat money, with power delegated to it by national governments, strikes me as a means so inappropriate as to outweigh any progress it might represent toward a unified global monetary system. Such a bank would render the supply of money no less a creature of politics, and possibly even more so. I would expect an international central bank's monetary policy-formation process to be even more muddled than the Federal Reserve's, if that is possible. Certainly the practical experience of the European Economic Community (the Common Market) does not give one any great hope for a "Eurocratic" monetary policy. An international central bank is unlikely to be aloof from games of power politics among national governments, which are anxious in various degrees to inflate away fiscal and re-election problems. It is even less likely to be aimed resolutely toward any academic policy target. Thus it would hardly enhance the predictability of the monetary system.

Fortunately, there are alternative means to global monetary unification. One, proposed by F. A. Hayek (1976), would be to free businesses and individuals everywhere to choose whichever existing national fiat currencies they find most attractive. If they use and hold German marks or Swiss francs, that verdict would give valuable feedback on what monetary policy they effectively prefer. Presumably, the currency of the best-behaved central bank would play a dominant role, at least in international transactions. It is difficult to understand how Cooper could consider that currency inferior (as an international medium of exchange and unit of account) to a currency controlled only 10 percent by the government of the best-behaved central bank and 90 percent by more inflationary governments.

For those who, understandably, feel uncomfortable with the prospect of a money managed by the bureaucracy of any foreign city, be it Brussels or Bonn, there is a modestly more sweeping reform available: Allow citizens everywhere to use a basic money that is not the liability of any central bank or governmental agency. A commodity standard makes such an international money of the market possible. Whether a single-commodity or a multi-commodity standard is better suited to the role is a secondary issue.

We can envision the results of such a reform by considering what would happen naturally between the United States and Canada if the same commodity monetary standard prevailed in both nations and if no barriers were erected to cross-border branch banking. Can anyone doubt that we would have a fully unified international monetary system? Exchanges between New York and Toronto would present no greater complexity than exchanges between New York and Chicago, especially with the same set of banks operating branch offices in all three cities. Transnational investments, just like interstate investments today, would be completely unfettered by exchange rate risk. The advantages of free trade in commodities and capital would be magnified appreciably, one would expect, by this monetary unification.

Perhaps the similarities and differences between Cooper's approach to global monetary unification and mine are best summarized the following way. Both of us would like the Federal Reserve, the Bank of Canada, and other central banks to give up their respective national monopoly powers over the supply of currency. He, however, would like the powers to be merged into a unitary international central bank cartel, a multinational monopoly issuer. I would like the powers to be surrendered so that no agency has a monopoly over money. Competitive provision of currency, responsive to the wants of moneyholders rather than to the exigencies of power politics, could then prevail both within each nation and across national boundaries.

## References

Barro, Robert J., and Gordon, David B. "A Positive Theory of Monetary Policy in a Natural Rate Model." *Journal of Political Economy* 91 (August 1983): 589–610.

Brainard, William C. "Uncertainty and the Effectiveness of Economic Policy." *American Economic Review* 57 (May 1967): 411–25.

Cooper, Richard N. "Is There a Need for Reform?" *In The International Monetary System: Forty Years after Bretton Woods*, pp. 21–39. Boston: Federal Reserve Bank of Boston, 1984.

Greenfield, Robert L., and Yeager, Leland B. "A Laissez-Faire Approach to Monetary Stability." *Journal of Money, Credit, and Banking* 15 (August 1983): 302–15.

Greenfield, Robert L., and Yeager, Leland B. "Competitive Payments Systems: Comment." *American Economic Review* 76 (September 1986): 848–49.

Hayek, F. A. *Choice in Currency*. London: Institute of Economic Affairs, 1976.

Kydland, Finn E., and Prescott, Edward C. "Rules Rather than Discretion: The Inconsistency of Optimal Plans." *Journal of Political Economy* 85 (June 1977): 473–91.

McCulloch, J. Huston. "Beyond the Historical Gold Standard." In *Alternative Monetary Regimes*, pp. 73–81. Edited by Colin D. Campbell and William R. Dougan. Baltimore: Johns Hopkins University Press, 1986.

Meltzer, Allan H. "Some Evidence on the Comparative Uncertainty Experienced under Different Monetary Regimes." In *Alternative Monetary Regimes*, pp. 122–53. Edited by Colin D. Campbell and William R. Dougan. Baltimore: Johns Hopkins University Press, 1986.

Romer, Christina D. "Is the Stabilization of the Postwar Economy a Figment of the Data?" *American Economic Review* 76 (June 1986): 314–34.

Selgin, George A. *The Theory of Free Banking: Money Supply under Competitive Note Issue*. Totowa, N.J.: Rowman and Littlefield, 1988.

Selgin, George A., and White, Lawrence H. "The Evolution of a Free Banking System." *Economic Inquiry* 25 (July 1987): 439–57.

Vaubel, Roland. "The Government's Money Monopoly: Externalities or Natural Monopoly?" *Kyklos* 37 (1984): 27–58.
White, Lawrence H. *Free Banking in Britain: Theory, Experience, and Debate, 1800–1845*. Cambridge: Cambridge University Press, 1984a.
White, Lawrence H. "Competitive Payments Systems and the Unit of Account." *American Economic Review* 74 (September 1984b): 699–712.
White, Lawrence H. "Competitive Payments Systems: Reply." *American Economic Review* 76 (September 1986): 850–53.
Willett, Thomas D., ed. *Political Business Cycles: The Political Economy of Money, Inflation, and Unemployment*. Durham: Duke University Press, 1988.
Yeager, Leland B. "Deregulation and Monetary Reform." *American Economic Review* 75 (May 1985): 103–07.

# COMMENT

# HOW ECONOMISTS WROUGHT A NONSYSTEM*

*Paul Craig Roberts*

I suppose that I am the leavening for the utopianism of Richard Cooper's single currency on the one hand and Lawrence White's private money on the other. Nothing is logically wrong with ideas that go to the heart of matters. If there are no exchange rates, we cannot be bedeviled with exchange rate volatility. If money is private, the market will winnow the good from the bad. In the real world we are a long way from formally adopting either a single currency or private money, but informally there is movement toward both. Along Cooper's lines, there is a sense in which the dollar is becoming the single currency. Many countries certainly prefer the dollar to their own national currencies. In some Latin American countries, major purchases such as housing cannot be made in the national currencies. For example, if you want to buy a house in Peru, you will probably need dollars. This example shows that even if the dollar looks bad to us, it looks very good to the majority of the world's population.

Private money will emerge when governments destroy the integrity of official monies. That, too, is happening. In many countries, the U.S. dollar performs the function of private money, and although not the legal tender, it is the preferred currency. More generally, the rise of parallel economies demonstrates that whenever governments make official economies too costly, people turn their backs and create unofficial activities that displace the official ones. In short, there is some reality in Cooper's and White's utopian schemes. The most successful mechanisms are probably those that develop on their own rather than those designed by politicians and economists. We can compare the market, for example, with the planning schemes of economists.

While we wait for an evolving world, what can we as economists contribute that might improve things on the margin? Our contribu-

---

*Reprinted from *Cato Journal* 8 (Fall 1988): 347–49.

The author holds the William E. Simon Chair in Political Economy at the Center for Strategic and International Studies.

tion is unlikely to be grand schemes of international cooperation. If the world could agree on monetary policy, we would not need Cooper's common currency. Moreover, I doubt many of us would favor concentrating power in a single central bank; it is hard to imagine a more surefire way of leveraging mistakes.

I have heard complaints that describe current international monetary arrangements as a "nonsystem." While I believe that this characterization exaggerates, I am willing to accept it if the reader can accept the role of economists in bringing about a nonsystem. Let's examine this interesting idea.

In 1981, the Federal Reserve took us off the dollar standard by driving up exchange rates and holding them up. When this policy changed, the Germans kept us off the dollar standard by adopting austerity policies as a defense against fears of importing U.S. inflation. Neither development could have occurred without the incorrect analysis and hysterical advice of economists.

The Fed collapsed inflation unexpectedly, sending the dollar through the roof, because lazy economists misinterpreted a supply-side policy as a huge demand-side fiscal stimulus coming on top of double-digit inflation. Moreover, Paul Volcker heard the chorus that "monetary policy is a junior partner that at best can conduct a weak, rear-guard action." Government policy was supposedly in the hands of crackpots, inflation was the order of the day, and the Fed would be blamed. With this expectation, the Fed went into a self-defensive posture, reasoning that an administration with monetarists in office could not blame inflation on the Fed if there was no growth in the money supply. This is the way the policy process really works. Governments do not have policies the way economists think; policy is what you discover in the next morning's newspaper.

The budget deficits were not intended. They were the consequence of unanticipated disinflation. The revenue loss from the tax cuts was fully anticipated; the administration's economic and budget forecasts were based on the treasury's static revenue analysis that tax cuts would lose revenues dollar-for-dollar. However, the loss of tax base from sudden disinflation was not anticipated.

Despite the facts, economists insisted on misinterpreting deficits, resulting from unanticipated disinflation, as "expansionary fiscal policy" and "excessive fiscal stimulus." Economists repeated these absurd mischaracterizations of policy while inflation collapsed in front of their eyes.

The result of this, perhaps willful, mischaracterization of the administration's fiscal policy was to convince the Germans that Reagan's policy was an escalation of the Keynesian policy of the 1970s, thereby threatening them with a new round of imported inflation. The American economic establishment worked overtime to grind this dangerous misinterpretation deep into German consciousness. German policymakers soon reached a point where they would not even listen to administration explanations, and they became impervious to factual analysis.

Like it or not, this description is an honest account of economists' responsibility for the current "nonsystem." If exchange rate stability is a goal, the G-7 will have to agree on a rate of economic expansion. Either the United States ceases to generate jobs or Europe starts to generate jobs. We are more likely to convince Europe to generate some jobs if our economists cease prattling about "major misalignments of fiscal policy."

# 7

# AN INTERNATIONAL GOLD STANDARD WITHOUT GOLD*

*Ronald I. McKinnon*

What can history tell us about the desirability, and feasibility, of maintaining fixed exchange rates between national currencies when capital is highly mobile? The workings of the international gold standard from the late 1870s to August 1914 provide the best example we have. Unlike the Bretton Woods system of pegged exchange rates in the 1950s and 1960s, or the residual controls of today's European Monetary System, no exchange controls impeded gross flows of financial capital. Moreover, net transfers of capital between countries were huge: Large net trade surpluses (deficits) opened and closed continually with no adjustments in nominal exchange rates and, by modern standards, with little change in real exchange rates. World trade grew rapidly.

Nevertheless, fixed exchange rates in general, and the gold standard in particular, remain as unpopular among American economists today as they were with the Populists who almost succeeded in electing William Jennings Bryan president in 1896. From 1873 onward America's acquiescence to the discipline of the gold standard and to British dominance of the international capital market was always somewhat grudging (Hale 1988). Even the formation of the Federal Reserve System in 1913 was an attempt to make American control over domestic money and credit somewhat more independent of international influences.

But this discrediting of fixed exchange rates, and subsequent refusal to bend American monetary policy toward maintaining a common international monetary standard, reflects, in part, a misassessment of the late 19th-century experience. How well the process of balancing payments between countries actually worked when exchange rates were fixed and capital markets were integrated has not been suffi-

---

*Reprinted from *Cato Journal* 8 (Fall 1988): 351–73.

The author is the William D. Eberle Professor of International Economics at Stanford University.

ciently distinguished from systemwide instability associated with gold itself.

In this paper I will contrast the classical Hume-Ricardo-Mill model of international payments adjustment under the gold standard—still the dominant textbook approach—with the modern (revisionist) view based on more integrated goods and financial markets. The case for or against flexible exchange rates largely depends on which of these perspectives one accepts.

First, however, I want to assess how well the 19th-century gold standard anchored the world price level. The problem of worldwide inflation and deflation is somewhat distinct from whether fixed exchange rates, based on mutual monetary adjustment, are desirable.

## The World Price Level

For the period before 1914, data on wholesale prices are much easier to obtain than is direct information on output and employment. Roy Jastram (1977) pieced together a long time series, based on both British and American price data, to show that the real purchasing power of gold over a general basket of primary commodities and simple manufactures was virtually the same at the beginning of World War I as it had been at the end of the Napoleonic wars a century earlier. Indeed, British data going back to the 18th century show a remarkable absence of any trend in gold's purchasing power.

A second characteristic of the gold standard—at least from the late 1870s to 1913 when exchange rates were securely fixed—was the strength of international arbitrage in markets for tradable goods other than precious metals. Table 1 shows that the wholesale price levels of the United States, Great Britain, Germany, and France fell *in parallel* by the order of 40 to 50 percent from 1873 to 1896, and then rose by a similar amount from 1896 to 1913. At a more microeconomic level, McCloskey and Zecher (1976) provide additional evidence that the absolute prices of individual commodities were generally aligned internationally about as well as they were among different regions within the same country.

Thus, in the late 19th century, the world economy was successfully unified to the extent that prices of a broad basket of tradable goods were aligned across countries. When nominal exchange rates were securely fixed by mutual monetary adjustment, international commodity arbitrage was sufficiently robust to create purchasing power parity (PPP): Any one national currency had about the same real purchasing power in domestic markets for tradable commodities as it did abroad. (This was most unlike our recent experience with

*TABLE 1*

WHOLESALE PRICE INDEXES FOR THE UNITED STATES, UNITED KINGDOM, GERMANY, AND FRANCE. SELECTED YEARS, 1816–1913

| Year and Period | United States | United Kingdom | Germany | France |
|---|---|---|---|---|
| Indexes (1913 = 100) | | | | |
| 1816 | 150 | 147 | 94 | 143 |
| 1849 | 82 | 86 | 67 | 94 |
| 1873 | 137 | 130 | 114 | 122 |
| 1896 | 64 | 72 | 69 | 69 |
| 1913 | 100 | 100 | 100 | 100 |
| Changes (%) | | | | |
| 1816–1849 | −45 | −41 | −29 | −33 |
| 1849–1873 | 67 | 51 | 70 | 30 |
| 1873–1896 | −53 | −45 | −40 | −45 |
| 1896–1913 | 56 | 39 | 45 | 45 |

SOURCE: Cooper (1982, p. 8).

floating exchange rates.) Since one may then talk sensibly about a common world price level, can the mechanisms of the gold standard per se be credited with systematically stabilizing it over the long run—as Jastram's statistics might suggest?

Barry Eichengreen (1985, p. 7) clearly summarizes the classical view of how the common price level was anchored:

> [Mill's] assumption was that the flow supply of newly mined gold would be responsive to relative prices. As the world economy expanded and the demand for money grew, downward pressure would be placed on the world price level. As the prices of other commodities fell in terms of the numeraire commodity gold, new supplies would be elicited by its rising value. . . . Similarly, to the extent that deflation causes the price of jewelry to fall in terms of gold coin, jewelry will be presented at the Mint for conversion into coin, increasing the quantity of coin in circulation and moderating the downward pressure on prices.

Robert Barro (1979) provides an algebraic exposition of these two forces and notes that "the determination of the absolute price level amounts to the determination of the relative price of the reserve commodity." Was then the price of gold relative to other commodities naturally constant so as to prevent secular change in the common price level?

From Table 2, Robert Triffin's (1964) analysis suggests the contrary. In the 19th century, only massive increases in the circulation of credit money (notes and deposits) prevented unending price-level deflation. Triffin shows that by 1885 token currency and demand deposits already constituted about 65 percent of the money supplies of Britain, France, and the United States, and that this proportion increased to 87 percent by 1913. Thus during this period, the mixed system had become largely a gold bullion standard with relatively slender reserves for meeting international payments concentrated in national treasuries and central banks.

These financial innovations were only loosely regulated at the national level. No authority with a worldwide view—not even the Bank of England—was monitoring or controlling the aggregate stock of credit money with an eye to stabilizing the world's price level. The fact that the world's price level was approximately the same in early 1914 as in 1814, therefore, seems to be largely accidental.

This absence of a dependable gold anchor for the common price level becomes evident once one looks at price movements over shorter time periods. In his thorough study of economic fluctuations under the pre-1914 gold standard, Richard Cooper (1982, p. 6) notes that

> Price stability was not attained, either in the short run or in the long run, either during the gold standard proper or over a longer period during which gold held dominant influence. In fact, in the United States short-run variations in wholesale prices were higher during the prewar gold standard than from 1949 to 1979. The standard deviation of annual movements in (wholesale) prices was 5.4 percent in the earlier period and only 4.8 percent in the latter period.

For longer-term cyclical fluctuations of a decade or two, Cooper offers the wholesale price index data in Table 1 for the United States, Great Britain, Germany, and France. The great deflations of the early 19th century were relieved only by the discovery of gold in California and Australia in 1849, and deflation was interspersed with depressions from 1873 to 1896 as more nations joined the gold standard, thereby causing a general shortage of gold reserves, which was not relieved until the South African and Yukon discoveries of the late 1890s. The inflations from 1849 to 1873 and from 1896 to 1913 were substantial, although not high by modern standards.

Periodic convertibility crises were a natural consequence of the buildup of credit money relative to the narrowing gold base. An "internal drain" within a country—not infrequently within some regions of the United States—could be triggered by a bank panic in which people rushed to cash in bank notes or deposits for gold. An "external drain" could arise out of (incipient) gold losses to foreigners through the balance of payments. Indeed, the development of central banking was largely a response to numerous convertibility crises. Whence Walter Bagehot's (1873) famous dictum that when a gold run developed, the national central bank should raise its discount rate to attract foreign funds, but then lend freely to domestic financial institutions to mitigate their reserve losses.

In summary, convertibility crises did not arise mainly because the gold standard was "international"—that is, because nations maintained fixed nominal exchange rates with each other and had to subordinate domestic money growth to the balance of payments. Individual countries could even, on occasion, meet an internal drain somewhat better if they could borrow in the London capital market. In the 19th century the world gold standard was less than fully stable because of the uneasy coexistence of gold and credit money. Moreover, the collective supply of the latter was not under the control of any supernational monetary authority that assumed responsibility for stabilizing the common price level.

## Two Views of International Adjustment

In the integrated world economy with fixed exchange rates of the late 19th century, the world price level and economic conditions were determined by cyclical fluctuations in the overall supply of and demand for gold and by uneven secular growth in gold-based credit monies. But how did payments between individual countries remain in balance?

The classical theory comes down from the full-bodied gold standard and price-specie flow mechanism of David Hume (1752). Sometimes called the Ricardo-Mill adjustment mechanism, it remains the standard textbook approach to interpreting how the gold standard worked. This theory presumes that gold movements themselves were instrumental in balancing international payments through their effects on net trade flows. If a country developed a payments deficit, a loss of gold to the outside world would force an internal deflation that induced a rise in exports and fall in imports, and vice versa for surplus countries.

The classical approach was extended to include the mixed system of the later 19th century, characterized by a narrow gold base and a larger superstructure of credit money. Under the "rules of the game," central banks or treasuries were not to sterilize: A gold inflow would be allowed to expand the domestic money supply by some multiple of the inflow itself, and vice versa. In Great Britain these rules were formalized under the Bank Act of 1844 where note issue by the Bank

*TABLE 2*

COMPARATIVE EVOLUTION OF MONEY AND RESERVE STRUCTURE, 1885 AND 1913

| Money and Reserves | Three Countries[a] 1885 | Three Countries[a] 1913 | Eleven Countries[b] 1885 | Eleven Countries[b] 1913 | World 1885 | World 1913 |
|---|---|---|---|---|---|---|
| In Billions of U.S. Dollars | | | | | | |
| 1. Money Supply | **6.3** | **19.8** | **8.4** | **26.3** | **14.2** | **33.1** |
| a. Gold | 1.4 | 2.0 | 1.8 | 2.7 | 2.4 | 3.2 |
| b. Silver | 0.7 | 0.6 | 1.0 | 1.2 | 3.0 | 2.3 |
| c. Credit Money | 4.1 | 17.2 | 5.6 | 22.4 | 8.8 | 27.6 |
| i. Currency[c] | *1.6* | *3.8* | *2.3* | *5.9* | *3.8* | *8.1* |
| ii. Demand Deposits | *2.6* | *13.3* | *3.3* | *16.5* | *5.0* | *19.6* |
| 2. Monetary Reserves | **1.0** | **2.7** | **1.5** | **4.0** | **2.0** | **5.3** |
| a. Gold | 0.6 | 2.1 | 0.9 | 3.2 | 1.3 | 4.1 |
| b. Silver | 0.4 | 0.6 | 0.6 | 0.8 | 0.7 | 1.2 |
| 3. Total Gold and Silver | **3.1** | **5.4** | **4.3** | **7.9** | **7.4** | **10.8** |
| a. Gold | 2.0 | 4.1 | 2.7 | 5.9 | 3.7 | 7.3 |
| b. Silver | 1.1 | 1.2 | 1.6 | 2.0 | 3.7 | 3.5 |

| | | | | | | |
|---|---|---|---|---|---|---|
| In % of Money Supply | | | | | | |
| 1. Money Supply | **100** | **100** | **100** | **100** | **100** | **100** |
| a. Gold | 23 | 10 | 21 | 10 | 17 | 10 |
| b. Silver | 11 | 3 | 12 | 5 | 21 | 7 |
| c. Credit Money | 66 | 87 | 67 | 85 | 62 | 83 |
| i. Currency[c] | *25* | *19* | *27* | *22* | *27* | *25* |
| ii. Demand Deposits | *41* | *67* | *39* | *63* | *35* | *59* |
| 2. Monetary Reserves | **16** | **14** | **18** | **15** | **14** | **16** |
| a. Gold | 9 | 11 | 11 | 12 | 9 | 12 |
| b. Silver | 7 | 3 | 7 | 3 | 5 | 4 |
| 3. Total Gold and Silver | **49** | **27** | **51** | **30** | **52** | **33** |
| a. Gold | 32 | 21 | 32 | 22 | 26 | 22 |
| b. Silver | 17 | 6 | 19 | 8 | 26 | 11 |

[a]United States, United Kingdom, and France.

[b]United States, United Kingdom, France, Germany, Italy, Netherlands, Belgium, Sweden, Switzerland, Canada, and Japan.

[c]Including subsidiary (nonsilver) coinage, except in last column.

SOURCE: Triffin (1964, p. 56).

of England was restricted one-for-one to any marginal changes in its gold reserves. Thus, internal inflation or deflation was ensured so as to maintain external equilibrium through changes in the net trade balance.

Consider a more precise example of a disturbance in the flow of international payments, say, a new ongoing transfer of long-term capital from country A to country B. According to classical theory, adjustment would occur because gold flows in the same direction as the capital transfer and the resulting fall in A's money supply would induce general price-level deflation—across both tradable goods and nontradable services—in country A and correspondingly general inflation in country B.

From the mid-18th century into the early 19th century, transport costs were perhaps such that only gold could be easily arbitraged to have a common price in both foreign and domestic markets (Marcuzzo and Rosselli 1987). Following gold movements, the prices of commodities other than precious metals could then fall in country A as they rose in country B, as might be predicted by the quantity theory of money applied on a purely national basis. (By the late 19th century, however, international markets in potentially tradable commodities were too unified for such divergent price movements to occur.)

In particular, the price of tradable goods produced in country A, measured at the prevailing fixed exchange rate, would decline relative to those produced in country B. This decline in A's terms of trade—the cheapening of A's export products relative to B's—is then seen (in the classical perspective) to be a principal mechanism by which A's exports increase and imports decrease so as to create a trade surplus. This surplus is the "real" counterpart of the capital transfer. Later authors in the classical tradition—from Viner (1924), Taussig (1927), and Keynes (1923, 1930) down to Friedman and Schwartz (1963)—place additional emphasis on absorption (and possibly income) decreases in country A and increases in country B. But induced changes in the relative prices of A's tradables vis-à-vis B's remained important for balancing international payments.

From this classical description of the adjustment mechanism, therefore, comes the popular image of the gold standard: In different countries domestic inflation rates continually moved in *opposite* directions. The stability of national price levels (and possibly employment and output) was hostage to (arbitrary) shifts in the international distribution of gold reserves arising out of disturbances in foreign trade or in capital flows. More generally, the classical view suggests that fixed exchange rates sacrifice domestic macroeconomic stability to the need for balancing international payments.

The revisionist view of how international payments remained balanced begins with the observation that the classical adjustment mechanism is inconsistent with price-level data of the sort displayed in Table 1. Instead of moving in opposite directions, national price levels moved up and down together over periods of several years (Triffin 1964; Cooper 1982), as did prices of individual tradable commodities (McCloskey and Zecher 1976; Dick and Floyd 1987). Indeed, therein lay the attractiveness of the fixed-rate 19th-century system: It provided a common international standard of value.

When exchange rates were fixed for a long period, generalized commodity arbitrage became sufficiently strong to prevent the prices (exclusive of tariffs) of any particular tradable good (for example, cotton shirts) from differing significantly more across countries than they did interregionally within a country.[1] Similarly, overall price levels of tradable goods, as measured by national wholesale price indices, remained aligned and did not change in a Humean fashion in response to gold flows.

With changes in relative national price levels thus restricted, what was the adjustment mechanism for the large net transfers of real capital from one country to another from 1870 to 1913? How did capital-receiving countries, such as those of North and South America, develop trade deficits while the capital-donating countries, largely in Western Europe, generated corresponding trade surpluses?

By the late 19th century, a large and sophisticated international capital market centered in London had developed for both short-term trade bills of exchange and longer-term bond and equity issues that could be, and were, purchased by foreigners as well as Britons (Arndt and Drake 1986). Through modest adjustments in relative interest rates, expenditure patterns across countries were coordinated so as to match trade surpluses and deficits with net capital flows (Whale 1937; Williamson 1964). In effect, the international integration of capital markets complemented the integration of markets in tradable goods so that little or no net gold flows—let alone changes in exchange rates—were necessary to effect these capital transfers. Adjustments in international payments were similar to adjustments within a country or a single currency area.

Consider the flotation of a large new issue of American railway bonds in the 19th-century London capital market. Under the classical adjustment mechanism, this transfer would be treated as an exogenous force inducing gold to flow into the United States, causing

[1]Only when exchange rates float freely and, thus, unpredictably is the law of one price systematically violated, as it has been in recent years (Isard 1977; Levich 1986).

inflation, and out of Great Britain, causing deflation. From the revisionist perspective of integrated financial and goods markets, however, the capital transfer would naturally reflect an upward propensity to spend for goods and services in the United States coupled with a similar reduction in Great Britain. That is, British financial saving, which would otherwise be transmuted to domestic investment, would simultaneously be diverted to support an increase in spending in the United States. So the changes in national levels of absorption (aggregate spending) would naturally create a British trade surplus with the United States that was a counterpart of the net capital transfer.

To the extent the British trade surplus fell short of (or exceeded) the total proceeds from the issue of railway bonds, an offsetting inflow (or outflow) of short-term capital to London would be the residual balancing item. Indeed, short-run interest rates could well adjust so that the funds were kept on deposit in London until disbursed "smoothly" through time to finance the American trade deficit. Only very small changes in international interest differentials would be necessary to maintain this payments balance as long as exchange rates remained credibly fixed.

In contrast to the classical view, gold flows would not be an instrumental or "forcing" variable in this adjustment process. Indeed, the initial flotation of railway bonds need not have any predictable impact on net gold flows, although they might respond ex post to differing rates of national income growth and increases in money demand (Abramovitz 1973; McCloskey and Zecher 1976).

What happens to relative prices in the revisionist adjustment process? Here it is important to distinguish between (1) the terms of trade: the relative price of a broad basket of British exports (largely manufactures) and American exports (largely primary products in the 19th century); and (2) the prices of tradable goods relative to nontradables within Great Britain and within the United States.

The classical adjustment mechanism does not distinguish between (1) and (2). That is, a forced gold flow, causing general price deflation in Great Britain and general price inflation in the United States, tends to lower British prices across the board relative to their American counterparts, with the possible exception of precious metals that can be easily arbitraged. Thus, the classical theory presumes that Great Britain's terms of trade would deteriorate, which imposes a secondary burden on the capital-donating country. Also, because some British goods have higher transport costs and are less tradable than other goods, their relative prices would fall further. The reverse pattern would hold in the United States.

In the revisionist view based on a more integrated world economy, however, there is no presumption that the terms of trade need change as a result of a capital transfer as long as exchange rates are fixed so that the law of one price holds for each tradable good. Although the relative prices of nontradables might be bid up in the United States and down in Great Britain, there is a presumption that all such changes would be moderate and possibly only temporary. To effect even large net transfers of capital, the "need" for broad changes in relative commodity prices would seem quite modest in final equilibrium when trade and capital movements are balanced.[2]

## The Law of One Price under Fixed and Floating Exchange Rates

One common justification for allowing exchange rates to float (Frenkel 1987) is to provide greater flexibility in allowing the prices of goods and services of country A to vary collectively vis-à-vis those in country B. In modern industrial economies, the invoice prices of manufactures, which are largely brand-specific, are quite rigid or "sticky" in the currency of the country where they originate (Grassman 1973; McKinnon 1979) and, temporarily, in the destination country. Thus a sudden (unexpected) depreciation of A's currency will

(i) violate the law of one price in a narrow sense: The same brand-name good will sell for days or weeks at a lower price in country A than the price in country B evaluated at the current exchange rate;

(ii) violate the law of one price in a broad sense: the prices of A's products similar (in the sense of models of monopolistic competition) to those in B will be sold at lower prices, possibly for many months or quarters; and

[2]This difference between the classical and the revisionist perspective parallels the famous 1929 debate between J. M. Keynes and Bertil Ohlin on whether the war reparations owed by Germany to the rest of Europe would necessarily turn the terms of trade against Germany and thus impose a secondary burden on the German economy beyond the transfer itself. By emphasizing the need for Germany's terms of trade to decline in order for a German trade surplus to develop, Keynes took the classical position on how the capital transfer would be effected.

Ohlin was the "revisionist." He argued as if the German economy were more fully integrated into the rest of Europe. The fall in absorption in Germany, coupled with a rise in the capital-receiving countries, would effect the transfer without substantially turning the terms of trade against Germany.

In retrospect, who was right seems to be more of an empirical question—how open was the postwar German economy—than a theoretical one. For the principal articles and rejoinders of Keynes and Ohlin, see *Economic Journal* 39 (1929): pp. 1–7, 172–82, and 400–408.

(iii) products unique to A will sell at lower prices compared with those unique to B, perhaps for several years if the depreciation were to persist.

In all three senses, the sudden depreciation of A's currency turns the terms of trade against country A. Moreover, under floating exchange rates with given national money supplies (present and future), the "normal" effect of an ex ante transfer of financial capital from A to B is to depreciate A's currency against B's (Johnson 1956). Thus, under floating, one expects a "forced" deterioration in A's terms of trade in response to a capital outflow—a deterioration similar to that posited by the classical theory of adjustment to a capital outflow under the gold standard. A modern example was the large 1980–84 depreciation of European currencies against the dollar in response to a flow of private capital into the United States. Thus, in a regime of floating exchange rates, there is a strong presumption that the terms of trade will turn against the transferor and in favor of the transferee.

But is such an abrupt change in relative prices, particularly in the terms of trade, warranted if economies could potentially be integrated under fixed exchange rates? Is the acute sensitivity of a floating exchange rate to shifts in international portfolio preferences a "correct" response for facilitating a trade surplus for A and a deficit for B? The late 19th-century experience with fixed exchange rates suggests otherwise: Capital flowed from Europe to Canada and the United States without inducing or requiring substantial increases in the North American terms of trade—certainly nothing like the U.S. dollar's 40 to 50 percent appreciation in the early 1980s.[3]

## Alternative Pure Trade Models of the Transfer Problem

For a moneyless world, pure trade theory offers several formal models based on barter and continuous full employment. To supplement historical experience, these models can throw additional light on how relative prices, including the terms of trade, should change in response to a capital transfer.

However, the implicit monetary mechanism that underlies, or is at least consistent with, the pure trade model must be made explicit.[4]

[3]For evidence on the Canadian experience, see Dick and Floyd (1987).

[4]As Samuelson (1971, pp. 327–28) noted, "Analytically, the discussion [of the transfer problem] remained confused, because models involving effective demand and financial considerations were rarely carefully separated from those involving pure barter." And in a series of articles beginning in the early 1950s, Samuelson himself could not make up his mind whether the orthodox presumption was correct: that a financial transfer would turn the terms of trade significantly against the transferor. To this day, a satisfactory general equilibrium model, incorporating real and financial considerations, remains to be constructed.

All of the pure trade models reviewed below assume that the law of one price for tradable goods always holds in both the narrow and broad senses discussed above. To this extent, therefore, these models implicitly assume a regime of fixed exchange rates (or a single currency area) linking foreign and domestic economies. This assumption, nevertheless, leaves open the possibility that terms of trade between dissimilar goods may vary. Although exchange rates are (implicitly) fixed, the prices of nontradable services, the provision of which requires close geographic proximity, may still vary.

In his article "Presumption and the Transfer Problem," Ronald Jones (1975) built a model with two trading economies. Each produced and consumed a nontradable commodity with prohibitively high international transport costs, an exportable (the other's importable), and an importable (the other's exportable) whose relative prices were free to vary. Because each produced nontradables as well as close substitutes for the other's exportables, Jones's model effectively assumed that the two were industrially diversified (as opposed to monoproduct) economies.

While fully mobile within each country, neither labor nor capital were internationally mobile in two important respects. First, there was no direct ongoing factor movement across national boundaries. To encapsulate the transfer problem, Jones did consider a one-time increase in the flow of capital out of the home country that was experiencing reduced domestic expenditures and corresponding increases abroad. But he assumed no ongoing financial linkage that would equalize interest rates between the two countries. Second, Jones did not assume that the two countries needed to be in the factor price equalization region: Trade alone does not equalize factor prices.

Instead, Jones simply posited that all three goods were gross substitutes in production and consumption within each country—with given, possibly heterogeneous, factor supplies. The two economies were integrated in trade flows but not in factor markets, thus leaving relative commodity prices free to vary.

Jones then demonstrated (1975, p. 265) that the transferor's or home country's terms of trade deteriorate if and only if

$$m_2^* + \theta^* m_3^* > m_2 + \theta m_3. \qquad (1)$$

The $m$ parameters are expenditure propensities (arising out of the capital transfer), asterisks represent the foreign country, commodity 2 is the home importable (foreign exportable), and commodity 3 is the nontraded good in each country. An alternative inequality condition could be restated in terms of commodities 1 (the home country's exportable) and 3. If (1) holds, the home country's terms of trade $P_1/P_2$ fall during the transfer—the orthodox presumption.

The parameters $\theta$ and $\theta^*$ are complex and reflect price substitution effects across the three commodities within each country. They would be identical if the two countries were symmetrically diversified in their production and consumption characteristics. Suppose they were so diversified.

Whether inequality (1) is satisfied, therefore, largely depends on whether each country's marginal propensity to spend on its own exportable exceeds the trading partner's propensity to spend on the same good (the partner's importable), that is, whether $m_2^* > m_2$. The fall in home country expenditures tends to reduce the relative price of the foreign exportable ($P_2$ tends to fall relative to $P_1$), but the rise in expenditures abroad tends to raise its relative price. And which effect is stronger remains an open empirical question for industrially diversified economies. There is no theoretical presumption that the terms of trade of the transferor need deteriorate, that is, for (1) to hold, unless one makes more specialized assumptions about patterns of production and consumption.

Paul Krugman (1987a, 1987b), for example, makes such specialized assumptions in order to support the orthodox (classical) presumption that the terms of trade of the transferor will deteriorate. In the modern context, he asks: "Suppose the United States were to increase tax revenues (reduce the fiscal deficit) by 100 billion dollars and stop borrowing that much in the international capital market. For the U.S. trade balance to improve by a similar amount, would the terms of trade have to turn against the United States?"

Krugman then assumes that the United States produces only one good, some of which it exports and most of which it consumes at home. The United States does not produce import substitutes while it consumes imports, nor is there a distinct category of nontradables. In contrast to the Jones model, the industrial structure in Krugman's model is not diversified. The rest of the world (ROW) is similarly a monoproduct economy. ROW consumes most of the single good it produces, while exporting the rest, and consumes some of the American good. (In common with the Jones model, however, Krugman's does not assume that factor markets are integrated with a tendency toward factor price equalization.)

With this analytical machinery based on nondiversified (monoproduct) economies in place, the orthodox presumption seems very strong: As the American trade balance adjusts to the reduced capital inflow, the terms of trade are likely to turn against the United States.

Specifically, Krugman shows that the orthodox presumption will hold if and only if

$$m + m^* < 1 \tag{2}$$

where the $m$ parameters are now distinguished from inequality (1) above. Here, $m$ is the more narrowly defined marginal propensity to import of the United States. (The $m$ parameter is identical to the marginal propensity to spend on importables, $m2$ above, only in monoproduct economies.) Parameter $m^*$ is ROW's similarly defined marginal propensity to import. Krugman provides empirical evidence to suggest that $m$ and $m^*$ are each much less than 0.5. Indeed, if one looks only at the share of imports in either American or ROW GNP, they are 0.2 or less, although Krugman recognizes that marginal propensities are likely to be a bit higher.

So (2) appears to be satisfied in practice, leading Krugman to take the orthodox view that the American terms of trade must deteriorate if the trade deficit is to be reduced by the full hypothetical increase in tax revenues. Further, because domestic prices of manufactured tradables are "sticky" in the United States and in ROW, he suggests some large nominal devaluation of the dollar would be justified to bring about the needed reduction in the American terms of trade. (This leaves open the important question of whether the requisite American fiscal adjustment is imminent, and whether dollar devaluation should precede, coincide with, or follow the $100 billion tax increase.)

But remember that inequality (2) is a sufficient condition for the orthodox presumption only if one accepts Krugman's simplifying assumption that both the United States and ROW are monoproduct economies. If, instead, both economies are diversified in the sense of Jones (1975) or Dornbusch (1975), then (2) may hold even if the orthodox presumption is invalid. Even though observed import shares in GNP are quite small, the transfer can be effected without having the terms of trade turn against the United States. Jones's model, based as it is on diversified free-trade economies, better represents the industrial world today as well as that of the late 19th century, although not necessarily in the intervening decades.

Left unanalyzed is the more naive, but commonly held, view that dollar devaluation alone—without a complementary change in the fiscal deficit—will reduce the dollar value of the American trade deficit. More generally, the old elasticities approach (Bickerdike 1920; Robinson 1939; Metzler 1949) suggested that exchange rate changes themselves have a systematic effect on net trade balances. That this latter presumption is false for open, diversified economies is demonstrated analytically in Dornbusch (1975) and McKinnon and Ohno (1986) and is borne out by the failure of the American trade deficit to respond to dollar devaluation from 1984 to 1988.

## An Exchange Rate Dilemma When Factor Markets Are Not Integrated

Barter models of exchange suggest that the terms of trade need not move substantially to bring about a capital transfer between economies with diversified foreign trade in goods and services. Whether the change in the terms of trade is negative or positive, the point at which final equilibrium is achieved remains unknown a priori. Unlike what Krugman's model suggests, using the nominal exchange rate as an instrument to influence the terms of trade during the transfer process seems neither necessary nor desirable.

When foreign and domestic factor markets are not integrated, however, the price of the domestic nontradable must still decrease (relative to tradables) in the transferor's economy and increase within the transferee's. In his pure trade model, Jones (1975) derives this unambiguous result algebraically, but it is clear intuitively under a fixed exchange rate regime. The capital transfer is associated with reduced spending in the home country, pressure from which then reduces the prices (using foreign exchange as the numeraire) of those goods and services not arbitraged in international markets. The home trade balance then improves as resources are released from the nontradables sector to produce more exportables and importables—with the reverse adjustment occurring abroad.

Now return to monetary economies where nominal prices may be quoted in different currencies. In addition, suppose that the domestic currency prices of both nontradables and domestically produced tradables are "sticky" at home and abroad. When the capital transfer occurs, would movement in the nominal exchange rate help speed the necessary adjustments in equilibrium relative prices by overcoming this price stickiness? Specifically, would the orthodox policy of having the home country devalue its currency reduce the relative prices of nontradables without causing "false" changes in other relative prices, and without impeding the process by which expenditures are naturally reduced at home and increased abroad? The short answer is "no." If substantial devaluation occurs, incidental price and absorption effects both go in wrong directions.

First, *the primary effect of devaluation is to reduce the transferor's terms of trade with the transferee—and not raise the relative price of tradables to nontradables within the home country while reduc-*

*ing it abroad.* The domestic currency prices of direct imports are typically sensitive to the exchange rate, even though prices of the great mass of domestically produced exportables and import substitutes are not. With full pass-through, a devaluation may quickly raise import prices vis-à-vis those of domestically produced tradables.[5] The law of one price is violated and the terms of trade turn against the transferor in the three senses discussed above. But there is no presumption that the terms of trade should or need to change in final equilibrium; thus, these price "misalignments" likely will need to be corrected at a later stage in the transfer process. In the short run, the devaluation introduces confusing noise into the price system.

At the same time, the devaluation succeeds in raising the prices of tradables relative to nontradables only in a limited, fragmented way. The prices of direct imports increase, but not the overall prices of domestically produced tradables. More important, the extreme changes observed in the mark/dollar and yen/dollar exchange rates in recent years—sometimes nearly 40 or 50 percent—seem to be much too high (see below) for any conceivable warranted adjustments in the average price of tradables relative to nontradables.

Second, *a devaluation may induce absorption to adjust the wrong way in both the transferor's and transferee's economies, and thus impede the capital transfer.* Because domestic invoice prices are sticky, they do not jump with the exchange rate. But they do adjust with a lag, albeit quite long. After devaluation by the transferor, expectations of ongoing domestic inflation will increase, raising the private propensity to spend for goods and services in that country. Similarly, expectations of deflation in the transferee will reduce peoples' propensity to spend there (McKinnon and Ohno 1986; Kim 1987). These perverse absorption effects then delay the emergence of the transferor's trade surplus, which is the real counterpart of the transfer of financial capital.

## Alternative Exchange Rate Systems and the International Integration of Factor Markets

However, if factor markets between economies with similar levels of technical proficiency are effectively integrated, even the relative

[5]Unlike other industrial economies such as Germany, immediate pass-through into the domestic prices of direct imports is not typical of the United States (Knetter 1988). Despite changes in the dollar exchange rate, exporters to the United States prefer to keep their dollar price quotes to American customers rather more rigid—perhaps because of the American economy's large size, and the dollar's central position in the world monetary system.

prices of tradables and nontradables need not adjust significantly when a transfer occurs. The ongoing international arbitrage in markets for tradable goods and in financial capital keeps both economies in the "factor-price equalization region." Because the nontradable goods industry in each country is then a price taker in factor markets facing the same real wage and real rental rate on capital, the relative price of nontradables need not change as their output varies during the transfer process (Samuelson 1971).

Whether international monetary arrangements support the ongoing arbitrage in goods and financial markets necessary to keep economies in, or close to, the equalization region is an open question. One condition is that the law of one price holds in international markets for tradable goods. A second is that financial arbitrage must be effective in equalizing *real* interest rates—nominal rates minus anticipated price inflation—across countries.

Unfortunately, both conditions have been continually violated under the system of fluctuating exchange rates we have observed over the past 15 years. Internal price and wage stickiness in the major industrial economies implies that unexpected changes in exchange rates continually disrupt commodity market arbitrage: The law of one price is violated in both the narrow and broad senses. This failure of tradable goods markets to remain integrated, that is, the failure of purchasing power parity between national monies, reduces indirect pressure to equalize factor prices across countries.

More subtly, *direct financial arbitrage—even today's massive (gross) capital flows among Europe, Japan, and the United States—fails to equate real interest rates across countries as long as exchange rates float and (relative) purchasing power parity is violated.* Because goods markets are imperfectly integrated, national rates of price inflation can differ from expected changes in exchange rates, which may dominate differences in nominal interest rates (Frenkel 1986). For example, from 1981 to mid-1985, the dollar was obviously overvalued against the yen and mark by the PPP criterion, and survey data showed that financiers expected the dollar to depreciate (Frenkel and Froot 1987). Thus, U.S. nominal interest rates remained much higher than in Japan or Germany, even though national rates of price inflation were not much different. Real interest rates were not equalized.

As a result, the modern system of fluctuating relative currency values severely impairs the allocative efficiency of the international capital market. Countries go through alternating cycles of underinvestment or overinvestment in tradable goods industries, depending on whether their currencies are overvalued or undervalued by the PPP criterion. The increased exchange risk inhibits industrial investment everywhere.

Here, the 19th-century system, based on fixed exchange rates and mutual monetary adjustment to provide a common standard of value, seems much preferred. Arbitrage in internationally tradable goods then became sufficient to approximate the law of one price. In financial markets the commitment to fixed nominal exchange rates had two related effects. First, nominal interest rates were closer together and, on average, lower. Second, price inflation was more uniform across countries. International financial arbitrage could succeed in keeping real interest rates closer together.

But is the present degree of economic integration among the principal industrial economies sufficient to warrant establishing a common monetary standard with fixed exchange rates? Table 3 indicates that the intensity of merchandise trade in the 1980s is again comparable to what had been achieved by 1913. With the elimination of exchange controls in Europe and Japan, arbitrage pressures in international financial markets seem at least as great as they were before World War I. If exchange rates were to become credibly fixed once more, commodity and financial arbitrage should again serve to keep industrial nations within, or close to, the region of factor price equalization.

Moreover, Table 4 indicates that the average net transfer of capital out of Britain between 1905 and 1914 was more than half of net national saving—proportionately much higher than the large trade surpluses generated by Japan and Germany (or trade deficit of the United States) in the mid-1980s. In this sense, the "need" for broad

*TABLE 3*

PROPORTIONS OF MERCHANDISE TRADE TO NATIONAL PRODUCT FOR MAJOR DEVELOPED ECONOMIES

| Ranked by Economic Size in 1984 | Pre–World War I | 1950s | 1984 |
|---|---|---|---|
| United States | 11.0 | 7.9 | 15.2 |
| Japan | 29.5 | 18.8 | 24.2 |
| Germany | 38.3 | 35.1 | 52.8 |
| France | 35.2 | n/a | 40.2 |
| United Kingdom | 43.5 | 30.4 | 47.0 |
| Italy | 28.1 | 25.0 | 44.6 |
| Canada | 32.2 | 31.2 | 47.3 |

SOURCE: Wolf (1987).

*TABLE 4*

NET CAPITAL OUTFLOWS

| | Gross National Savings | Gross Domestic Fixed Investment | Current Account |
|---|---|---|---|
| United States 1985 | 16.5 | 18.6 | −2.9 |
| Japan 1985 | 31.4 | 27.5 | 3.7 |
| West Germany 1985 | 22.2 | 19.5 | 2.2 |
| United Kingdom 1905–14 | 16.0 | 7.0 | 8.0 |

SOURCE: Wolf (1987).

changes in relative prices to help effect capital transfers would seem to be less now than in the earlier era. And, among modern industrial economies, this paper suggests that exchange rate changes can be ambiguous, even perverse, in bringing about whatever adjustments in relative prices that might be needed to keep net trade balances in line with warranted net capital flows.

## Lessons from the 19th Century

The strengths and weaknesses of the 19th-century gold standard must be carefully assessed to draw any useful lessons for present-day monetary arrangements.

Consider the positive side first. By binding nations together—albeit sometimes grudgingly—with what was a common price level, the system completely avoided the sudden and dramatic changes in relative international competitiveness characteristic of floating rates in the 1970s and 1980s. This common monetary standard permitted a much more efficient international allocation of capital: Financial arbitrage could better succeed in equalizing real interest rates while keeping European and North American economies within (or close to) the region of factor price equalizaton.

Moreover, the reality of international adjustment was quite different from its usual treatment in modern textbooks. Large net transfers of capital from country A to country B did not require a major deflation for A to run a trade surplus, nor a major inflation for B to run a trade deficit. At unchanged nominal exchange rates, capital transfers took place quite smoothly with apparently little need for one country's price level to change in any substantial way vis-à-vis another's. In short, that the gold standard was truly international was its greatest virtue.

But worldwide deflation or inflation was a problem for the 19th-century system because the underlying base of gold and credit monies was not properly anchored. Much American Populist hostility at the time—with present-day echoes—was concerned with strong deflationary pressure and recurrent depressions from the 1870s to the mid-1890s. Because these pressures were not peculiar to the United States, fixed exchange rates per se, requiring American monetary policy to adjust to an international standard, have been "unfairly" identified as creating excessive domestic cycles of inflation or deflation. Rather, the problem lay with basing the international standard on gold.

Now North America, Western Europe, and Japan are as mutually dependent on trade and finance as were the former two a century ago. If exchange rates were again credibly fixed through mutual monetary adjustment, the "natural" nominal anchor for the system as a whole would be the common price level over internationally tradable goods, which can be approximated by wholesale or producer price indices. And, through joint management of the underlying base of national credit monies, the triumvirate could keep the new international monetary standard more stable than its 19th-century counterpart.[6]

## References

Abramovitz, Moses. "The Monetary Side of Long Swings in U.S. Economic Growth." Memorandum 146. Center for Research on Economic Growth, Stanford University, 1973.

Arndt, Helmut, and Drake, Peter. "Bank Loans or Bonds: Some Lessons of Historical Experience." Banca Naziorale del Lavoro *Quarterly Review* (December 1985): 373–92.

Bagehot, Walter. *Lombard Street*. Reprint of 1915 edition. New York: Arno Press, 1969.

Barro, Robert. "Money and Price Level under the Gold Standard." *Economic Journal* 89 (March 1979): 13–27.

Bickerdike, C. F. "The Instability of Foreign Exchange." *Economic Journal* 30 (March 1920): 118–22.

Cooper, Richard N. "The Gold Standard: Historical Facts and Future Prospects." *Brookings Papers on Economic Activity* (1982): 1–45. Reprinted in Richard N. Cooper, *The International Monetary System*. Cambridge: MIT Press, 1987.

[6]See McKinnon (1984, 1988) for an overall description of how mutual monetary adjustment could be organized; and McKinnon and Ohno (1988) on the specific question of how "starting" exchange rates could be set so as to bring national price and wage levels into approximate alignment.

Dick, Trevor, and Floyd, John. "Canada and the Gold Standard: 1871–1913." Manuscript. July 1987.
Dornbusch, Rudiger. "Exchange Rates and Fiscal Policy in a Popular Model of International Trade." *American Economic Review* 65 (December 1975): 859–71.
Eichengreen, Barry. "Editor's Introduction." In *The Gold Standard in Theory and History*, pp. 1–36. Edited by B. Eichengreen. New York: Methuen Press, 1987.
Frenkel, Jacob A. "International Capital Mobility and Crowding Out in the U.S. Economy." In *The Increasing Openness of the U.S. Economy*, pp. 33–69. Edited by R. Hafer. Federal Reserve Bank of St. Louis, 1986.
Frenkel Jacob, A. "The International Monetary System: Should It Be Reformed?" *American Economic Review* 77 (May 1987): 205–10.
Frenkel, Jacob A., and Froot, Kenneth. "Using Survey Data to Test Standard Propositions Regarding Exchange Rate Expectations." *American Economic Review* 77 (March 1987): 93–106.
Friedman, Milton, and Schwartz, Anna. *A Monetary History of the United States, 1867–1960*. Princeton: Princeton University Press, 1963.
Grassman, Sven. "A Fundamental Symmetry in International Payments Patterns." *Journal of International Economics* 6 (May 1976): 105–6.
Hale, David. "Will We Hate Japan as We Hated Britain?" *The International Economy* 2 (January/February 1988): 84–91.
Hume, David. *Of the Balance of Trade*. 1752. Reprinted in *Writings on Economics*. Edited by E. Rotwein. Madison: Wisconsin University Press, 1955.
Isard, Peter. "How Far Can We Push the Law of One Price?" *American Economic Review* 67 (1977): 942–48.
Jastram, Roy. *The Golden Constant: The English and American Experience, 1560–1976*. New York: John Wiley and Sons, 1977.
Johnson, Harry. "The Transfer Problem and Exchange Stability." *Journal of Political Economy* 64 (June 1956): 212–25.
Jones, Ronald. "Presumption and the Transfer Problem." *Journal of International Economics* 5 (1975): 263–74.
Keynes, John M. *A Tract on Monetary Reform*. London: Macmillan, 1923.
Keynes, John M. "The German Transfer Problem." *Economic Journal* 39 (March 1929): 1–7.
Keynes, John M. *A Treatise on Money*. London: Macmillan, 1930.
Kim, Yoonbai. "International Transfers of Capital and the Role of the Terms of Trade." Economics Department, Stanford University, February 1987.
Knetter, Michael. *Export Price Dynamics: Theory and Evidence*. Ph.D. diss., Stanford University, 1988.
Krugman, Paul. "Adjustment in the World Economy." *Occasional Paper 24*, Group of 30, 1987.
Krugman, Paul. "Exchange Rates and International Adjustment." Manuscript. September 1987.
Levich, Richard. "Gauging the Evidence on Recent Movements in the Value of the Dollar." In *The U.S. Dollar: Recent Developments, Outlook, and Policy Options*, pp. 1–28. Federal Reserve Bank of Kansas City, 1986.

McCloskey, Donald, and Zecher, Richard. "How the Gold Standard Worked: 1880–1913." In *The Monetary Approach to the Balance of Payment.* Edited by Jacob A. Frenkel and Harry G. Johnson. London: Allen and Unwin, 1976.
McKinnon, Ronald I. *Money in International Exchange: The Convertible Currency System.* New York: Oxford University Press, 1979.
McKinnon, Ronald I. *An International Standard for Monetary Stabilization.* Washington, D.C.: Institute for International Economics, 1984.
McKinnon, Ronald I. "Monetary and Exchange Rate Policies for International Financial Stability: A Proposal." *Journal of Economic Perspectives* 2 (Winter 1988): 83–103.
McKinnon, Ronald I., "Purchasing Power Parity as a Monetary Standard." Economics Department, Stanford University, October 1988.
McKinnon, Ronald I., and Ohno, Kenichi. "Getting the Exchange Rate Right: Insular Versus Open Economies." Economics Department, Stanford University, December 1986.
Marcuzzo, Maria, and Rosselli, Annalisa. "Profitability in the Early History of the International Gold Standard." *Economica* 54 (August 1987): 367–80.
Metzler, Lloyd A. "The Theory of International Trade." In *A Survey of Contemporary Economics*, pp. 210–14. Edited by H. Ellis. Philadelphia: Richard Irwin for the American Economic Association, 1949.
Ohlin, Bertil. "The Reparation Problem: A Discussion." *Economic Journal* 39 (June 1929): 170–78.
Robinson, Joan. "The Foreign Exchanges." In *Readings in the Theory of International Trade*, pp. 83–103. Edited by H. Ellis and L. A. Metzler. Homewood, Ill.: Blakiston, 1950.
Samuelson, Paul. "On the Trail of Conventional Beliefs about the Transfer Problem." In *Trade, Balance of Payments, and Growth.* Edited by Jagdish Bhagwati, et al. Amsterdam: North-Holland, 1971.
Taussig, Frank W. *International Trade.* New York: Macmillan, 1927.
Triffin, Robert. "The Evolution of the International Monetary System: Historical Reappraisal and Future Perspectives." *Princeton Studies in International Finance*, no. 18, June 1964.
Viner, Jacob. *Studies in the Theory of International Trade.* New York: Harper and Brothers, 1937.
Whale, Philip B. "The Working of the Prewar Gold Standard." *Economica* 6 (February 1937): 18–32.
Williamson, Jeffrey G. *American Growth and the Balance of Payments, 1820–1913.* Chapel Hill: University of North Carolina Press, 1964.
Wolf, Martin. "The Need to Look to the Long Term." *Financial Times*, 16 November 1987.

## COMMENT

# THE MCKINNON STANDARD: HOW PERSUASIVE?*

*Rudiger Dornbusch*

Ronald McKinnon never fails to be insightful and provocative at the same time. His highly suggestive discussion of relative price variability under alternative monetary regimes forms part of a new research direction that was initiated in particular by Alan Stockman (1983) and Michael Mussa (1986). His discussion of a new monetary standard, a gold standard without gold, is a challenge to the current nonsystem.

I will in my comments touch on three issues: First, what can be said of adjustment mechanisms in international payments theory. Second, what do we know about relative price variability under alternative regimes and how does this variability relate to the law of one price. Third, how persuasive is the case for the McKinnon standard.

## The Adjustment Mechanism in International Payments

McKinnon makes much of a distinction between traditional and revisionist interpretations of the adjustment mechanism under the gold standard: Do relative prices have to move in the course of payments adjustment, or to effect a transfer? And if so, which relative prices must move: exports relative to imports, or home goods relative to tradables?

As in all interpretations of classical literature, and more generally in talmudic pursuits, different scholars emerge with different findings, the ones coming late usually calling themselves revisionist. I have little doubt that Jacob Viner, the great scholar of classical writing

*Reprinted from *Cato Journal* 8 (Fall 1988): 375–83.

The author is the Ford International Professor of Economics at the Massachusetts Institute of Technology.

on the adjustment mechanism,[1] would have dismissed the McKinnon revisionism with little sympathy.

A standard rendition of the payments mechanism under Ricardian assumptions goes as follows:[2] An income transfer, reparation payment, or loan from A to B raises spending in B and reduces it in A. The spending increase in B raises demand for home goods and for tradables as well; abroad spending on nontradables and tradables declines. With identical tastes (the central classical assumption), the spending changes in the world traded goods markets offset each other. But there will be excess demand in B's home goods market and in the market for labor, and an excess supply in A. Wages and *all* prices of goods produced in B will rise, and in A they will decline. Thus in B the terms of trade will improve and the price of home goods will rise in terms of importables, though not in terms of exportables under Ricardian assumptions about technology. In A, the transferring country, the real price of home goods will decline in terms of importables.

The price level as measured by consumer prices will decline in the transferring country, while it will rise in the country receiving the loan. Thus Ricardo's dictum "in borrowing countries prices are high" is borne out by the analysis. Much of the discussion of Viner (1924), Graham (1922), Taussig (1928), and Williams (1920) revolves around the question of what precisely the evidence is. None of that literature offers evidence to support that, contrary to classical writing, relative prices did not play a role in the adjustment process. It is regrettable that McKinnon did not dig deeper into this rich literature and fell all too quickly for revisionism.

## Relative Prices and Monetary Regimes

Michael Mussa (1986) showed persuasively that the variability of real exchange rates, measured for example by bilateral relative price levels, increases sharply in the transition from fixed to flexible rates. Figure 1 shows the example of the U.S.–German real exchange rate. The immediate objection might be that the increased volatility might be the result not of the exchange rate regime per se, but rather of an increased level of noise in the world economy—oil shocks being the obvious example. But Mussa persuasively shows that for countries like Canada who have used flexible rates at various times increased variability is *always* the consequence of moving to a flexible rate

[1]See Viner (1955), Angell (1965), Harrod (1934), Hawtrey (1928), Mints (1945), and, especially, Iversen (1935).

[2]See Dornbusch, Fischer, and Samuelson (1977).

*FIGURE 1*

U.S.–GERMANY: REAL EXCHANGE RATE CHANGES
(PERCENT PER MONTH)

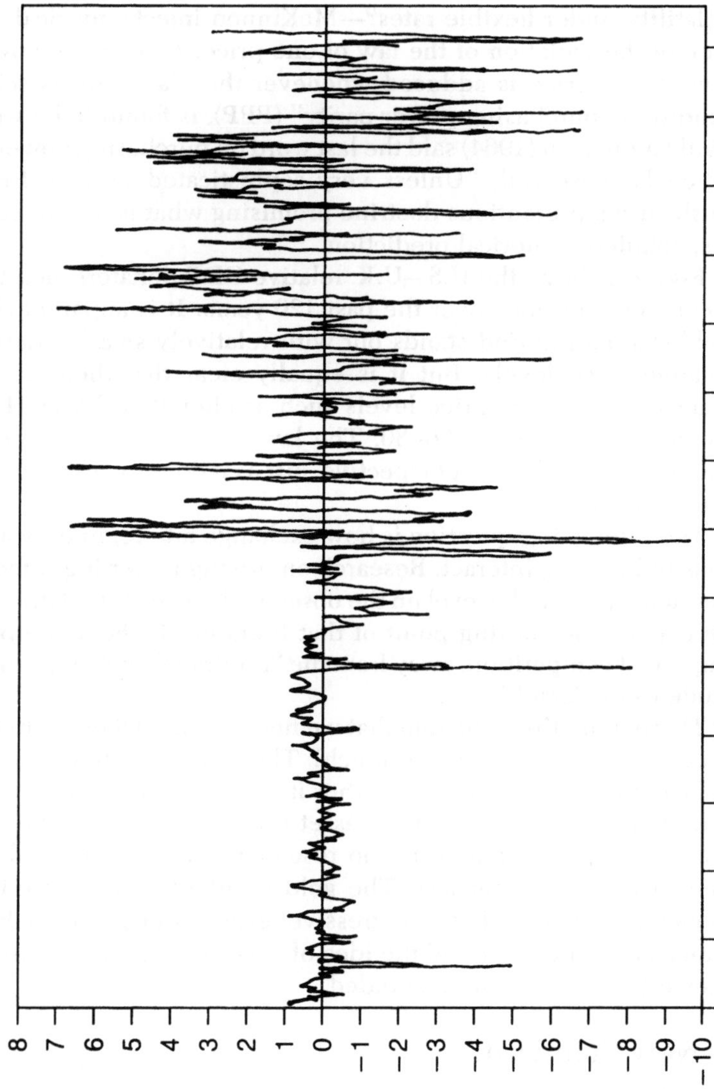

regime. The evidence may not be ironclad, but the case is made with sufficient persuasion to move an open-minded jury.

McKinnon picks up this same theme. But where Mussa had shown evidence and opened up the puzzling question—why is there more volatility under flexible rates?—McKinnon injects mystical discussion of the violation of the law of one price. As is well-known, the law of one price is adduced whenever the "law," or its scientific rendition "purchasing power parity" (PPP), is found to be wanting. Paul Samuelson (1964) said the last word on purchasing power parity when he observed, "Unless very sophisticated indeed, PPP is a misleading, pretentious doctrine promising what is rare in economics, detailed numerical prediction."[3]

Figure 2 shows the U.S.–U.K. relative GDP deflators measured in a common currency over the past 120 years. It is apparent that the gold standard period stands out with relatively small variations in relative price levels. But it is equally clear that there are major changes in relative price levels such as after World War II or the trend in the period 1950–80. The law of one price has a bit of a problem in this longer perspective, just as it does in month-to-month fluctuations.

The interesting question is how exchange rate regimes, wage setting and pricing interact. Research on pricing under imperfect competition has started to explain the observed behavior of relative prices. Of course, the starting point of that literature is the assumption of imperfect competition, away from the "arbitrage" view that animates students of Cassel.[4]

There is another question that we need to understand better: Why do exchange rates move so much? The same question extends, of course, to all asset prices, whether it be real estate, stocks, or long-term bonds. The instability of asset prices may well be tied to the monetary regime, but so far no researcher has offered a plausible demonstration of that fact. The gold standard may have offered a monetary framework for regressive expectations and stabilizing expectations built around the idea of a flat trend in prices. But even then crises and crashes abounded.

## A New Standard?

McKinnon has made on various occasions proposals for a new monetary regime: fixed exchange rates among the United States,

[3]For a detailed evaluation of PPP see Samuelson (1964) and Dornbusch (1988a).

[4]See Dornbusch (1988b) and Dornbusch and Giovannini (1988).

FIGURE 2

THE U.S.–U.K. REAL EXCHANGE RATE

(INDEX 1980 = 100)

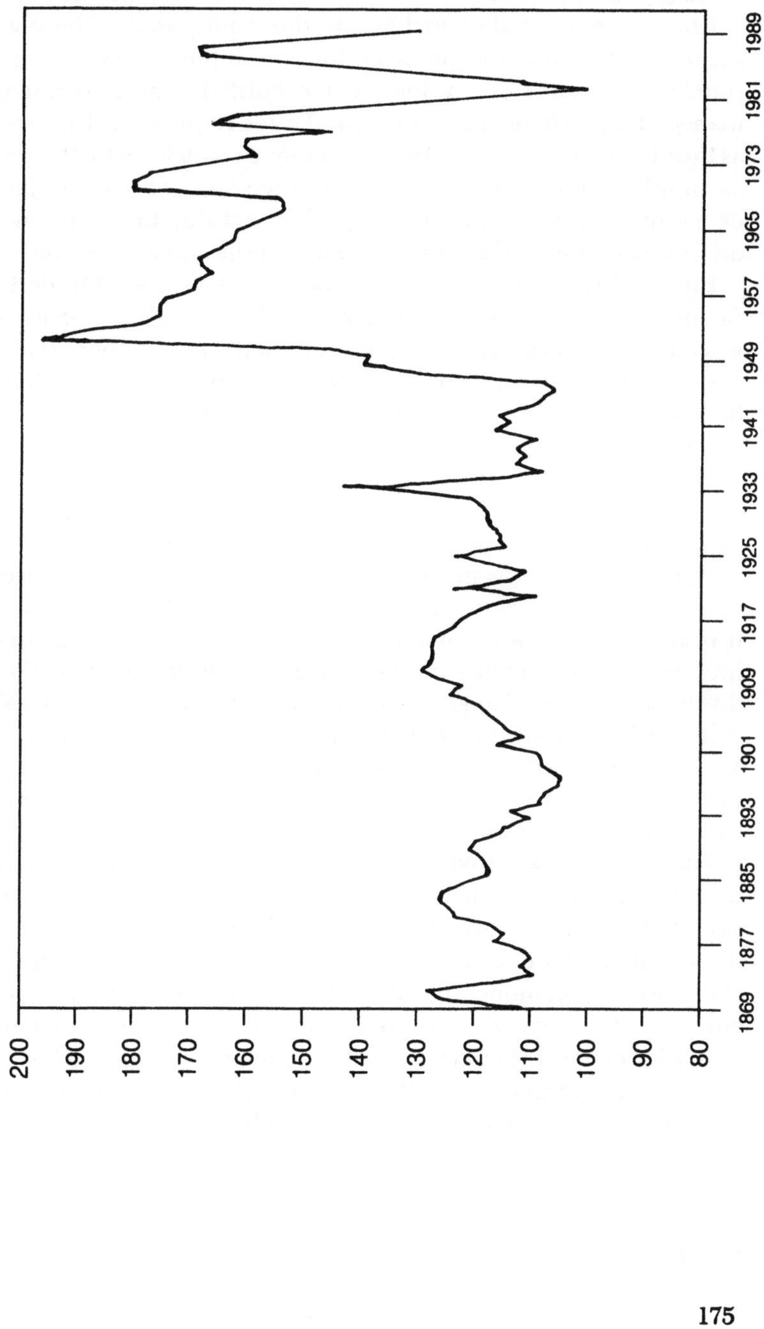

Japan, and Germany combined with a world monetary rule and exchange rate-oriented domestic credit policy. In the latest versions these proposals have been accompanied by the recommendation of a sharp yen devaluation (!) to return to purchasing power parity.

I have commented elsewhere on these proposals.[5] There are two major issues. First, the proposal for yen depreciation as a return to purchasing power parity leaves one baffled. The superior performance of Japan in manufacturing and trade requires real appreciation as the classical response. Precisely a move *away* from PPP is required as an adjustment to these favorable developments for the Japanese economy. The terms of trade improvement due to much lower real oil prices in the world economy point in the same direction.

Figure 3 shows the ratio of export prices to the GDP deflator in Japan. The downward trend reflects the Ricardo-Balassa-Samuelson-Kravis effect: In countries with rapidly rising productivity real appreciation is the rule. Any crude PPP comparisons based on a "common basket of tradables" cannot possibly suggest the right level for the real exchange rate. Equilibrium real exchange rates, just as in barter theory, have to do with full employment, absorption, and intertemporal budget constraints. In that perspective real appreciation is the appropriate price response to favorable developments.

I am similarly unpersuaded by the argument that we need exchange rate-oriented monetary policy. From the work of William Poole (1970) it is known that the optimal monetary rule—targeting aggregates or interest rates—depends on the source of the disturbance. Carrying this idea over to exchange rates as intermediate targets, the McKinnon rule would be perfect if all disturbances are shifts from one country's $M_1$ to another's. But if we deal with portfolio shifts, then sterilized intervention is appropriate; and if they are real disturbances, then exchange rate targeting is altogether inappropriate.

The flexible exchange rate experience has left many observers unsatisfied. One alternative is a move to a far more managed system, say fixed exchange rates with rules. The common response is that there is insufficient coordination to make such a system work. Especially relying on monetary integration alone may be highly undesirable. Anna Schwartz (1986) has made a very forceful case against reviving the gold standard. Another response is to leave the system as is on the argument that there is no better arrangement, but that there is room to pursue more stable policies within a flexible rate system.

[5]See Dornbusch (1988b).

*FIGURE 3*

RATIO OF EXPORT PRICES TO DEFLATOR
(INDEX 1980 = 100)

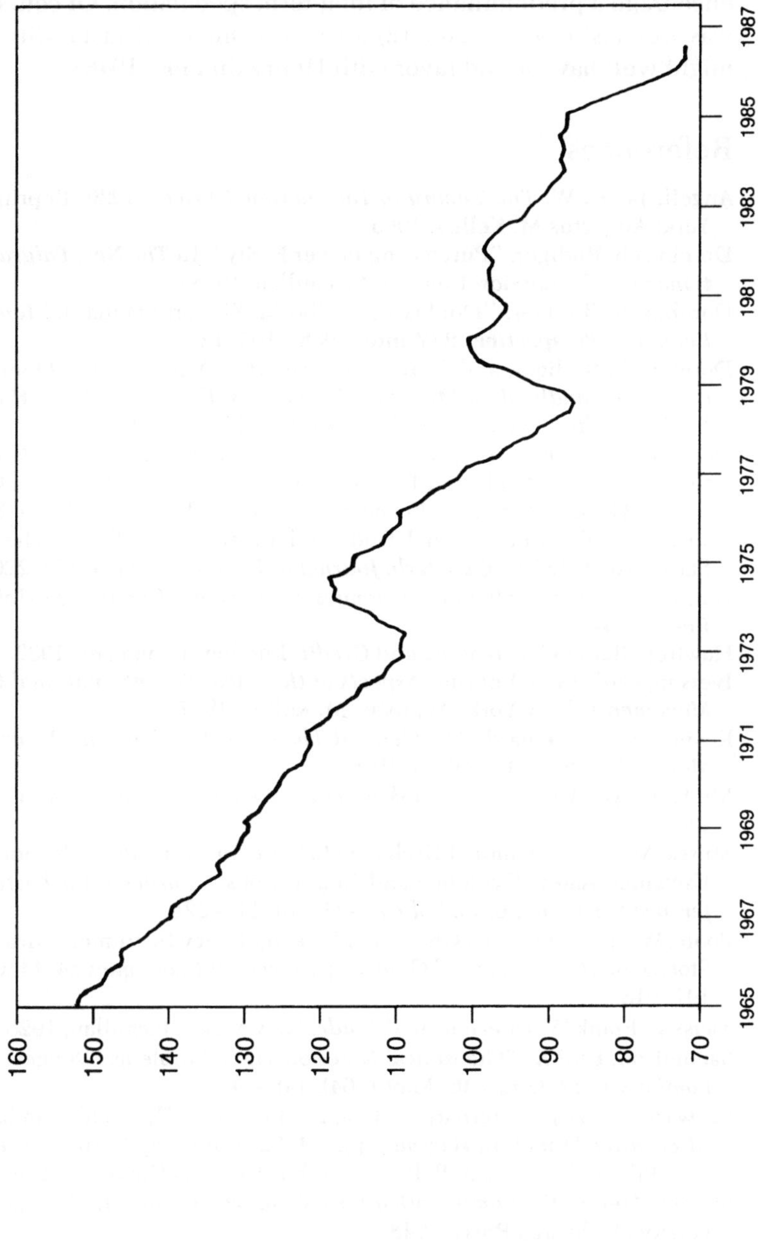

A third direction is to view exchange rate instability in the broader perspective of excessively speculative markets. In that view one would argue for a very moderate financial transactions tax (on all financial transactions) so as to lengthen speculative horizons and thus encourage a predominance of long-term speculation. Of course, that was Keynes' (1936, chap. 12) answer to financial instability and it might well have found favor with Henry Simons (1948).

## References

Angell, James W. *The Theory of International Prices.* 1926. Reprint. New York: Augustus M. Kelley, 1965.

Dornbusch, Rudiger. "Purchasing Power Parity." In *The New Palgrave Dictionary of Economics.* London: Macmillan, 1988a.

Dornbusch, Rudiger. "Doubts about the McKinnon Standard." *Journal of Economic Perspectives* 2 (Winter 1988): 105–12.

Dornbusch, Rudiger, and Giovannini, Alberto. "Money in the Open Economy." In *Handbook of Monetary Economics.* Edited by Frank Hahn and Benjamin Friedman. Amsterdam: North-Holland, forthcoming.

Dornbusch, Rudiger; Fischer, Stanley; and Samuelson, Paul A. "Comparative Advantage, Trade and Payments in a Ricardian Model with a Continuum of Goods." *American Economic Review* 67 (December 1977): 823–39.

Graham, Frank. "International Trade under Depreciated Paper: The United States, 1862–1879." *Quarterly Journal of Economics* 34 (1922): 220–73.

Harrod, Roy. *International Economics.* Cambridge: Cambridge University Press, 1934.

Hawtrey, Ralph G. *Currency and Credit.* London: Longmans, 1933.

Iversen, Carl. 1935. Reprint. *Aspects of the Theory of International Capital Movements.* New York: Augustus M. Kelley, 1967.

Keynes, John Maynard. *The General Theory of Employment, Interest and Money.* London: Macmillan, 1936.

Mints, Lloyd. *A History of Banking Theory.* Chicago: University of Chicago Press, 1945.

Mussa, Michael. "Nominal Exchange Rate Regimes and the Behavior of Real Exchange Rates: Evidence and Implications." *Carnegie Rochester Conference Series on Public Policy* 24 (1986): 117–224.

Poole, William. "Optimal Choice of Monetary Policy Instruments in a Simple Stochastic Macro Model." *Quarterly Journal of Economics* 84 (May 1970): 197–216.

Taussig, Frank W. *International Trade.* New York: Macmillan, 1928.

Samuelson, Paul A. "Theoretical Notes on Trade Problems." *Review of Economics and Statistics* 46 (May 1964): 145–54.

Schwartz, Anna J. "Alternative Monetary Regimes: The Gold Standard." In *Alternative Monetary Regimes*, pp. 44–72. Edited by Colin D. Campbell and William R. Dougan. Baltimore: Johns Hopkins University Press, 1986.

Simons, Henry. *Economic Policy for a Competitive Society.* Chicago: University of Chicago Press, 1948.

Stockman, Alan. "Real Exchange Rates under Alternative Nominal Exchange Rate Regimes." *Journal of International Money and Finance* 2 (1983): 147–66.
Viner, Jacob. *Canada's Balance of International Indebtedness*. Cambridge: Harvard University Press, 1924.
Viner, Jacob. *Studies in the Theory of International Trade*. London: George Allen & Unwin, 1955.
Williams, John. *Argentine International Trade under Inconvertible Paper Money, 1880–1900*. Cambridge: Harvard University Press, 1922.

# COMMENT

# PRICE LEVEL CHANGES AND THE ADJUSTMENT PROCESS UNDER FIXED RATES*

*Robert E. Keleher*

The topic of Professor McKinnon's paper is considerably narrower than suggested by its title. It addresses the role of price level movements in the balance-of-payments adjustment process under fixed exchange rates. Yet it is importantly related to McKinnon's earlier proposals for international monetary reform.[1] Accordingly, in commenting on McKinnon's paper, I will first indicate how it relates to his earlier proposal and why his paper is important. Second, I will discuss two specific aspects of his paper: (1) the role of price level changes in the balance-of-payments adjustment mechanism under fixed exchange rates, and (2) the assertion that price level volatility under the pre–World War I gold standard was due to global monetary instability and is not an inherent feature of fixed exchange rates.

## Performance of Exchange Rate Regimes and Proposals for Reform

It is now well recognized that flexible exchange rates have not performed as many had expected. In particular:

1. Exchange rates have displayed more short-run volatility (or variability) than expected. This is the case whether exchange rates are measured in nominal or real terms, bilateral or multilateral terms. Moreover, there is little evidence to suggest that this short-run exchange rate volatility has declined as traders have become more accustomed to flexibility.
2. Exchange rates have been characterized by long-term overshooting or persistent misalignment.[2]
3. Neither the short-term exchange rate volatility nor the long-term overshooting of exchange rates has been predicted; the

*Reprinted from *Cato Journal* 8 (Fall 1988): 385–92.

The author is Economist for the Board of Governors of the Federal Reserve System.

[1]See, for example, McKinnon (1984, 1988).

[2]Bernholz (1982) indicates that such overshooting is the historical norm.

explanatory power of existing exchange rate models has been poor.

4. Demands for international reserves have not diminished to the extent that some had expected. Governments have continued to intervene more than had been expected.
5. Economies are not as insulated and macroeconomic policies are not as independent as some had expected.
6. Trade and current account imbalances are larger in size and receive more public attention than they did under the Bretton Woods System.
7. Research suggests that relative to fixed exchange rate regimes, flexible exchange rates have been associated with much greater variability of real exchange rates and higher average levels of inflation.[3]

Given this performance, it is no wonder that McKinnon and others have proposed international monetary reform. The two fundamental components of his proposal are fixed exchange rates and a monetary or price rule to serve as an anchor for the international monetary system. Since McKinnon advocates fixed exchange rates with an anchor, his proposal is not novel but essentially a variant of the classical scheme.

McKinnon's paper relates to his broader reform proposal in that he discusses both fixed exchange rates and global monetary stability. His argument is that fixed exchange rates have wrongly been identified with price level variability. In supporting this contention, McKinnon examines the pre–World War I gold standard that he views as the best example of integrated economies under fixed exchange rates. The prewar period, he points out, was associated with minimal artificial restrictions on the mobility of commodities, capital, and labor. Moreover, large net flows of capital actually occurred during the period without requiring changes in nominal exchange rates and with little variability of real exchange rates.

In examining the gold standard, McKinnon contends that while price level variability certainly did occur, it was brought about by unstable global monetary conditions and not by the functioning of fixed exchange rates. According to McKinnon, price level variability is not an inherent part of the fixed exchange rate balance-of-payments adjustment mechanism.

McKinnon contends that this adjustment mechanism has been long misinterpreted. Specifically, the common textbook interpretation

[3]See, for example, Mussa (1986), Giovannini (1987), Meltzer (1986), and Meltzer and Robinson (1987).

includes changes in the general price level as a fundamental element of the adjustment process. This misperception results from a common interpretation of Hume's price-specie-flow mechanism that McKinnon refers to as classical. In this view, a balance-of-payments deficit leads to an outflow of gold. The gold outflow in turn causes a contraction of the domestic money supply and hence a decline of the general price level. Deflation causes exports to become cheaper and imports *relatively* more expensive thereby working to reduce the trade deficit. Since the opposite happens in surplus countries, *divergent movements in the general price level are commonly viewed as part of the adjustment mechanism.*

The implications of this interpretation are very important. First, this view implies that fixed exchange rates necessarily are associated with price level variability (or volatility) and not price level stability. Such price level variability is seen as an inherent element of fixed exchange rates. Second, this view has led some well-known monetary writers to contend that the choice between fixed and flexible exchange rates is the choice between exchange rate stability and price stability.

McKinnon, contends that this interpretation of the adjustment process is incorrect and misleading. Divergent movements of general prices are not part of the adjustment mechanism of an open economy under fixed exchange rates in an integrated world. In such circumstances there is a common price level (for tradable goods) maintained by active arbitrage. Divergent price level movements would violate the law of one price and purchasing power parity. Instead of divergent price level movements, adjustment occurs via flows of goods and capital. Accordingly, the choice between fixed and flexible exchange rates is not a choice between stable exchange rates and stable prices.

## The Classical Position

I believe McKinnon is correct on this commonly misunderstood point. Before examining the empirical evidence, however, it is important to mention that McKinnon fosters the common misperception that the divergent price level view of the adjustment process was endorsed by classical monetary writers. He refers to the view that price levels do not diverge as "revisionist." I believe these labels are misleading and incorrect.

A careful reading of original classical monetary writers leaves little doubt that these writers did not support the divergent price level view.[4] These writers all endorsed the natural distribution of specie

[4]See Keleher (1978), Humphrey and Keleher (1982), and Glasner (1985).

hypothesis and the law of one price. Moreover, they explicitly stated that divergent movements of general price levels (or prices of tradable goods) were not part of the adjustment mechanism under fixed exchange rates. Divergent price level movements were not possible because of the constraints of arbitrage.

This nonprice-diverging view applies to David Hume as well as to Adam Smith and the Bullionist writers. Banking School writers, John Stuart Mill, Knut Wicksell, and J. Laurence Laughlin also held this interpretation. This view, therefore, was the orthodox view from Hume until the early 20th century when it fell into eclipse for a number of reasons.[5] In fact, empirical evidence was provided by John Wheatley, Thomas Tooke, John Cairnes, and Laughlin to show that divergent price level adjustments never received factual support. In short, the interpretation that classical monetary writers endorsed a divergent price level adjustment mechanism is incorrect. The view supported by McKinnon and those writers adopting the modern monetary approach to the balance of payments is classical, not revisionist.

## The Pre–World War I Evidence

To support his contentions, McKinnon examines the pre–World War I gold standard. The prewar case is appropriate since it is an example where exchange rates were fixed, economies were well integrated, and minimal tariffs, capital controls, and immigration restrictions existed. McKinnon contends that common misinterpretations of the operation of fixed exchange rates is epitomized by interpretations of this period. More specifically, he contends that while it is common to attribute the period's price level volatility to fixed exchange rates, the operation of fixed exchange rates has not been sufficiently distinguished from the period's global monetary and price instability. While the period is characterized by price level variability, this was due to unstable world monetary conditions rather than to fixed exchange rates.

As evidence to support his view, McKinnon cites the work of Richard Cooper (1982) and Robert Triffin, which suggests that price levels of various countries moved together during the prewar period rather than diverging. Furthermore, McKinnon cites evidence from McCloskey and Zecher as well as from Dick and Floyd that show parallel, not divergent, movement in the prices of tradable goods.

While this evidence does suggest that prices move together rather than diverging, McKinnon has not produced empirical evidence to

[5]See Humphrey and Keleher (1982, pp. 200–202) for a discussion of these reasons.

support his contention that unstable global monetary conditions produced short-term price level variability. Some evidence (Bordo 1981, Cooper 1982, Meltzer 1986, Meltzer and Robinson 1987) does indicate that short-term price variability was higher during the gold standard years. But other evidence (Bernholz 1983) suggests that such variability may not have been the case for all countries.[6] Moreover, part of the reason for the short-term price variability may have been due to the domination of agricultural prices in the periods' wholesale price indices and hence related to agricultural instability rather than global monetary instability.[7] The method of measuring variability in one of these studies is also open to question.[8]

In contending that global monetary conditions were unstable, McKinnon points out that the gold base became smaller during the 1885–1913 period. While this may increase the vulnerability of the system to shocks, it does not necessarily imply anything about actual price variability or volatility. Moreover, while gold production increased sharply from about 1890 to World War I, this in itself does not imply anything about short-term price variability. Yet, as Michael Bordo (1986) has shown, financial crises including stock market crashes and bank runs occurred nearly simultaneously in numerous countries during the prewar period, which seems to support McKinnon's position.

Finally, if the period did experience global monetary instability as McKinnon suggests, he should indicate how such short-term price variability is reconciled with the well-documented long-run price stability found by several researchers. It is difficult to believe that this stability is accidental as McKinnon seems to suggest.[9]

In sum, while McKinnon's assertions about the adjustment mechanism under fixed exchange rates seem well founded, one has to

[6]Bernholz (1983) found that the variance of price movements during the gold standard period was higher only for the United States and Germany but not for France and England. Similarly, Cooper (1982) indicated that in England, the standard deviation of price change was *lower* during the gold standard period than in the postwar period. Moreover, Meltzer (1986) indicated that the variance of the price level was *lower* under the gold standard than under the recent fluctuating exchange rate regime: "The variance of the price level increased under pegged interest rates, but it is highest in the recent period of fluctuating exchange rates and relatively high inflation" (p. 139).

[7]Notably, recent research by Romer (1985, 1986) and Sheffrin (1988) has shown that economic fluctuations were not more severe under the gold standard as compared to more recent experience.

[8]The measurement of price variability used by Meltzer has been questioned by Carl Christ (1986).

[9]Most interpreters of the classical gold standard contend that fixing the price of gold creates incentives for the working of a self-regulating mechanism that ensures long-run price stability. See, for example, Aliber (1982, pp. 152–53).

remain skeptical of his contention concerning global monetary instability. Indeed, such skepticism must persist until McKinnon provides us with more empirical evidence to support his claim and until he reconciles short-run global instability with long-run, secular price stability.

## Regional Price Evidence

In order to assess the working of an unhampered fixed exchange rate system, the examination of the pre–World War I period is certainly appropriate. It is, after all, a period when economies were integrated, exchange rates were fixed, and artificial barriers to the movement of commodities, capital, and labor were minimal. But another, perhaps even better, example exists that should be mentioned. In particular, the set of regions within the U.S. economy satisfy all of these characteristics. Specifically, these regions are well integrated and effectively function as if in a common currency area (i.e., as if immutably fixed exchange rates existed). No tariffs or capital controls exist and since factor mobility is prevalent, there is an automaticity in the balance-of-payment adjustment process. Finally, some relatively consistent and reliable data is available to assess the working of these regions.

If regional price data are examined, the following conclusions seem readily apparent:

1. There is no evidence of divergent price level movements as part of a balance-of-payments adjustment process. There is a common price level.
2. Tradable good prices move together and do not diverge.
3. The only prices that differ significantly are nontradable prices of such goods as housing, rent, labor services, and so forth.
4. Adjustments to balance-of-payments disturbances between regions have apparently taken place smoothly despite common views as to the severity of such adjustments under fixed exchange rates. Apparently, the transfer problem works as McKinnon suggests; that is, it does not necessarily require price level adjustments.
5. Finally, if price levels are variable, it is because the price level in the United States as a whole is variable.

In short, the regional price evidence seems to support McKinnon's (or the classical) view of the balance-of-payment adjustment process under fixed exchange rates.

## Conclusion

There is both contemporary and historical theoretical precedent as well as empirical evidence to support McKinnon's classical view that divergent price level movements are not part of the adjustment process under fixed exchange rates. However, one must remain skeptical of McKinnon's contention about global monetary and price instability during the pre–World War I period until he provides more convincing evidence to support his assertions.

McKinnon's assessment is appropriate for circumstances where exchange rates are immutably fixed and there exists little expectation that government will alter the exchange rate or manipulate it as a policy tool. Unfortunately, these circumstances do not exist today and it is unlikely that they will in the near future. Nonetheless, McKinnon's paper suggests that in considering proposals for reform as well as in properly comparing fixed versus flexible exchange rates, economists ought at least to understand how fixed exchange rates worked.

## References

Aliber, Robert Z. "Inflationary Expectations and the Price of Gold." In *The Gold Problem: Economic Perspectives*. Edited by Alberto Quadrio-Cruzio. New York: Oxford University Press, 1982.

Bernholz, Peter. *Flexible Exchange Rates in Historical Perspective*. Princeton Studies in International Finance, no. 49. Princeton, N.J., July 1982.

Bernholz, Peter, "Inflation and Monetary Constitutions in Historical Perspective." *Kyklos* 36 (1983): 397–419.

Bordo, Michael D. "Financial Crises, Banking Crises, Stock Market Crashes, and the Money Supply: Some International Evidence, 1870–1933." In *Financial Crises and the World Banking System*. Edited by Forrest Capie and Geoffrey E. Wood. London: Macmillan, 1986.

Bordo, Michael D. "The Classical Gold Standard: Some Lesson for Today." *Federal Reserve Bank of St. Louis Review* 63 (May 1981): 2–17.

Christ, Carl F. "Accuracy of Forecasting as a Measure of Economic Uncertainty." In *Alternative Monetary Regimes*, pp. 154–60. Edited by Colin D. Campbell and William R. Dougan. Baltimore: Johns Hopkins University Press, 1986.

Cooper, Richard N. "The Gold Standard: Historical Facts and Future Prospect." *Brookings Papers on Economic Activity* 1 (1982): 1–56.

Giovannini, Alberto. "Prices and Exchange Rates: What Theory Needs to Explain." Paper prepared for the 1987 ASSA Meetings, Chicago, Ill., December 1987.

Glasner, David. "A Reinterpretation of Classical Monetary Theory." *Southern Economic Journal* 51 (July 1985): 46–67.

Humphrey, Thomas M., and Robert E. Keleher. *The Monetary Approach to the Balance of Payments, Exchange Rates, and World Inflation*. New York: Praeger, 1982.

Keleher, Robert E. "A Framework for Examining the Small, Open Regional Economy: An Application of the Macroeconomics of Open Systems." Working Paper Series, Federal Reserve Bank of Atlanta, December 1977.

Keleher, Robert E. "Of Money and Prices: Some Historical Perspectives." In *The Monetary Approach to International Adjustment*. Edited by Bluford Putnam and Sykes Wilford. New York: Praeger, 1978.

McKinnon, Ronald I. *An International Standard for Monetary Stabilization*. Washington, D.C.: Institute for International Economics, 1984.

McKinnon, Ronald I. "Monetary and Exchange Rate Policies for International Financial Stability: A Proposal." *Journal of Economic Perspectives* 2 (Winter 1988): 83–103.

Meltzer, Alan H. "Some Evidence on the Comparative Uncertainty Experienced under Different Monetary Regimes." In *Alternative Monetary Regimes*, pp. 122–53. Edited by Colin D. Campbell and William R. Dougan. Baltimore: John Hopkins University Press, 1986.

Meltzer, Alan H., and Saranna Robinson. "Stability under the Gold Standard in Practice." Working Paper, Carnegie-Mellon University, September 1987.

Mussa, Michael L. "The Exchange Rate Regime and the Real Exchange Rate." Paper presented at American Economic Association Meetings, New Orleans, December 1986.

Romer, Christina. "Is the Stabilization of the Postwar Economy a Figment of the Data?" *American Economic Review* 76 (June 1986): 314–34.

Romer, Christina, "The Prewar Business Cycle Reconsidered: New Estimates of Gross National Product, 1872–1918." Working Paper, Princeton University, 1985.

Sheffrin, Steven M. "Have Economic Fluctuations Been Dampened?" *Journal of Monetary Economics* 21 (1988): 73–83.

# PART III

# EXCHANGE RATE REGIMES: RULES AND CONSEQUENCES

# 8

# KEY EXCHANGE RATE REGIMES: A CONSTITUTIONAL PERSPECTIVE*

*Thomas D. Willett*

After a decade and a half of experience with the widespread use of flexible exchange rates among the major industrial countries, we have learned a great deal. But disputes about exchange rate policies and calls for international monetary reform are as frequent and heated as ever. The range of views about flexible exchange rates has narrowed somewhat, and the experience clearly has not been as disastrous as feared by many critics who foresaw a repeat of the disasters of the 1930s. Nor have flexible exchange rates been a complete solution to international monetary issues by eliminating the need for international monetary cooperation and by generating international monetary stability as the strongest supporters had hoped.

While supporters can plausibly argue that floating rates helped the world economy survive severe strains, few can be happy with the absolute level of performance of our international monetary arrangements over the past decade. Thus, continuing interest in evaluating alternative exchange rate policies and regimes and in considering proposals for reform is quite understandable.

## Developments in Exchange Rate Analysis

While the views that are held by international monetary experts about preferred exchange rate arrangements have narrowed only modestly, our understanding has improved considerably about how to analyze exchange rate issues. I hasten to add that the previous statement is meant in the broad sense of conceptual frameworks in which exchange rate issues can be analyzed most fruitfully. On the other hand, at the level of more specific questions such as how are exchange rates determined or what are optimal coordination strate-

*Reprinted from *Cato Journal* 8 (Fall 1988): 405–20.

The author is the Horton Professor of Economics at the Claremont Graduate School and Claremont McKenna College and Director of the Claremont Center for Economic Policy Studies.

gies, our advances in theoretical and exchange research have often left us feeling less, rather than more, sure that we know the answers. As theoretical models of exchange rate determination and exchange rate dynamics have proliferated, we have gained a much better appreciation of the complex issues involved in discussing equilibrium levels and time paths of exchange ranges. But we have gained little in our ability to empirically implement such analysis.

A number of models initially appeared to fit important aspects of the data well, but in each case more systematic testing failed to confirm their robustness. Indeed we can argue that a major message of the recent exchange rate literature, with its emphasis on the role of expectations and news and on the delineation of numerous channels of influence on exchange rates, is that we should not expect to be able to give very precise empirical implementation to exchange rate models. We can still argue that there were many good reasons, having largely to do with U.S. economic policies, why the dollar fell substantially in the late 1970s and then soared in the early 1980s. However, we can say much less about the short-run dynamics of exchange rate behavior.[1]

Perhaps the major analytical lesson we learned is the severe danger of analyzing exchange rate issues in isolation. Now we better understand that the effects of exchange rate changes on major economic variables such as price levels, volume of international trade, and domestic employment will often depend crucially on the causes of the changes.[2] This understanding applies not only to the quantitative magnitudes of the effects but also to their direction in terms of whether they tend to have a stabilizing or a destabilizing influence. As a result of this recognition, debates over issues such as the inflationary effects of fixed versus flexible exchange rates can rest on much firmer foundations than in earlier periods.[3] Modern analysis also makes us wary of sweeping generalizations about the effects of fixed versus flexible rates. As is emphasized in the literature on optimum currency areas and on optimal stabilization policy in open economies, evaluations

[1]I am not arguing that theoretical and empirical research on exchange rate dynamics and speculative behavior is a waste of time, but rather that we should not expect highly accurate short-term forecasts or strong consensus on equilibrium levels of rates to emerge from this process. For recent analysis and references to the literature on exchange rate modeling and forecasting, see Arndt, Sweeney, and Willett (1985); Bhandari (1987); Bhandari and Putnam (1983); Bigman and Taya (1983); Bilson and Marston (1984); and Jones and Kenen (1985).

[2]See Arndt, Sweeney, and Willett (1985) and Willett (1982).

[3]See Corden (1977), Crockett and Goldstein (1976), Darby et al. (1983), and Willett and Wolf (1983).

of the effects of alternative exchange rate regimes can vary substantially depending on the assumptions made about the patterns of economic shocks, structure of the economy, and the weights given to different policy objectives.[4]

Such analysis also highlights another consideration, which will be the central focus of this paper. One cannot usefully analyze the performance of an exchange rate regime independent of its interrelationships with national monetary and fiscal policies. A paper written 15 or 20 years ago with a title such as "Key Exchange Rate Regimes" would probably have focused primarily on the various forms that exchange rates arrangements might take, from the extremes of genuinely fixed and freely floating rates through various intermediate forms such as the adjustable peg, wider bands, crawling pegs, and managed floating.[5] Today that list would be expanded to include proposals for reference rates, target zones and indicator systems, and alternative intervention strategies for managed floating.[6] While these issues are clearly important, they are not of primary concern for those interested in how we can best reduce international monetary instability.

National economic policies must be considered in any meaningful analysis of alternative exchange rate regimes. The same set of exchange rate arrangements may work well or poorly depending on the behavior of other economic policies. We now widely recognize, for example, that fixed exchange rates are just not workable among countries that insist on maintaining highly divergent domestic monetary and fiscal policies. Arguments for fixed exchange rates are often made on the (frequently implicit) assumption that they will be accompanied by internationally coordinated, national macroeconomic policies. We must carefully spell out and analyze the mechanisms by which such policy coordination might come about.

In examining alternative exchange rate regimes, then, we need to distinguish between two types of analysis: (1) the mode of analysis designed to show how alternative exchange rate arrangements may be expected to operate under different patterns of economic policies and shocks, and (2) the mode of analysis focusing on the likely patterns of policies and how these patterns may in turn be influenced by the exchange rate regime and policy understandings that go with it. It is in this second mode that political economy becomes crucially

[4]See the analysis and references in Arndt, Sweeney, and Willett (1985); Buiter and Marston (1985); Jones and Kenen (1985); and Willett (1985b).

[5]See Halm (1970).

[6]See Frenkel and Goldstein (1986), Kenen (1987), and Williamson (1986, 1987).

important for analyzing both the likely course of unconstrained national policies and how alternative exchange regimes are likely to influence the course of these policies.[7]

## International Monetary Reform: Conflicting Traditions

There have been two strong and conflicting traditions in the literature on alternative exchange rate systems and international monetary reform. One tradition views the major objective of exchange rate and international monetary arrangements to be to interfere as little as possible with national macroeconomic policymaking. The other views the international monetary system as a much-needed source of discipline over otherwise unconstrained national policymaking.[8] These views differ, of course, on whether they see national economic policymaking as taking place more in line with the public interest view (typically assumed, for example, by Keynesians) or with the perverse political pressures view held by many public choice analysts and hard money advocates.[9]

The public interest view of the operation of the political process, combined with the (Keynesian) theory of economic policy as applied to open economics, generally leads to optimally managed flexibility as the preferred exchange rate regime (for countries large enough to make an independent currency viable),[10] although the content of optimal management strategies is highly model specific. Those concerned with using the international monetary system to provide discipline over national macroeconomic policies have, in turn, generally favored a gold standard or some other form of fixed exchange rate system.

Unfortunately, the writers in these two traditions have paid relatively little attention to each others' analysis. Compared with the volume of international monetary writings in these two traditions, relatively little analysis has been presented from the perspective of an intersection of these views. This perspective sees a need for institutional reforms to discipline the domestic policymaking pro-

[7]For examples and references to the literature that takes political economy approaches to domestic and international monetary relations, see Cohen (1977), Lombra and Witte (1982), and Willett (1983, 1988).

[8]For discussions and references to the literature on the discipline debate, see Willett and Mullen (1982).

[9]On these different views, see Buchanan and Wagner (1977) and the papers by Willett and Banaian in Willett (1988).

[10]See Tower and Willett (1976).

cess, but questions whether international rules are the best way to attempt to impose such discipline.[11] (Different dimensions of the meaning of the best way will be discussed later.)

Conceptually, we may distinguish among several different types or levels of political analysis needed to "close" the analysis of alternative international monetary regimes. One, of course, involves considering whether or not domestic political pressures tend to generate noneconomically optimal economic policies from the perspective of a closed economy.[12] A second type, quite unrealistic in my opinion but commonly adopted (often implicitly) in international monetary literature, assumes political problems only at the international level with self-interested national governments tending to engage in suboptimal (from a global perspective) levels of internationally cooperative actions.[13]

Where political problems are assumed at both the national and international levels, the analysis can become quite complex. In my judgment this third type of political analysis deserves much greater attention. Depending on the issue in question and the nature of the political forces assumed to be at work, we see that "biases" at the national and international levels may be either additive or offsetting. Judgments on this issue may also differ depending on the criterion for judgment adopted. For example, it is frequently argued that nationalist concerns will tend to lead to an underprovision of short-run exchange rate stability. On the other hand, recent analysis of political business cycles and other incentives for time inconsistency problems can generate pressures for self-interested national governments to seek arrangements for short-run exchange rate fixity, which would increase the incentives for unconstrained national macroeconomic policies to follow strategies with an inflationary bias.[14] One lesson that we certainly should have learned is that greater short-run exchange rate fixity by itself is not a sure contributor to greater longer-run stability.

Political analysis can interact with economic analysis on issues of both feasibility and enforcement. From one perspective, discussions of what is currently politically feasible may be used to narrow the range of policy options to be seriously considered in the short term.

[11]Milton Friedman has long advocated such an approach with his emphasis on domestic monetary rules. For recent analysis along these lines, see Genberg and Swoboda (1987), Gutowski (1978, 1979), and Willett (1987a).

[12]For analysis and references to the literature on this question, see Willett (1988).

[13]A number of examples of such analysis may be found in Buiter and Marston (1985).

[14]See Rogoff (1985), Vaubel (1986), and Willett and Mullen (1982).

From another, analysis of political realities can be crucial to discussions of the need for possible institutional reforms to change the operation of, or to constrain the outcomes from, the political process. Complementary to such analyses are considerations of the likely operation (i.e., enforceability and workability) of institutional reforms, if adopted, and of the political feasibility of adopting such institutional reforms in the first place. Unfortunately, there often is a tradeoff between the latter two considerations (i.e., the more binding a reform is likely to be, the more difficult it will be to reach agreement on its adoption). Thus, for example, our historical experience suggests that it is much easier to get agreement among governments for fixing their exchange rates in the short run than it is to negotiate the constraints on national macroeconomic policies that would be necessary to make these exchange rates sustainable over the longer run.

There is an urgent need for all three types of political analysis. No one of them is the sole correct level of analysis. What is important, however, is that analysts are clear on what type of analysis they are presenting. There are more than enough grounds for disagreements over particular political analysis, just as with economic analysis, without further adding to the scope for controversy by failing to make clear the specific type of analysis and the political-economic interrelationships being considered.

This difficulty has frequently occurred with proposals for various exchange rate and monetary policy rules. Some proposals have clearly been motivated primarily by concerns about optimal policy strategies, while others have been more concerned with promoting discipline or rules of the game to limit the use of "beggar-thy-neighbor" policies. Often, however, the motivation for particular proposals has not been made sufficiently clear.

## Rationales for Alternative Exchange Rate Regimes

### *Optimal Discretion*

Let us consider some major possible rationales or objectives for exchange rate regimes. From the standpoint of public interest (or ideal political process) decisionmaking, the question would be one of facilitating optimal discretionary policy responses. From a traditional Keynesian optimal policy perspective, the content of such policy strategies would include official intervention to offset destabilizing speculation and internationally coordinated monetary, fiscal, and intervention policies to optimally offset other economic and financial shocks.

*Policy Rules*

With imperfect information, case-by-case discretion would move toward and, in the limit, be replaced with policy rules that determine policies on the basis of estimates of or views about the average pattern of disturbances.[15] These rules might become quite complicated, focusing on a large number of indicators as in some of the current indicator proposals.

When the problem of imperfect information is combined with imperfectly and internationally oriented national decisionmakers, a case emerges for forums for discussion and enforcement of internationally coordinated discretionary policies or policy rules. In the absence of willingness by national governments to cede such authority to an international body, rules limiting the range of permissible national policy actions or requiring particular policy actions under specified conditions become an attractive strategy.

Commonly proposed examples of such international rules or guidelines of a negative type are limits on the cumulative amount of or circumstances of official intervention in the foreign exchange market (e.g., prohibitions on aggressive as opposed to "leaning-against-the-wind" intervention).[16] Requirements to intervene if exchange rates move outside an internationally agreed target zone are an example of a frequently proposed positive rule. With a still lower level of international cooperation, such rules might be given a presumptive role as a basis for marshaling moral suasion.

*Constraint Systems*

While a great deal more analysis of this issue is needed, I would conjecture that the case for focusing on exchange rates as the basis for policy rules is likely to be substantially reduced when imperfections in the operation of domestic political processes are systematically introduced. Conceptually, the discipline argument for institutional reforms presents more of a case for the imposition of constraints on policy outcomes rather than for policy rules per se.[17] In other than new classical economic models, the particular form of a policy rule adopted will typically have a substantial influence on the performance of the economy (and this can occur in some new classical

[15]See Tower and Willett (1976).

[16]For examples of discussions of these issues during the Committee of Twenty Negotiations over international monetary reform during the 1970s, see de Vries (1985), Willett (1977), and Williamson (1977).

[17]The ideal institutional reform would be one that removes the biases in the decisionmaking process in the first place. For this paper I shall assume that the scope for much first-best reforms is quite limited.

models as well). Ideally, one would like a constraint system to allow economically optimal policy outcomes while limiting the scope for deviation from this outcome because of political pressures. Unfortunately, much of the literature fails to make a clear distinction between the case for optimal policy rules from the standpoint of the traditional theory of economic policy and the case for national or international constraint systems to offset political biases or beggar-thy-neighbor policies.

## Converting Optimal Policy Rules to Sensible Constraint Systems

With a particular dominant type of disturbance, we may be able to achieve both the optimal rule and constraint objectives with a particular policy rule. For example, if international currency substitution and portfolio shifts were the only major sources of disturbance, then Ronald McKinnon's proposal of fixed exchange with nonsterilized intervention to determine the domestic money supply would be an optimal (or at least quite reasonable) policy rule.[18] However, a domestic monetarist like Milton Friedman sees a quite different pattern of disturbance than does an international or global monetarist like McKinnon.[19] Thus Friedman prefers a fixed national money supply rule for the major industrial countries, combined with flexible exchange rates among them. Likewise, gold standard advocates and Keynesians assume still different perponderant patterns of disturbances.[20] It is certainly difficult and probably inappropriate to try to obtain fundamental institutional reforms whose desirability highly depends on the answers to questions that are open to considerable controversy among mainstream economists. On this view one should seek to reach agreement on constraint systems that seem reasonable albeit nonoptimal to a substantial proportion of experts. Taking such a constitutional perspective also suggests the desirability of simplicity and enforceability in the design of institutional reforms.[21] The combination of these considerations presents a strong case for domestic rather than international constraint systems.

[18]See McKinnon (1984, 1985) and Willett (1985a).

[19]While some initial empirical research did support McKinnon's view on the importance of international currency substitution for the United States, these findings did not hold up strongly in light of subsequent research. For recent critical surveys of this empirical literature, see Willett et al. (1987).

[20]See Mayer and Willett (1988).

[21]Such a perspective refers to the analysis of fundamental rules of the game. These rules need not be formally embedded in constitutional provisions. For recent examples of analysis taking such a perspective, see Dorn and Schwartz (1987).

On the basis of simplicity and easy technical enforceability, the pure form of McKinnon's fixed-rate proposal is quite attractive. As he himself describes it, his proposal presents the basic attractive features of the gold standard rules of the game while doing away with the need to depend on the vagaries of the gold market. But after the conversion from a policy rule to a constraint system, this attraction quickly disappears. How do we allow a loose version of this approach? Systematic partial sterilization would make little economic sense and would make even less as a political rule. Mandatory nonsterilized intervention at the limits of some target zone for exchange rates would be more attractive as a constraint system. However, as with gold-based systems, such a regime would still be subject to the problems of making reasonable estimates of initial equilibrium rates and of the disequilibrating effects on domestic money growth, which would result from changes in equilibrium real exchange rates. Recent empirical studies on purchasing power parity and exchange rate behavior suggest that this is a possibility that must be taken very seriously.[22]

Looking at the behavior of exchange rates along with that of many other variables makes considerable sense in the formulation of discretionary monetary policy, including discretionary behavior within a broader constraint system. The design of a sensible mechanical relationship between the exchange rate and domestic monetary policy is a quite different question. For example, consider that the dollar in 1985 was high but falling. Did this indicate a stronger case for monetary ease or tightness?

The case becomes even more difficult in looking at the relationship between the exchange rate and fiscal policy. While proposals for target zones for exchange rates were initially put forth largely to deal with perceived problems of destabilizing or insufficiently stabilizing speculation, in his recent writings John Williamson has stressed the potential role of target zones in promoting fiscal discipline.[23] A set of mechanical rules for adjusting fiscal policy in response to exchange rate movements could certainly be devised, but it seems unlikely that one would find a rule that produced desirable behavior under a plausible range of circumstances. Still more difficult perhaps would be trying to sell such a rule for fiscal discipline to national legislatures. As a presumptive guideline there could be some value to such

[22]See the analysis and references in Arndt, Sweeney, and Willett (1985); and Darby et al. (1983).

[23]See Williamson (1986, 1987) and, for critical analysis, Branson (1986), Cooper (1986), Fischer (1986), Frenkel (1987), and Frenkel and Goldstein (1986).

an approach, but my reading of the situation is that much stronger forms of reform are required for us to reasonably expect a substantial sustained reduction in international monetary instability. This issue of fiscally produced instability would remain a problem even under the adoption of a system of rigidly fixed exchange rates based on McKinnon's set of rules for monetary policy.

## Domestic Versus International Constraint Systems

Concern with the technical feasibility of ensuring consistency among policies complements optimal policy and simplicity arguments for domestic constraint systems. The simplicity argument may be expressed relatively straightforwardly in terms of limits on the size of (possibly full employment) budget deficits and rates of monetary growth. Money growth rules could specify a range on the permissible average rate of growth of some monetary variable or allow for deviations from a target range for average rates of inflation or nominal income to force adjustment in the growth rates of a monetary variable.[24] With a constraint system approach, this type of feedback system need not give rise to the type of dynamic instability likely to occur from a tight short-term linkage between price and money growth variables.

Such a domestic constraint system would allow exchange rates to move consistently with underlying economic conditions. Exchange rate variability would not be eliminated, but it would be reasonable to expect that much of the dollar's plunge in the late 1970s and its surge in the first half of the 1980s would have been avoided because variability in U.S. monetary and fiscal policies would have been reduced. Residual concerns about possible excessive short-term exchange rate variability because of destabilizing speculation could still be addressed through official intervention, perhaps even geared to a soft system of target zones. Considerable analysis of the details of both domestic constraint systems and exchange market provisions would be needed to formulate the best system. But the system's essential characteristic would be that exchange market provisions would be secondary to the domestic monetary and fiscal policy constraints.

The fundamental alternative is the set of proposals under which exchange market developments drive domestic monetary and fiscal policy. Historical experience suggests that, with support from the United States, an international agreement placing considerable lim-

[24]For discussion and references to the literature on the alternative possible forms and targets of such constraint systems, see Dorn and Schwartz (1987).

its on short-term exchange rate variability would be much easier to achieve than would the type of domestic constraint system described above. It seems doubtful, however, that effective agreement would be reached on the types of rules for domestic monetary and fiscal policy that would be necessary to make the system of short-term exchange rate fixity consistent with longer-term stability. There is considerable question whether one could overcome the technical difficulties involved in designing the quantitative specification of policy rules that would avoid dynamic instability or persistent payments disequilibrium and would overcome the forcing of changes in monetary and fiscal policy that would have serious destabilizing effects on the domestic economies.[25] Nor would these seem to be the types of reforms that would generate substantial political support.

## Fundamental Choices in a Politicized World

While many fascinating details of alternative sets of exchange rate arrangements deserve attention, at the most fundamental level we have a choice among four types of exchange rate and international monetary regimes in a world in which biases in the operation of political pressures play a major role in the determination of unconstrained domestic macroeconomic policies.

We may have either of two variants of disciplined or constrained systems: one focused on exchange rates and the other domestically oriented. We may likewise have two types of regimes with relatively unconstrained domestic monetary and fiscal policy. These unconstrained variants may have either pegged or flexible rates in the short run, but historical experience suggests that both would produce considerable global economic instability over the long run. In a world of political economic policies, the case is strong for fundamental institutional reforms to help promote long-run economic and financial stability, including exchange rate stability.

In my judgment, for the major industrial countries we should look for greater exchange rate stability primarily as a consequence of, rather than as a means to, greater domestic financial stability. Conceptually, domestic monetary and fiscal policies can be geared to the exchange rate regime, but on grounds both of best promoting macroeconomic stability, if followed, and of the political likelihood that consistent policies actually would be followed, the weight of historical experience suggests to me that exchange rate regimes should be designed in light of domestic financial considerations rather than

[25]See, however, Edison et al. (1987).

vice versa. If this view is correct, then the most fundamental issues concerning the design of exchange rate regimes strongly depend on the analysis of domestic monetary and fiscal policy and of institutions.

Adoption of floating exchange rates was not the cause of the acceleration of worldwide inflation in the 1970s as some have argued. Since national monetary and fiscal policies were not systematically linked in practice to obligations to maintain pegged rates, little systematic discipline was imposed, and the major U.S. pressures that generated the acceleration of inflation (associated with the financing of the Vietnam War) were initiated under pegged rates.[26] While it is a debatable issue, it seems likely that floating rates have generated more discipline on average than have pegged rates unaccompanied by specific linkages to national macroeconomic policies.

What seems clear, however, is that even if floating rates promoted more rather than less discipline, this discipline was still woefully inadequate. Floating rates in and of themselves are not sufficient to provide adequate financial discipline. Further institutional reform is urgently needed to place explicit limits on the range of permissible discretionary variations in national monetary and fiscal policies. While such reforms would conflict with the short-run political advantages of many powerful officials, and hence would be difficult to achieve, the reforms would be in the long-run interests of countries adopting the disciplinary measures. By reducing the export of instability such reforms would also be desirable from the standpoint of a country's trading partners.

While ultimately such reforms would be national decisions and the specifics could vary from one country to another, it would be desirable to approach such reform efforts within a cooperative international framework rather than exclusively as matters of unilateral national actions.

I have argued that for the major industrial countries such reforms should be focused primarily on domestic rather than exchange rate criteria. There are two major caveats to this proposition. As is stressed in the theory of optimum currency areas, one caveat is that it may be more economically desirable for smaller countries to peg to a relatively stable larger country or to join with other small countries to form a currency area.

A second caveat is that in the dynamic of establishing a political and economic climate within which the adoption of more fundamen-

[26]See Barro (1982) and Calleo (1982) for statements that the breakdown of pegged rates and gold convertibility played an important role in reducing discipline in the United States. For empirical work reaching the opposite conclusion, see Briggs et al. (1988) and Darby et al. (1983).

tal institutional reforms would become feasible, it is possible that coordination on exchange rates could prove useful. This type of argument, however, should be approached with considerable caution. The experiences with the European Economic Community have found the linkages from economic reform to political integration to be much weaker than many advocates had hoped. Also, there is always a danger that such evolutionary strategies will succumb to the promises of quick political fixes that fail to produce longer-run stability while diverting attention from more fundamental issues. Still the avoidance of economic warfare after the breakdown of pegged rates in the 1970s is an important example that there can be some truths to such evolutionary arguments. The fact that the most recent experiences of the European Monetary System were not obvious failures (albeit the "success" depended on widespread use of capital controls) suggests that efforts at evolutionary strategies related to exchange rates deserve further attention.

Except for small countries, however, such strategies should be seen as complements to, rather than substitutes for, concerns with directly establishing limits over the range of discretion for national monetary and fiscal policies. The behavior of the latter determines the feasibility of alternative exchange rate regimes.

## References


Arndt, Sven; Sweeney, Richard J.; and Willett, Thomas D. *Exchange Rates, Trade, and the U.S. Economy.* Cambridge, Mass.: Institute for Public Policy Research, 1985.

Barro, Robert. "United States Inflation and the Choice of Monetary Standard." In *Inflation, Causes and Effects,* pp. 99–110. Edited by Robert Hall. Chicago: University of Chicago Press, 1982.

Bernholz, Peter. "The Implementation and Maintenance of a Monetary Constitution." In Dorn and Schwartz (1987, pp. 83–118).

Bhandari, Jagdeep S., ed. *Exchange Rate Management under Uncertainty.* Cambridge: MIT Press, 1987.

Bhandari, Jagdeep S., and Putnam, Bluford, eds. *Economic Interdependence and Flexible Exchange Rates.* Cambridge: MIT Press, 1983.

Bigman, D., and Taya, T., eds. *Exchange Rate and Trade Instability: Causes, Consequences, and Remedies.* Cambridge, Mass.: Ballinger Press, 1983.

Bilson, J., and Marston, R., eds. *Exchange Rate Theory and Practice.* Chicago: University of Chicago Press, 1984.

Branson, William H. "The Limits of Monetary Coordination as Exchange Rate Policy." *Brookings Papers on Economic Activity* 1 (1986): 175–94.

Briggs, John; Christenson, D. B.; Martin, Pamela; and Willett, Thomas D. "The Decline of Gold as a Source of Monetary Discipline." In Willett (1988, pp. 186–99).

Buchanan, James M., and Wagner, Richard E. *Democracy in Deficit: The Political Legacy of Lord Keynes*. New York: Academic Press, 1977.

Buchanan, James M.; Rowley, Charles K.; and Tollison, Robert D., eds. *Deficits*. Oxford: Basil Blackwell, 1987.

Buiter, Willem H., and Marston, Richard C. *International Economic Policy Coordination*. Cambridge: Cambridge University Press, 1985.

Calleo, David. *The Imperious Economy*. Cambridge: Harvard University Press, 1982.

Campbell, Colin D., and Dougan, William K., eds. *Alternative Monetary Regimes*. Baltimore: Johns Hopkins University Press, 1986.

Christ, Carl. "Rules vs. Discretion in Monetary Policy." *Cato Journal* 3 (Spring 1983): 121–41.

Cohen, Benjamin J. *Organizing the World's Money: The Political Economy of International Monetary Relations*. New York: Basic Books, 1977.

Cooper, Richard N. "Dealing with the Trade Deficit in a Floating Rate System." *Brookings Papers on Economic Activity* 1 (1986): 195–207.

Corden, M. W. *Inflation, Exchange Rates, and the World Economy*. Chicago: University of Chicago Press, 1977.

Crockett, Andrew, and Goldstein, Morris. "Inflation under Fixed and Flexible Exchange Rates." *IMF Staff Papers* 23 (November 1976): 509–44.

Darby, Michael; Lothian, A. E. Gandolfi; Schartz, A. J.; and Stockman, A. C., eds. *The International Transmission of Inflation*. Chicago: National Bureau of Economic Research, University of Chicago Press, 1983.

de Vries, Margaret G. *The International Monetary Fund, 1972–1978. Cooperation on Trial. Volume I: Narrative and Analysis*. Washington, D.C.: International Monetary Fund, 1985.

Dorn, James A., and Schwartz, Anna J., eds. *The Search for Stable Money*. Chicago: University of Chicago Press, 1987.

Dornbusch, Rudiger. "Flexible Exchange Rates and Excess Capital Mobility." *Brookings Papers on Economic Activity* 1 (1986): 209–26.

Edison, Hali J., et al. "On Evaluating and Extending the Target Zone Proposal." *Journal of Policy Modeling* 9(1) (1987): 199–224.

Fischer, Stanley. "Symposium on Exchange Rates, Trade, and Capital Flows: Discussion." *Brookings Papers on Economic Activity* 1 (1986): 227–32.

Frenkel, Jacob A. "The International Monetary System: Should It Be Reformed? *American Economic Review* 77 (May 1987): 205–10.

Frenkel, Jacob A., and Goldstein, Morris. "A Guide to Target Zones." International Monetary Fund *Staff Papers* 33, no. 4 (December 1986): 633–73.

Genberg, Hans, and Swoboda, Alexander K. "Fixed Exchange Rates, Flexible Exchange Rates, or the Middle of the Road: A Reexamination of the Arguments in View of Recent Experience." In *The Reconstruction of International Monetary Arrangements*, pp. 92–116. Edited by Robert Z. Aliber. New York: St. Martin's Press, 1987.

Gutowski, Armin. "International Guidelines and Principles for National Financial and Exchange Rate Policies: Discussion." In *Exchange Rate Flexibility*, pp. 197–200. Edited by Jacob Dreyer, Gottfried Haberler, and Thomas D. Willett. Washington, D.C.: American Enterprise Institute, 1978.

Gutowski, Armin. "Commentary." In *U.S.-European Monetary Relations*. pp. 70–74. Edited by Samuel I. Katz. Washington, D.C.: American Enterprise Institute, 1979.

Halm, George N., ed. *Approaches to Greater Flexibility of Exchange Rates: The Burgenstock Papers*. Princeton: Princeton University Press, 1970.

Jones, Ronald W., and Kenen, Peter B., eds. *Handbook of International Economics*, vol. 2. Amsterdam: North-Holland, 1985.

Kenen, Peter B. "Exchange Rate Management: What Role for Intervention?" *American Economic Review* 77 (May 1987): 194–99.

Lombra, Raymond E., and Witte, Willard D., eds. *Political Economy of International and Domestic Monetary Relations*. Ames: Iowa State University Press, 1982.

Mayer, Thomas, and Willett, Thomas D. "Evaluating Proposals for Fundamental Monetary Reform." In Willett (1988, pp. 398–423).

McKinnon, Ronald I. *An International Standard for Monetary Stabilization*. Washington, D.C.: Institute for International Economics, 1984.

McKinnon, Ronald I. "The Dollar Exchange Rate as a Leading Indicator for American Monetary Policy." San Francisco Federal Reserve Bank, *Academic Conference Volume* (Fall 1985): 161–206.

Rogoff, Kenneth. "Can International Monetary Policy Cooperation Be Counterproductive?" *Journal of International Economics* 18 (1985): 199–217.

Tower, Edward, and Willett, Thomas D. "The Theory of Optimum Currency Areas and Exchange Rate Flexibility." Special Papers in International Economics. Princeton: Princeton University, Department of Economics, 1976.

Vaubel, Roland. "A Public Choice Approach to International Organization." *Public Choice* 51 (1986): 39–57.

Willett, Thomas D. *Floating Exchange Rates and International Monetary Reform*. Washington, D.C.: American Enterprise Institute, 1977.

Willett, Thomas D. "Functioning of the Current International Financial Systems." In *International Money and Credit*. Edited by George von Furstenberg. Washington, D.C.: International Monetary Fund, 1983.

Willett, Thomas D. "The Dollar Exchange Rate as a Leading Indicator for American Monetary Policy: Comment." San Francisco Federal Reserve Bank, Academic Conference (Fall 1985a): 207–14.

Willett, Thomas D. "Macroeconomic Policy Coordination Issues under Flexible Exchange Rates." *ORDO* 35 (1985b): 137–49.

Willett, Thomas D. "The Causes and Effects of Exchange Rate Volatility." In *The International Monetary System*, pp. 24–64. Edited by Jacob Dreyer, Gottfried Haberler, and Thomas D. Willett. Washington, D.C.: American Enterprise Institute, 1982.

Willett, Thomas D. "A Public Choice Analysis of Strategies for Restoring International Economic Stability." Prepared for the Konstanz Conference on "New Institutional Arrangements for the World Economy," 1–4 July 1987a.

Willett, Thomas D. "National Macroeconomic Policy Preferences and International Coordination Issues." Prepared for the National Bureau of Economic Research Interdisciplinary Conference on "The Political Economy of International Macroeconomic Policy Coordination," November 1987b.

Willett, Thomas D., ed. *Political Business Cycles: The Political Economy of Money, Inflation, and Unemployment*. Durham: Duke University Press for Pacific Research Institute, 1988.

Willett, Thomas D., and Mullen, John E. "The Effects of Alternative International Monetary Systems on Macroeconomic Discipline and the Political Business Cycle." In Lombra and Witte (1982, pp. 143–59).

Willett, Thomas D., and Wolf, Matthais. "The Vicious Circle Debate." *Kyklos* 2 (1983): 231–48.

Willett, Thomas D., and Banaian, King. "Models of the Political Process and Their Implications for Stagflation: A Public Choice Perspective." In Willett (1988, pp. 100–16).

Willett, Thomas D., et al. "Currency Substitution, U.S. Money Demand, and International Interdependence." *Contemporary Policy Issues*, 5 (July 1987): 76–82.

Williamson, John. *The Failure of World Monetary Reform, 1971–1974*. New York: New York University Press, 1977.

Williamson, John. "Target Zones and the Management of the Dollar." *Brookings Papers on Economic Activity* 1 (1986): 165–74.

Williamson, John. "Exchange Rate Management: The Role of Target Zones." *American Economic Review* 77 (May 1987): 200–204.

# 9

# TRADE AND INVESTMENT UNDER FLOATING RATES: THE U.S. EXPERIENCE*

*Martin J. Bailey and George S. Tavlas*

## Introduction

Since the move to a managed floating exchange rate system in 1973, world financial markets have been characterized by large movements in nominal exchange rates. These movements have been accompanied by large swings in real exchange rates, reflecting the fact that nominal exchange rate variations have not closely followed changes in relative prices of traded goods. The short-run variability of exchange rates—whether measured in real or nominal terms, in bilateral or effective terms—has been substantially higher in the post-1973 period than it was under the Bretton Woods system (Frenkel and Goldstein 1986). Moreover, exchange rate variations have been much greater than the early advocates of floating had expected. For example, in an influential article, Harry Johnson (1969, pp. 19–20) argued that the allegation that a flexible-rate system would result in unstable rates ignored "the crucial point that a rate that is free to move under influences of changes in demand and supply is not forced to move erratically, but instead will move only in response to such changes in demand and supply . . . and normally will move only slowly and predictably."[1]

This paper assesses the causes of exchange rate variability and examines its consequences for trade and investment. Following John Williamson (1985), we distinguish between two concepts of vari-

---

*Reprinted from *Cato Journal* 8 (Fall 1988): 421–42.

Martin J. Bailey is an Economic Adviser to the Undersecretary for Economic Affairs at the Department of State and an Adjunct Professor of Economics at the University of Maryland. George S. Tavlas is an economist in the European Department of the International Monetary Fund. The authors are grateful to William Gavin, Peter Isard, Guy Stevens, Michael Ulan, and John Wilson for helpful comments. The views expressed are the authors' and are not to be interpreted as those of their respective institutions.

[1]Perceptively, Johnson (1969, p. 17) also recognized that exchange rates would be stable only as long as "underlying economic conditions (including government policies)" remained stable.

ability—short-term volatility and longer-term misalignment. Volatility involves short-term (monthly, weekly, or even hourly) fluctuations in exchange rates as measured, say, by their absolute percentage changes during a particular period. In contrast, misalignment is a subjective concept and, as such, difficult to quantify. Misalignment has been defined as a departure over a substantial period of time of the exchange rate from its "fundamental equilibrium value" (i.e., the exchange rate that yields a cyclically adjusted current-account balance equal to normal private capital flows—those capital flows that exist in the absence of undue restrictions on trade and special incentives to incoming or outgoing capital) (Williamson 1985, Crockett and Goldstein 1987). For example, the value of the U.S. dollar in 1984 and early 1985 was considered by many commentators to be considerably higher than justified by the fundamentals; hence, the value of the dollar was perceived by these commentators as bound to come down. The problem with getting a grip on misalignment is, as Crockett and Goldstein (1987) have observed, the difficulty entailed in measuring such concepts as a "substantial" period of time, the "cyclically adjusted" current-account balance, "normal" private capital flows, "undue" restrictions on trade, and "special incentives" on capital flows.

The remainder of the paper discusses, in turn, the various explanations of exchange rate behavior, the effects of exchange rate variability, and the impact of exchange rate movements on U.S. exports and investment. We note that if exchange rate variability has been in some sense "excessive," it must have been unpredicted by theories of exchange rate determination, or at least inconsistent with the stylized explanations posited by those theories. Moreover, in considering the possible costs of exchange rate variability and misalignment, we observe that the main costs are usually associated with allocation effects on trade and investment; theoretically, the costs of exchange rate variability on trade and investment are ambiguous. Our empirical results of the effects of exchange rate variability on trade and direct investment in the U.S. economy do not support the hypothesis that exchange rate variations (defined in terms of either short-term volatility and longer-term misalignment) have hampered trade and investment in the U.S. economy.

## Explanations of Exchange Rate Behavior

Why have exchange rates moved so much and for such long periods of time? In what follows, we will review six explanations of exchange rate behavior. Before doing so, however, several observations are in order.

The first pertains to the characterization of the present international exchange rate regime. At the outset, we described the current system as one of managed floating—not one of freely floating—currencies. This description is apt because most countries (almost all of which are developing countries) adhere to pegged exchange rate arrangements while a number of countries (including the eight members of the European Monetary System) follow limited flexibility vis-à-vis a single currency or group of currencies.[2] Further, even among the floating currency countries, exchange rates have not been permitted to float cleanly, as evidenced by recent efforts to talk the U.S. dollar up or down (sometimes within the same day); by informal agreements among the Big Five (the Plaza Agreement, the Louvre Accord); and by large interventions of central banks. Indeed, intervention strategies have differed among countries and over time, ranging from free floating, to short-term smoothing, to heavy intervention aimed at achieving a targeted rate (Shafer and Loopeska 1983, p. 6).

The second observation is that the world operating environment since 1973 has differed substantially from that characterizing the Bretton Woods era. As Shafer and Loopeska argue, floating rates should not be blamed for the slowdown in world growth and trade that accompanied the move to managed floating. Specifically, they note that the rapid growth of the economies of Europe and Japan in the 1950s and 1960s was, in part, a catching up after World War II and was unlikely to be sustained, that the floating rate period inherited international disequilibrium and inflation, and that the world economy suffered two oil price shocks during the floating rate period. Also, the post-1973 period has been characterized by developments that contributed to exchange rate variability. These developments include the technological advances in communications that provide fast, high-volume linkages among world financial markets, enabling events in any one market to have an almost instantaneous impact on other markets. This rapid advance in communications technology has, not surprisingly, been accompanied by a relaxation of controls on capital movements.

Finally, as Frenkel and Goldstein (1986) note, exchange rates are financial asset prices and, therefore, are flexible and forward looking—unlike many goods prices that are sticky and backward looking

[2]See Tavlas (1987). However, as Goldstein (1984, pp. 3–4) reports, most of world trade is conducted at unpegged currencies.

(reflecting previous contractural agreements).[3] Volatility is to be expected in an auction market, such as the exchange market, under floating rates simply because of continuous surprises. William Nordhaus (1978, p. 250) made this point explicitly: "In those pure auction markets where prices are the main shock absorber, considerable price volatility is the result. These conditions generally prevail in raw foods and commodities markets, in markets for many financial instruments such as common stocks, or when a regime of pure floating exchange rates exists. Such volatility is an intrinsic feature of real world auction markets—markets in which there are incessant surprises due to weather, changes in taste, inventions, political upheaval, inflation, recession, and boom, etc." Indeed, Gottfried Haberler (1986, p. v) argues that the ability of flexible exchange rates to absorb shocks has eased quantity and price adjustments in goods and labor markets. Further, Maurice Obstfeld (1985) argues that it is doubtful whether the fixed exchange rate system would have survived the changed world environment since 1973 without the imposition of controls on capital movements and restrictions on trade.

The auction market characteristic is important, but it certainly does not account fully for the magnitude of exchange rate movements. To understand why instability may be an inherent characteristic of flexible rates, we turn to a brief overview of theories of exchange rate behavior.

A useful starting point for considering theories of exchange rate determination is the portfolio balance model.[4] The model is built around the determinants of net outside supplies of stocks of assets denominated in different currencies and the demands for them. Individuals are assumed to allocate their wealth, which has a given total value at each moment, among alternative assets including, most generally, domestic and foreign money and domestic and foreign securities. Assets denominated in different currencies are viewed by investors as perfect substitutes (i.e., uncovered interest rate parity holds). Thus, if one country has a higher expected monetary growth

[3]Frenkel and Goldstein (1986, p. 647) also point out that exchange rate changes have been smaller than changes in other asset prices, such as national stock markets and short-term interest rates.

[4]The portfolio balance model is an extension of the vintage 1970s' monetary model. As Krueger (1983, p. 50) observes, "At the present time it is difficult to distinguish an adherent of the monetary approach from the author of a portfolio balance model." An important bridge between the two approaches was provided in the article by Frenkel and Rodriguez (1975), which incorporated the treatment of asset accumulation and current account determination within the monetary approach. For an interesting appraisal of the monetary approach, see Boughton (1988).

rate and consequently a higher expected inflation rate, assets denominated in its currency will carry an interest-rate differential that is equal to the expected depreciation in its exchange rate. Expectations play a key role in the determination of equilibrium. Another component of the portfolio model is that goods of different countries are essentially perfect substitutes, and there are virtually no barriers to instantaneous (price) adjustment in goods markets (see Krueger 1983, pp. 86–90). The assumptions with respect to both asset prices and goods prices will be relaxed below.

*Rational Speculative Bubbles*

By treating exchange rates as financial asset prices, the portfolio approach draws attention to the substantial influence of expectations. A number of writers including Mussa (1976), Frenkel and Mussa (1980), and Dornbusch (1980) have argued that the exchange rate market, as any asset market, is efficient; a market is considered to be efficient when prices reflect all available information, including expectations about economic policies. Consequently, the behavior of exchange rates is affected in an important way by new information that is continuously being processed by economic agents. Short-term fluctuations in exchange rates, according to the efficient markets view, are to be expected if the forces that lie behind exchange market equilibrium are themselves subject to substantial short-term fluctuation. As Michael Mussa (1976, p. 203) has stated, "under a floating exchange rate regime, private agents must continuously revise their expectations of the future behavior of money supplies and other relevant variables in forming their expectations about the appropriate level of the nominal exchange rate." Continuous revisions in expectations make for continually changing exchange rates. Indeed, if exchange rate variations were exclusively determined by new and unanticipated information, the exchange rate would follow a random walk—today's exchange rate would be the best predictor of expected future exchange rates.

One should note that if expectations are continuously revised in the same direction for a substantial period of time—for example, if expectations of interest rates are modified repeatedly in the direction of higher and higher rates, thereby reflecting an expected progressive tightening of monetary policy—the efficient markets view gives rise to what is referred to as rational speculative bubbles. Consequently, the efficient markets framework can account for both short-term volatility in exchange rates and longer-term movements, although the latter do not imply deviation from any fundamental equilibrium value.

*Irrational Speculative Bubbles*

The efficient markets view assumes that private agents process all information in a rational manner. Therefore, the market equilibrium exchange rate reflects the underlying economic fundamentals. By contrast, the irrational speculative bubbles story views economic agents as myopic. Ronald McKinnon (1976) had argued that exchange rate instability might be caused by an inadequate supply of private capital available for taking net positions in either the forward or spot markets on the basis of long-term exchange rate expectations. Thus, as Artus and Young (1979, p. 678) observed, the McKinnon hypothesis indicates that "cyclical variations in the demand for foreign exchange originating from trade or financial activities that may be sustained for a number of years may lead to large exchange rate movements because of a lack of investors with both the funds and the willingness to take a longer-run open position."

Paul Krugman (1985) has recently applied McKinnon's hypothesis to the context of the "high" value of the U.S. dollar of late 1984 and early 1985. According to Krugman (p. 106), "the case for a [speculative bubble] ... is in fact the argument that there is *insufficient* speculation." His argument runs as follows. The large U.S. trade deficits of the mid-1980s had produced a situation where the dollar was unsustainably high. The dollar was bound to fall in value, but investors' expectations were irrational. Had these expectations been rational, recognizing that the dollar needed (on the basis of long-run fundamentals) to come down, the expected future depreciation of the dollar would have inhibited the holding of dollar-denominated assets, thereby putting downward pressure on the dollar's value. Instead, market participants paid "more attention to the higher [relative] yield on dollar securities than to the forces which [would] eventually weaken the dollar. Thus, the dollar [was] high because investors [paid] too little attention to the prospect of future exchange rate changes, not too much" (Krugman 1985, p. 106). The market had reached a consensus that the dollar would come down slowly. If the long-term fundamentals pointed to the need for a rapidly falling dollar, then the market had overreacted to the then-existing interest differential because of a lack of forward-looking speculation, producing an irrational speculative bubble. Krugman used this argument to predict correctly that "the dollar must at some point plunge" (1985, p. 107).[5] Assuredly Krugman's expectations proved to be more accurate than the representative market expectation. We are not sure,

[5]A hard landing was also predicted by Marris (1985).

however, that this fact establishes that speculation was either irrational or insufficient.

*Overshooting: The Case of Sticky Prices*

Overshooting can occur in any portfolio model in which some markets do not adjust instantaneously. For example, Branson (1977), Dornbusch (1976), and Kouri (1976) have focused on the slow speed of price adjustment in the goods market to explain exchange rate instability; this focus reflects the view that goods prices are backward looking in the short to medium term while exchange rates are flexible and forward looking. The sticky price argument runs as follows: An unanticipated change in the nominal money supply produces an increase in the real quantity of money because prices do not adjust promptly. As a result, real interest rates fall, leading to an incipient capital outflow and a depreciation in the real exchange rate, which is proportionately more than the change in money (Dornbusch 1986, p. 213). With lower real interest rates, the demand for goods picks up. In parallel, real exchange depreciation causes a substitution from foreign goods in favor of home country goods in both the domestic and export markets. Over time, as goods prices increase, the real money supply will contract and the real exchange rate will appreciate until real equilibrium is regained (Dornbusch 1986).

As Jeffrey Frankel (1985) has argued, if the market is foresighted, it anticipates that the expansion in demand will set prices in motion above their previously expected path. If we assume rational expectations, the anticipation of further exchange rate appreciation must be sufficient to offset the interest rate differential between domestic and foreign rates, so that opportunities for profits do not exist by holding either domestic or foreign assets. What accounts for the exchange rate overshooting is the fact that, following the monetary innovation, the exchange rate fell below the level that was expected in the long run (Frankel 1985, p. 7).

*Overshooting: The Case of Asset Accumulation*

Now we assume flexible goods prices but relax the assumption of perfect substitutability between domestic and foreign assets. Consequently, the variable that is not free to adjust instantanteously is the level of domestic claims on foreign assets. Next we assume, for purposes of illustration, an expansionary domestic fiscal policy leading to cumulative current-account imbalances. In the context of the Mundell-Fleming framework, the fiscal expansion results in a rise in domestic interest rates, an excess supply of foreign assets and an appreciation of the currency. Jeffery Frankel (1985) and Rudiger

Dornbusch (1987) have shown that the accumulated net external indebtedness, which accompanies the current account deficits, will decrease the level of domestic claims on foreign assets, eventually undoing their initial excess supply and with it the appreciation of the domestic currency. But the currency will not just fall back to its original value because the current account deficits result in reduced income from net foreign assets. As Dornbusch (1987, p. 7) has argued: "The reduction in net external assets means that following a period of deficits, the current account cannot be balanced simply by returning to the initial real exchange rate. Now there will be a deficit from the increased debt service. Therefore, to restore current account balance, an overdepreciation is required."

Both of the overshooting hypotheses are able to account for exchange rate variability and long-term movements in rates. Short-term variability arises because both hypotheses emphasize the role of news. For example, as Artus and Young (1979, p. 679) observe with respect to the current account story: "Market participants—continually reassess their views of the needed exchange rate change on the basis of actual current balance developments without always being able to discount properly the effects of temporary divergences in economic cycles, J-curve effects of exchange rate changes, and so forth." Moreover, the fact that the overshooting hypotheses are able to explain short-term and long-term movements in the exchange rate should not be taken to imply that the exchange rate deviates in any way from its equilibrium value (Williamson 1985). Richard Levich (1985, p. 1018) makes this point explicitly: "[The] definition of overshooting draws a distinction between short-run and long-run equilibria while retaining the notion that the exchange rate is priced fairly at all times, a perfect reflection of all information."

### *The Safe-Haven Hypothesis*

Michael Dooley and Peter Isard (1987) extend the portfolio balance model, focusing on international portfolio shifts. In particular, the safe haven approach "departs from other portfolio balance models of exchange rates by shifting attention away from the financial characteristics of assets. . . . Instead, the approach emphasizes that variations over time in the prospective income streams on physical capital in different countries can generate changes in observed holdings of claims to those income streams, giving rise to desired net international capital flows and associated changes in relative prices and exchange rates" (Dooley and Isard 1987, p. 71). Consequently, the exchange rate is determined in such a manner as to give rise to a current account deficit that is equal to the rate at which foreigners wish to acquire claims on the domestic country. As such, the approach stresses the "safe-haven phenomenon" whereby the strength of the U.S. dollar in the first half of the 1980s is ascribed to the perceived relative strengthening of the U.S. economic and political situation. The transmission of such perceptions included a shift of bank lending from less-developed countries to the U.S. capital market and increased direct investment in the United States. One important implication of the safe-haven hypothesis is that "the choice between a fixed or flexible exchange rate regime may not have a very significant influence, ceteris paribus, on the variability of the real terms of international competition as characterized by the relative prices of tradable goods and the real balance of trade" (Dooley and Isard 1987, p. 79).

*Demand Shifts and Other Influences*

Alan Stockman (1987a, 1987b) provides a thorough, textbook-like review of explanations of exchange rate movements, summarizing most of the foregoing approaches and adding other detailed cases. His analysis includes shifts of demand in each country for internationally traded goods, plus other real shifts, but does not include irrational bubbles. He concentrates solely on shifts of fundamentals like those in the previous three cases just considered. The result adds to the richness and complexity of the issues we are considering, and it calls into question any approach that considers only one or two influences on exchange rates.

Stockman develops an equilibrium model of the determination of exchange rates and prices of goods.[6] Changes in relative prices of goods, because of supply or demand shifts, induce changes in exchange rates and deviations from purchasing power parity. According to Stockman (1987a, p. 12), "Repeated disturbances to supplies or demands . . . thereby create a correlation between changes in real and nominal exchange rates. This correlation is consistent with equilibrium in the economy, in the sense that markets clear through price adjustments."

A number of important policy inferences can be drawn from the equilibrium model of exchange rates. For purposes of this paper, the relevant inferences are that changes in exchange rates do not cause changes in relative prices but are themselves dependent variables driven by fundamentals (i.e., by exogenous variables). Further, the issue of whether exchange rate variability has detrimental effects on

[6]Disequilibrium theories of the exchange rate are based on sluggish adjustment of nominal prices and imply that the correlation between real and nominal exchange rate changes is exploitable by government interventions in the foreign exchange market (Stockman 1987a, p. 13).

the economy—either through its effects on trade or investment—is not the relevant question "because the exchange rate is an *endogenous* variable. The right question is whether the underlying disturbances to the economy are 'good' or 'bad,' so (of course) the answer lies with the disturbance" (Stockman 1987a, p. 17). We would add that if "fundamentals" refer to consumer preferences, comparative advantage, other supply conditions, and comparative rates of inflation among different trading partners, then the associated changes in exchange rates are efficient (i.e., they increase world output). Whether these changes affect trade and investment (as they sometimes would) is less interesting than whether *other* changes in exchange rates affect trade and investment.

## Effects of Exchange Rate Variability

In the light of the foregoing discussion of the causes of exchange rate volatility, we would prefer, so far as possible, to divide exchange rate changes into those caused by fundamentals and those caused by other factors (i.e., misguided speculation). Ideally, we would represent each such influence accurately by a right-hand-side variable in a regression; these variables would be exogenous, while exchange rates, trade, and investment would be a subset of the jointly determined (endogenous) variables of a comprehensive model. The regression, in that case, would be one of the reduced form equations, with, say, direct investment as the dependent variable. Besides the difficulty in trying to specify and measure the relevant exogenous variables, however, we are faced with the impossible task of finding a measure of the speculative influence. Consequently, we need a proxy for it, and the only proxy available is exchange rate variation not explained by the exogenous variables that represent fundamentals. Although this residual variability is not the fundamental cause of whatever effects we might observe in trade and investment, it can be viewed as the proximate cause, in its role as a proxy for misguided speculation. We can then address the question of what happens if governments adopt policies that stabilize exchange rates around the equilibrium rates determined by fundamentals. Would trade increase, and would international investment be larger or better allocated as a result? This approach has two clear advantages. First is the practical consideration just mentioned—that we can measure exchange rate variability whereas we cannot measure the amount of misguided speculation. Second, if all of the variability not explained by specified exogenous variables is due to irrational speculative bubbles or to other such causes, it is not clear that this variability should be considered endogenous; there would be no prima facie reason to suppose that treating it as endogenous would bias the analysis. Of course, not all of the fundamentals can be measured, so that some bias may result from our approach; but we see no alternative.

In a recent paper with Ulan (Bailey, Tavlas, and Ulan 1987), we reviewed many of the arguments for and against the proposition that short-term exchange rate volatility reduces trade because of the risks and costs it involves.[7] The argument that exchange rate volatility hampers trade is simple and almost self-evident: Because contracts to sell goods, movement of the goods themselves, and payments for them rarely all coincide, there will be an element of exchange risk in foreign trade. This risk is equivalent to a cost to a risk-averse trader, and the trader will sometimes bear an actual cost to avoid it. Although this cost may be small for short-term transactions (because transactions costs are low for foreign exchange), the bid-ask spread widens with volatility; also, forward exchange markets exist for only about a year or so into the future. Being like a transportation cost, in that exchange risk affects trade in both directions, exchange rate volatility will tend to reduce a country's exports and imports.

However, the arguments are not all on one side. For example, exporters may gain knowledge through trade that would help them anticipate future exchange rate movements better than can the average participant in the foreign exchange market. If so, the profitability of this knowledge could offset the risk of exchange rate volatility. If they wish to hedge longer-term investment or other transactions rather than use the forward exchange market, exporters can borrow and lend in local currency to offset their other commitments. For example, a plant in a foreign country can be financed mainly with local capital, so that investors limit their exchange risk in the basic investment. An additional counter-argument of especially great weight is that we have to specify the alternative to volatility. If the volatility is due to fundamental factors influencing the exchange rate, intervention by the authorities to reduce it would be unsustainable and eventually disruptive. To achieve a reduction of apparent, observed volatility, authorities would have to intervene with exchange controls or other restrictions on trade and payments. That intervention could be more harmful to trade, and reduce it more, than would unrestrained movement of the exchange rate.

Furthermore, volatility of a single exchange rate is a poor measure of the risk of trade with the country involved, because of portfolio considerations. In general, a firm will be involved in trade with

[7]See also Yeager (1976) for a discussion of the issue.

several countries and so will have a mixed portfolio of foreign claims and obligations. What additional exposure in one country adds to the risk of the portfolio depends both on the variability of the direct bilateral exchange rate and on its correlation with other exchange rates. Hence, the effect of exchange rate volatility on trade cannot be determined a priori, but is an empirical question.

If the effect of exchange rate volatility on trade is uncertain, the effect on investment flows is even more so. (In fact, we have found very little systematic published or unpublished discussion of this effect). Besides not being sure whether exchange rate volatility reduces trade, we cannot be sure, if it does, whether this effect would tend to increase or reduce international direct investment. A reduction in trade might mean more concentration on the home market by exporting firms, or it might mean that multinationals dispersed their production more completely into overseas markets and exported less from their major production plants in the home country. The first of these two cases would mean less international investment, presumably, whereas the second would mean more. This uncertainty augments the uncertainty resulting from the ambiguous effect of exchange rate volatility on trade.

This point came out clearly in a recent paper by David Cushman (1985), the one empirical article that we were able to find that deals with direct investment as a function of exchange rate volatility. Cushman notes that actual trade is more complex than simple models would suggest. Although a firm may export a good whose inputs consist exclusively of domestic goods and services, its trade may also involve intermediate goods in various ways. The effect of exchange rate volatility or other factors on the location of economic activity (i.e., on the location of value added) can, therefore, be complicated, which also complicates the analysis of investment flows. This consideration gives further scope for the effect to run in either direction.

Cushman's analysis emphasized, as did ours (Bailey, Tavlas, and Ulan 1987), that businesses or portfolio investors will balance risk against expected profit when they plan a transaction. Suppose, as Williamson (1985) suggests, that floating exchange rates result in significant "misalignments"—real exchange rates pushed out of line by temporary capital movements. Potential direct investors across national boundaries may share this view. Those who feel able to anticipate future changes of misaligned exchange rates will take this expectation into account in calculating expected and risk-adjusted rates of return (see Frankel 1985). If the profit expectation were uncorrelated with the risk, the effect of risk itself would be predictable for each transaction, taken separately. However, the Williamson argument is that misalignments are more frequent and more serious when exchange rates, freely floating, are volatile than when they are not. If so, risk will be positively correlated with expected profits for many transactions, so that the net effect is indeterminate until one has the specific numbers and the degree of risk aversion.

These points help highlight the central importance of the notion of misalignment to the analysis. If all variability of exchange rates were due to variation in the fundamentals, such as independent, unpredictable changes in monetary and fiscal policies in different countries, exchange rates would approximate a random walk. Without misalignment, there would be few opportunities for profitable anticipation, by traders or direct investors, of future exchange rate changes. Although some firms or households may believe that they can foresee shifts in such fundamentals, only in a few exceptional cases would the ability to do so be related to a firm's volume of foreign trade or investment. (Also, it would be harder to argue, as a rule, that the effects on trade and resource allocation, if any, of this type of exchange rate variability were harmful and distortive.)

Because it appears that "variability" has implicitly been almost synonymous with misalignment in much of the previous conceptual work on this issue, we have based our discussion on misalignment and on short-term volatility. With that approach, exchange rate variability can affect trade in either direction. Its effect on direct investment is still more uncertain, inasmuch as it could go in either direction even if the effect of variability were to reduce trade. With the consequences of both short-term volatility and misalignment on trade and investment conceptually uncertain, we turn to some empirical results concerning the effects of these two measures of exchange rate movements on trade and investment in the case of the United States.

## Exchange Rate Movements and U.S. Export and Investment Performance

In recent years, a number of empirical studies dealing with the post-1973 period have been produced; they examine the issue of whether short-term exchange rate volatility hampers trade. Only one study has investigated the relationship between volatility and investment. To our knowledge, not a single empirical study has examined the effects of misalignment, per se, on either trade or investment.

Most recent empirical studies have supported the proposition that short-term volatility does indeed impede trade (Cushman 1983, Akhtar and Hilton 1984, Kenen and Rodrik 1986, Maskus 1986, Thursby and Thursby 1987, and De Grauwe and de Bellefroid 1987). The coverage of these studies has been impressive: It has encompassed both total and bilateral trade flows, differences in sampling data (i.e., time series and pooled time series cross-sectional), bilateral and trade-weighted measures of exchange rates, real and nominal exchange rates, and a range of industrial countries. Studies that have rejected the hypothesis that volatility has had an adverse impact on trade include the IMF (1984), Gotur (1985), and several papers with which we have been associated—Bailey, Tavlas, and Ulan (1986); Aschheim, Bailey, and Tavlas (1987); and Bailey, Tavlas, and Ulan (1987).

In the most comprehensive of our studies—Bailey, Tavlas, and Ulan (1987)—we tested for the impact of exchange rate volatility on real exports of 11 OECD countries, using for most countries two measures of volatility for both real and nominal exchange rates.[8] In all, over the managed floating period we presented 33 regression equations. In addition to exchange rate volatility, the factors that were posited to affect exports of these countries were real GDP in partner industrial countries, real export earnings of oil-producing countries, and relative prices (defined as the ratio of the dollar-denominated export unit values of each country relative to the dollar-denominated export unit values for the IMF's "industrial country" aggregate). Of the 33 regressions estimated, only 3 showed a significant and negative impact of volatility on exports. These 3 regressions each involved real volatility. So perhaps real volatility is the culprit. Considering only those equations with real exchange rate volatility variables, that still left only 3 instances out of 16 in which exchange rate volatility negatively and significantly affected real exports.

Despite the diversity of empirical results, some generalizations can be drawn from the current status of empirical work. First, most studies (including our work) that find a significant effect for volatility on trade find it only for *real* exchange rate volatility. But as our aforementioned results indicate, even in the case of real volatility, the evidence is anything but overwhelming. Second, of the studies that do find a negative effect of exchange rate volatility on trade, most do so using bilateral trade data (e.g., Cushman 1983, Akhtar and Hilton 1984, Maskus 1986, and Thursby and Thursby 1987). Thus it may be that volatility affects the pattern of trade, but not its overall level. Regarding the aggregate trade studies that find a negative impact of volatility on trade, Kenen and Rodrik (1986) examine the effects of exchange rate volatility on imports—not exports. Still, in

[8]The countries examined were Australia, Canada, France, Germany, Italy, Japan, the Netherlands, New Zealand, Switzerland, the United Kingdom, and the United States.

only 4 of the 11 countries examined did the results show a negative and significant impact. On the other hand, De Grauwe and de Bellefroid (1987) find less ambiguous effects of volatility on exports. However, their study does not include a relative price term. In their words, "The reader may wonder why no relative price (or competitiveness) variables appear in the equation. The reason is that we concentrate here on the determinants of the long-run growth rates of trade. . . . Over very long periods . . . these relative price effects are likely to have disappeared" (De Grauwe and de Bellefroid 1987, p. 195). The theoretical motivation behind this argument escapes us. At the very least, the effect of relative prices should have been empirically tested. By failing to do so, it is likely that the results obtained by De Grauwe and de Bellefroid comingled the effects of relative prices with exchange rate volatility, obtaining an exaggerated or spurious impact for the latter.

The final generalization to be drawn from empirical work is that the primary determinants of trade are real output in trading partner countries and the terms of trade. In this context, equations (1a), (1b), and (1c) in Table 1 provide estimates on the determinants of U.S. export volumes over the managed floating rate period.[9] Equation (1a) shows that some 93 percent of the variance of real exports from the United States is explained by real output in other industrial countries, real export earnings of oil-exporting nations (a proxy for their ability to buy other nations' exports), and relative export prices between the United States and its industrial-country trading partners adjusted for exchange rate changes. (Thus, relative prices reflect real exchange rates in terms of traded goods.)[10] Equation (1b) adds the volatility of the real effective exchange rate to the previous specification. While the coefficient is negative, it is insignificant and does not change the coefficients of the other variables. Because the relative price term is adjusted for exchange rate changes, it may be that the relative price term is biasing the volatility coefficient toward zero. Accordingly, in equation (1c) we drop the relative price term while retaining the volatility term. The coefficient on the latter variable remains insignificant; meanwhile, the significance of the coefficients on the other

[9]Equations (1a) through (1c) are estimated over the quarterly period, 1975:1 through 1986:1. We began the estimation period in 1975:1 because exchange rate volatility is entered with an eight-period (i.e., two-year) lag, taking us back to 1973:1, the beginning of managed floating. We ended the estimation period in 1986:1, as export earnings of oil-exporting nations (a term in the equations) were available only through 1985:4. We were able to estimate that term through 1986:1, however, because it was entered with a one-quarter lag.

[10]See the notes to Table 1 for additional details.

*TABLE 1*

EFFECTS OF EXCHANGE RATE VARIABILITY ON U.S. EXPORT VOLUMES

| Equation | Constant | Real OECD GDP | Relative Export Prices | Real Oil Revenues | Exchange Rate Variability: Short-Term Volatility | Exchange Rate Variability: Long-Term Misalignment | Rho | $\bar{R}^2$ | D.W. | Estimation Period |
|---|---|---|---|---|---|---|---|---|---|---|
| (1a) | −2.46 | 1.05 | −0.77 | 0.11 | | | 0.62 | 0.926 | 1.70 | 1975:1–1986:1 |
| | (3.0) | (7.9) | (5.9) | (2.5) | | | (4.6) | | | |
| (1b) | −2.23 | 1.02 | −0.72 | 0.12 | −0.84 | | 0.62 | 0.923 | 1.75 | 1975:1–1986:1 |
| | (2.6) | (7.0) | (4.8) | (2.5) | (0.7) | | (4.1) | | | |
| (1c) | 0.70 | 10.55 | | 0.08 | −1.64 | | 0.89 | 0.900 | 1.73 | 1975:1–1986:1 |
| | (0.4) | (1.9) | | (1.4) | (0.9) | | (12.5) | | | |
| (1d) | −2.18 | 1.01 | −0.73 | 0.09 | | | 0.69 | 0.908 | 1.65 | 1976:1–1986:1 |
| | (1.9) | (5.5) | (4.8) | (1.8) | | | (5.1) | | | |
| (1e) | −2.24 | 1.02 | −0.78 | 0.09 | | 0.0005 | 0.67 | 0.906 | 1.67 | 1976:1–1986:1 |
| | (2.0) | (5.7) | (4.3) | (1.8) | | (0.4) | (4.8) | | | |
| (1f) | 0.54 | 0.59 | | 0.04 | | −0.0003 | 0.93 | 0.889 | 1.44 | 1976:1–1986:1 |
| | (0.2) | (1.6) | | (0.7) | | (0.2) | (16.1) | | | |

NOTES: Numbers in parentheses are t-ratios. Real OECD is real GDP (current period) in national currency units for 11 industrial-country trading partners converted to U.S. dollars at 1985:1 exchange rates. Relative prices are the dollar-denominated export-unit value index divided by the IMF's "industrial country" export-unit value series. Relative prices are entered with a two-quarter lag. Real oil revenues are the dollar value of oil exporters' export earnings (as provided by the IMF) deflated by the dollar-denominated export-unit value index of the "industrial nations" taken as a whole to represent the real purchasing power of the oil exporters as it relates to industrial-country exports. The figure is entered with a one-quarter lag. Short-term exchange rate variability is the absolute value of the quarterly percentage change in the real effective exchange rate (as constructed by Morgan Guaranty Bank). It is estimated by using an eight-period (t-1 through t-9) second-degree Almon lag. Long-term exchange rate misalignment is the deviation of the real effective exchange rate (REER) from the fundamental equilibrium exchange rate (FEER) as constructed by Williamson (1985). Williamson (1985) provides data on REER and FEER for the period 1976:1–1984:4. For 1985:1–1986:1, figures for REER and FEER have been updated by the authors, extrapolating data on the basis of figures contained in Williamson (1986). The export volume series (IMF) was seasonally adjusted using the X-11 ARIMA technique. Rho was estimated using a maximum likelihood procedure.

SOURCES: IMF, *International Financial Statistics;* Morgan Guaranty Bank; Williamson (1985, 1986); and authors' calculations.

remaining variables declines while serial correlation increases, suggesting a misspecification problem.

If short-term volatility of the exchange rate has not adversely affected U.S. exports over the managed floating period, what about exchange rate misalignment, defined as the difference between the real effective exchange rate (REER) and the real "fundamental equilibrium" exchange rate (FEER)? As Frenkel and Goldstein (1986) have noted, there is an assortment of problems associated with measuring an equilibrium exchange rate; any such measure is bound to be only an approximate one. Undaunted by the difficulties, Williamson (1986) provides estimates of the FEER and the REER over the period 1976:1 through 1984:4. We have updated Williamson's estimates of these two series by using data contained in Williamson (1986). The effects of deviations from the equilibrium exchange rate (i.e., REER minus FEER) are provided in equations (1d) through (1f). Equation (1d) is merely the specification in (1a), but it is estimated over the now shorter estimation period. Equation (1e) adds the misalignment series; the misalignment variable is insignificant and has a positive coefficient. Finally, equation (1f) drops the relative price term while retaining the misalignment variable. The latter remains insignificant; meanwhile the properties of the equation (coefficients on other variables, serial correlation) deteriorate, again suggesting that misspecification results from dropping relative prices.

As noted, with the exception of Cushman (1985), empirical work dealing with the determinants of direct investment in the U.S. economy in recent years is nonexistent.[11] Indeed, Cushman's paper dealt with bilateral direct investment outflows from the United States to five countries over the period 1963 through 1978; thus his data were drawn largely from the managed rate period. In Table 2, we present results on the determinants of aggregate direct investment inflows into the United States over the quarterly interval, 1976:1 through 1986:1 (see the notes to Table 2 for the reason why we began with 1976:1). We test for the effects of short-term exchange rate volatility and long-term misalignment on real direct investment inflows.

We use a stock adjustment model to estimate the determinants of real direct investment—manipulation of the stock adjustment model results in a lagged dependent variable as one determinant of direct investment. In addition, we posit that direct investment is determined by the expected performance of the U.S. economy (proxied

[11]Cushman (1985, p. 298) observed that "empirical work concerning exchange rate uncertainty on direct investment is rare." The few studies that Cushman was able to find were published during the 1970s.

*TABLE 2*

EFFECTS OF EXCHANGE RATE VARIABILITY ON REAL DIRECT INVESTMENT IN THE UNITED STATES (1976:1–1986:1)

| Equation | Constant | Anticipated Real GDP | Relative Export Prices | Real Interest Rate Spread | Lagged Dependent Variable | Oil Shock Dummy | Short-Term Volatility | Long-Term Misalignment | Rho 1 | Rho 2 | $\bar{R}^2$ | DW |
|---|---|---|---|---|---|---|---|---|---|---|---|---|
| (2a) | −3.00 | 0.87 | −2.95 | 0.08 | 0.54 | 0.21 | | | −0.44 | −0.40 | 0.522 | 2.03 |
| | (1.4) | (2.2) | (3.1) | (2.0) | (3.2) | (1.4) | | | (2.1) | (2.1) | | |
| (2b) | −1.15 | 0.68 | −4.00 | 0.14 | 0.49 | 0.35 | 9.45 | | −0.55 | −0.47 | 0.555 | 2.08 |
| | (0.5) | (1.9) | (3.3) | (2.4) | (3.0) | (2.1) | (1.4) | | (2.7) | (2.6) | | |
| (2c) | −3.39 | 0.81 | | −0.04 | 0.63 | 0.17 | −6.96 | | −0.36 | −0.28 | 0.411 | 1.89 |
| | (1.1) | (1.6) | | (0.9) | (3.0) | (0.8) | (1.1) | | (1.5) | (1.3) | | |
| (2d) | −2.74 | 0.93 | −4.35 | 0.06 | 0.45 | 0.27 | | 0.02 | −0.41 | −0.42 | 0.566 | 2.16 |
| | (1.4) | (2.4) | (3.5) | (1.3) | (2.5) | (1.8) | | (1.8) | (1.8) | (2.3) | | |
| (2e) | −2.00 | 0.72 | | −0.03 | 0.53 | 0.28 | | −0.001 | −0.22 | −0.20 | 0.384 | 1.85 |
| | (0.7) | (1.3) | | (0.4) | (1.9) | (1.3) | | (0.1) | (0.7) | (0.8) | | |

NOTES: Numbers in parentheses are t-ratios. Dependent variable is nominal direct investment inflow into the United States (Federal Reserve Board's flow of funds series, seasonally adjusted) divided by the GDP deflator. Anticipated real GDP was constructed by regressing the logarithm of real U.S. GDP on its past values in periods t-1 through t-13, using a second-degree Almon polynomial distributed lag with no end-point restrictions. The predicted series made by that regression was used as the anticipated series. Relative export prices are the same series used in Table 1; as with the regressions contained in Table 1, the figure is entered with a two-quarter lag in the regressions reported above. Real interest rate spread is the differential between the real average market yield on U.S. government 10-year bonds (constant maturity) and the real average yield on long-term government bonds of major U.S. trading partners. The spread series is from Data Resources, Inc., U.S. model data bank. Because it is available beginning only in 1976:1, all of the above regressions were estimated beginning in 1976:1. The oil shock dummy variable is a shift dummy representing the second oil price shock. It equals unity from 1979:2 through 1980:2, and it equals zero for all other observations. The volatility and misalignment series are the same as used in the equations in Table 1. Rho 1 and Rho 2 were estimated using a maximum likelihood procedure since the widely used Cochrane-Orcutt procedure results in inconsistent parameter estimates in the presence of lagged dependent variables (see Aschheim and Tavlas 1988). We are grateful to John Wilson of the Federal Reserve Board for providing us with the nominal direct investment series.

SOURCES: Data Resources, Inc.; Federal Reserve Board; IMF, *International Financial Statistics;* Morgan Guaranty Bank; Williamson (1985, 1986); and authors' calculations.

by "anticipated" real GDP in the United States), by real relative export prices (the same variable that was used in the equations for export volumes), by the real interest rate differential between long-term rates in the United States and those in the main trading partners of the United States, and by an oil shock term, which was aimed at capturing the effects of the oil price hike of the late 1970s. Through their effects on trade and investment, these variables also happen to be variables that help determine real exchange rates. With such variables in the equations, the regression coefficients for exchange rate variability and misalignment capture the effects of speculative errors for given fundamentals.

A general observation concerning the empirical results is that the explained proportions of the variances of the regressions are considerably below those obtained for the export equations. Equation (2a) presents our basic specification. Anticipated real GDP, the real interest rate spread series, and the lagged dependent variable all have positive (as expected) and significant coefficients. The oil price shock series also has a positive coefficient, but it is only marginally significant; the implication is that the oil price shock of the late 1970s increased direct investment into the United States either in accord with the safe-haven hypothesis or as part of the financing of the enlarged trade deficit. The relative price (real terms of trade) series has a negative coefficient (as expected) and is significant.

Equation (2b) tests for the impact of short-term exchange rate volatility on direct investment; the coefficient on the volatility variable is marginally significant—and positive. In equation (2c) we drop the relative price term in order to test whether its inclusion in equation (2b) was biasing the impact of the volatility term. (This is the same procedure that we undertook for the export equations.) The volatility term has a negative, but insignificant, coefficient in equation (2c). Finally, equations (2d) and (2c), with and without relative prices, respectively, test for the impact of the misalignment series. In equation (2d) the misalignment series is marginally significant, but with a positive coefficient. In equation (2e) it is negative and insignificant. In sum, we were unable to find any adverse impact of either exchange rate volatility or misalignment on real direct investment into the United States during the managed floating rate period.

## Conclusion

We have argued that exchange rates vary both because of long-term fundamental influences and because of speculative and other transitory influences. These influences, especially the latter, are unpredictable, and they vary more sharply at some times than others. Consequently, the volatility of exchange rates is itself variable, and one can easily understand the rationale for an international policy regime that aims to reduce it.

To the extent that the size and variance of movements in exchange rates have been unpredictable, have they also been harmful? Advocates of fixed exchange rates posit that exchange rate variations are harmful because they entail resource allocation effects on trade and investment. For the U.S. economy, our results indicate that exchange rate variations have not had significant effects on trade and direct investment. Of course, we doubt whether a fixed exchange regime would have been able to survive during a period that has included huge disturbances, such as the two oil price shocks to the world economy. Our results on investment are exploratory and may be revised if progress should be made on the difficult specification problems involved. The issue is empirical and must eventually be resolved by testing the various claims against the data.

## References

Akhtar, M., and Hilton, R. S. "Effects of Exchange Rate Uncertainty on German and U.S. Trade." Federal Reserve Bank of New York *Quarterly Review* 9 (Spring 1984): 7–16.

Artus, Jacques R., and Young, John H. "Fixed and Flexible Exchange Rates: A Renewal of the Debate." International Monetary Fund *Staff Papers* 26 (December 1979): 654–98.

Aschheim, Joseph; Bailey, Martin J.; and Tavlas, George S. "Dollar Variability, the New Protectionism, Trade, and Financial Performance." In *The New Protectionist Threat to World Welfare*. Edited by D. Salvatore. Amsterdam: North Holland, 1987.

Aschheim, Joseph, and Tavlas, George S. "Econometric Modelling of Partial Adjustment: The Cochrane-Orcutt Procedure, Flaws, and Remedies." *Economic Modelling* 5 (January 1988): 1–8.

Bailey, Martin J.; Tavlas, George S.; and Ulan, Michael. "Exchange Rate Variability and Trade Performance: Evidence for the Big Seven Industrial Countries." *Weltwirtschaftliches Archiv* 122 (1986): 466–77.

Bailey, Martin J.; Tavlas, George S.; and Ulan, Michael. "The Impact of Exchange Rate Volatility on Export Growth: Some Theoretical Considerations and Empirical Results." *Journal of Policy Modeling* 9 (Spring 1987): 225–43.

Boughton, James M. "The Monetary Approach to Exchange Rates: What Now Remains?" International Finance Section *Essays in International Finance*. Princeton: Princeton University, 1988.

Branson, William H. "Asset Markets and Relative Prices in Exchange Rate Determination." *Sozialwissenschaftlich Annalen* 1 (1977): 69–89.

Crockett, Andrew, and Goldstein, Morris. *Strengthening the International Monetary System: Exchange Rates, Surveillance, and Objective Indicators.* International Monetary Fund, Occasional Paper no. 50, 1987.

Cushman, David O. "The Effects of Real Exchange Rate Risk on International Trade." *Journal of International Economics* 15 (August 1983): 45–63.

Cushman, David. O. "Real Exchange Rate Risk, Expectations, and the Level of Direct Investment." *Review of Economics and Statistics* 67 (May 1985): 297–308.

De Grauwe, Paul, and de Bellefroid, Bernard. "Long-Run Exchange Rate Variability and International Trade." In *Real Financial Linkages among Open Economies.* Edited by Sven Arndt and J. David Richardson. Cambridge: MIT Press, 1987.

Dooley, Michael, and Isard, Peter. "Country Preferences, Currency Values, and Policy Issues." *Journal of Policy Modeling* 9 (Spring 1987): 65–82.

Dornbusch, Rudiger. "Expectations and Exchange Rate Dynamics." *Journal of Political Economy* 84 (December 1976): 1161–76.

Dornbusch, Rudiger. "Exchange Rate Economics: Where Do We Stand?" *Brookings Papers on Economic Activity* 1 (1980): 143–85.

Dornbusch, Rudiger. "Flexible Exchange Rates and Excess Capital Mobility," *Brookings Papers on Economic Activity* 1 (1986): 209–26.

Dornbusch, Rudiger. "Exchange Rate Economics: 1986." *Economic Journal* 97 (March 1987): 1–18.

Frankel, Jeffrey. *Six Possible Meanings of "Overvaluation": The 1981–85 Dollar.* Princeton Essays in International Finance. Princeton: Princeton University, 1986.

Frenkel, Jacob, and Goldstein, Morris. "A Guide to Target Zones." International Monetary Fund *Staff Papers* 33 (December 1985): 633–73.

Frenkel, Jacob, and Mussa, Michael L. "The Efficiency of Foreign Exchange Markets and Measures of Turbulence." *American Economic Review* 70 (May 1980): 374–81.

Frenkel, Jacob, and Rodriguez, Carlos. "Portfolio Equilibrium and the Balance of Payments: A Monetary Approach." *American Economic Review* 65 (September 1975): 674–88.

Goldstein, Morris. *The Exchange Rate System: Lessons of the Past and Options for the Future,* International Monetary Fund, Occasional Paper no. 30, 1984.

Gotur, Padma. "Effects of Exchange Rate Volatility on Trade: Some Further Evidence." International Monetary Fund *Staff Papers* 32 (September 1985): 475–512.

Haberler, Gottfried. "The International Monetary System and Prospects for International Policy Coordination." American Enterprise Institute, Washington, D.C., December 1986.

International Monetary Fund. *Exchange Rate Volatility and World Trade.* Occasional Paper no. 29, 1984.

Johnson, Harry. "The Case for Flexible Exchange Rates, 1969." Federal Reserve Bank of St. Louis, *Review* 51 (June 1969): 12–24.

Kenen, Peter, and Rodrik, Davis. "Measuring and Analyzing the Effects of Short-Term Volatility in Real Exchange Rates," *Review of Economics and Statistics* 68 (May 1986): 311–15.

Kouri, Pentti. "The Exchange Rate and the Balance of Payments in the Short Run and in the Long Run." *Scandinavian Journal of Economics* 78, no. 2 (1976): 280–304.

Krueger, Anne O. *Exchange Rate Determination.* Cambridge: Cambridge University Press, 1983.

Krugman, Paul R. "Is the Strong Dollar Sustainable?" Federal Reserve Bank of Kansas City *The U.S. Dollar—Recent Developments, Outlook, and Policy Options* (August 1985): 103–32.

Levich, Richard M. "Empirical Studies of Exchange Rates: Price Behavior, Rate Determination, and Market Efficiency." In *Handbook of International Economics,* vol. 2. Edited by R. W. Jones and P. B. Kenen. Amsterdam: North Holland, 1985.

Marris, Stephen. *Deficits and the Dollar: The World Economy at Risk.* Washington, D.C.: Institute for International Economics, 1985.

Maskus, K. E. "Exchange Rate Risk and U.S. Trade: A Sectoral Analysis." Federal Reserve Bank of Kansas City, *Economic Review* 71 (March 1986): 16–23.

McKinnon, Ronald. "Floating Foreign Exchange Rates, 1973–74: The Emperor's New Clothes." In *Institutional Arrangements and the Inflation Problem,* vol. 3. Edited by Karl Brunner and Allen H. Meltzer. Carnegie-Rochester Conference on Public Policy. Amsterdam: North Holland, 1976.

Mussa, Michael. "The Exchange Rate, the Balance of Payments, and Monetary and Fiscal Policy under a Regime of Controlled Floating." *Scandinavian Journal of Economics* 78, no. 2 (1976): 229–48.

Nordhaus, William D. "Statement." In *The Decline of the Dollar,* pp. 249–53. Hearings before the Subcommittee on Foreign Economic Policy. 95th Cong., 2d sess. Washington, June 1978.

Obstfeld, Maurice. "Floating Exchange Rates: Performance and Prospects." *Brookings Papers on Economic Activity* 2 (1985): 369–464.

Shafer, Jeffrey, and Loopeska, Bonnie. "Floating Exchange Rates after Ten Years," *Brookings Papers on Economic Activity* 1 (1983): 1–70.

Stockman, Alan C. "The Equilibrium Approach to Exchange Rates." Federal Reserve Bank of Richmond *Economic Review* 73 (March/April 1987a): 12–30.

Stockman, Alan C. "Exchange Rate Systems and Relative Prices." *Journal of Policy Modeling* 9 (Spring 1987b): 245–56.

Tavlas, George S. "Policy Aspects of Alternative Exchange Rate Regimes: Introduction." *Journal of Policy Modeling* 9 (Spring 1987): 1–5.

Thursby, J., and Thursby, M. "Bilateral Trade Flows, the Linder Hypothesis, and Exchange Risk." *Review of Economics and Statistics* 69 (August 1987): 488–95.

Williamson, John. *The Exchange Rate System.* Washington, D.C.: Institute for International Economics, 1985, revised.

Williamson, John. "Target Zones and the Management of the Dollar." *Brookings Papers on Economic Activity* 1 (1986): 165–74.

Yeager, Leland B. *International Monetary Relations: Theory, History, and Policy,* 2nd ed. New York: Harper and Row, 1976.

# COMMENT

# REFORMING THE EXCHANGE RATE SYSTEM*

*Maurice Obstfeld*

The title of the paper by Martin Bailey and George Tavlas gives a somewhat inaccurate picture of its contents. Trade and investment performance is a key criterion for evaluating floating exchange rates since 1973, but the discussion and new empirical evidence related to this issue come only at the end of the paper. Instead, we find a broad survey covering the theory of floating exchange rates, speculative bubbles, and risk diversification. All these issues are central to the *theory* of how exchange rate variability affects trade, so the coverage given to them in the paper is appropriate. In my comment, I will go a step further than the authors and place their results in the context of the debate over reforming the exchange rate system.

## Arguments Against Floating

When the move to floating took place over the 1971–73 period, it seemed a necessary temporary measure in the face of severe speculative pressures on the fixed exchange rate system. That "temporary" measure, however, turned out to be fairly permanent. It is in part the memory of the 1971–73 experience that has convinced most people that a return to rigidly fixed exchange rates is impracticable. Nevertheless, in recent years policymakers and economists increasingly have been asking whether there is a better way of running the exchange rate system, and whether possible improvements should involve limiting the flexibility of exchange rates.

The potential negative features of floating rates had been pointed out quite clearly before the early 1970s. These features were noticed during the interwar period and motivated the Bretton Woods conference to design a system based on fixed rates. The major arguments advanced against floating rates centered around five (overlapping) issues: discipline, the illusion of autonomy under floating rates, inter-

*Reprinted from *Cato Journal* 8 (Fall 1988): 443–49.
The author is Professor of Economics at the University of Pennsylvania.

nationally uncoordinated policies, destabilizing speculation, and injury to international trade and investment.

*Discipline*

Fixed rates served as an automatic brake on overexpansionary monetary policies, since countries whose government policies led to balance-of-payments deficits would lose international reserves and soon be forced to adjust. Under floating rates this discipline would be absent.

*The Illusion of Autonomy under Floating Rates*

Proponents of floating argued that fixed rates restricted not only license (by imposing discipline) but also liberty. Foes of floating replied that it was unrealistic to think governments would really have greater freedom to set policies in a world of floating: The exchange rate's macroeconomic effects—on inflation, income distribution, industrial structure, and so on—are so important that no government, not even the U.S. government, can allow it to be a freely determined residual of monetary and fiscal policy choices.

*Internationally Uncoordinated Policies*

Just as governments had engaged in competitive currency depreciations between the world wars, a new era of floating might lead to economic policy warfare in which individual governments, pursuing nationalistic goals, might take mutually offsetting actions harmful to the international community.

*Macroeconomic Consequences of Destabilizing Speculation*

Critics of floating thought that speculators would not be a stabilizing influence on exchange rates, but would have the opposite effect, causing wild gyrations in their individual attempts to stay a step ahead of the market's psychology. These speculative rate movements, unrelated to market fundamentals, would destabilize the trade sector and the price level.

*Injury to International Trade and Investment*

A closely related fear was that excessive exchange rate variability would discourage the international flow of goods and capital.

## Would Fixed Rates Have Performed Better?

Experience since 1973 has indicated that there is much truth in all of the negative forecasts of how floating rates would perform. What is less clear is how, and if, fixed rates would have performed better.

Consider the discipline argument, for example. It makes little sense to blame exchange rate movements for resource misallocations when faulty policies lie behind the rate movements *and* the misallocations. One should still ask, however, whether less exchange rate flexibility would have promoted better policies. An affirmative answer is hard to support. Much recent strain in the world economy has been caused by the undisciplined increase in the federal fiscal deficit under the Reagan administration. Not only did this increase contribute to dollar overvaluation up until the dollar's about-face in early 1985, it helped bring about the current stubborn pattern of trade imbalances that is a source of uncertainty and turbulence in the foreign exchange market and in other asset markets. But would less flexibility in dollar exchange rates have prevented this disastrous fiscal course? Almost certainly the answer is, No.[1]

Imagine, to take the most extreme case, a fixed dollar exchange rate. The immediate effect of the fiscal expansion would have been a large surplus in the U.S. balance of payments, hardly an event to discipline the United States. Had the Federal Reserve intervened to keep the dollar down—operations that would have led to a ballooning U.S. money supply—the result would have been inflation. This inflation would have become evident only a couple of years *after* the fiscal stimulus, but too late to have discouraged it. And we now would have the deficit *and* roaring inflation, had the Fed prevented the dollar's 1981–85 appreciation.

Alternatively, the European and Japanese central banks might have intervened to fix the dollar's exchange rate by shrinking their own money supplies. Such an approach would have been unsustainable for long, given the contractionary effect on foreign economies, and would have ended in a devaluation of their currencies against the dollar. It is hard to see why this action would have led America to modify its fiscal plans. The Johnson administration's post-1965 fiscal expansion, which many believe was the beginning of the Bretton Woods system's end, was certainly not restrained by the discipline of a fixed exchange rate.

One key caveat concerns the case in which a fiscal deficit is financed, not by borrowing, but by running the monetary printing presses. In this case a fixed exchange rate can impose discipline on fiscal policy, but once again, it need not. The current situation in Italy illustrates this point. Membership in the European Monetary System has led the Italian authorities to partially substitute bond issue for seigniorage in deficit financing. The necessity of limiting seigniorage has not

[1]See Obstfeld (1985).

tamed the deficit, however, and as a result, Italy's public debt has by now assumed alarming proportions.

The proposition that greater exchange rate variability has impeded the growth in international trade under floating rates has received very little solid empirical support, as Bailey and Tavlas document. At a very crude level, the trend growth rate of world trade in merchandise and services shows no noticeable decline after the early 1970s. Regression equations purporting to link trade volume measures to exchange rate variability yield conflicting conclusions and fail to be robust with respect to specification or choice of the variability measure. Even a reliably negative statistical correlation between variability and trade volume would be a very imperfect indicator of welfare effects. Under some circumstances international capital movements can substitute for trade, and in this connection there has been a large increase since the mid-1960s in the foreign sales of foreign affiliates of American firms.[2]

The lack of empirical support for the proposition that floating rates have impeded international trade is not surprising, because the theoretical case behind the proposition being tested by Bailey and Tavlas is slim. In particular, with regard to the impact of exchange rate variability on U.S. exports, it is unclear what the appropriate measure of the risk faced by exporters is, whether increased exchange rate variability necessarily increases that risk, and how exporters alter production and sales decisions when the risk they face increases.

Here I want to record, however, a disagreement with some arguments Bailey and Tavlas apparently make with regard to the resource misallocations that might arise under floating exchange rates. They seem to argue that the only exchange rate changes that give rise to resource misallocation are those that are not dictated by fundamentals such as monetary policy, fiscal policy, and demand conditions—only such "spurious" exchange rate changes communicate the wrong price signals. This argument would be correct in an economy that functioned smoothly and efficiently in the absence of exchange market misbehavior. But that is not the world we live in.

Perhaps the most important market imperfection is the short-run stickiness of wages and the prices of many manufactured goods.[3] In a sticky-price world, a rise in the demand for domestic money—one possible example of a change in a fundamental—causes the domestic currency to appreciate against foreign currencies, reducing domestic competitiveness and causing unemployment. This resource misal-

[2]The evidence is presented by Lipsey and Kravis (1987).

[3]Mussa (1986) makes a particularly convincing empirical case for price stickiness.

location would not occur if the price level could fall immediately to help equilibrate the home money market; but the exchange rate change is completely justified by fundamentals, and it is necessary to prevent any abnormal profit opportunities from opening up in the foreign exchange market.[4]

In fact, one of the important criteria for choosing between exchange rate systems in a world of imperfect markets revolves around the nature of the shocks hitting the economy and the resulting role of the exchange rate in promoting or discouraging an efficient use of economic resources. If most shocks originate in asset markets—as in the example of a rise in the demand for money given above—fixed exchange rates indeed do better. Under a fixed rate, an increase in money demand, rather than appreciating the currency and causing unemployment, causes an inflow of capital that raises the home money supply in line with the money demand increase. If most shocks come from the economy's demand side, however (e.g., fiscal policy shifts or shifts in the demand for home exports), a floating rate generally promotes good resource allocations by partially offsetting these shocks. In the latter type of environment, a floating exchange rate could actually reduce the risk faced by exporters. Because their effects are felt throughout the economy, it is often hard to tell where the shocks that cause fluctuations originate, in the asset markets or in the output markets; but there is evidence that both types of shock have been important. This means that a significant degree of exchange rate flexibility is warranted.

## Exchange Rate Variability and Protectionism

One important channel through which large misalignments under floating rates may lead to resource misallocations is ignored by the authors, but the channel is of great importance in our recent experience, and was perhaps the key factor in reversing the noninterventionist attitude toward exchange rates that the Reagan administration maintained until September 1985. Protracted swings in real exchange rates may strengthen the hand of those pressing the government for protection from foreign imports. While the problem is a political one, it certainly deserves attention and analysis in any study of the choice of exchange rate arrangements.

[4]This discussion does not deny, of course, that exchange rate changes unrelated to fundamentals can have adverse allocative effects.

## The Credibility Problem

A clear improvement in the functioning of the current exchange rate system would be a more cooperative mode of decisionmaking among the governments of the main industrial countries. It is far from clear, however, that such cooperation would optimally take the form of agreement on approximate exchange rate targets, the approach that apparently formed the basis of the February 1987 Louvre accord. Successive exchange rate agreements have lacked credibility in the face of persistent failures convincingly to rectify fiscal positions so as to hasten trade-balance adjustment. As exchange rate targets have been breached, governments have, in effect, looked to the market for guidance on "appropriate" exchange rate levels, while markets, in turn, have set exchange rates by trying to forecast official currency targets. Under the circumstances the market loses any anchor for long-run forecasts: Basically it is chasing its own tail. Noncredible exchange rate targets may be behind the extreme exchange rate volatility we have recently witnessed.

## Policy Imbalances and the Exchange Rate Puzzle

Participants in the debate over floating rates, as well as future historians, face the puzzle of why currencies have been so much more volatile since the early 1980s. Circumstantial evidence certainly points to the unprecedented policy imbalances characterizing the period as a major part of the story. It does not help matters that these imbalances have occurred in a setting of rapid financial innovation, a setting in which the consequences of policies became unusually hard to predict. A credible commitment to more rigid exchange rates, if possible, would probably have reduced exchange rate instability. It is not at all clear, however, that such a commitment would have led to policies better than those that still await full correction. Nor is it clear how governments could have purchased again the credibility they so clearly lacked when the Bretton Woods system broke down.

## References

Lipsey, Robert E., and Kravis, Irving B. "The Competitiveness and Comparative Advantage of U.S. Multinationals, 1957–1984." *Banca Nazionale del Lavoro Quarterly Review*, no. 161 (June 1987): 147–65.

Mussa, Michael. "Nominal Exchange Rate Regimes and the Behavior of Real Exchange Rates: Evidence and Implications." In *Real Business Cycles, Real Exchange Rates, and Actual Policies*, pp. 117–214. Edited by Karl

Brunner and Allan H. Meltzer. Carnegie-Rochester Conference Series on Public Policy 25. Amsterdam: North-Holland, 1986.
Obstfeld, Maurice. "Floating Exchange Rates: Experience and Prospects." *Brookings Papers on Economic Activity* 2 (1985): 369–450.

# 10

# Transmission of Real and Monetary Disturbances under Fixed and Floating Exchange Rates*

*Michael D. Bordo and Anna J. Schwartz*

The world economy since the 19th century has been characterized by varying degrees of interdependence. In the pre–World War I world, individual economies to a great extent were exposed to economic events in the rest of the world. Countries were linked together through trade in goods and services; flows of human, financial, and physical capital; and information transfers. World War I fundamentally contracted each of these links. That process accelerated during the interwar period, when countries sought to insulate themselves from what they perceived to be negative impulses transmitted from abroad. One of the hallmarks of the Bretton Woods years, in reaction to the interwar experience, was a drive to liberate trade and immigration flows while preserving barriers to capital flows. Although the record is mixed because of actual steps and threats of further steps to restrict the channels of transmission, a distinctive feature of the period of floating exchange rates since 1973 is said to be a high and rising degree of interdependence.

Theoretical channels of transmission differ under alternative exchange rate arrangements as well as in an open world economy, as compared with a world economy in which restrictions on international trade and capital controls are mandated. The types of theory economists have constructed reflect the differences in conditions that have arisen in the world economy, possibly in response to their

---

*Reprinted from *Cato Journal* 8 (Fall 1988): 451–72.

Michael D. Bordo is Professor of Economics at the University of South Carolina and a Research Associate of the National Bureau of Economic Research. He completed this article while Visiting Professor of Economics in the Graduate School of Industrial Administration at Carnegie-Mellon University. Anna J. Schwartz is a Research Associate at the National Bureau of Economic Research and was 1987–88 President of the Western Economic Association.

doctrines.[1] One objective of this paper is to relate the changing content of the theory of transmission to these differences. We neglect the views of "real business cycle" theorists who assert that the transmission is unaffected by exchange rate regimes or monetary forces.

Disturbances are both monetary and real in nature. They are transmitted by a number of channels, of which the most prominent is the current account of the balance of payments with effects on relative prices, output, and income, and by capital flows induced by interest rate differentials that establish interest rate equality except for differences in risk premia, taxes, or transaction costs.

Foreign exchange rate arrangements traditionally were regarded as crucial in assessing the role of transmission through various channels—transmission that occurred under fixed exchange rates and was mostly prevented when exchange rates floated. The insulation property of floating exchange rates and the expectation that monetary independence would be granted to countries that floated were key reasons for the shift to the present regime of floating. The experience of recent years, however, suggests that floating rates may not provide the degree of insulation once believed. Reasons given for interdependence under floating rates include increased capital mobility, exchange rate expectations, and policy interdependence.

This paper examines the operation of channels of transmission under fixed and floating rates according to two standard approaches: a traditional one of long standing designed for an open world economy, and the other derived from Keynesian thinking influenced by a closed world outlook associated with the interwar period. The Keynesian approach has undergone significant change since the advent of floating exchange rates. We trace the policy implications of each approach, focusing on the role each assigns to government intervention in promoting or blocking the transmission mechanism. Following a historical overview of empirical channels of transmission during the past two centuries, we conclude with a discussion of the policy lessons that the historical record suggests.

## Transmission Channels in an Open and Closed World Economy

### *Traditional Approach in an Open World Economy*

Under the conditions of the fixed exchange-rate specie standard that (in one form or another) characterized an open world economy

[1]Keynes, for example, early in his career advocated a gold exchange standard with limited intervention, but by the 1940s he proposed extensive intervention and made the case for exchange and capital controls. See Keynes ([1913] 1971, [1941] 1980).

for most of the two centuries preceding World War I, both monetary and real shocks were transmitted through the balance of payments, thereby affecting domestic money supplies, expenditure, price levels, and real income. The adjustment mechanism worked through the current account supplemented by the capital account.

An example of a monetary disturbance is the case of a large country on a specie standard, which temporarily issues fiat money to finance a war. Under fixed exchange rates, the increase in the money supply raises domestic expenditures, nominal income, and, ultimately, the price level. The rise in the domestic price level leads to an improvement in the terms of trade, but a balance-of-trade deficit results. In its trading partners, the same forces produce a balance-of-trade surplus.

The deficit is financed by a specie outflow from the inflating country to its trading partners, reducing the monetary gold stock in the former and raising it in the latter. As a consequence, in the trading partners, money supply increases, raising domestic expenditure, nominal income, and, ultimately, the price level. Depending on the relative share of the inflating country's monetary gold stock in the world total, world prices and income rise. The initial effects of monetary change may fall on real output, reflecting possible rigidities, but eventually the full effect is on the price level.

An alternative channel is price arbitrage. To the extent that the law of one price holds, the prices of traded goods are continuously equated across the world, without the need for relative prices of exports and imports to adjust. However, relative prices of traded and nontraded goods are altered.

Since the initial effects of increases in the money supply tend to lower interest rates, capital flows abroad are also a channel of transmission. A short-term capital inflow, however, may provide temporary financing of the current account deficit.

An example of a real disturbance is a new technology that exploits an existing resource, raising the expected real rate of return in the home country. Investors in other countries, with a lower real rate of interest, purchase securities issued by the home country. Under fixed exchange rates, the capital flow is financed by a specie flow from the foreign countries to the home country. The specie inflow raises the home country's money supply and price level, in turn raising the price of exports relative to the price of imports. The demand for imports in the home country rises, with a resulting transfer of real resources from the foreign to the home country.

In the long run, whether the disturbances are monetary or real, the balance of payments under fixed exchange rates returns to equilibrium. In the case of a monetary disturbance, the rise in the price level of the inflating country is reversed as its money supply contracts with a falling monetary gold stock. Specie is redistributed from the inflating country to the recipient countries. In the case of a real disturbance, both short-term capital flows from the home country to foreign countries (reverse specie flows consequent upon the higher price level in the former) and interest payments to service the capital imports will restore equilibrium.

Under floating rates, the issue of fiat money, if it continues beyond the point where all monetary gold is displaced, will force the country off the specie standard. The consequent rise in the domestic price level will manifest itself in a depreciating currency (Taussig 1917, Graham 1922). In the case of a real disturbance, capital inflows to the home country in response to the new technology will appreciate the country's currency. A negative supply shock will depreciate the country's currency, with contractionary effects on the rest of the world's goods, specie, and capital.

*Keynesian Approach to Transmission in a Closed World Economy*

A more recent and widespread view of how transmission works is the Keynesian approach developed by Meade (1951), Mundell (1968), and Fleming (1962), which was designed for those inward-looking countries of the world economy of the interwar years that were expected to behave similarly in the post–World War II era. Based on the IS-LM framework, the Mundell-Fleming model in its original version assumed Keynesian unemployment, demand-determined output short of feasible capacity utilization, and rigid wages and prices. Domestic wages, which were determined in domestic labor markets, determined domestic prices. Commodity arbitrage was neglected, and changes in exchange rates had little effect on domestic prices. Private capital outflows were held to be insufficient to finance current account imbalances. National monetary systems were assumed to be insulated. Short-term interest rates were controlled by domestic monetary authorities and were not influenced by foreign interest rates or exchange rate expectations (Kenen 1985). The model was consistent with recommendations to policymakers to restrict capital flows in the post–World War II period. The recommendations were based on the difference between transmission in the presence and in the absence of capital mobility that was featured.

Under fixed exchange rates a monetary disturbance is exemplified by an increase in the money supply in one country that lowers interest rates and raises real expenditure, including the purchase of imports. That process leads to a current account deficit at home, financed by decumulation of official reserves, and to a surplus abroad, financed by accumulation of official reserves. Real income rises both at home and abroad; the extent of its rise is determined by a multiplier, which in turn depends on the relative sizes of the marginal propensities to import and save. The home country increases its consumption of domestic plus imported goods. The output of the foreign country responds to the increased demand from abroad by an amount that exceeds the initial increase in demand. This is transmission in the absence of capital mobility. In its presence, the fall in interest rates at home leads to a capital outflow, which in turn reduces official reserves. This reserve loss then forces a contraction of the money supply, which offsets the effects on income of the initial monetary expansion. The foreign country's surplus is increased by the capital outflow from the home country, so its income is raised even more than is the case in the absence of capital mobility.

Under fixed exchange rates a real disturbance is exemplified by an increase in government expenditure in one country that raises real expenditure and income, including the demand for imports, leading to a balance-of-trade deficit at home and a surplus abroad. Real income rises in both countries through the multiplier. In both cases the balance-of-payments disequilibrium cannot be sustained. The decline in reserves in the deficit country (rise in the surplus country) will cause the domestic money supply to fall (rise), reversing the process. This is the case in the absence of capital mobility. With perfect capital mobility, the rise in real government expenditure raises the domestic interest rate, which induces a capital inflow, which in turn enhances the rise in income at home but offsets the rise in income abroad. Thus capital mobility under fixed exchange rates enhances the transmission abroad of a domestic monetary disturbance and offsets the transmission abroad of a domestic real disturbance.

Under floating exchange rates, insulation against both monetary and real shocks results, provided capital mobility is absent. An increase in the domestic money supply lowers interest rates and raises real expenditure, including the demand for imports, leading to an incipient balance-of-payments deficit at home and a surplus abroad. The home currency then depreciates, which lowers the price of domestic goods relative to the domestic price of foreign goods. Demand shifts from foreign to domestic goods, offsetting the increase in foreign income induced through the current account. Similarly, an increase in government expenditure in one country raises real expenditure, including the demand for imports, thus depreciating the exchange rate. Demand shifts from foreign to domestic goods, offsetting the increase in foreign income.

However, under floating exchange rates with perfect capital mobility, although a rise in the domestic money supply creates an incipient balance-of-payments deficit at home and surplus abroad (leading to a depreciation of the home currency), the concomitant decline in interest rates induces a capital outflow, which further depreciates the home currency. Demand for the home country's goods is thereby stimulated and demand for the foreign country's goods is reduced, raising income at home and reducing it abroad. With capital mobility, monetary expansion at home leads to a recession abroad.

Under floating exchange rates, an increase in government expenditure in one country raises real expenditure, including the demand for imports, hence depreciating the exchange rate. With capital mobility, however, the rise in interest rates induced by the increase in government expenditure leads to a capital inflow, which offsets the effect of the current account imbalance on the exchange rate. At the same time, the capital outflow from the foreign country depreciates its exchange rate, stimulating the demand for its goods. Hence real output abroad rises. Thus under floating exchange rates with perfect capital mobility, in contrast to the traditional approach, the Mundell-Fleming model predicts perverse effects on foreign countries' income from monetary disturbances in the home country and positive effects from real aggregate demand disturbances in the home country. Insulation no longer prevails.

In recent years, the Mundell-Fleming model has been modified in an attempt to correct its shortcomings (Frenkel and Razin 1987a, 1987b). These shortcomings include the failure of the model to base the money demand function and savings, the investment, and the trade balance on intertemporal optimizing behavior. Expectations in the model are static. It does not take into account country size, which is an important determinant of the effectiveness of monetary and fiscal policies. The results of a model in which capital flows alter capital stocks are different from one in which flow equilibrium alone is examined. In addition, the model ignores not only the distribution of assets and money across countries but also wealth effects. The rigid price and wage assumptions of the model have been relaxed, and the treatment of government expenditures has been broadened to distinguish financing of expenditures by taxation rather than bonds.

The original Mundell-Fleming model accordingly has been the inspiration for a host of recent models that vary some or many of its conditions. One direction of change has been to incorporate rational expectations and uncertainty in two-country general equilibrium approaches with full employment and flexible prices (Lucas 1982, Svensson 1985, Stockman and Svensson 1985). Another direction retains the assumption of sticky goods prices and demand-determined output but with proper microeconomic foundations, which are derived from optimizing behavior in a rational expectations context (Svensson and van Wijnbergen 1986). Some models assume wages that are temporarily fixed due to contract lags or wage indexation (Flood and Marion 1982). Models vary according to the degree of substitutability assumed between domestic and foreign goods and between domestic and foreign money and assets denominated in different currencies.

In addition to the choice of model assumptions, the results obtained depend on the elaboration of the character of the disturbances: anticipated or unanticipated, temporary or permanent, current or future. Does the monetary disturbance originate on the supply side or on the demand side? Is it a domestic or foreign disturbance? Is the real disturbance created by a supply rather than a demand disruption? (Fischer 1976)

With such an array of variables, it is no simple task to summarize the effects on transmission under fixed or floating exchange rates. The current state of the art reflects the ingenuity of the investigator in ringing changes on the original or modified versions already reported.

How complicated the analysis becomes, even when limited to two effects of transmission, may be illustrated by the question of whether a foreign country is benefited or harmed by high interest rates in the United States (Corden 1985). The answer depends in part on whether the foreign country is a net creditor or debtor, which must be considered in relation to a terms-of-trade effect. Terms of trade might deteriorate for the period during which additional capital flows from the foreign country to the United States—the channel of transmission that generates a current account surplus. Although a worsened terms of trade would be adverse, the gain to the foreign country as a net creditor at a variable interest rate, thanks to its capital exports, would be offsetting. The total effect of transmission is thus not easy to determine even in theory.

In addition to the modifications of the Mundell-Fleming model in the recent literature, analyses of floating exchange rates have proposed at least two channels of transmission that have not been recognized in that literature. One channel is possible interdependence of money demand through direct currency substitution (Miles 1978, Brittain 1981) and indirect currency substitution: the substitution of foreign and domestic assets, which in turn are close money substitutes (McKinnon 1982). The other channel is interdependence of money supply through policy reaction functions that incorporate exchange rates and foreign interest rates (McKinnon 1982) or through buffer stock effects (Bordo, Choudhri, and Schwartz 1987).

Direct transmission of real disturbances under floating has also been proposed (Swoboda 1979). Examples are a fall in expected rates of return on investment in an important foreign country as well as at home, an increase in uncertainty at home and abroad, and changes in prospective profitability for a large industrial sector at home and abroad. Direct transmission is also possible when international capital flows are interrupted for domestic reasons from the countries of outflows.

Whether the theoretical effect of international transmission is positive or negative is thus ambiguous. The results obtained appear to reflect the model-builders' priors.

## Policy Implications of the Two Approaches with Respect to Intervention

In efforts to block transmission, governments and central banks have engaged in intervention to a limited extent under fixed exchange rates and more extensively under floating exchange rates when insulation was regarded as porous.

### *Intervention under the Traditional Approach*

Under the traditional gold standard model, the only role for monetary policy was observance of the "rules of the game" by the central bank—to facilitate internal adjustment to a balance-of-payments deficit or surplus. In the case of a current account deficit (surplus), the prescription was to contract (expand) the domestic money supply. (How faithfully the prescription was followed will be examined in the historical-overview section.) Before 1914 intervention was not extensive. In the interwar regime of the gold exchange standard, it was the rule rather than the exception.

Before 1914, when governments were expected to balance their budgets, national fiscal policy did not entail adjustments that were conventionally considered necessary for monetary policy. Worldwide peacetime fiscal policy did not usually veer from budget balance. In the interwar gold exchange standard regime, concern to avoid budget deficits as inflationary gradually diminished as theory shifted to according government expenditure and tax policy primacy over monetary policy. Intervention in exchange and capital markets and the imposition of controls were legitimized.

### *Intervention under the Keynesian Approach*

Under fixed exchange rates, according to the Mundell-Fleming model, with perfect capital mobility, monetary policy in a small, open economy has no effect on the rest of the world. The larger the economy, the greater will be the impact of its monetary policy on the rest of the world. The result is qualified by the immobility of factors of production, imperfect substitution of assets, and lags in adjustment (Mussa 1979). Under fixed rates, however, monetary disturbances are imported from abroad, establishing the case for sterilization of reserve flows in the short run and, ultimately, the abandonment of fixed rates to achieve monetary independence.

Under floating rates with perfect capital mobility, monetary disturbances can produce perverse effects on foreign countries' incomes, while fiscal policy changes produce positive effects. Capital flows link interest rates in different countries, thereby preventing independent manipulation of interest rates by any one country to achieve its own domestic macroeconomic goals. These results underlie the case for coordinated intervention (Fischer 1987).

Other arguments for intervention in exchange markets are the prevention of exchange rate turbulence and overshooting, offsetting wide swings of exchange rates, and inflationary effects of exchange rate depreciation (John Williamson 1983, Frenkel and Mussa 1980).

Under fixed exchange rates, intervention to prevent effective transmission eventually involves resorting to exchange and capital controls and other forms of protectionism.[2] Under floating rates, intervention is designed to protect export-market shares when the exchange rate appreciates and to preclude inflation when the exchange rate depreciates. This course ignores the fact that movements in exchange rates and prices are a consequence of the choices that countries make with respect to monetary policy, public sector expenditures and taxes, protection of property rights, and regulation. Intervention under floating rates shifts adjustment away from the exchange rate back to the real economy, abandoning the benefits of floating.

### *The Case for and against Policy Coordination*

The case for policy coordination under fixed exchange rates was based on inconsistency of Phillips curve ambitions of individual nations or, for fiscal policy, incompatibility of independent policy. Policies adopted for their impacts on domestic targets would spill over to affect policy instruments or targets of other countries. There are externalities. To rectify the effects of externalities, countries

[2]A deficit country following a policy of sterilization ultimately will be drained of international reserves. In this predicament, such countries sometimes opt for dual exchange rates and controls on capital export. In a surplus country, the accumulation of international reserves will produce inflationary pressure. Controls on capital inflow are a likely response.

would have an incentive to trade off policies (Caves 1968). Policy harmonization thus would promote efficient adjustment by all countries in maintaining fixed exchange rates.

Another argument, based on game theory, was that nations following their own objectives in a regime of fixed exchange rates would not achieve optimal results in an interdependent world. One model demonstrated that if two countries tried to achieve, for instance, balance-of-payments surpluses to increase their international reserves in excess of the growth of world reserves, monetary policy in a noncooperative solution would be more contractionary and inflation rates would be lower than desired. The result would be avoided in a cooperative solution (Hamada 1979).

Under floating rates with capital mobility, the case for policy coordination also rests on spillover effects of monetary and fiscal policies. Again game theory has been introduced to show that coordination can yield better results than independent national policies. It has been used to suggest that decentralized decisionmaking in a floating rate world will lead to excessive economic contraction in response to an exogenous world supply shock (Cooper 1985).

The game-theoretic analysis of policy coordination treats countries as if they were persons, bypassing the question of how to coordinate capital flows and other transactions involving decisions by many agents.[3] The main problem with this approach, however, is the lack of agreement in the literature on the effects of alternative policies. It is not clear whether the difference among the models on the theoretical size and sign of gains from coordination arises from special assumptions or from the need to modify the models to make estimation tractable. Measures of spillover effects, moreover, are not overwhelming (Fischer 1987). If there are negative spillover effects, the likely reason is that domestic policies from which they originate are misguided.

If policymakers in a floating exchange rate world cannot agree on the cause of current values of real exchange rates or real interest rates or the consequences of policy actions either domestically or internationally, what possible guidance can game-theoretic analysis give?

A cynical justification offered for policy coordination is that it is politically advantageous to adduce foreign considerations to lessen opposition to unpopular domestic policies. A special case for international monetary coordination to achieve exchange rate stability has been proposed by McKinnon (1984). Coordination in his view requires

[3]We are indebted to Allan H. Meltzer for this insight.

offsetting U.S. money growth rates vis-à-vis those of Germany and Japan.

Advocates of policy coordination sometimes have as their real goal agreement by participating countries on a system of pegged exchange rates. They do not face up to the fact that the costs of the restoration of fixed exchange rates may well exceed the benefits of overcoming negative spillovers through policy coordination.

Policy coordination as a proposal to improve the international monetary system is visionary. As long as there are separate countries, each with its own currency and its own economic objectives, conflicts of interest are inevitable. Theoretical demonstrations of improved outcomes when national interests are submerged for the projected greater common good have had little practical success because they ignore the vested interest of politicians in safeguarding their home country sovereignty.

## Historical Overview of Empirical Channels of Transmission

### *The Classical Gold Standard*

Many examples may be cited of transmission of both monetary and real disturbances during the 19th century, when major countries adhered to the gold standard. A prime example of monetary transmission is the analysis by Cairnes and Jevons of the 19th-century gold discoveries in Australia and California. (There are elements of a real disturbance in gold discoveries, which we neglect here.) They demonstrated how increased gold output altered money supplies, expenditures, and prices in country after country in the manner predicted by Hume and Ricardo (Bordo 1975; Laidler 1982; for a counter view, see Glasner 1985).

A frequent case of a pure monetary disturbance with domestic effects transmitted abroad was the Bank of England's action of raising the Bank Rate (1837–38, 1857, 1890) to stem a drain of its gold reserves. The rapid curtailment of capital flows precipitated financial stringency and, on occasion, panic in peripheral countries such as, for example, the United States in 1838 (Levy-Leboyer 1982) and Australia in 1890 (Kindleberger 1984).

Monetary-induced business cycles were transmitted through the specie standard from Great Britain to the United States before the Civil War and in the reverse direction thereafter (Huffman and Lothian 1984). In addition, financial crises including stock market crashes and bank runs occurred nearly simultaneously in numerous countries linked together under the classical gold standard (Bordo 1986). Evidence linking financial market disturbances through interest-rate arbitrage is documented (Morgenstern 1959).

Real shocks, such as harvest failures in England, had consequences on numerous other countries closely linked to gold. The shocks were transmitted through the current account and the Bank of England reaction to an external drain (Dornbusch and Frenkel 1984).

The transfer of real resources associated with long-term capital flows is an important theme in the economic development of the United States (Jeffrey Williamson 1963); Australia (Butlin 1962, Cairncross 1953); Argentina (Ford 1962); and Canada (Viner 1924). Long-term capital flows, however, were subject to decisions by the exporting countries to redirect capital from one part of the world to another or to reduce or halt the flow, with consequent disruption of investment plans in the affected capital importers.

Viner's analysis of the adjustment mechanism in Canada in 1900–13 is still regarded as the classic description. According to Viner, an investment boom, consequent on the opening of the prairies by railroad construction, was financed by long-term capital flows from the United States and the United Kingdom. The capital inflows were accompanied by a specie inflow that raised the reserves of the Canadian banking system. The increase in the money supply, domestic price level, and terms of trade that followed produced a balance-of-trade deficit allowing a real transfer of goods. Debate continues over the question of whether the rise in prices was related to the investment boom rather than the increase in bank reserves (Ingram 1957, Rich 1989, Dick and Floyd 1987).

Emigration and immigration characterized the pre-1914 world, with real effects on housing demand and supply and on wages and incomes in countries losing and gaining population (Thomas 1973).

Whether the channels of transmission under the classical gold standard invariably operated as theory prescribed is doubtful. Central banks did not systematically follow the rules of the game but periodically engaged in sterilization to shield the domestic money supply from external disequilibrium (Bloomfield 1959). Sterilization, however, was possible only as a temporary maneuver. In the case of a balance-of-payments deficit, sterilization was bounded by the stock of international reserves that the central bank held, and in the case of a surplus, by changes in domestic credit. In most cases before 1914, as noted, intervention was never extensive enough to threaten convertibility.

### *The Greenback Episode, 1862–78*

From 1862 through 1878, the U.S. greenback dollar floated against the British pound and other European currencies that were on a specie standard. Graham (1922) analyzed the balance-of-payments adjustment mechanism during the greenback episode. According to him, heavy capital inflows, such as occurred from 1863 to 1873, reduced the premium on gold (the price of foreign exchange) and their cessation raised it. Moreover, the relative price of exports, imports, and domestic goods changed as the dollar depreciated, as predicted by classical theory. The relative price adjustment differed, as predicted, from that occurring under the gold standard. Huffman and Lothian (1984, pp. 471–75, 478) provide evidence of insulation from foreign disturbances during this period: A pronounced cyclical downturn in the United Kingdom in 1866 was not reflected in the United States, while the severe contraction of 1873 in the United States had little impact on the United Kingdom.

*The Gold Exchange Standard*

Irving Fisher (1935) first clearly stated the case that the Great Depression was transmitted from the United States to the rest of the world by the gold standard, and he gave evidence of insulation from declining income and prices in countries not linked to gold. Confirmation for a number of European countries of Fisher's insight is found in Choudhri and Kochin (1980). The depression was transmitted through relative price and income effects. The gold exchange standard did not survive the gold hoarding policies of the United States and France, and it misaligned exchange rates (an overvalued pound and an undervalued French franc). Universal sterilization (Nurkse 1944) exacerbated the effects of inappropriate policies in the United States and France (Eichengreen 1987).

*Bretton Woods*

The Bretton Woods fixed exchange rate system provided ample evidence of transmission of monetary shocks. Michael Darby, James Lothian, et al. (1984) show, based on simulations of their eight-country model, over the period of 1955 to 1976 that U.S. monetary policy was responsible for transmitting inflationary shocks from country to country. The dominant mechanism of transmission, they find, was a variant of the Humean mechanism through changes in relative prices and capital flows. They also find that other channels including currency substitution and direct income effects were negligible. Though the seven countries other than the United States maintained some short-run control over domestic monetary policy by sterilization, the dominant impulse originated in the United States.

As for transmission of real shocks under the Bretton Woods system, the main one on which empirical evidence exists is the effect of a shift in foreign demand for the home country's output. The finding is that distributed lag coefficients on real export shocks in a real income equation are insignificant in the sample of countries studied by Darby, Lothian, et al. (1984), with the possible exceptions of the United Kingdom and Canada.

*Canada's Experience under Floating Exchange Rates, 1950–62*

To avoid the inflationary consequences of a massive capital inflow, Canada shifted to a floating exchange rate in 1950. The evidence on insulation in this episode is mixed. Paul Wonnacott (1965, pp. 78–79) reports a decline in the average amplitude of cycles relative to U.S. cycles in the 1950s compared to the interwar period (1946–54 vs. 1929–39). He provides limited evidence of monetary independence in the trends of short-term interest rates. However, he concludes that Canada's success at stabilization policy during the floating rate period may have stemmed from following conservative monetary and fiscal policies not dissimilar to those in the United States. Using spectral analysis, on the other hand, Bonomo and Tanner (1972) find little evidence of reduced Canadian cyclical sensitivity to U.S. cycles in the 1950s.

*Floating Rates since 1973*

Since the advent of general floating in 1973, evidence has been presented of increased independence of monetary policy and a tendency for long-run independence in the movements of nominal magnitudes (interest rates and price levels). However, there is also evidence of increased short-run interdependence of nominal and real magnitudes (Darby and Lothian 1989).

Among the factors accounting for the high degree of short-run interdependence are the reaction to common real shocks, such as the oil price shocks of 1974 and 1979; increased capital mobility (Fischer 1987); and the presence of foreign variables in policy reaction functions in different countries (Hodgman 1983). Interdependence has been related to changes in world commodity supplies: oil in 1974 and 1979, sugar in 1973–74, and grain in 1972–73 (Cooper 1986). Presumably, similar changes also characterized earlier periods in economic history.

The international money multiplier—the response of foreign money growth to U.S. money growth—has been cited as contributing to interdependence (McKinnon 1984): World depression results when the exchange value of the dollar appreciates and growth in world money contracts; world inflation results when the exchange value of the dollar depreciates and world money increases. Likewise, with an increase in the dollar exchange rate, debt-service payments in dollars of debtor countries become more burdensome, and the reverse for a decrease in the dollar exchange rate.

Fiscal policy interdependence, as predicted by the Mundell-Fleming model, is generally taken for granted. U.S. fiscal expansion since 1982 is implicated in producing an increase in real interest rates that attracted foreign capital and created a demand for dollar securities. The capital inflow caused a dollar appreciation and, by drawing capital out of foreign economies, raised interest rates abroad too. High real U.S. interest rates and a high real interest rate differential between the United States and the rest of the world produced the dollar appreciation. The evidence is an annual regression of the dollar-DM exchange rate, 1973–84, on a five-year foward-looking measure of the U.S. budget deficit and other variables including money growth and inflation forecasts. The budget deficit in this regression has the most explanatory power (Feldstein 1986).

Several problems with this mainstream view cast doubt on the fiscal channel. The domestic link between fiscal deficits and real interest rates has not been established (Evans 1986, Mascaro and Meltzer 1983). In any event, the rate of interest is not set by the market for the flow of new debt, but for the existing stock of debt. Through early 1985, dollar investment opportunities were more advantageous than foreign investments, thanks to favorable tax provisions. Combined with declining U.S. inflation, the investment opportunities stimulated the rise in foreign demand for dollars. The U.S. experience of 1982–85 is not an exception to the historical inverse relationship between fiscal deficits and the external strength of a currency. The depreciation of the dollar since early 1985 is inconsistent with the commonly held view that high budget deficits drive up the U.S. dollar. The depreciation since 1985 reflects a lower foreign demand for dollars in view of weaker U.S. real growth and less favorable tax provisions.

The fiscal deficit approach ignores effects related to the stock of government debt, to the use of resources for consumption or investment arising from government expenditure and tax policies, and to the effects of increased monetary uncertainty that accompanied the growth in the fiscal deficit.

Nevertheless, the available evidence on transmission focuses on fiscal shocks. Using simulations for a number of multicountry econometric models, Stanley Fischer (1987) shows that fiscal shocks in the United States have positive significant and lasting effects on real income in U.S. major trading partners, although the reverse effect from foreign fiscal shocks on the United States is negligible. However, there is great diversity of views among the individual empirical models. One finds that a bond-financed increase in U.S. government spending leads to a small negative effect on output at home and abroad, while another obtains strong positive effects (Minford 1985, Oudiz and Sachs 1985).

There is even greater diversity of views among the individual models with respect to the effects of monetary expansion than with respect to the effects of fiscal expansion. Expansionary U.S. monetary policy leads to worsened current accounts of the United States and OECD countries, and presumably improved current accounts of non-OECD countries, according to Fischer's simulations of 12 models. Again, one model reports strong positive spillover effects of monetary expansion in the United States; the other, small negative effects.

The conclusion that emerges is that little firm evidence exists on the actual effects of transmission under the present floating exchange rate system. Theory can outline the mechanisms of transmission, but with no agreed-upon econometric model, the results are far from established. Moreover, theory distinguishes between fixed and floating exchange rate regimes. The quantitative effects, however, are estimated for the actual world. The results showing interdependence may not be a contradiction of theory. Since the post-1973 regime cannot be characterized as a pure float, much of the interdependence may be a consequence of policy management and U.S. policy instability.

## Lessons from History

The chief difference between the pre-1914 world and the world we now know is that the former was characterized by a relatively free international flow of factors and goods. Countries did not then believe that they had the leeway to resist the adjustments required to maintain gold convertibility. Countries accepted the burden (discipline) of fixed exchange rates. Higher priority was assigned to maintenance of external balance than to stabilizing the internal level of prices and income. In the gold exchange regime and the Bretton Woods system that followed, intervention was widely accepted as needed to achieve domestic economic objectives. That concern has carried over into the current floating regime.

In the past, under fixed exchange rates, the channels of transmission were mainly shifts in foreign demand for the home country's output, changes in international commodity supplies, arbitrage because of substitutability in goods and financial assets among countries, and international money flows (gold or foreign exchange) that bridged the gap between imports and exports. Monetary contraction in response to a current account deficit was not unusual. An imbalance on current account could, however, be fully offset by a flow of short-term capital to a deficit country experiencing a boom and a higher interest rate than elsewhere.

Long-term capital flows under fixed exchange rates from a country with surplus savings to a country with a deficit of savings relative to investment opportunities was another channel of transmission. If capital flows shifted from one country to another, the results were cyclical contraction in the country from which capital was withheld and cyclical expansion in the country to which capital was redirected. Human capital flows could have a similar effect, stimulating the country of inflows and depressing the country of outflows. Under fixed exchange rates, deficit-country money supplies, domestic demand, real output, and prices had to fall, while interest rates rose; surplus-country money supplies, domestic demand, real output, and prices had to rise, while real interest rates fell. Investment declined in deficit countries and rose in surplus countries. None of these influences on domestic demand were expected to occur if imbalances in international payments on current account were corrected by movements in exchange rates.

In recent analyses of the floating exchange rate system, this conclusion does not hold. The reason is that the analysis takes for granted slow adjustment to monetary change of prices and wages, so while the nominal exchange rate adjusts rapidly to policy changes, wages and prices do not; hence the real exchange rate moves closely with the nominal one. Since the real exchange rate determines the profitability of exports, foreign countries are thought to be quickly affected by changes in it. In addition, as prices of imports change, so do overall price indexes.

Whether price and wage stickiness is as pervasive as is assumed is not examined in current analyses. More rapid inflation should shorten the time between price revisions, and large monetary shocks should induce more agents to revise their nominal prices in a given period.

Despite the emphasis in current analyses on sluggish wage and price adjustment, the effects of exchange rate changes on domestic inflation are supposed to be quickly transmitted. Therefore, depreciation of the currency leads to an increase in the prices of imports and an increase in wage claims as exports become more profitable and increase aggregate demand. Why should the response of wages and prices to exchange rate changes be more rapid than to monetary changes?

Especially under floating exchange rates, expectations of policy decisions affecting interest rates, asset prices, and exchange rates are given an important role as a channel of transmission. Much has been made of this channel in recent analyses, focusing in particular on U.S. policy decisions. One problem is that expectations of similar policy decisions in other countries do not match the effects assumed to occur in the United States.

The role of expectations with respect to fiscal policy has been especially prominent in recent discussion. Current analysis of channels of transmission pays much attention to fiscal influences. This emphasis was not present in discussions of either the pre-1914 gold standard or the Bretton Woods system.

Though we can state confidently that one obvious international interaction is widely recognized—the current accounts of both oil-importing and oil-exporting countries are affected by OPEC pricing decisions—we conclude that, more generally, our understanding of international interactions is limited both theoretically and empirically. The effects of transmission are diverse, and our ability to measure them is primitive. Moreover, if economists cannot agree on the links among variables domestically, the extent of spillover of these connections to the rest of the world is even more doubtful.

The exercises in model building that have occupied specialists in international economics seem designed to impress readers with the ingenuity of the effort rather than the value of the analytical contribution. The theoretical predictions in many cases conflict because they are model specific. Similarly, the empirical evidence on channels of transmission based on these theories has not yet resulted in a consensus. This suggests that policy advice, particularly with respect to support for exchange market intervention and policy coordination, should be forsworn.

The reasons for the massive swings in the dollar exchange rate—depreciation in 1977–79, appreciation from the summer of 1980 through the first quarter of 1985, and depreciation thereafter—are not well understood by economists. Disillusionment by some with floating exchange rates, however, has prompted proposals to fix or manage them.

Fluctuations in real exchange rates, however, do not imply instability. Output and prices are not more variable in the United States under floating than under fixed exchange rates. In Germany and Japan output and prices are more stable than in the United States because their policies are more stable. If markets are not permitted to adjust exchange rates freely, adjustment will take place in other markets: debt, equity, commodity, labor, money. A change in exchange rates may have lower costs of adjustment than a change in wholesale prices.

A preference for one's own economic objectives seems to characterize the nations of the world. A stable international order is achievable with a floating rate system that provides independence to pursue stable domestic policies consistent with that preference. For international economic stability, policy coordination is neither necessary nor attainable.

## References


Bloomfield, Arthur I. *Monetary Policy under the International Gold Standard.* New York: Federal Reserve Bank of New York, 1959.

Bonomo, Vittorio, and Ernest, Tanner J. "Canadian Sensitivity to Economic Cycles in the United States." *Review of Economics and Statistics* 54 (February 1972): 1–8.

Bordo, Michael D. "John E. Cairnes on the Effects of the Australian Gold Discoveries, 1851–73: An Early Application of the Methodology of Positive Economics." *History of Political Economy* 7 (Fall 1975): 337–59.

Bordo, Michael D. "Financial Crises, Banking Crises, Stock Market Crashes, and the Money Supply: Some International Evidence, 1870–1933." In *Financial Crises and the World Banking System*, pp. 190–248. Edited by F. Capie and G. E. Wood. London: Macmillan, 1986.

Bordo, Michael D.; Choudhri, Ehsan U.; and Schwartz, Anna J. "The Behavior of Money Stock under Interest Rate Control." *Journal of Money, Credit, and Banking* 19 (May 1987): 181–97.

Brittain, Bruce. "International Currency Substitution and the Apparent Instability of Velocity in Some Western European Economies and the United States." *Journal of Money, Credit, and Banking* 13 (May 1981): 135–55.

Butlin, Noel G. *Australian Domestic Product, Investment, and Foreign Borrowing, 1861–1938/39.* Cambridge: Cambridge University Press, 1962.

Cairncross, Alec. *Home and Foreign Investment, 1870–1913.* Cambridge: Cambridge University Press, 1953.

Caves, Richard E. "Comments on Niehans and Jones." *Journal of Political Economy* 76 (July/August 1968): 946–50.

Choudhri, Ehsan U., and Kochin, Levis A. "The Exchange Rate and the International Transmission of Business Cycle Disturbances." *Journal of Money, Credit, and Banking* 12 (Part I, November 1980): 565–74.

Cooper, Richard N. "Economic Interdependence and Coordination of Economic Policies." In *Handbook of International Economics*, vol. 2, pp. 1195–1234. Edited by R. W. Jones and P. B. Kenen. Amsterdam: North-Holland, 1985.

Cooper, Richard N. "The United States as an Open Economy." In *How Open is the U.S. Economy?* pp. 3–24. Edited by R. W. Hafer. Lexington: Heath, 1986.

Corden, W. Max. "On Transmission and Coordination under Flexible Exchange Rates." In *International Economic Policy Coordination*, pp. 8–24. Edited by W. H. Buiter and R. C. Marston. Cambridge: Cambridge University Press, 1985.

Darby, Michael R.; Lothian, James R.; et al. *The International Transmission of Inflation*. Chicago: University of Chicago Press, 1984.

Darby, Michael R., and Lothian, James R. "The International Transmission of Inflation Afloat." In *Money, History and International Finance: Essays in Honor of Anna J. Schwartz*, pp. 203–36. Edited by M. D. Bordo. Chicago: University of Chicago Press, 1989.

Dick, Trevor J. O., and Floyd, John E. "Canada and the Gold Standard, 1871–1913." Toronto, July 1987. Mimeographed.

Dornbusch, Rudiger, and Frenkel, Jacob A. "The Gold Standard and the Bank of England in the Crisis of 1847." In *A Retrospective on the Classical Gold Standard, 1821–1931*, pp. 233–64. Edited by M. D. Bordo and A. J. Schwartz. Chicago: University of Chicago Press, 1984.

Eichengreen, Barry. "Trade Deficits in the Long Run." In *U.S. Trade Deficit: Causes, Consequences, and Cures*. Edited by A. E. Burger. Norwell, Mass.: Kluwer Academic Publishers, 1989 (in press).

Evans, Paul. "Is the Dollar High Because of Large Budget Deficits?" *Journal of Monetary Economics* 18 (November 1986): 227–49.

Feldstein, Martin. "The Budget Deficit and the Dollar." In *NBER Macroeconomics Annual 1986*, pp. 355–92.

Fischer, Stanley. "Comment on R. Dornbusch." *Scandinavian Journal of Economics* 78 (1976): 276–79.

Fisher, Stanley. "International Macroeconomic Policy Coordination." NBER Working Paper 2244, May 1987.

Fisher, Irving. "Are Booms and Depressions Transmitted Internationally through Monetary Standards?" *Bulletin of the International Statistical Institute* 28, no. 2 (1935): 1–29.

Fleming, John M. "Domestic Financial Policies under Fixed and under Floating Exchange Rates." *IMF Staff Papers* 9 (November 1962): 369–79.

Flood, Robert P., and Marion, Nancy P. "The Transmission of Disturbances under Alternative Exchange-Rate Regimes with Optimal Indexing." *Quarterly Journal of Economics*, 97 (February 1982): 43–66.

Ford, Alec G. *The Gold Standard, 1880–1914: Britain and Argentina*. Oxford: Clarendon Press, 1962.

Frenkel, Jacob A., and Mussa, Michael. "The Efficiency of Foreign Exchange Markets and Measures of Turbulence." *American Economic Review* 70 (May 1980): 374–81.

Frenkel, Jacob A., and Razin, Assaf. *Fiscal Policies and the World Economy*. Cambridge: MIT Press, 1987a.

Frenkel, Jacob A., and Razin, Assaf. "The Mundell-Fleming Model a Quarter Century Later: A Unified Exposition." *IMF Staff Papers* 34 (December 1987b): 567–620.

Glasner, David. "A Reinterpretation of Classical Monetary Theory." *Southern Economic Journal* 52 (July 1985): 46–67.

Graham, Frank D. "International Trade under Depreciated Paper: The United States, 1862–79." *Quarterly Journal of Economics* 36 (February 1922): 220–73.

Hamada, Koichi. "Macroeconomic Strategy and Coordination under Alternative Exchange Rates." In *International Economic Policy: Theory and Evidence*, pp. 292–324. Edited by R. Dornbusch and J. A. Frenkel. Baltimore: Johns Hopkins University Press, 1979.

Hodgman, Donald, ed. *The Political Economy of Monetary Policy: National and International Aspects*. Federal Reserve Bank of Boston Conference Series, no. 26, 1983.

Huffman, Wallace E., and Lothian, James R. "The Gold Standard and the Transmission of Business Cycles, 1833–1932." In *A Retrospective on the Classical Gold Standard, 1821–1931*, pp. 455–507. Edited by M. D. Bordo and A. J. Schwartz. Chicago: University of Chicago Press, 1984.

Ingram, James C. "Growth in Capacity and Canada's Balance of Payments." *American Economic Review* 47 (March 1957): 93–104.

Kenen, Peter B. "Macroeconomic Theory and Policy: How the Closed Economy was Opened." In *Handbook of International Economics*, vol. 2, pp. 625–77. Edited by R. W. Jones and P. B. Kenen. Amsterdam: North-Holland, 1985.

Keynes, J. M. *The Collected Writings of John Maynard Keynes*. Vol. 1, *Indian Currency and Finance*. Vol. 25, *Activities 1940–44: Shaping the Post-War World: The Clearing Union*. Edited by E. Johnson and D. Moggridge. Macmillan, [1913] 1971, [1940–44] 1980.

Kindleberger, Charles P. "International Propagation of Financial Crisis in the Experience of 1888–93." In *International Capital Movements, Debt, and the Monetary System*. Edited by W. E. Engel et al. Mainz: Hase and Koehler Verlag, 1984.

Laidler, David. "Jevons on Money." *The Manchester School* 50 (4) (December 1982): 326–53.

Levy-Leboyer, Maurice. "Central Banking and Foreign Trade: The Anglo-American Cycle in the 1830s." In *Financial Crises: Theory, History and Policy*. Edited by C. P. Kindleberger and J. P. Laffargue. Cambridge: Cambridge University Press, 1982.

Lucas, R. E., Jr. "Interest Rates and Currency Prices in a Two-Country World." *Journal of Monetary Economics* 10 (November 1982): 335–60.

Mascaro, Angelo, and Meltzer, Allan H. "Long- and Short-Term Interest Rates in a Risky World." *Journal of Monetary Economics* 12 (November 1983): 485–518.

McKinnon, Ronald. "Currency Substitution and Instability in the World Dollar Standard." *American Economic Review* 72 (June 1982): 320–33.

McKinnon, Ronald. *An International Standard for Monetary Stabilization*. Institute for International Economics, 1984.

McKinnon, Ronald; Radcliffe, C.; Tan, Kong-Yam; Warga, A. D.; and Willett, Thomas D. "International Influences on the U.S. Economy: Summary of an Exchange." *American Economic Review* 74 (December 1984): 1132–34.

Meade, James. *The Theory of International Policy*, vol. 1 (Supplement), *The Balance of Payments*. 1951. Reprint. New York: Oxford University Press, 1965.

Miles, M. A. "Currency Substitution, Flexible Exchange Rates, and Monetary Independence." *American Economic Review* 68 (June 1978): 428–36.

Minford, Patrick. "The Effects of American Policies—A New Classical Interpretation." In *International Economic Policy Coordination*, pp. 84–130. Edited by W. H. Buiter and R. C. Marston. Cambridge: Cambridge University Press, 1985.

Morgenstern, Oskar. *International Financial Transactions and Business Cycles*. Princeton: Princeton University Press, 1959.

Mundell, Robert A. *International Economics*. New York: Macmillan, 1968.

Mussa, Michael. "Macroeconomic Interdependence and the Exchange Rate Regime." In *International Economic Policy*, pp. 160–204. Edited by R. Dornbusch and J. A. Frenkel. Baltimore: The Johns Hopkins Press, 1979.

Nurkse, Ragnar. *International Currency Experience*. 1944. Reprint. New York: Arno Press, 1978.

Oudiz, Gilles, and Sachs, Jeffrey. "International Policy Coordination in Dynamic Macroeconomic Models." In *International Economic Policy Coordination*, pp. 274–319. Edited by W. H. Buiter and R. C. Marston. Cambridge: Cambridge University Press, 1985.

Rich, George. *The Cross of Gold: Money and the Canadian Business Cycle, 1867–1913*. Ottawa: Carleton Library, 1989.

Stockman, Alan C., and Svensson, Lars. "Capital Flows, Investment, and Exchange Rates." NBER Working Paper, no. 1598, *1985*.

Svensson, Lars E. O. "Currency Prices, Terms of Trade, and Interest Rates: A General-Equilibrium Asset-Pricing Cash-in-Advance Approach." *Journal of International Economics* 18 (February 1985): 17–41.

Svensson, Lars E. O., and van Wijnbergen, Sweder. "International Transmission of Monetary Policy." Seminar Paper no. 362. Institute for International Economic Studies, University of Stockholm, 1986.

Swoboda, Alexander K. "Comment." In *International Economic Policy*, pp. 204–208. Edited by R. Dornbusch and J. A. Frenkel. Baltimore: The Johns Hopkins Press, 1979.

Taussig, Frank W. "International Trade under Depreciated Paper: A Contribution to Theory." *Quarterly Journal of Economics* 21 (May 1917): 380–403.

Thomas, Brinley. *Migration and Economic Growth*. 2d ed. Cambridge: Cambridge University Press, 1973.

Viner, Jacob. *Canada's Balance of International Indebtedness, 1900–1913*. Cambridge: Harvard University Press, 1924.

Williamson, Jeffrey G. "Real Growth, Monetary Disturbances, and the Transfer Process: The United States, 1879–1900." *Southern Economic Journal* 29 (January 1963), 167–80.

Williamson, John. *The Exchange Rate System*. Washington, D.C.: Institute for International Economics, 1983.

Wonnacott, Paul. *The Canadian Dollar, 1948–58*. Toronto: University of Toronto Press, 1965.

# COMMENT

# REAL EXCHANGE RATES AND FREEDOM OF INTERNATIONAL TRADE AND CAPITAL FLOWS*

*Michael R. Darby*

I would like to respond to rather than comment in detail on the paper by my former colleagues Michael Bordo and Anna Schwartz. While I agree with most and disagree with some of their presentation, I fear that there is real potential of a forest and trees problem if I attempt to distinguish which is which. Instead, I would like to present a different way of looking at economic transmission under alternative systems.

## A Four-Way Classification

Bordo and Schwartz arrange their taxonomy around whether the economy is on a floating or fixed exchange rate system. I would argue that across this dichotomy lies a much more fundamental dichotomy of whether there is an open or closed trading system for goods and financial assets. Both dichotomies suggest black or white cases where there may be shades of grey in between, but I think they are useful because one or another philosophy or strategy predominates at a given place and time.

Open trading systems differ from closed systems in that changes in fundamentals have strong effects on the real exchange rate between two countries. The real exchange rate is the amount of goods in one country that trades for a given amount of goods in the other. An increase in taxes on capital or decrease in the international value of a dominant national product will tend to depreciate the real exchange rate. If the country has a floating exchange rate, its nominal exchange rate will depreciate as required by the assumed change in fundmentals. Alternatively, if there is a fixed exchange rate system, the depreciation will be achieved by a reduction in money supply and prices

---

*Reprinted from *Cato Journal* 8 (Fall 1988): 473–75.

The author is Assistant Secretary for Economic Policy at the U.S. Treasury Department. The paper represents the author's personal opinions and should not be construed as necessarily representing the position of the Treasury Department.

at home—a deflation—or increase in money supply and prices abroad—an inflation—according to which is the nonreserve country. The timing and sectors that are affected in the transition depend on whether a fixed or floating exchange rate system is followed but not the ultimate size of the real depreciation of the domestic currency or real appreciation of the foreign currency.

Under a closed trading system, capital and trade flows are restricted so that the assumed changes in fundamentals may cause smaller moves in the equilibrium real exchange rate. Indeed the controls—which are part of the fundamentals in this system—are likely to be adjusted to offset pressures on the nominal exchange rate if we are to judge from the historical precedent of the Bretton Woods system or other present-day examples.

## The Evolution of Systems

Now, I have suggested a four-way classification—fixed open, floating open, fixed closed, and floating closed—but only the first three really seem to be observed much in the real world. If there is only one independent central bank with any other monetary authorities passively adjusting their money supplies as required to maintain the nominal exchange rate, then one has a fixed open system. The ultimate example would be the linkage of the other 11 Federal Reserve districts to that headquartered in New York, but some observers would characterize the European Monetary System this way as well as certain countries that independently have chosen to define their national currencies as a certain quantity of dollars or pounds.

When there are sovereign nations involved, each has the right to set up a central bank with the power to determine its own money supply so that inflation or deflation reflects national goals, not the choices of a foreign central bank or the implications for the real exchange rate of changing tax policies or other fundamentals. This is why sovereign nations rarely operate for long under fixed open systems.

There is a strong impulse for a nonreserve country to resist an unwanted inflation or deflation by imposing capital controls. At the same time a bit of protectionism is likely to be added. As time goes on these controls build up until the system can only be characterized as closed. This is the sad history of the Bretton Woods system. That system was broken both by the growing gap between the inflationary impulse in the reserve country and the lower inflation goals in many major nonreserve countries as well as by technological innovations that made capital controls increasingly difficult to enforce.

With the advent of floating rates, there is little to be gained to offset the costs of operating a closed system, so we should not be surprised that the controls were dismantled and that international trade boomed. The costs of dealing with fluctuating real exchange rates while real proved much less a burden on trade than the costs of the controls needed to prevent the fluctuations. As Bordo and Schwartz report, in work with James Lothian I have recently developed evidence that the floating open regime has indeed resulted in a much more integrated world real economy even as nations have pursued much more divergent inflation goals than were possible under the Bretton Woods system.

## Conclusion

I believe that the basic distinction is between open trading systems in which real exchange rates fluctuate and closed trading systems in which the effects on the real exchange rate of changing fundamentals are attenuated or offset by variable controls on the flows of goods and capital. While both fixed and floating exchange rates are consistent with open trading systems, the fixed system requires acceptance of substantial fluctuations in the price level of the nonreserve countries. For this reason, we observe historically major sovereign nations linked primarily either by fixed closed or floating open systems. It seems preferable to me when analyzing transmission under fixed and floating exchange rates to account simultaneously for the differences in capital and goods controls that are associated with the two systems. There is little gain and much potential mischief in comparing real systems with imaginary alternatives: After all, even democracy and capitalism suffer by comparison to idealized utopias instead of real alternatives.

# 11

# THE EUROPEAN MONETARY SYSTEM: HOW WELL HAS IT WORKED?*

*Michele Fratianni*

## Introduction

The Treaty of Rome makes no reference to monetary union or specific exchange rate arrangements. In 1968 Raymond Barre, then commissioner of the European Community (EC), wrote a proposal advocating tighter consultations of member governments concerning macroeconomic policy and in particular monetary policy. The celebrated Werner Report of 1970 was an outgrowth of Barre's ideas. Although this report set monetary union as the ultimate EC objective, it was careful to emphasize (1) preconditions in the form of coordinated policies and (2) the establishment of narrower margins of fluctuations around exchange rate par values. The so-called snake arrangement, instituted in 1972, was believed to be the Werner Report in action. In fact, from the Werner Report the "snake" system borrows only the idea of reducing currency fluctuations without setting a machinery to coordinate policies. The "snake" failed.

The decision taken in 1978 by Chancellor Helmut Schmidt and President Giscard d'Estaing to create a "zone of monetary stability" came as a surprise, not only to the general public but also to central banks. Samuel Brittan (1979) speculated that the birth of the European Monetary System (EMS) had less to do with a desire for monetary stability than a Franco-German reaction to the weakness of the dollar and the unreliability of the Carter Administration. Whatever the reasons, the EMS became a reality on March 13, 1979.

Several authors predicted failure or at least modest success. Benjamin Cohen (1981, p. 21) stated that "the potential for an inflationary bias is there and, unlike the hypothethical reverse danger of a deflationary bias, could well become serious in practical terms. . . . Any

*Reprinted from *Cato Journal* 8 (Fall 1988): 477–501.

The author is Professor of Business Economics and Public Policy at Indiana University. He gratefully acknowledges the comments by Juergen von Hagen and Alan Walters on earlier versions of the paper.

disciplinary effect of the joint float on a deficit member would probably be more than offset by the 'safety valve' of access to the credit facilities." In 1980, I predicted that "the EMS is destined to become an adjustable-peg system. How well this system will fare depends on the disparity of inflation rates and timeliness of parity adjustments. The current disparity of inflation rates and underlying policies among EEC countries suggests frequent realignments. Yet history teaches us that decisionmakers perceive parity changes as costly political decisions and, therefore, postpone taking action" (Fratianni 1980, p. 165). Roland Vaubel (1980) identified in the EMS the emergence of "egalitarianism, collectivism, and *etatism*" and worried about the built-in moral hazard incentives and inflation bias.

The EMS has not failed. Many economists and policymakers consider it a success, partly on the strength of the evidence I will review in this paper. Yet, the relevant question is not whether the EMS has survived or done well according to some absolute criterion, but whether it has performed better or worse than an alternative exchange rate regime. Needless to say, this is a demanding task because of the difficulty of holding other things constant.

In the remainder of the paper, I first compare the performance of the EMS countries both with the countries' own pre-EMS history and with non-EMS countries. Next, I consider the workings and merit of the EMS relative to the free-floating alternative. While there is a considerable amount of theoretical work on the relative desirability between an EMS-type and a free-floating arrangement (with and without credible monetary authorities), the empirical work bearing on this proposition is still in its infancy. In the concluding section, I offer speculations concerning the motives of each EMS country in being part of the present arrangement.

## The Record

This section reviews the EMS record on exchange rate variability, inflation rates, money growth, interest rates, and economic growth.

### *Exchange Rates*

There have been 11 parity changes or realignments during the life of the EMS; 7 occurred during the first four years and 4 in the subsequent four years (see Appendix Table 1). In the approximately 8-year period from March 1979 to January 12, 1987, the Italian lira experienced the largest parity depreciation, 45 percent, vis-à-vis the

Deutsche mark; the Dutch guilder had the smallest depreciation, 4 percent (see Appendix Table 2).[1]

Did these parity changes evolve to take into consideration inflation differentials within the EMS countries? In Appendix Tables 3 and 4, I have shown cumulative bilateral inflation rate differences—over the period of 1979–86—measured by percentage changes of the wholesale price index and the consumer price index, respectively. Italy, again, has had the highest inflation differential in relation to Germany (64 and 84 percentage points, respectively); the Netherlands, the smallest (1 and 3 percentage points, respectively). A comparison of Appendix Table 2 with Appendix Tables 3 and 4 reveals that bilateral depreciations were positively associated with a higher domestic inflation rate.[2] This positive association, however, was far from being complete and left room for real exchange rate changes (see Appendix Table 5). In particular, the French franc, the Italian lira, and the Irish pound have had sizeable real appreciations vis-à-vis the other EMS currencies. With respect to the Deutsche mark, the French franc has appreciated 8 percentage points, the Italian lira 38 percentage points, and the Irish pound 35 percentage points.[3]

One interpretation of the EMS is that monetary authorities of the participating countries do not understand the EMS to be a fixed exchange rate arrangement, but rather as one aimed at preventing high variability of exchange rates. If high variability implies that exchange rate movements have a large unexpected component, risk-averse individuals will move resources away from the riskier trade sector to the less risky nontraded sector (provided mean and variance of the exchange rate change are independent of each other). Hence high variability of exchange rates—despite the existence of future or forward markets—hampers the growth of trade.

Horst Ungerer et al. (1986) give detailed evidence about exchange rate variability within the EMS countries, within the non-EMS

[1]The parity realignment of 2.6 percent between the Irish pound and the French franc was the smallest absolute parity change.

[2]The co-movement between nominal exchange rate realignments and inflation rate differentials was tested by regressing the cross-section data of Appendix Table 2 (Exr) on the cross-section data of Appendix Tables 3 and 4 (wpi and cpi, respectively):

$$\text{Exr} = -5.59 + .65^{*}\text{wpi} \qquad \text{SEE} = 10.3$$

t values (2.45) (9.86)

$$\text{Exr} = -6.8 + .50^{*}\text{cpi} \qquad \text{SEE} = 9.6$$

(3.17) (10.7)

where Exr = nominal exchange rate; wpi = wholesale price index; cpi = consumer price index.

[3]These were the real exchange rate changes based on the consumer price index.

countries, and between them. Here are the salient results of this study. First, intra-EMS exchange rate variability—both nominal and real—declined after the creation of the EMS. This decline is particularly so for bilateral exchange rates, which is evidence that corroborates the earlier study by Kenneth Rogoff (1985) who had, instead, concentrated on predictability. The evidence shows that the variance of the forecast error of the risk-neutral rational expectations model was lower during the first five years of the EMS than during the preceding five years. In contrast, non-EMS exchange rate variability went up after the creation of the EMS.

Much more subtle is the evidence concerning the interaction between EMS and non-EMS countries. On the basis of the IMF's multilateral exchange rate model, there is little evidence in Ungerer et al. to suggest that the pre-EMS period behaves different from the post-EMS period.[4] As an alternative, I computed the standard deviation and the coefficient of variations of the annual percentage change of the effective exchange rate as defined by the OECD (see below for a description of the data). My computation was for the seven EMS countries; three European non-EMS countries (Austria, the United Kingdom, and Switzerland); and three non-European countries (Canada, Japan, and the United States). The results, presented in Appendix Table 6, indicate a sizeable increase in variability for two of the EMS countries (Belgium and the Netherlands) in contrast to the rather stable pattern in non-EMS countries. This fact implies that part of the gain in reduced exchange rate variability within the EMS countries came at the expense of a higher variability of exchange rates between EMS and non-EMS countries.[5]

Why has there been a significant decline in the growth rate of intra-EMS trade after 1979, in relation to both its own past and to non-EMS trade growth, despite the achieved lower (within the EMS) exchange rate variability?[6] De Grauwe and Verfaille (1987) tackle this issue by testing a cross-sectional model of bilateral export flows. The determinants of the export flows were the growth of demand of

[4]See Tables 28 and 29 in Ungerer et al. (1986).

[5]In support of this point Ungerer et al. (1986, Table 22) show that the coefficient of variation of bilateral exchange rates, measured with respect to non-EMS countries' currencies, rises from 36.3 in the period 1974–78 to 46.7 in the period 1979–85 for the average EMS countries, and from 39.6 to 42.8 for the average non-EMS countries.

[6]See DeGrauwe (1985) for a report on the relevant trade statistics. Denmark, Ireland, and the United Kingdom (the new members of the EEC) have experienced larger trade growth rates with the EEC countries than the old members. Their late entry into customs union may explain in part the difference in performance. There is the possibility, applicable only to the United Kingdom, that the EMS arrangement has, in fact, retarded trade growth within the EEC.

the importing country, the growth of output supply of the exporting country, the exchange rate variability, the nature of the trade arrangement between the pairs of countries, and an indicator of protectionism. The latter determinant was quantified by cumulative percentage overvaluation of the currency of the importing country. Overvaluation is defined in terms of productivity-adjusted real exchange rate. The main findings are that the slowdown in the growth of output in the EMS and the slowdown in the integration process had a larger impact on intra-EMS trade growth than the beneficial effect of lower exchange rate variability. What remains to be explained, according to the authors, is "whether the EMS arrangement might have induced both low exchange rate variability and low growth of output."

*Inflation Rates and Money Growth*

Proponents of the EMS have pointed to the reduction in inflation rates in the EMS countries as a sign of the system's success. Statements of this kind need to be carefully scrutinized in two ways. First, is the inflation rate during the EMS period significantly lower than in the pre-EMS period? Meaningful statistical inferences cannot be made by simply comparing two periods. Naturally, these periods will differ by the number, size, and nature of the shocks, as well as by the exchange rate regime under consideration. Only under the heroic assumption of equivalent shocks can we attribute to the exchange rate regime the decline in the inflation rate. To relax in part the assumption of homogeneous shocks—and this is the second point—one can compare the performance of the EMS economies with economies that are "similar" to the EMS economies, except for the exchange rate regime.[7]

In Appendix Table 7, I have reported the average inflation rates—measured in terms of the consumption deflator—of the eight EMS countries, the EMS average, and the averages of the non-EMS countries for the pre-EMS period 1974–78 and the post-EMS period 1979–86. The data are annual and come from the diskettes of the OECD, *Economic Outlook* no. 41, June 1987. The aggregation over countries was made by multiplying the country's growth rate by the country's weight, which was based on GNP share calculated in 1982 prices and exchange rates.[8] In addition to the two sample averages, Appen-

[7]A more meaningful exercise, which is beyond the task of this paper, would require analyzing the disinflation of the EMS countries relative to that of the non-EMS countries in terms of the relative costs of disinflation.

[8]These weights are Belgium = 1.1, Denmark = 0.7, France = 7.0, Germany = 8.5, Ireland = 0.2, Italy = 4.5, Netherlands = 1.8, Austria = 0.9, United Kingdom = 6.3, Switzerland = 1.2, Canada = 3.9, Japan = 14.0, United States = 40.9.

dix Table 7 shows the difference between the two periods and indicates whether this difference is significantly different from zero.[9]

The essential point emerging from the table is that the small, two percentage-point decline in the inflation rate in the EMS is not statistically significant, whereas the large declines in the other six countries are. These results may not do justice to the drastic disinflation that has taken place in the EMS countries in the several years, and indeed the outcome would drastically change if we ignored the first four years of the EMS. Belgium had an inflation rate of 1.4 percent in 1986 compared to an inflation rate of 7.1 percent in 1982. For the following countries the first percentage is for 1986 and the second for 1982: Denmark, 3.6 percent compared to 9.8 percent; France, 2.2 percent compared to 10.6 percent; Germany, −0.4 percent compared to 4.7 percent; Ireland, 3.7 percent compared to 14.7 percent; Italy, 6.0 percent compared to 15.7 percent; and the Netherlands, 0 percent compared to 5.1 percent.

Different considerations can be made with respect to the growth rate of the money stock, which slows down significantly in Belgium, Germany, Italy, and the Netherlands but rises in the other three European non-EMS countries (see Appendix Table 7). The incompleteness of money data for Denmark and France, however, prevents us from making statistically relevant comparisons between EMS and non-EMS aggregates. As an alternative to the money stock, I considered the growth rate of the monetary base, which has the advantage of closely reflecting the policy actions of the central banks.[10] In Appendix Table 8, I report the sample averages of the annualized growth rate of the monetary base of each EMS country and the relative growth rates of each as defined by the difference of the country's growth rate and by the growth rate of the EMS aggregate, excluding the country in question.

Italy and Ireland experienced significant (but at the relatively high 20 percent confidence level) declines in the growth of the monetary base; France, in contrast, had an increase in the relative growth. The interplay of these forces within the EMS left the EMS monetary base

[9]The following $t$ statistic was employed:

$$t = (x_1 - x_2)/[std(1/n_1 + 1/n_2)^{1/2}]$$

where $std = [n_1{*}var_1 + n_2{*}var_2)/(n_1 + n_2 - 2)]^{1/2}$, $x_1$ = sample average of the pre-EMS period, $x_2$ = sample average of the EMS period, $var_1$ = variance of the pre-EMS period, $var_2$ = variance of the EMS period, $n_1$ = number of observations in the pre-EMS period, and $n_2$ = number of observations in the EMS period.

[10]These are quarterly data obtained from the *International Financial Statistics* (line 14) of the IMF.

growth in the 1979–86 period virtually unchanged with respect to the pre-EMS period.[11]

*Interest Rates*

Integration of the financial markets implies that, in the absence of expected real exchange rate changes, real rates of interest cannot differ among countries. Rogoff (1985) shows that the difference between German and French and between German and Italian short-term real interest rates increased during the EMS period. Furthermore, the conditional variance of these interest rates—based on two alternative ways to proxy the expected rate of inflation—rose as well in the post-EMS period.[12] Giavazzi and Pagano (1985) present evidence that the spread between offshore and onshore interest rates widens and becomes more variable when an expectation of a parity realignment sets in. By tying the evidence produced by Giavazzi and Pagano with that of Rogoff, one arrives at the conclusion that the reduced variability of the exchange rates cannot be credited to coordinated monetary policy, but rather to the existence of capital controls that have effectively put a wedge between German interest rates, on the one hand, and French and Italian interest rates, on the other hand. Charles Goodhart (1986), on the strength of this evidence, argues against the entry of the United Kingdom in the EMS, because the crucial role of London as a major financial center requires freedom of capital movement.[13] To put it differently, if the cost of joining the EMS is the application of exchange controls, the EMS is not worth it.

The evidence on interest rates cited above was based on data going up to 1984. What has happened more recently? The most important development is the exchange liberalization process that has taken place both in Italy and France. This liberalization forces the real interest rates in these countries to rise relative to those abroad. In Appendix Table 9, I have calculated the short-term real rate of interest using two alternative data sets: the annual data of the OECD, and the monthly three-month Treasury rates published by Harris Bank's *Weekly Review*. In both instances I have assumed that individuals were blessed with perfect foresight as to the next period's rate of

[11]There is a slowdown in the growth rate of the monetary base of the "rest of the world," but it is not statistically significant. We should note that the growth rate of the monetary base has large variances in all countries, a fact that explains why apparently large drops in the sample means are not statistically significant.

[12]See Appendix Table 5.

[13]Walters (1986) rejects the EMS on these grounds, as well as on political-economy considerations.

inflation. While the two data sets yield different quantitative results, qualitatively they concur in pointing to a narrowing of the differentials.

The narrowing of the interest-rate differential is consistent with the hypothesis that countries like France and Italy have used the exchange rate as an exogenous variable and have adopted a policy of letting their domestic currencies appreciate in real terms vis-à-vis the Deutsche mark.

*Economic Growth and Unemployment*

How have the EMS countries performed on the real side of the economy? The evidence is very clear concerning unemployment, less so about output growth. Unemployment rates have increased substantially in the post-EMS period: In each of the EMS countries the increase is statistically significant at the 5 percent level (see Appendix Table 10). But this statement is also true for the other three European countries that are not part of the EMS, in contrast with the experience of the Canada-Japan-U.S. group. The unemployment story does not carry over, however, to the growth of real GNP where the slowdown is statistically significant for France, Ireland, and the Netherlands. We should note that the growth rates of output in the 1974–78 period were low to begin with, making the economic slowdown even more pronounced.

The nature and size of the real slowdown in Europe is very controversial and is the subject of ongoing research. One critical issue is whether the higher unemployment results from high real wage rates (classical explanation) or from inadequate spending (Keynesian explanation). We should note that unemployment in Europe is largely concentrated among the young and the unskilled, particularly in well-defined geographical areas. In a recent paper Jacques Drèze et al. (1987) argue that European unemployment exhibits both classical and Keynesian characteristics. These economists propose a series of supply-side measures aimed at reducing the high wedge between the private cost of labor (inclusive of taxes) and the social cost (i.e., net of tax). But they also propose that Germany, France, and the United Kingdom should generate additional government spending for future expansion of productive capacity, which is currently almost fully used.[14]

From the perspective of this paper the above discussion highlights that the EMS is a monetary arrangement, not a fiscal one. Indeed

[14]The proposal entails higher public debt today and more taxes in the future. The higher public debt today serves to induce an intertemporal substitution of labor away from the future (when the economy will be at full employment) and toward the present (when resources are unemployed).

there is evidence that fiscal policies among the EMS countries were more divergent after 1979 than before.

## An Interpretation of the EMS

The EMS was created to achieve "a zone of monetary stability in Europe" that would eventually culminate into the establishment of a European Monetary Fund. Central banks have interpreted "a zone of monetary stability" to mean (1) lower variability of exchange rates, and (2) lower and converging inflation rates among EMS countries.

The EMS has been successful in reducing nominal and real exchange rate variability. Yet, intra-EMS trade growth has fallen. It is conceivable that trade growth would have fallen even more with more exchange rate variability. As to inflation, the facts are more ambiguous. The achieved reduction in the inflation rates turns out to be not as significant as the reduction in inflation rates among non-EMS countries when the entire post-EMS period is considered. If, instead, one isolates the 1982–86 period, the story becomes much more favorable for the EMS. Finally, there is some evidence that France and Italy have used the EMS as a disinflationary mechanism, by letting their currencies appreciate in real terms vis-à-vis the Deutsche mark and letting their real rates of interest rise relative to the real rates of interest prevailing in Germany.

Two questions immediately come to mind. Why would France and Italy accept the discipline of the EMS in preference to appropriate domestic disinflationary policies? Why would Germany be part of a scheme that makes it a potential importer of inflation? The rest of the paper is devoted to answering these two questions.

### *The Reputation Hypothesis*

The key issue underlying the first of the two questions is whether or not membership in the EMS facilitates disinflation relative to an independent policy of disinflation. High-inflation countries may find it worthwhile to join an EMS-type arrangement because of the benefit derived by linking their currencies to that of a low-inflation country. These benefits stem from the reputation that the low-inflation country's central bank has earned in the market place.

A central bank with little or no reputation faces an inflation rate higher than would prevail if the central bank had committed itself to a credible strategy of disinflation.[15] This central bank can borrow

[15]There is one branch of the literature on reputation that considers conditions under which policy shifts are credible (e.g., Barro and Gordon 1983), while another branch emphasizes that the central bank is free to follow discretionary policies and determine its level of credibility (e.g., Cukierman and Meltzer 1986). The latter view does not make it clear that the EMS enjoys a comparative advantage in generating reputation over an independent monetary policy of disinflation.

reputation by committing its country's currency to a policy of real exchange rate appreciation with respect to the currency of a low-inflation credible central bank. The EMS can be interpreted as an arrangement of this type, with the relatively high-inflation countries of France and Italy borrowing reputation from low-inflation Germany.

Giavazzi and Pagano (1986) explore theoretically the advantage of high-inflation countries of tying their hands as far as monetary policy is concerned. The critical point for these economists is not whether the EMS is an effective disciplinary force, but whether the high-inflation countries gain from the arrangement.

The gain of reputation is only one aspect of joining the EMS; high-inflation countries also have to consider the losses in competitiveness implied by real exchange rate appreciations. The Giavazzi-Pagano model postulates that monetary authorities prefer more output to less output, value a positive rate of inflation because it creates revenues, but dislike inflation variability because of its adverse effects on output. The latter responds positively to real exchange rate depreciation and inflation "surprises."

Finally, the real exchange rate of the high-inflation countries appreciates between realignments, but returns to its initial value at the time of a realignment (i.e., changes in parities are set equal to cumulative inflation differentials). Under these conditions, the EMS is worth joining if the authorities do not seek to extract revenues from inflation, an intuitive outcome. Equally intuitive is the result that the payoff of joining the EMS is ambiguous if the authorities value the inflation tax. The final outcome depends on the relative strength of the seigniorage, the present value of output loss because of inflation variability, and the tightness of the EMS regime. Unfortunately, no empirical measures of the three forces are critical in the determination of EMS membership. Only through revealed preference can we deduce that the seigniorage incentives are small enough, relative to the gain in reputation, to have made it worthwhile for France and Italy to remain in the EMS so far.

*Benefits to the Supplier of Reputation*

Let us turn to the second question raised earlier: What does Germany gain by being in the EMS? Participation in the EMS poses a complex problem to Germany. As a supplier of monetary credibility the Bundesbank receives no reward from the EMS. In fact, the workings of the EMS make it "natural" for Germany to import inflation from high-inflation countries. On the other hand, the EMS makes it possible for the Deutsche mark (DM) to have smaller real appreciations than would be true under free floating.

This competitive advantage may justify why the German government has been more favorable toward the EMS than the Bundesbank. The Bundesbank does not have exclusive authority to set priorities for the economy as a whole. In reality there are conflicts within branches of the executive. Germany, as represented by the Ministry of Finance, is more favorable to a DM real depreciation than Germany represented by the Bundesbank (see Tsoukalis 1987). By German law, the Ministry of Finance, not the Bundesbank, decides the exchange rate arrangement. Indeed, as I mentioned before, Chancellor Schmidt's original decision to join the EMS—against the opposition of the Bundesbank—might have had less to do with monetary unification than with searching for an expedient way to diffuse the brunt of heavy speculative flows into Germany (Brittan 1979).

The EMS may generate another benefit for Germany: the integration of financial markets in Europe and, hence, smaller German vulnerability to changes in foreign economic policy. It is not surprising that German authorities have consistently pushed for the integration of financial markets, with France and Italy relaxing exchange controls. The unfolding of tighter financial integration ought to raise the substitutability between DM-denominated assets and assets denominated in French francs and in liras. The benefit for Germany will be less vulnerability to changes in U.S. economic policies.[16]

*Evidence on Reputation*

Giavazzi and Giovannini (1987) address the issue of how important reputation has been in the EMS. They test for the empirical size of reputation by employing the famous Lucas (1979) critique to econometric practice in a positive manner. Since the institution of the EMS represents a new policy regime, it follows that any well-specified model of inflation estimated before the EMS will tend to overpredict inflation during the EMS period for countries borrowing reputation and to underpredict for reputation-supplying Germany. Giavazzi and Giovannini estimate vector-autoregressive models that act as "idealized" reduced-form equations for changes in the price level, nominal wages, and output. These variables are postulated to depend on their lagged values, money growth, changes in the relative price of imported raw materials, and changes in the relative price of imported finished goods, as well as on a smattering of country-specific dummy variables.

The authors find only one significant change in the overall values of the estimated coefficients before and after the establishment of

[16]The asymmetries noted by Giavazzi and Pagano (1985) will have then disappeared.

the EMS; that change occurs for the French price inflation. As Giavazzi and Giovannini admit (p. 16), "This result might suggest that the EMS has not brought about any of the changes in expectations that we describe in the sections above, except for the price equation in France." Since the authors do not provide statistics about the relative forecast accuracy of the models before and after the EMS, the issue of the effectiveness of the regime change cannot be explored more deeply.

What we are left with are graphs of the actual and predicted values of the models in the post-EMS period. These graphs, in the absence of formal statistics, become the evidence upon which Giavazzi and Giovannini evaluate the reputation hypothesis. The graphs for Danish and German inflation "appear" to be consistent with the hypothesis. Besides importing inflation from the other EMS countries, Germany also seems to be a loser on the real side of the economy.

This conclusion runs counter to the popular notion that Germany is a deflationary force on the system.

Curiously enough, the United Kingdom appears to have been able to have its cake and eat it too with systematic negative forecast errors in the inflation rate and with positive forecast errors in output. This result at face value vindicates Mrs. Thatcher's insistence in not being part of the EMS; and it is consistent with Alan Walter's (1986) assessment of the EMS.

*Bundesbank Leadership*

There is virtual unanimity in the literature that, despite the intentions of the founding fathers to create a democratic institution, the EMS behaves as if Germany were a price leader.

France has been more than vociferous in denouncing the dominant role of Germany. In January 1987, France refused to intervene as the franc fell to the compulsory intervention floor; the Bundesbank had to intervene. Inspired by France, the finance ministers of the EC in September 1987 modified the rules governing interventions and their financing.[17]

The key change concerns the access of weak-currency countries to automatic credit through the Very Short-term Financing Facility. Mr. Balladur, the French finance minister, has interpreted the change as

[17]Masera (1987) outlines the principal institutional changes of the September 12–13, 1987, decision by the EC Council of Finance Ministers. In addition to the change discussed in the text, there is a time extension of the Very Short-term Financing Facility; a larger role given to the "official" ECU; and an engagement to monitor exchange rates, external imbalances, and monetary conditions in each of the EMS countries. The decision was written with unusually guarded language.

meaning "a presumption of automaticity" (an oxymoron?), whereas Mr. Poehl has interpreted the September decision as giving the Bundesbank the discretion to decide each case on its merit, the criterion being that "the main pre-condition will be that it does not threaten price stability in Germany" (*The Economist* 1987). It is too early to judge whether the institutional innovations pushed by France and backed by other countries will nudge the Bundesbank to alter its monetary policy. Much will depend on the Bundesbank's ability to sterilize interventions in the exchange markets.

## Conclusion

The European Monetary System has not failed. The potential for an inflationary bias predicted by many economists has not materialized. So much is clear. Less clear is the matter of whether the EMS has been a success. The evidence marshalled in this paper indicates that the EMS has achieved lower exchange rate variability. Yet, intra-EMS trade growth has declined. The reduction in inflation rates, greatly praised by proponents of the EMS, turns out to be modest when compared to the reduction achieved by other countries. The stronger evidence pertains to the willingness of high-inflation France and Italy to have used the EMS as a disinflationary mechanism. The real value of the franc and the lira has appreciated in relation to the mark, while the wedge between German real interest rates, on the one hand, and French and Italian real interest rates, on the other hand, has shrunk. The early reliance of France and Italy on exchange controls has given way to later efforts to open up their financial markets.

The preference of France and Italy to join the EMS over a domestically driven disinflation suggests that the Banque de France and Banca d'Italia are relatively weak institutions and lack the reputation of the Bundesbank. By committing themselves to a policy of real exchange rate appreciations, France and Italy use the reputation of the Bundesbank in lowering the inflation rate at a lesser cost than would be possible through an independent monetary policy.

German participation in the EMS is problematic. The Bundesbank supplies credibility to the system but gains virtually nothing. As we have shown, the impetus to join the EMS came from the German government, not from the Bundesbank. The government has supported the EMS because the arrangement has provided for smaller real appreciations of the Deutsche mark than under a regime of free floating. Germany also benefits from the integration of European financial markets, giving it a further justification for joining and remaining in the EMS.

Belgium, Luxembourg, the Netherlands, and Denmark are small countries that have embraced, to different degrees, a Deutsche mark standard. The United Kingdom has refused to join the EMS for fear of losing independence of monetary policy. The evidence reviewed in this paper does not indicate that the United Kingdom has lost by staying out. Ireland, a small country not linked to the Deutsche mark area, remains a puzzle as to its gain from EMS participation.

The EMS so far has run as a German-dominated system. While there are pressures to make the arrangement more democratic, it is too early to predict any fundamental changes. However, should democratization come about without an adequate amount of shared reputation, a great deal of the *raison d'être* of the EMS would have disappeared.

## Appendix Tables

The following tables provide information on the performance of the EMS since its inception in 1979. Performance is viewed both within the EMS and relative to non-EMS countries. The data pertain to exchange rate variability, monetary growth and inflation, real interest rates, economic growth, and unemployment.

*APPENDIX TABLE 1*

EXCHANGE RATE REALIGNMENTS WITHIN THE EMS

| | DM | HFL | FF | BFR | LIT | DKR | IRL |
|---|---|---|---|---|---|---|---|
| 24 Sept. 1979 | 2.0 | — | — | — | — | −2.9 | — |
| 30 Nov. 1979 | — | — | — | — | — | −4.8 | — |
| 23 Mar. 1981 | — | — | — | — | −6.0 | — | — |
| 5 Oct. 1981 | 5.5 | 5.5 | −3.0 | — | −3.0 | — | — |
| 22 Feb. 1982 | — | — | — | −8.5 | — | −3.0 | — |
| 14 Jun. 1982 | 4.25 | 4.25 | −5.75 | — | −2.75 | — | — |
| 21 Mar. 1983 | 5.5 | 3.5 | −2.5 | 1.5 | −2.5 | 2.5 | −3.5 |
| 22 Jul. 1985 | 2.0 | 2.0 | 2.0 | 2.0 | −6.0 | 2.0 | 2.0 |
| 7 Apr. 1986 | 3.0 | 3.0 | −3.0 | 1.0 | — | 1.0 | — |
| 4 Aug. 1986 | — | — | — | — | — | — | −8.0 |
| 12 Jan. 1987 | 3.0 | 3.0 | — | 2.0 | — | — | — |

NOTE: The numbers are percentage changes of a given currency's bilateral central rate against those currencies whose bilateral parities were not realigned. A positive number denotes an appreciation, and a negative number denotes a depreciation. On March 21, 1983, and on July 22, 1986, all parities were realigned. BFR—Belgium/Luxembourg franc, DKR—Danish kroner, DM—Deutsche mark, FF—French franc, LIT—Italian lira, IRISH £—Irish pound, HFL—Netherlands guilder.

SOURCE: Commission of the European Communities.

*APPENDIX TABLE 2*

PERCENTAGE CHANGE IN BILATERAL PARITIES FROM MARCH 13, 1979, TO JANUARY 12, 1987

| | BFR | DKR | DM | FF | LIT | IRISH £ | HFL |
|---|---|---|---|---|---|---|---|
| BFR | | 2.94 | −27.18 | 10.13 | 18.30 | 7.48 | −23.29 |
| DKR | | | −30.12 | 7.19 | 14.75 | 4.54 | −26.23 |
| DM | | | | 37.31 | 45.48 | 34.16 | 3.89 |
| FF | | | | | 8.18 | −2.64 | −34.81 |
| LIT | | | | | | −10.82 | −41.59 |
| IRISH £ | | | | | | | −30.77 |

NOTE: A positive number denotes a devaluation, and a minus sign denotes an appreciation of the currency shown in the column heading with respect to the currency shown in the row heading.

SOURCE: Ungener et al. (1986, Table 6) and San Paolo, *ECU Newsletter*, January 1987.

*APPENDIX TABLE 3*

CUMULATIVE BILATERAL INFLATION DIFFERENTIAL MEASURED BY THE WHOLESALE PRICE INDEX OVER THE PERIOD 1979–1986

| | BFR | DKR | DM | FF | LIT | IRISH £ | HFL |
|---|---|---|---|---|---|---|---|
| BFR | | 28.1 | −4.3 | 37.9 | 59.3 | 33.1 | −2.9 |
| DKR | | | −32.4 | 9.8 | 31.2 | 5.0 | −31.0 |
| DM | | | | 42.2 | 63.6 | 37.4 | 1.4 |
| FF | | | | | 21.4 | −4.8 | −40.8 |
| LIT | | | | | | −26.2 | −62.2 |
| IRISH £ | | | | | | | −36.0 |

NOTE: A positive (negative) number indicates that the inflation rate of the country shown in the column heading is cumulatively higher (lower) than that of the country shown in the row heading.

SOURCE: International Monetary Fund, *International Financial Statistics*, Yearbook 1987.

*APPENDIX TABLE 4*

CUMULATIVE BILATERAL INFLATION DIFFERENTIAL MEASURED BY THE CONSUMER PRICE INDEX OVER THE PERIOD 1979–86

| | BFR | DKR | DM | FF | LIT | IRISH £ | HFL |
|---|---|---|---|---|---|---|---|
| BFR | | 17.7 | −18.8 | 27.0 | 65.0 | 69.6 | −15.8 |
| DKR | | | −36.5 | 9.3 | 47.3 | 31.9 | −33.5 |
| DM | | | | 45.8 | 83.8 | 68.8 | 3.0 |
| FF | | | | | 38.0 | 22.6 | −42.8 |
| LIT | | | | | | −15.4 | −80.8 |
| IRISH £ | | | | | | | −65.4 |

NOTE: A positive (negative) number indicates that the inflation rate of the country shown in the column heading is cumulatively higher (lower) than that of the country shown in the row heading.

SOURCE: International Monetary Fund, *International Financial Statistics*, Yearbook 1987.

*APPENDIX TABLE 5*

PERCENTAGE CHANGE IN BILATERAL REAL EXCHANGE RATE REALIGNMENT FROM MARCH 13, 1979, TO JANUARY 12, 1987

| | Wholesale Price Index | | | | | | |
|---|---|---|---|---|---|---|---|
| | BFR | DKR | DM | FF | LIT | IRISH £ | HFL |
| BFR | | −25.16 | −22.88 | −27.77 | −41.00 | −25.62 | −20.39 |
| DKR | | | 2.28 | − 2.61 | −16.45 | − 0.46 | 4.77 |
| DM | | | | − 4.89 | −18.12 | − 3.24 | 2.49 |
| FF | | | | | −13.22 | 2.16 | 5.99 |
| LIT | | | | | | 15.38 | 20.61 |
| IRISH £ | | | | | | | 5.23 |
| | Consumer Price Index | | | | | | |
| | BFR | DKR | DM | FF | LIT | IRISH £ | HFL |
| BFR | | −14.76 | − 8.38 | −16.87 | −46.7 | −62.12 | − 7.49 |
| DKR | | | 6.38 | − 2.11 | −32.55 | −27.36 | 7.27 |
| DM | | | | − 8.49 | −38.32 | −34.64 | 0.89 |
| FF | | | | | −29.82 | −25.24 | 7.99 |
| LIT | | | | | | 4.58 | 39.21 |
| IRISH £ | | | | | | | 34.63 |

NOTE: A positive number indicates a real depreciation of the country's currency shown in the column heading with respect to the country's currency shown in the row heading. The real exchange rate changes were obtained by subtracting the cumulative inflation differences of Appendix Table 3 and Appendix Table 4 from the cumulative nominal parity changes shown in Appendix Table 2.

*APPENDIX TABLE 6*

VARIABILITY OF THE ANNUAL GROWTH OF THE EFFECTIVE EXCHANGE RATE

| Countries | Period 1974–78 | | Period 1979–86 | | F Ratio[a] |
|---|---|---|---|---|---|
| | Standard Deviation | Standard Deviation / Mean | Standard Deviation | Standard Deviation / Mean | |
| Belgium | 1.40 | 0.53 | 4.68 | 3.78 | 11.15 |
| Denmark | 1.61 | 3.36 | 3.68 | 1.77 | 5.19 |
| France | 5.73 | 3.31 | 3.77 | 2.04 | 0.43 |
| Germany | 2.15 | 0.45 | 3.32 | 1.14 | 2.38 |
| Ireland | 2.02 | 0.63 | 4.25 | 1.81 | 4.43 |
| Italy | 4.31 | 0.44 | 3.03 | 0.82 | 0.50 |
| The Netherlands | 0.91 | 0.28 | 3.42 | 1.81 | 14.09 |
| Sum EMS | 1.55 | 5.33 | 2.72 | 13.69 | 3.07 |
| Austria | 1.34 | 0.49 | 1.54 | 0.74 | 1.34 |
| Switzerland | 6.50 | 0.61 | 3.14 | 1.07 | 0.23 |
| United Kingdom | 5.17 | 0.83 | 6.00 | 11.64 | 1.34 |
| Sum Euro Non-EMS | 4.11 | 1.44 | 4.18 | 16.27 | 1.04 |
| Canada | 6.16 | 2.21 | 2.98 | 1.31 | 0.23 |
| Japan | 9.83 | 1.88 | 10.51 | 2.18 | 1.14 |
| United States | 4.64 | 5.31 | 1.42 | 1.35 | 0.09 |
| Sum Non-Euro Non-EMS | 2.41 | 5.34 | 4.81 | 2.77 | 3.99 |

[a]F ratio is the ratio of the variance of the 1979–86 period to the variance of the 1974–78 period. The value of the F(7,4) statistic at the 1 percent level = 14.98; at 5 percent level = 6.09.

SOURCE: OECD, *Economic Outlook* no. 41, June 1987, data diskettes.

*APPENDIX TABLE 7*

EMS vs. NON-EMS COUNTRIES:
A COMPARISON OF INFLATION AND MONEY GROWTH RATES

| Countries | Annual Percentage Change Consumption Deflator 1974–78 | 1979–86 | Difference | Annual Percentage Change Money Stock 1974–78 | 1979–86 | Difference |
|---|---|---|---|---|---|---|
| Belgium | 8.54 | 5.53 | −3.01** | 11.77 | 6.14 | −5.63* |
| Luxembourg | 7.49 | 6.03 | −1.46 | — | — | — |
| Denmark | 10.37 | 7.79 | −2.58 | — | 15.87 | |
| France | 9.93 | 8.57 | −1.36 | — | 9.79 | |
| Germany | 4.66 | 3.43 | −1.23 | 8.83 | 5.92 | −2.91* |
| Ireland | 14.87 | 11.00 | −3.87 | 17.14 | 10.96 | −6.18 |
| Italy | 16.12 | 13.17 | −2.95 | 19.05 | 12.89 | −6.16* |
| The Netherlands | 7.65 | 3.75 | −3.9* | 12.07 | 7.05 | −5.02** |
| EMS Countries | 9.04 | 7.10 | −1.94 | — | — | — |
| European Non-EMS Countries[a] | 12.40 | 7.15 | −5.25* | 4.91 | 11.63 | 6.72* |
| Non-European Countries[b] | 8.04 | 5.24 | −2.80** | 10.30 | 8.75 | −1.55** |

[a]Austria, United Kingdom, and Switzerland.
[b]Canada, Japan, and the United States.
*Statistically different from zero at the 5 percent significance level (t distribution, 11 degrees of freedom).
**Statistically different from zero at the 10 percent significance level (t distribution, 11 degrees of freedom).
SOURCE: OECD, *Economic Outlook* no. 41, June 1987, data diskettes.

*APPENDIX TABLE 8*

GROWTH OF THE MONETARY BASE IN THE EMS COUNTRIES
(QUARTERLY DATA 1974:2–1986:4)

| | Own Growth Rate | | | Relative Growth Rate | | |
|---|---|---|---|---|---|---|
| Countries | 1974–78 | 1979–86 | Difference | 1974–78 | 1979–86 | Difference |
| Belgium | 6.00 | 2.40 | −3.60 | −1.38 | −5.3 | −3.92 |
| Denmark | 11.58 | 12.37 | 0.79 | 4.39 | 5.06 | 0.67 |
| France | 0.34 | 8.19 | 7.85 | −9.88 | 1.04 | 10.92*** |
| Germany | 4.84 | 4.00 | −0.83 | −3.86 | −5.37 | −1.51 |
| Ireland | 16.83 | 7.59 | −9.24*** | 9.59 | 0.13 | −9.46*** |
| Italy | 21.46 | 13.97 | −7.49*** | 17.44 | 8.03 | −9.41* |
| The Netherlands | 8.88 | 5.78 | −3.10 | 1.69 | −1.82 | −3.51 |
| Sum EMS | 7.32 | 7.46 | 0.14 | | | |
| Rest of the World | 8.07 | 7.25 | −0.82 | | | |

NOTE: The first three columns refer to the annual percentage change of the monetary base of the indicated country; the second three columns refer to the difference between the country's growth rate and that of the rest of the EMS. Rest of the world is defined as the weighted sum of Canada, Japan, the United Kingdom, and the United States.

*Statistically different from zero at the 5 percent significance level (t distribution, 49 degrees of freedom).
***Statistically different from zero at the 20 percent significance level (t distribution, 49 degrees of freedom).

SOURCE: International Monetary Fund, *International Financial Statistics*, line 14, various issues.

*APPENDIX TABLE 9*

EMS VS. NON-EMS COUNTRIES:
A COMPARISON OF REAL INTEREST RATES

| | OECD Data | | | | | |
|---|---|---|---|---|---|---|
| | 1974–78 | | 1979–86 | | | |
| Countries | Mean | Std. | Mean | Std. | t Stat.[a] | F Ratio[b] |
| Belgium | 1.31 | 2.03 | 6.11 | 1.35 | −4.61 | 0.44 |
| France | −0.13 | 1.32 | 3.61 | 3.49 | −2.14 | 6.99 |
| Germany | 1.33 | 1.27 | 4.27 | 1.91 | −2.80 | 2.26 |
| Ireland | −4.00 | 2.99 | 3.17 | 4.51 | −2.90 | 2.28 |
| Italy | −1.58 | 2.20 | 3.65 | 4.73 | −2.13 | 4.62 |
| The Netherlands | −1.09 | 1.75 | 4.02 | 1.44 | −5.26 | 0.68 |
| EMS Countries | 0.08 | 1.04 | 4.04 | 2.63 | −2.96 | 6.40 |
| European Non-EMS Countries | −2.85 | 1.95 | 3.51 | 2.48 | −4.48 | 1.62 |
| Non-European Countries | 0.10 | 0.28 | 2.45 | 1.12 | −4.23 | 16.00 |

*APPENDIX TABLE 9 (cont.)*

EMS VS. NON-EMS COUNTRIES:
A COMPARISON OF REAL INTEREST RATES

| | Harris Bank Data | | | | | |
|---|---|---|---|---|---|---|
| | 1974–78 | | 1979–86 | | | |
| | Mean | Std. | Mean | Std. | t Stat.[a] | F Ratio[b] |
| Belgium | 0.206 | 3.718 | 5.87 | 3.08 | −63.06 | 0.69 |
| France | −1.26 | 2.07 | 4.18 | 4.25 | −57.43 | 4.22 |
| Germany | 0.22 | 2.34 | 3.25 | 2.61 | −45.16 | 1.24 |
| Ireland | N.A. | | | | | |
| Italy | −4.49 | 7.94 | 1.51 | 5.44 | −34.11 | 0.47 |
| The Netherlands | N.A. | | | | | |
| UK | −4.91 | 6.25 | 3.18 | 5.78 | −50.54 | 0.86 |
| Canada | −0.98 | 3.09 | 4.42 | 2.76 | −69.55 | 0.80 |
| Japan | −2.65 | 5.41 | 2.84 | 3.87 | −44.99 | 0.51 |
| USA | 1.70 | 2.20 | 3.44 | 86.12 | −0.98 | 1,532.37 |

[a]t Statistic: The critical values with 11 degrees of freedom (OECD data) are 2.2 (5 percent) and 1.8 (10 percent); with 154 degrees of freedom (Harris Bank data) the values are 1.98 (5 percent) and 1.65 (10 percent).

[b]F Ratio: The critical values with (7,4) degrees of freedom (OECD data) are 14.98 (1 percent) and 6.09 (5 percent); with (92,62) degrees of freedom (Harris Bank data) the values are approximately 1.71 (1 percent) and 1.46 (5 percent).

SOURCE: OECD, *Economic Outlook* no. 41, June 1987, data diskettes; Harris Bank, *Weekly Review*, various issues.

*APPENDIX TABLE 10*

EMS VS. NON-EMS COUNTRIES:
A COMPARISON OF OUTPUT GROWTH AND UNEMPLOYMENT RATES

| Countries | Annual Percentage Change of Real GNP 1974–78 | 1979–86 | Difference | Unemployment Rate 1974–78 | 1979–86 | Difference |
|---|---|---|---|---|---|---|
| Belgium | 2.31 | 1.42 | −0.89 | 5.25 | 10.75 | 5.5 * |
| Luxembourg | 1.18 | 2.28 | 1.1 | 0.37 | 1.24 | 0.87* |
| Denmark | 1.55 | 2.31 | 0.76 | 5.16 | 8.69 | 3.53* |
| France | 3.03 | 1.52 | −1.51** | 4.42 | 8.41 | 3.99* |
| Germany | 2.00 | 1.74 | −0.26 | 3.54 | 6.30 | 2.76* |
| Ireland | 3.77 | 0.55 | 3.22* | 7.72 | 12.56 | 4.84* |
| Italy | 2.12 | 1.99 | −0.13 | 6.38 | 9.14 | 2.76* |
| The Netherlands | 2.55 | 1.04 | −1.51*** | 5.15 | 11.45 | 6.3 * |
| EMS Countries | 2.38 | 1.66 | −0.72 | 4.62 | 8.18 | 3.56* |
| European Non-EMS Countries[a] | 0.99 | 1.70 | 0.71 | 3.46 | 7.76 | 4.3 * |
| Non-European Countries[b] | 2.81 | 2.54 | −0.27 | 5.76 | 6.57 | .81 |

[a]Austria, the United Kingdom, and Switzerland.
[b]Canada, Japan, and the United States.
*Statistically different from zero at the 5 percent significance level (t distribution, 11 degrees of freedom).
**Statistically different from zero at the 10 percent significance level (t distribution, 11 degrees of freedom).
***Statistically different from zero at the 20 percent significance level (t distribution, 11 degrees of freedom).
SOURCE: OECD, *Economic Outlook* no. 41, June 1987, data diskettes.

## References


Barro, Robert, and Gordon, David. "Rules, Discretion, and Reputation in a Model of Monetary Policy." *Journal of Monetary Economics* 12 (July 1983): 101–21.

Brittan, Samuel. "European Monetary System: A Compromise that Could Be Worse than Either Extreme." *The World Economy* 2 (1979): 1–30.

Cohen, Benjamin J. "The European Monetary System: An Outsider's View." *Essays in International Finance* no. 142. Princeton: International Finance Section, Princeton University, 1981.

Cukierman, Alex, and Meltzer, Allan H. "A Theory of Ambiguity, Credibility, and Inflation under Discretion and Asymmetric Information." *Econometrica* 5 (September 1986): 1099–128.

De Grauwe, Paul. "Memorandum." In Memoranda on the European Monetary System, House of Commons, Treasury and Civil Service Committee, the Financial and Economic Consequences of U.K. Membership of the European Communities, pp. 5–11. London, 1985.

De Grauwe, Paul, and Verfaille, Guy. "Exchange Rate Variability, Misalignment, and the European Monetary System." Katholieke Universiteit te Leuven, 1987.

Dreze, Jacques; Wypslosz, Charles; Bean, Charles; Giavazzi, Francesco; and Giersch, Herbert. "The Two-Handed Growth Strategy for Europe: Autonomy through Flexible Cooperation." Economic Papers, no. 60. Brussels: Commission of the European Communities, October 1987.

*The Economist.* "No Parity of Power in the EMS." 19 September 1987.

Fratianni, Michele. "The European Monetary System: A Return to an Adjustable-Peg Arrangement." In *Monetary Institutions and the Policy Process*, pp. 139–72. Edited by Karl Brunner and Allan H. Meltzer. Carnegie-Rochester Conference Series on Public Policy, vol. 13, 1980.

Giavazzi, Francesco, and Giovannini, Alberto. "The Role of the Exchange-Rate Regime in a Disinflation: Empirical Evidence on the European Monetary System." Paper presented at the American Economic Association Meetings, Chicago, 28–30 December 1987.

Giavazzi, Francesco, and Pagano, Marco. "Capital Controls and the European Monetary System." In *Capital Controls and Foreign Exchange Legislation.* Euromobiliare, Occasional Paper, June 1985.

Giavazzi, Francesco, and Pagano, Marco. "The Advantage of Tying One's Hands: EMS Discipline and Central Bank Credibility." Center for Economic Policy Research Discussion Paper no. 135. London, October 1986.

Goodhart, Charles. "Has the Time Come for the U.K. to Join the EMS?" *The Banker*, February 1986.

Harris Bank. International money market and foreign exchange rates, *Weekly Review*. Chicago, various issues.

International Monetary Fund. *International Financial Statistics*. Washington, D.C., various issues.

Lucas, Robert E. "Econometric Policy Evaluation: A Critique." In *The Phillips Curve and Labor Markets*, pp. 19–46. Edited by Karl Brunner and Allan H. Meltzer. Carnegie-Rochester Conference Series on Public Policy, vol. 1, 1976.

Masera, Rainer. *L'unificazione monetaria europea*. Bologna: il Mulino, 1987.
Organization for Economic Cooperation and Development. *Economic Outlook* no. 41, Paris, June 1987, data diskettes.
Rogoff, Kenneth. "Can Exchange Rate Predictability Be Achieved without Monetary Convergence?" *European Economic Review* 28 (June–July 1985): 93–115.
San Paolo. *ECU Newsletter*. Torino, January 1987.
Tsoukalis, Loukas, "The Political Economy of the European Monetary System." Paper presented at the conference on the Political Economy of International Macroeconomic Policy Coordination, Andover, Mass., 5–7 November 1987.
Ungerer, Horst; Evans, Owens; Mayer, Thomas; and Young, Philip. *The European Monetary System: Recent Developments*. Washington, D.C.: International Monetary Fund, December 1986.
Vaubel, Roland. "The Return to the New European Monetary System: Objectives, Incentives, Perspectives." In *Monetary Institutions and the Policy Process*, pp. 173–221. Edited by Karl Brunner and Allan H. Meltzer. Carnegie-Rochester Conference Series on Public Policy, vol. 13, 1980.
Walters, Alan. *Britain's Economic Renaissance: Margaret Thatcher's Reforms 1979–1984*. New York: Oxford University Press, 1986.

# Comment

# A Critical View of the EMS*

*Alan Walters*

With the exception of one or two reservations, I find myself in substantial agreement with Michele Fratianni's paper. My main concern is that it did not provide a sharp and concise description of this reptilian descendant of the deceased snake. Let us try to fill this gap.

## A Caricature of the EMS

Clearly, the purpose of the European Monetary System (EMS) was to provide intermember exchange rate stability until the occasion of realignment. Let us therefore suppose that realignments take place at the end of the year, and that the EMS currencies have fixed exchange rates for that year. Let us also assume that there are no capital controls and no regulations inhibiting or taxing foreign acquisition of financial assets. Then the fixed exchange rates will necessarily imply that nominal interest rates, for periods of maturity less than one year, will be equal. Arbitrage will ensure such equality.

To suffuse an air of verisimilitude, let us suppose the two countries, Italy and Germany, are locked into this EMS-induced equality of interest rates. This equality will occur whatever the ambient rates of inflation in the two countries. Let us therefore suppose that the ambient rate of inflation in Italy is 10 percent and that Germany has stable prices. The common nominal interest rate, we may assume, is 5 percent.

This implies that the real interest rate in Germany is positive at 5 percent, whereas in Italy there is a *negative* real interest rate of 5 percent. Such interest rates are, of course, precisely the opposite of those that are required for reducing the rate of inflation in Italy and for promoting growth in Germany. With the short interest rate as the most important instrument of monetary control, the low real interest rates in Italy would stimulate a rapid expansion of lira, whereas the

---

*Reprinted from *Cato Journal* 8 (Fall 1988): 503–6.

The author is Professor of Economics at Johns Hopkins University and a Senior Fellow at the American Enterprise Institute.

high real rates in Germany would depress the demand for marks. Thus it appears that the EMS would induce monetary incentives that are exactly the opposite of those required for "harmonization" of inflation rates.

One may concede this point but argue that the domestic pressures on interest rates would surely give rise to a narrowing of the real interest rate gap. (One would also need to concede that there are costs of capital crossing frontiers to violate the one-price result of perfect arbitrage.) Let us imagine therefore that nominal rates are 3 percent in Germany and 7 percent in Italy. Although the real rates are plus 3 percent in Germany and minus 3 percent in Italy, there is still an incentive for owners of mark deposits to overcome the costs of capital crossing the Italian frontier since deposits in lira earn 7 percent, which can be converted at the end of the year to marks at the fixed exchange rate. Thus the pressure is for capital to move from Germany to Italy. This is the reverse of an equilibriating flow of reserves. Again it will enhance the disparity in inflation rates. (One of the effects of the automaticity, which was recently negotiated, is to make sure official capital flows quickly offset the private flows.)

With monetary policy so emasculated, the main weight of adjustment must be taken over by fiscal policy that is aided and abetted by direct controls over wages and prices. To contain and reduce the inflation in Italy, tight fiscal policies would cause unemployment to rise. Again one would expect disparate fiscal policies—and Fratianni has observed evidence of this during 1979–87.

This pure fixed exchange rate system is, of course, a caricature of the EMS. In particular, there is considerable room (2.25 percent and, for Italy, 6 percent) within which the exchange rates can move from the central parity. Furthermore, the realignments of new parities can come at unexpected times. All these considerations blur the perversity we outlined in the pure caricature. But, at the same time, they destroy the one advantage of the EMS: namely, the fixity of exchange rates in the short run.

Fratianni says that the members of the EMS now regard it not as a short-run stabilizer, but as a mechanism aimed at "preventing high variability of exchange rates." But, as he points out, the reduction in variability within the EMS was eroded by a higher variability between the EMS and non-EMS countries. There is little enough stability to credit to the EMS account.

## Speculation, Capital Movements, and Reputation

One of the frequent claims is that the EMS reduces speculation against currencies. It is, of course, very difficult to know precisely what this claim means. But surely the EMS process of realignments—as in the devaluations of the franc and lira and the revaluation of the mark—provides the most risk-free speculation for any asset owner. Everyone knows the approximate date and direction of the change. It is not surprising that overnight interest rates of the franc shoot sky-high as investors borrow to bet on such a sure thing. I suspect that the opportunity to join periodically in such a sure thing against sterling may explain some of the enthusiasm in the City of London for Britain joining the exchange rate mechanism.

The pressure of capital movements in the EMS and the difficulty of maintaining exchange rates encourage resorting to other methods for reducing the pressure. Both Italy and France have maintained capital controls and exercise considerable restrictions over domestic credit markets. Attempts to abolish capital controls *and* to deregulate domestic capital markets have yet to be realized. One suspects also that the increased trade barriers in Europe, compared with the sharp decreases in the 1970s, have been in part due to the pressures of the EMS.

On the issue of reputation and discipline, Fratianni nicely confirms my own conjectures.[1] Before 1979, the main European nation outside the EMS, the United Kingdom, grew at half the rate of Germany and France, but since the recession of 1982, it has grown at twice the rate of Germany and France. British unemployment has been falling dramatically for three years, whereas in Germany, France, and Italy it is still increasing. The reduction in inflation has been quite as impressive as in those countries in the EMS. But I would attribute this British renaissance not entirely to its freedom from EMS entanglements, as in the study of Giavazzi and Giovannini, but primarily to Mrs. Thatcher. I refuse to regard Mrs. Thatcher as simply a realization of a random variable. She is neither random nor variable.

## Politicization of Exchange Rates

Compared with a floating system, the EMS entails a considerable politicization of exchange rates. The occasion for realignments involves a great political bargaining session rather than an occasion on which to review the fundamentals of real exchange rates. The French denouncing the dominant role of Germany and the attempts to make the Bundesbank pursue more inflationary policies seem to point to a political Achilles' heel. Any departure from German hegemony would, as Fratianni hints, make a nonsense of what little rationale there is for the EMS.

[1]See Walters (1986, chap. 7).

## The Currency Board Alternative

If the ultimate objective is the monetary integration of Europe through a European Central Bank (ECB) in a single currency area, then the EMS seems to be hardly a step in the right direction. It creates too many tensions, both economic and political. On the other hand, it is possible to develop sensible institutional arrangements that would usher in the integrated monetary system. One such institution, with massive historical precedent, is the currency board arrangement. Using the Bundesbank as the de facto ECB, member nations would hold 100 percent mark reserves against their own currency issues and would, at all times, exchange their currency against marks at a fixed rate. Such a fixed-rate system would provide automatic adjustments of the money supply to support the fixed rates. But, as everyone would agree, such integration is far beyond the bounds of the politically possible.

I can agree with Fratianni that the EMS "has not failed," but only in the sense that it has not broken down in mutual acrimony. In every other sense, which he examines so patiently, I would regard the EMS as a failure.

## Reference

Walters, Alan. *Britain's Economic Renaissance.* New York: Oxford University Press, 1986.

# 12

# SHOULD FLOATING CONTINUE?*

*Gottfried Haberler*

## Critics of the Present System

In the last two or three years the present system, or nonsystem as its critics say, of loosely managed floating has come under increasing criticism. The latest blast came from a totally unexpected source. His Holiness Pope John Paul II, in his Encyclical "The Social Concerns of the Church," says, "The world monetary and financial system is marked by excessive fluctuations of exchange rates and interest rates, to the detriment of the balance of payments and the debt situation of the poorer countries."[1] Naturally, the Pope does not make concrete proposals for change. The Encyclical says, "The Church does not have technical solutions to offer for the problem of underdevelopment as such. . . . For the Church does not propose economic and political systems or programs." Still the statement has been widely interpreted as a rejection of the present system of floating exchange rates.

French governments under the presidency of Francois Mitterrand, both socialist and conservative, also have expressed a distaste for floating rates and urged a return to some sort of fixed exchange system.

Naturally, the gold bugs at the *Wall Street Journal* have been delighted with the anti-float mentality of the Pope and the French. Indeed, they awarded a gold medal to French Minister of Finance Edouard Balladur and a silver medal to Pope John Paul II, citing them as among "the world's notable economic thinkers." The *Journal* then went on to criticize Beryl Sprinkel, a leading proponent of floating, awarding him a medal to "be fashioned in Styrofoam."[2]

---

*This article is an updated version of a paper that appeared under the same title in the *Cato Journal* 8 (Fall 1988): 307–14.

The author is a Resident Scholar at the American Enterprise Institute and Galen L. Stone Professor of International Trade, emeritus, at Harvard University.

[1]Cited in the *New York Times*, 20 February 1988, p. 4.

[2]*Wall Street Journal*, 23 February 1988, p. 30.

Mr. Balladur (1988) has spelled out the French position in considerable detail. Since his article has received widespread attention and reflects the general case against floating, his proposals should be carefully examined.[3] He starts by mentioning several alleged failures of floating exchange rates to achieve expected results: Never have international balances been so large, nor fluctuations of these imbalances so wide as during the period of floating exchange rates. I could go through the list of alleged failures and show that what happened was not the consequence of floating. But I shall not take the time to do that, because his criticism of floating falls to the ground when we consider the nature of proposed alternatives to floating and what would have happened if any one of them had been in force in the 1980s.

## Alternatives to Floating Rates

The suggested alternatives for floating rates are variants of the Bretton Woods system of "stable but adjustable exchange rates," embellished by target zones and guided—or misguided—by commodity price indexes, including the price of gold. There is no reason to assume that in the 1980s a Bretton Woods type system would have functioned better than it did in the 1960s and 1970s. On the contrary, it is easy to see that it would have broken down just as it did in the early 1970s.

In 1982 the U.S. economy took off on a vigorous, non-inflationary expansion. Foreign capital from Europe and other countries poured into the United States, the dollar soared, and a large trade deficit developed. Thus the U.S. economy pulled the world economy out of the recession.

Now consider what would have happened if in that situation the world economy had been in a straight jacket of fixed exchange rates. Europe would have come under severe deflationary pressure and any fixed rate system, with or without a target zone, would have collapsed. The response would have been imposition of controls and the world economy probably would have been plunged into a recession.

The Achilles' heel of the system of stable but adjustable exchange rates à la Bretton Woods is its vulnerability to destabilizing speculation. Very briefly, if under that system a currency weakens and the country loses reserves, the speculators (market participants) know that the currency can only go down; it cannot go up. Furthermore,

[3]See Solomon (1988) for a critical analysis of Balladur's proposals.

they have learned from experience that a devaluation is bound to be large, because the authorities want to make sure that they will not have to go soon again through the painful operation. Therefore, if the speculators have guessed correctly and the currency is devalued, they make a large profit. If they have misguessed, they merely lose transactions costs.

Under floating the situation is different. A currency under pressure goes down immediately. Therefore, the speculators can never be sure whether the market has not already overshot and the currency will go up again. Thus the speculation becomes much more risky.

The existence of target zones does not change the situation, unless it is sufficiently wide and otherwise flexible so as to approach a free float. John Williamson, the chief and most persuasive proponent of the target zone system, has been fully aware of the vulnerabilities of Bretton Woods and of a rigid target zone to speculative capital flows. In a recent proposal for reforming the international monetary system, Williamson and Miller (1987) suggest five modifications of the target zone scheme to make it more flexible and less vulnerable to speculative capital flows. First, increase the width of the target zone. For example, a 20 percent band compared with a 2 percent band under Bretton Woods would sharply increase the risk for speculators. Second, give the zone "soft buffers," so that "the authorities would be entitled to cease defending the zone" if some unexpected disturbance threatened to push the exchange rate out of the zone. Third, apply the principle of the crawling peg to the target zone. Fourth, provide for regular reviews of the real exchange rate target. Fifth, adjust policy so as to preclude major interventions.[4]

To be sure, if the width of the zone is sufficiently large, the buffers sufficiently soft, the crawl sufficiently fast, the policy reviews sufficiently frequent, and the policy adjustment sufficiently prompt, ample flexibility of the system would be assured. But in my opinion all this is much too complicated to be put into a multilateral agreement such as the Group of Seven (G-7).

Jacob Frenkel and Morris Goldstein (in the present volume) rightly say that the effectiveness of "a system of target zones" depends "on knowledge of equilibrium exchange rates."[5] The fact is that we, economists as well as ministers of finance and central bankers, do not know what the equilibrium rates are. But many economists, Rudiger Dornbusch and Martin Feldstein among them, are con-

[4]This fifth point was discussed in a letter by John Williamson to the author dated March 2, 1988.

[5]For a detailed discussion of target zones, see Frenkel and Goldstein (1987).

vinced that the dollar has to fall a good deal more to sharply reduce the U.S. current account deficit. A few others, on the basis of some purchasing power parity calculations believe that the dollar is already undervalued. In my opinion PPP has some long-term uses, but is much too crude an instrument to be of any use for short- or medium-term problems.

Official statements that this or that exchange rate is right have in most cases turned out to be incorrect. Time and again high U.S. officials and their German or Japanese counterparts have declared that the dollar–Deutsche mark or dollar-yen exchange rate was right, and they were soon contradicted by the facts.

Declarations of prestigious groups about exchange rates have not been much better. For example, the G-7 major industrial countries declared in their famous Louvre Agreement (February 1987) that exchange rates of the G-7 currencies, in particular the dollar-mark and the dollar-yen rates, are "consistent with the underlying fundamentals." True, the dollar-mark and dollar-yen rates remained stable for a year or so. But it required very large interventions in the foreign exchange market by the German and Japanese central banks—and later in 1988 and 1989 there occurred large fluctuations of the dollar-mark and dollar-yen rates.

The fact is that "the open-mouth policy," as frequent official pronouncements of the proper exchange rates was called, has lost credibility and has become counter-productive; that is to say, the policy has not reduced but increased the volatility of exchange rates. Noboru Takeshita, Japan's prime minister, hit the nail on its head. When asked whether the dollar-yen rate was about right, he responded: "Only God knows!"

I conclude that markets, if left alone, do a better job setting exchange rates than governments. True, markets, too, occasionally make mistakes; they sometimes overshoot. But markets correct themselves, because if a mistake has been made, more and more market participants (speculators) realize that the situation is becoming precarious. In sharp contrast, it is in the nature of the political process that governments are slow to recognize that they have made a mistake and are even slower correcting it.

It has been widely suggested that the dollar be anchored on, or linked to, an index of commodity prices including the price of gold. Mr. Balladur has mentioned that the monetary system as a whole might be given such an anchor. But as far as I know, nobody has spelled out how such a system would work.

I mention a few questions that have not been thoroughly discussed, let alone satisfactorily answered. First, which commodities should be included in the index? Take oil, one of the most important internationally traded commodities. The price of oil is very volatile, because it fluctuates with the ups and downs of the OPEC cartel. Does that not disqualify the oil price for inclusion in the index? There are other prices, such as the prices of coffee and tin, that are manipulated, or at least sharply influenced, by dominant producers. Moreover, large export subsidies influence the prices of many agricultural commodities.

Second, what is the rationale of including the gold price? If exchange rates between the major currencies are not fixed, in which currency should the price of gold be expressed?

Third, is the commodity price index a proper measure of world inflation and one that should guide monetary policy in all countries? Proponents of the indexing scheme seem to think so, but in most countries the consumer price index is regarded as the proper measure of inflation. The two price indexes often diverge sharply over extended periods. I do not think it would be reasonable to recommend that the national monetary authorities should pay more attention to commodity price indexes than to the consumer price index, and there surely is no chance that such an advice would be heeded.

Where does that leave the suggestion that the dollar or some other currency should be anchored on, or linked to, commodity prices? The answer seems to be that the commodity price index is just one of several economic "indicators" that should guide policymakers in their decisions.

The notion of "indicators," often called "objective indicators," has been playing a considerable role in the drive for international policy coordination. Thus at the Tokyo Summit (May 1986) the heads of state of the seven summit countries "requested" the ministers of finance of the G-7 "to review their economic objectives and forecasts at least once a year . . . to ensure their mutual compatibility . . . taking into account indicators such as GNP growth rates, inflation rates, interest rates, unemployment rates, fiscal deficit ratios, current account and trade balances, monetary growth rates, reserves, and exchange rates."

The proposed use of "indicators" has been hailed as a new approach and a major advance of policymaking in general and of international coordination of policies in particular. In my opinion there is nothing new in this "approach," not even the term "indicators" is new. As early as 1973, a report for the Committee of Twenty on Reform of the International Monetary System and Related Issues by "The Technical Group on Indicators" (under the chairmanship of Robert Solomon) discussed the use of indicators in the adjustment process.[6]

[6]See International Monetary Fund (1974, pp. 51–76).

Actually, hardly anything has been heard about a development and use of indicators by later meetings of the ministers of finance. True, in September 1986 the ministers of finance of the Group of Seven met "to conduct the first exercise of multilateral surveillance pursuant to the Tokyo Economic Summit Declaration of the heads of state of May 6, 1986." But the one-page official statement of the meeting is a collection of generalities, evidently a compromise that, according to press reports, was reached after spirited, even somewhat acrimonious discussions.[7]

Later meetings of the seven ministers like the one at the Louvre in Paris (February 1987) reached the conclusion that "the exchange rates were just about right, that they are consistent with the underlying fundamentals." Whether "objective indicators" were used to reach this conclusion is not known. But three things are clear: (1) The collective statements about equilibrium exchange rates turned out to be wrong; (2) the main thrust for international policy coordination is not to be found in the statements of the G-7, but in the pressure on Japan and especially on Germany by the United States, joined sometimes by other countries, to stimulate their economy; and (3) it is utopian to assume that these questions can be settled by setting up an agreed system of "indicators" that will tell every country what it has to do.

## Floating Should Continue

My conclusion from all this is that the present international monetary system does not require a radical change and that floating should continue, which I think it will. A Bretton Woods type conference to set up a new fixed rate system as has been suggested by French governments, both socialist and conservative, is out of the question.

The 1944 Bretton Woods conference was run by Britain and the United States (by John Maynard Keynes and Harry Dexter White). Today it would be the Group of Seven or the Group of Ten, and it would be hard to keep out representatives of the Third World. It is inconceivable that such a group could agree on something so ambitious as a new Bretton Woods scheme. In the present world the alternative to floating is in most cases direct controls, not fixed rates with free convertibility.

But I do not want to overstate the case for floating exchange rates; in a sense floating is merely a second best. Fixed exchange rates

[7]See Haberler (1987, pp. 86–87) for details.

would be the best system. If two or more countries can agree to fix the exchange rates of their currencies, it would be the best arrangement—provided, *first,* that the currencies are fully and freely convertible into each other at the fixed rate (in other words, that there are no exchange controls and no trade restrictions "to protect the balance of payments") and, *second,* that the fixed rate does not impose excessive unemployment or inflation on any participating country.

Unfortunately, in the present-day world these conditions are rarely fulfilled among sovereign states. It would require, as a minimum, close harmonization of monetary policy. The European Monetary System (EMS) is no exception because exchange rates are subject to periodic realignment and there is still exchange control in some member countries (for example, in France).[8] A few real exceptions can be found among the many countries that peg their currencies to the dollar, the Deutsche mark, or the yen. Austria is a good example: The Austrian schilling is pegged to the German mark. For a small country to peg its currency to that of its largest trading partner is a sensible policy. It is true Austria still has some exchange controls, but the controls are mild; and if the schilling lacked the firm anchor on the prestigious German mark, confidence in the soundness of the schilling would suffer and the controls would be tightened.

I repeat, in most cases the only realistic alternative to floating is not a fixed rate with full and free convertibility, but a pseudo fixity propped up by a battery of exchange and trade restrictions—the worst system. This was, of course, different before 1914; under the gold standard, exchange control was unknown. But those who want to go back, beyond Bretton Woods to the gold standard, face still another stumbling block. The Soviet Union and South Africa are by far the largest gold producers. As such, their output of gold would determine the long-term course of the world price level. Who would want to take that chance?

## Postscript

Controversies about the problem of fixed versus flexible exchange rates have been simmering since the breakdown of the Bretton Woods system in the early 1970s. From time to time the simmer has come to a boil, and it will almost certainly do so again later this year.

The European Community (EC) in 1987 agreed to create a single European market (that is, to abolish all trade restrictions by 1992). At a European summit in Hanover in June 1988, the EC agreed that

[8]See the excellent contribution by Michele Fratianni to the present volume and his article "Europe's Non-Model for Stable World Money" (1988).

by mid-1990 all restrictions on capital flows will be eliminated (in other words, that exchange controls will be lifted). The Committee of 17, a group of central bank governors chaired by Jacques Delors, president of the European Commission in Brussels, was set up to consider how to achieve economic and monetary union. The committee's report, due in May 1989, will be reviewed by the EC's ministers of finance and submitted to the European summit in Madrid in June 1989.

Lifting controls on capital flows obviously creates major monetary problems, especially for EC countries that still have exchange controls, notably France. These problems have been discussed under the heading "The Inconsistent Tercet." One cannot at the same time have free mobility of capital, fixed exchange rates, and national autonomy of monetary policy.

Two radical solutions of the problem have been proposed.[9] At one extreme is the creation of a single European central bank, which would issue a single European currency. This proposal has found astonishingly wide support, even from high officials. I find it inconceivable, however, that anything like that could be set up by mid-1990, or even by 1992.

The other extreme solution would be to scrap the EMS and go back to floating exchange rates, giving each country the choice of letting its currency float independently or of pegging it to the German mark or the French franc. From the economic point of view, this would be the best solution in my opinion. But I have no illusion that it is politically acceptable. It will be very interesting to see what the Committee of 17 proposes.

## References

Balladur, Edouard. "Rebuilding an International Monetary System: Three Possible Approaches." *Wall Street Journal,* 23 February 1988.

"Economic Olympiad." *Wall Street Journal,* 23 February 1988, p. 30.

"Excerpts from Papal Encyclical on Social Concerns of Church." *New York Times,* 20 February 1988, p. 4.

Fratianni, Michele. "Europe's Non-Model for Stable World Money." *Wall Street Journal,* 4 April 1988.

Frenkel, Jacob A., and Goldstein, Morris. "A Guide to Target Zones." NBER Reprint no. 907. Cambridge, Mass.: National Bureau of Economic Research, 1987. Reprinted from *IMF Staff Papers* 33 (1986).

Haberler, Gottfried. "The International Monetary System and Proposals for International Policy Coordination." In *Deficits, Taxes, and Economic Adjustments: Contemporary Economic Problems,* pp. 63–98. Edited by Phillip Cagan. Washington, D.C.: American Enterprise Institute, 1987.

[9]For a more elaborate discussion, see Haberler (forthcoming).

Haberler, Gottfried. "The International Monetary System, The European Monetary System (EMS), and a Single European Currency in a 'Single European Market,' " forthcoming.

International Monetary Fund. *International Monetary Reform*. Washington, D.C.: IMF, 1974.

Solomon, Robert. "Minister Balladur on International Monetary Reform." *International Economic Letter* 8 (15 March 1988).

Williamson, John. Letter to Gottfried Haberler, 2 March 1988.

Williamson, John, and Miller, Marcus H. *Targets and Indicators: A Blue Print for the International Coordination of Economic Policy*. Policy Analyses in International Economics, no. 22. Washington, D.C.: Institute for International Economics, September 1987.

# PART IV

# THE POLITICAL ECONOMY OF DEFICITS AND TRADE

# 13

# THE UNEASY RELATION BETWEEN THE BUDGET AND TRADE DEFICITS*

*William A. Niskanen*

Popular and political perceptions about the relation of the U.S. budget and trade deficits are based on the observation that both deficits have been unusually high during the past several years. Our professional perception of this relation is based on the combination of an accounting identity and a plausible hypothesis about the chain of effects that might lead an increased budget deficit to increase the trade deficit.

These two perceptions, however, provide neither an adequate understanding of this relation nor a sufficient guide for economic policy. The observed combination of large budget and trade deficits may have been a coincidence, in that both deficits may have been due to unrelated changes in other conditions. The two pillars of our professional understanding of this relation are more useful but are not sufficient. This paper summarizes our professional understanding of this relation and concludes that much of what we "know" about this relation is not consistent with the available evidence.

## The Accounting Identity

For several years, economists have been trying to educate politicians and journalists (without much success) about the implications of a basic accounting identity. This identity demonstrates that the foreign balance of any country in any year, an amount equal to the exports minus the (broadly defined) imports of that country, is also equal to saving *by* that country minus investment *in* that country. In other words, a country will have a trade surplus if saving is greater than domestic investment, and it will have a trade deficit if saving is

*Reprinted from *Cato Journal* 8 (Fall 1988): 507–19.

The author is Chairman of the Cato Institute and a former member of the President's Council of Economic Advisers.

less than domestic investment. Two implications of this identity are the following:

- A change in conditions or policies that increases exports or reduces imports will *not* increase the trade balance unless it also increases the balance of domestic saving and investment. Specifically, trade policy, by itself, may affect the level, product composition, and bilateral balances of trade but cannot change the balance of total exports and imports. Most politicians, unfortunately, either do not understand this implication or they are using a more general concern about the trade deficit as cover for policies that serve some sectoral interest.
- For our purpose, the more relevant implication is that a change in conditions or policies that increase the government-sector deficit will increase the trade deficit by an *equal* amount, unless such changes also affect private saving or investment. This identity, thus, provides a basis for expecting a strong positive relation between the government-sector balance of receipts and expenditures and the foreign-sector balance of exports and imports.

While these implications are important, they tell us nothing about the *direction* of the relation between the foreign and domestic balances. Specifically, changes in the domestic balance may be the result of changes in the foreign balance and vice versa. As it turns out, moreover, the expected relation between the government-sector balance and the foreign balance is not consistent with the available evidence.

An examination of the relevant data for the two most recent U.S. recovery periods provides some insights into why the relation between the government-sector balance and the foreign balance has not been stable. Table 1 summarizes the relation between the U.S. foreign and domestic balances during the recovery from the recessions of 1974–75 and of 1981–82, periods during which other economic conditions and policies were quite different.

The recovery from the 1974–75 recession illustrates the usual cyclical pattern. From 1975 through 1979, net foreign investment by the United States declined substantially, despite a strong increase in the government balance from a record peacetime deficit to a small surplus. During this recovery, in other words, there was a strong *negative* relation between the foreign balance and the government balance. Other characteristics of this recovery were also rather typical. The rate of private saving declined gradually during the recovery, and the rate of private investment increased sharply. The single condition most closely associated with net foreign investment is the level of private domestic investment. In brief, the United States invests more abroad when it invests less at home and vice versa.

*TABLE 1*

THE RELATION OF U.S. FOREIGN AND DOMESTIC BALANCES

| Year | F | = | X | − | M | = | S | + G | − | I |
|---|---|---|---|---|---|---|---|---|---|---|
| | | | | | Percent of GNP | | | | | |
| 1975 | 1.4 | | 10.1 | | 8.7 | | 19.2 | − 4.1 | | 13.7 |
| 1976 | 0.5 | | 10.0 | | 9.5 | | 18.2 | − 2.2 | | 15.6 |
| 1977 | −0.4 | | 9.6 | | 10.1 | | 17.8 | − 1.0 | | 17.3 |
| 1978 | −0.4 | | 10.1 | | 10.6 | | 18.1 | − 0.0 | | 18.5 |
| 1979 | 0.1 | | 11.7 | | 11.6 | | 17.7 | 0.5 | | 18.1 |
| 1982 | 0.0 | | 11.4 | | 11.5 | | 17.6 | − 3.5 | | 14.1 |
| 1983 | −1.0 | | 10.4 | | 11.3 | | 17.5 | − 3.8 | | 14.7 |
| 1984 | −2.4 | | 10.2 | | 12.6 | | 18.0 | − 2.8 | | 17.6 |
| 1985 | −2.9 | | 9.2 | | 12.1 | | 16.4 | − 3.3 | | 16.0 |
| 1986 | −3.4 | | 8.9 | | 12.3 | | 15.9 | − 3.5 | | 15.8 |
| 1987 | −3.5 | | 9.5 | | 13.0 | | 14.9 | − 2.4 | | 16.0 |

F = net foreign investment
X = exports plus capital grants received by the United States
M = imports plus transfer payments and interest payments by the government to foreigners
S = gross private saving plus the statistical discrepancy
G = total government-sector (federal, state, and local) surplus (+) or deficit (−)
I = gross private domestic investment

NOTE: Details may not add to totals because of rounding.

SOURCE: U.S. Bureau of Economic Analysis, *Survey of Current Business*.

The recovery from the 1981–82 recession reflects a quite different pattern. From 1982 through 1987, net foreign investment by the United States declined substantially, although the government deficit share of GNP also declined somewhat. During this recovery there was little apparent relation between the foreign balance and the government balance. The decline in the foreign balance through 1984 was primarily due to a strong increase in domestic investment. The continued decline in the foreign balance through 1987, however, was primarily due to an unusually strong decline in the rate of private saving, a condition that has yet to be explained.

These comparisons indicate that changes in the government balance have not been the primary causes of short-term changes in the foreign balance. A comparison of the comparable recovery years of 1979 and 1986, however, illustrates the expected relation: Net foreign investment by the United States in 1986 was lower than in 1979 by about 3.5 percent of GNP, in combination with a reduction of the government balance by about 4 percent of GNP. This last comparison indicates that the large recent decline in net foreign investment by the United States was due, not to an increase in the government deficit, but to the fact that the deficit did not decline as much as is usual during the current recovery.

The longer-term U.S. experience, as well as a cross-country comparison, does not indicate any significant direct relation of the foreign balance and the government balance. Figure 1 illustrates the U.S. data from 1947 through 1986. Figure 2 illustrates the cross-country data, based on the 1970–84 averages.[1] (The dashed line in Figure 1 reflects the relation between the first-differences of these variables, to be discussed later. The dashed line in Figure 2 reflects the relation between the average levels of these variables.) In both cases there is a very small positive relation between the foreign and government balances, but in neither case is this relation significant. How does one reconcile the strong positive relation between these balances, as suggested by the accounting identity, with the very weak and insignificant direct relation indicated by the empirical data? One step at a time.

From the accounting identity

$$F = S + G - I,$$

the effect on $F$ of an increase in $G$ is

$$\delta F/\delta G = \delta S/\delta G + 1 - \delta I/\delta G.$$

As mentioned above, one should expect a strong positive relation between the foreign balance and the government balance only if private saving and investment are not strongly related to the government balance. The observed direct relation between the foreign balance and the government balance will be the sum of these three effects. If the Ricardo-Barro effect ($\delta S/\delta G$), for example, is equal to $-1$, an increase in government borrowing is offset by an equal increase in private saving, with no effect on either foreign or domestic investment. Similarly, if an increase in government borrowing displaces an equal amount of domestic investment ($\delta I/\delta G = 1$) with no effect on private saving, changes in the government balance will have no effect on the foreign balance. Some of the more serious controversies among economists involve the magnitude of these two "crowding-out" effects. I do not expect here to resolve these controversies.

The results of the simple first-difference regressions reported in Table 2, however, provide an important insight into why the government balance in the United States does not appear to have had a

[1]Figure 2 is from Darby (1987).

*FIGURE 1*

U.S. FOREIGN AND GOVERNMENT BALANCES, 1947–87

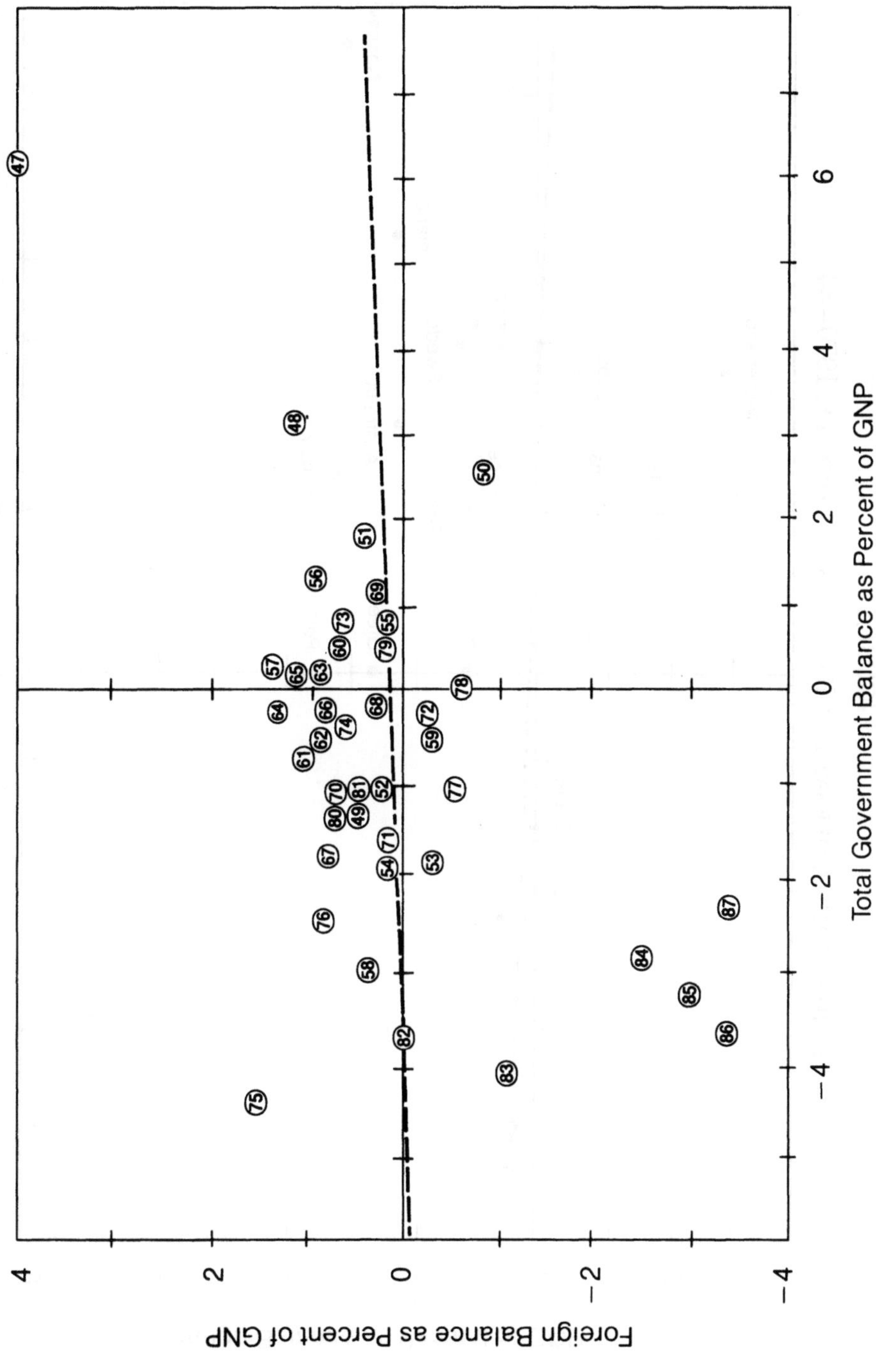

*FIGURE 2*

FOREIGN AND GOVERNMENT BALANCES BY COUNTRY, 1970–84

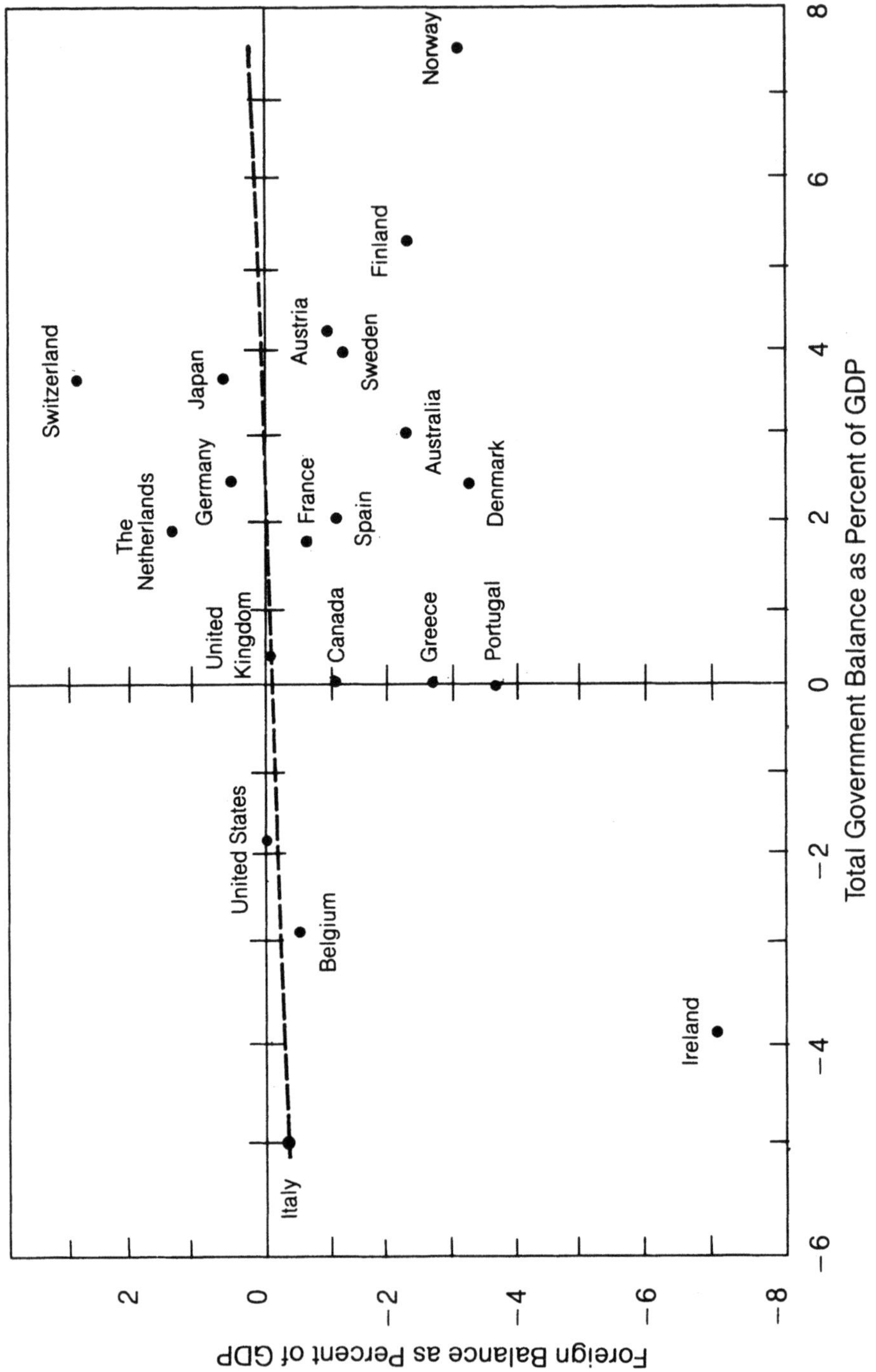


SOURCE: Darby (1987).

*TABLE 2*

MARGINAL EFFECTS OF CHANGES IN THE GOVERNMENT BALANCE

| Dependent Variables | *F* | *S* | *I* |
|---|---|---|---|
| Samples | | | |
| 1947–80 | | | |
| Annual Change | −.07 | .07 | .11 |
| Marginal Effects | .06 | −.27 | .67 |
| $r^2$ | .021 | .335 | .539 |
| 1947–87 | | | |
| Annual Change | −.16 | .00 | .13 |
| Marginal Effects | .05 | −.24 | .71 |
| $r^2$ | .015 | .239 | .544 |

NOTE: All variables are deflated by nominal GNP.

significant effect on the U.S. foreign balance: Specifically, the marginal effect of changes in the government balance on changes in private saving minus the marginal effect on domestic investment appears to be close to −1. In other words, most of the changes in the government balance appear to have been offset by changes in private saving and domestic investment, with little effect on the foreign balance. (The results reported in Table 2 are best described as descriptive statistics, because they do not control for cyclical conditions that affect each of these variables. The cross-country data presented in Figure 2, however, are the average of these variables over a 15-year period and reflect a similar weak relation between the foreign and domestic balances.) Moreover, the marginal effects of changes in the government balance do not appear to have changed significantly during the 1980s. For the total postwar period, thus, almost all the variation in the U.S. foreign balance appears to have been due to changes in U.S. private saving and investment that were independent of changes in the government balance.

The constant terms in these simple first-difference regressions also deserve attention. Both samples indicate a small secular decline in U.S. foreign investment and a small secular increase in U.S. domestic investment. This outcome reflects the gradual decline in the real post-tax return on foreign investment relative to the return on U.S. domestic investment—a condition that, in turn, reflects the relative increase in the foreign capital stock after the destruction of World War II. The corresponding small secular decline in the U.S. trade balance, therefore, was due more to a realignment in the relative capital stocks than to a relative decline in the U.S. government balance.

Since 1980, however, U.S. private saving has been lower and U.S. domestic investment has been higher than would have been anticipated based on the prior postwar sample. From 1947 through 1980, for example, there was a small secular increase in the private saving rate, a condition that was sharply reversed in the 1980s. The reasons for the sharp decline in the U.S. private saving rate since 1980 are not clear, but this decline was probably associated with the large increase in the real value of financial assets. The relative increase in U.S. private investment through 1984 was most directly attributable to the reduction in the effective tax rates on new business investment in the 1981 tax legislation—a condition that was reversed by the 1986 tax legislation. The resulting sharp decline in the U.S. foreign balance during the 1980s, in summary, appears to have been primarily due to conditions other than the decline in the government balance. The "twin deficits" of the 1980s, in brief, were primarily a coincidence of unrelated conditions, rather than the result of a significant relation between the trade and budget deficits.

## The Plausible Hypothesis

The economist's characteristic hypothesis about the relation between the foreign and government balances is based on the following sequence of effects: Real budget deficits increase real interest rates, which increase the real exchange rate, which increases the real trade deficit.[2] This might best be described as "the Feldstein chain," after Martin Feldstein's explanation of this relation.[3] The problem of this hypothesis, however plausible, is that the evidence for each link in this chain is extraordinarily weak.

There is ample theoretical reason to expect that increased government borrowing will increase real interest rates by some amount, except in the extreme case in which the increased borrowing is fully offset by increased private saving. The best tests of this relation, however, fail to find any significant effects of past, current, or future

[2]The relation between the budget and trade deficits may also operate through other channels. Specifically, many economists maintain that an increase in the budget deficit increases total domestic demand, which increases imports and the trade deficit for any given level of interest and exchange rates. My reading of the evidence, especially during the 1980s, is that the relation between budget deficits and total domestic demand is even weaker than the relations operating through interest and exchange rates. In any case, whatever the channels of effects of the budget deficit, the aggregate data do not indicate a significant effect of budget deficits on the foreign balance.

[3]Feldstein's position was first summarized in the 1984 *Economic Report of the President* and later in Feldstein (1986).

government deficits on rates.[4] The characteristic focus on net saving, rather than on the total stock of debt, has led many economists to expect a larger effect. A focus on how government borrowing changes the total supply of debt, however, provides a more accurate perspective on the magnitude of the potential effects on interest rates.

The following example illustrates this point. Assume a total world supply of debt of $20 trillion and a real interest rate of 4 percent. An increase in the real government debt of $100 billion, in this case, increases the total supply of debt to $20.1 trillion, a 0.5 percent increase. In the absence of an increase in the world demand for debt, this increase in the supply of debt would increase real interest rates by only 2 basis points on a consul or about 5 basis points on a 10-year bond, plus some portfolio effect specific to the debt of the borrowing government. A precise estimate of the effect of a given increase in government debt would have to control for the conditions affecting the total world demand for debt and the supply of debt by the world's private sector and other governments, a task that is now beyond the most sophisticated econometric techniques. Variations in other conditions that affect the world demand for debt and the supply of debt by others apparently swamp the small effects of the large recent U.S. government deficits on real interest rates. This conclusion should surprise only those who continue to use a model based on saving and investment flows rather than the stock of debt to analyze these effects.

The theoretical relation between interest rates and exchange rates is more complex than is usually recognized. Specifically, the difference between the current and forward exchange rate with respect to another currency tends to equal the difference between domestic and foreign interest rates. In other words, an increase in domestic interest rates will increase the current exchange rate by an equal amount only when the forward exchange rate does not change, such as when the increase in the domestic interest rate is expected to be temporary. This relation, called the "covered parity" condition, is strongly consistent with the evidence and was about the same in the late 1970s and the early 1980s.[5] In both periods, changes in the current and forward exchange rates were closely related, explaining why there has been so little relation between interest rates and exchange rates. Moreover, the combined effect of these first two links does not appear to be significant. In other words, there does not

[4]The best studies of this issue are by Evans (1985, 1987).

[5]For the relation between exchange rates and interest rates, see Somensatto (1985) and Meese and Rogoff (1987).

appear to be any significant direct effect of budget deficits on exchange rates.[6]

Finally, the relation between the real exchange rate and the real trade deficit has also turned out to be weaker than expected. Economists have long recognized that a change in exchange rates would have a "J-curve" effect on the *nominal* trade deficit, but the lag between changes in the real exchange rate and changes in the real trade deficit was expected to be relatively short. The U.S. experience of the past several years, however, suggests that this relation is weaker and operates with a longer lag than earlier expected. Although the real foreign exchange value of the dollar peaked in early 1985, for example, the real U.S. trade deficit continued to increase through the summer of 1986. A continued decline in the real dollar exchange rate to a level about equal to that in 1980 has only reduced the real trade deficit, to date, to a level about equal to that in early 1986.

The reasons for this weak recent relation between the real exchange rate and the real trade deficit are not clear. One plausible explanation is the increased relative importance of quantitative restraints on international trade in a large number of products. Another reason may be the increased international sourcing of components of traded products, a practice that offsets part of the foreign price effect of changes in the exchange rate. A third reason may be a pricing strategy by some firms to maintain their market share, especially if the changes in the exchange rate are expected to be temporary. For whatever reason, the substantial decline in the real exchange value of the dollar since early 1985 has not, to date, reduced the real U.S. trade deficit as much as one would have expected from prior experience. In general, a lower real exchange rate will reduce the real trade deficit, but this relation is apparently weaker than was previously expected.

In summary, the characteristic explanation of the relation between the budget deficit and the trade deficit is plausible, but the evidence for each link in this chain of effects is surprisingly weak. One should not be surprised, therefore, that there does not appear to be significant direct relation between these two deficits.

## What to Do?

The "twin deficits" of the 1980s represent only one problem: The increase in private and government consumption, financed in part by borrowing abroad, will not provide a stream of returns to finance the increased debt. A reduction in the growth of either private or

[6]For a direct test of the relation between exchange rates and budget deficits, see Evans (1986).

government consumption relative to the growth of output will be necessary to resolve this problem, and the choice between these two approaches will be the central political issue for some years. The trade deficit, by itself, is not a problem. Given U.S. economic policies during the early 1980s, we were much better off with a large trade deficit; in the absence of a larger flow of goods and services from abroad, U.S. domestic investment would have been much lower and real interest rates would have been somewhat higher. If U.S. economic policies during this period were correct, the increased trade deficit should have been regarded as a desirable, albeit not anticipated, effect of these policies. The trade deficit has become a problem only because popular and political perceptions have misattributed this deficit to "unfair" foreign trade practices, with the consequent increase in actual and potential protectionist actions by the United States.

The remaining problem, however, is serious and will become more serious the longer we delay addressing it. This problem is the result of the growth of total debt relative to the growth of output, not the small but growing proportion of this debt owed to foreigners. The primary challenge will be to focus on the budget deficit, not the trade deficit. Some measures that would reduce the trade deficit would not be desirable, and some measures that would increase the trade deficit may be desirable. A recession, for example, would increase the budget deficit but would probably reduce the trade deficit. In contrast, a reduction in the capital gains tax rate would probably reduce the budget deficit but would increase the trade deficit.

Moreover, it is important to focus on measures to reduce the budget deficit that have the least adverse effects on economic growth, whatever their effects on the trade deficit. The primary candidates for government spending restraint, I suggest, are those programs that increased most rapidly during the Reagan years—defense, medical care, and agriculture. Defense spending (adjusted for general inflation) is now about 60 percent higher than in 1978 and about 20 percent higher than the peak Vietnam War spending in 1968, and there is reason to question whether the value of this record peacetime buildup was worth the cost. In effect, our large share of the defense burden of the West is one of our largest exports, but is one for which we are not compensated. At the margin of current spending for medical care, there does not appear to be any relation between most dimensions of health status and medical care, and most of the incremental benefits accrue to the providers of medical care. Our agricultural programs are a national scandal, and most of the benefits of these programs accrue to owners of farm land (and their creditors).

Spending for these and other smaller federal programs could probably be reduced by some amount without significant effects on our national security, health status, private consumption, or economic growth.

Some increase in tax revenues is necessary only if our politicians choose to maintain the current path of total real federal spending. The choice among alternative means to increase tax revenues, however, is very important. As much as possible, revenues should be increased by continuing to broaden the tax base, rather than by increasing tax rates. As much as possible, tax measures should be designed to restrain private consumption, rather than private saving or domestic investment. Again, the effects of such measures on the trade deficit should be irrelevant. An increased tax on domestic business investment, for example, would reduce the trade deficit by more than the decline in the budget deficit, but at the expense of U.S. economic growth.

One might hope that some presidential candidate would at least address these issues. In any case, a new administration of either party can avoid these hard choices only at the expense of increasing the problem for some later administration. A sustained reduction of the budget deficit may or may not reduce the trade deficit but is necessary to reduce the growth of total debt. Our objective, in summary, should be to put our own fiscal house in order without concern for the consequent effects on exchange rates and the trade deficit.

## References

Darby, Michael. "The Shaky Foundations of the Twin Towers." Department of the Treasury, Washington, D.C., 2 October 1987.

*Economic Report of the President*. Washington, D.C.: Government Printing Office, 1984.

Evans, Paul. "Do Large Deficits Produce High Interest Rates?" *American Economic Review* 75 (March 1985): 68–87.

Evans, Paul. "Is the Dollar High Because of Large Budget Deficits?" *Journal of Monetary Economics* 18 (November 1986): 227–49.

Evans, Paul. "Interest Rates and Expected Future Deficits in the United States." *Journal of Political Economy* 95 (February 1987): 34–58.

Feldstein, Martin. "The Budget Deficit and the Dollar." In *NBER Macroeconomics Annual*. Edited by Stanley Fisher. Cambridge: MIT Press, 1986.

Meese, Richard, and Rogoff, Kenneth. "Was It Real? The Exchange Rate-Interest Differential Relation over the Modern Floating Rate Period." Hoover Institution Working Papers in Economics, E-87-49, November 1987.

Somensatto, Eduardo. "Budget Deficits, Exchange Rates, International Capital Flows, and Trade." In *Contemporary Economic Problems*. Edited by Phillip Cagan. Washington, D.C.: American Enterprise Institute, 1985.

# COMMENT

# BUDGET POLICY AND THE ECONOMY*

*Gary H. Stern*

Based only on his conclusions, I judge William Niskanen to have written a wise paper. That is because I reached many of the same conclusions in recent articles in our Bank's *Annual Report* and *Quarterly Review* (Stern 1986, 1987). But this agreement is reached despite significant differences in our views about how budget policy affects the economy. So in my brief comments, I will recite some of our common conclusions, describe how I arrived at them, and then explain where I disagree with Niskanen's analysis.

## Common Conclusions

Let me recite just a few of our common conclusions:

1. A GNP identity is useful in relating the trade deficit, government deficit, and savings/investment gap.
2. Assuming that private savings are fixed, the identity indicates that a rise in the government deficit must either crowd out domestic investment or worsen the trade deficit.
3. In the Reagan years, private savings as a percent of GNP in fact did not increase when the government deficit increased.
4. Because of a resulting decline in total savings (private plus government), the root problem caused by the higher government deficits is the sacrifice of future consumption for the sake of higher current consumption. In other words, our policies are impoverishing future generations to the benefit of current generations.
5. The trade deficit is not a root problem; it is a possibly optimal adjustment to the (mis)match of monetary and budget policies both here and abroad.
6. Policies that attempt to deal with the trade deficit directly, such as trade protectionism, without addressing the fundamental

*Reprinted from *Cato Journal* 8 (Fall 1988): 521–27.

The author is President of the Federal Reserve Bank of Minneapolis. His views do not necessarily reflect those of the Federal Reserve System.

problem will likely reduce investment and thus are likely to be counterproductive.

7. The appropriate policy course, then, and one which will result in a lower trade deficit, is to raise total U.S. savings. Since our efforts to raise private savings have not met notable success, this prescription suggests we must raise government savings—or, in other words, reduce the federal deficit.

## A General Model

I was careful in my *Annual Report* article to indicate the limitations of analysis by identity. Without some additional restrictions based on theory or empirical evidence, the identity provides no predictions about the effects of budget policy changes. In the *Annual Report* article I merely assumed that a higher deficit policy would not bring forth an equivalent rise in private savings; in the *Quarterly Review* article I explained why.

Let me briefly describe the general model I had in mind when I wrote those articles. My purpose is to help illustrate and clarify some of the differences I have with Niskanen's analysis.

Based on available theories and evidence, I reasoned that the best model of fiscal policy is a hybrid of a Barro-type Ricardian model and a Samuelson-type non-Ricardian model. (See, for example, Barro 1974 and Samuelson 1958.) In a Barro-type model all generations are linked by operative bequests, and it can be shown that a policy of higher budget deficits will be offset one-for-one by higher private savings. In a Samuelson-type model no bequests are operative and higher budget deficits are not offset one-for-one.

While both theories are coherent and internally consistent, evidence and common sense suggest that a more realistic model is somewhere between the two extremes. There are obvious shortcomings with Barro's model. A Barro-type model cannot explain why private savings did not increase in response to the Reagan deficits. Poterba and Summers (1987) have shown that this finding obtains no matter how private savings are reasonably defined. Moreover, as Bernheim and Bagwell (1988) point out, there would be no distorting taxes of any kind if Barro's model were true. Finally, we are all aware of people who leave no bequests. But, in the same vein, the Samuelson world is not realistic either. We know from micro data that a lot of people do leave bequests. In fact, Kotlikoff and Summers (see Kotlikoff 1987) estimate that without bequests, a Samuelson-type model can explain only about 20 percent of actual savings.

A hybrid of these two models, one in which some bequests are operative and some are not, seems the best bet. But such a hybrid should yield policy predictions that are qualitatively like those of the Samuelson model. That is because the weighted sum of the neutral Barro effects and nonneutral Samuelson effects will be nonneutral, just as the weighted sum of zero and a positive number is still a positive number.

Thus, my conclusions are consistent with a well-specified Samuelson-type model similar to that of Miller and Wallace (1985). In that model a permanent rise in the U.S. budget deficit, with no immediate response in monetary policy, raises the stock of real debt in the world capital market, and this causes the real interest rate to rise. Some of the additional real debt is bought by foreigners, and so there is an increase in the current account deficit. Exchange rate effects are determined by domestic and foreign monetary policy responses to the budget policy change. Total U.S. savings decline as private savings do not rise to offset the rise in the deficit.

## Criticisms of Niskanen's Analysis

On the basis of my just-described analysis, I believe Niskanen makes too much of the chain by which higher budget deficits lead to a higher trade deficit, and I think he grossly misinterprets the data. Let me explain each of these criticisms.

I believe Niskanen's causal chain is overemphasized for three reasons. First, my model makes clear that the changes in the real interest rate, debt, exchange rates, and trade deficit constitute a single equilibrium response to a single external disturbance, the latter being the change in federal budget policy. What Niskanen should analyze is the response of these variables to a change in budget policy, not the average correlations these variables have had historically with one another. My model does not predict that the responses of these variables to a budget policy change will follow in any particular order.

Second, the crucial factor in determining whether budget policy matters is how private savings respond to policy changes and not how the trade deficit responds. If private savings do not rise one-for-one with higher budget deficits, as both Niskanen and I find, there is a problem with a higher deficit policy, and the nature of that problem does not depend on whether the trade deficit increases or private investment falls. In either case the problem is that we are sacrificing future consumption for the sake of more current consumption. On the one hand, if we have a higher trade deficit, we could maintain the same capital stock, but foreigners will own more of the returns on it. On the other hand, if we have less investment, we will have a smaller capital stock. As long as savings do not behave in a Ricardian fashion, a policy of higher budget deficits makes future generations poorer.

Third, I do not believe we can dismiss, as Niskanen does, that our higher budget deficits did in fact lead to higher trade deficits. Theory and past relationships gave us little guidance on what the outcome of this policy change would be. Using the identity and my theory, we could conclude that such a policy change would result in some mix of higher trade deficits and lower investment. The theory does not say much about what that mix would be. And we have very little evidence to guide us in how the change in policy would affect the two. But, that gets me into my next main criticism.

I think Niskanen grossly misinterprets the data. The purpose of the analysis is to examine the proposition that a policy of higher budget deficits in the face of an unchanged monetary policy will lead to certain real effects. We get no evidence on whether this proposition is true by examining, as Niskanen does, simple correlations between realized values of deficits and other variables. Those correlations are essentially meaningless. (An appendix, available on request, supports my criticisms more explicitly.)

Budget deficits can change for essentially three reasons, but the proposition applies to only one such change. The correlations Niskanen examines just confound the effects of deficit changes from the three separate sources.

Budget deficits are affected by the economy. A weaker economy, for instance, implies lower government revenues and higher expenditures for unemployment compensation. Budget deficits are also affected by policy actions within a given policy regime. For much of the postwar period, for instance, tax rates were cut when the economy was weak and raised when it was strong, all within a regime of approximate budget balance over the business cycle. And finally, budget deficits can be affected by a change in budget regimes, such as a permanent cut in taxes.

The reason this distinction among the three types of deficit changes is important is that each can be expected to be related differently to other real economic variables. For example, budget deficits caused by a weak economy should go along with low interest rates as a fall in demand affects both; budget deficits caused by policy actions within a given policy regime may have little effect on interest rates since people come to expect the actions and adjust to them; but budget deficits caused by a regime change could have large effects on interest rates as the allocation of goods across time is altered.

*FIGURE 1*

DEFICITS AND INTEREST RATES
QUARTERLY 1948–1987:4

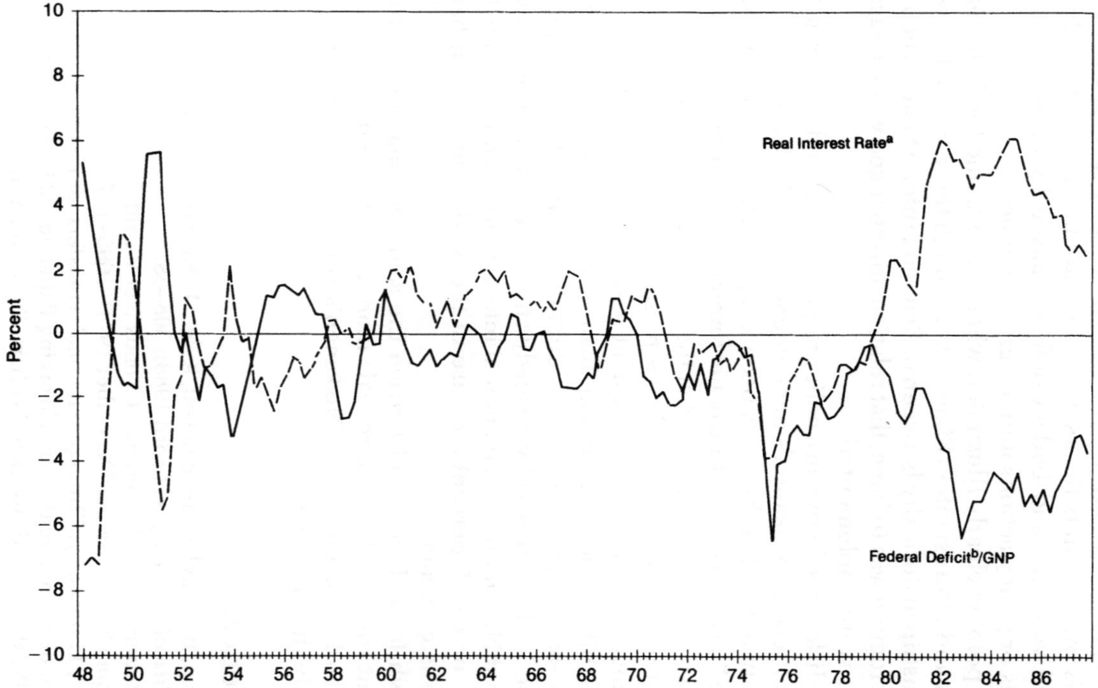


[a]Difference between four-quarter moving average in the three-month Treasury-bill rate and the four-quarter percentage change in the gross national product (GNP) implicit price deflator.
[b]As reported in the national income accounts.

Because Niskanen's evidence does not make these distinctions about deficits, I find it unconvincing. There is empirical evidence that the budget policy regime changed when Reagan came into office (see Miller and Roberds 1987). And there is evidence that real variables responded as my theory predicted. All that Niskanen's evidence is picking up is the average correlations historically between selected variables and budget deficits caused by either economic changes or policy actions under a given regime.

This point is clearly illustrated when we examine the behavior of deficits and interest rates (Figure 1). Although there was only a weak relationship historically between deficits and interest rates when one budget regime was in force, that relationship changed when Reagan's policies were implemented.

This difference between a policy regime change and a policy action is also crucial in Niskanen's incremental debt calculation. He seems to acknowledge that there has been a regime change when he states that the "large recent decline in net foreign investment by the United States was due . . . to the fact that the deficit did not decline as usual during the current recovery." We might then want to characterize the change in policy as a permanent real increase in budget deficits of $100 billion per year rather than a one-time increase of $100 billion—as Niskanen uses in his debt calculation. The incremental increase in debt caused by a steady stream of $100 billion per year forever at Niskanen's 4 percent real interest rate is equivalent to $2.5 trillion, or a 12.5 percent increase in the world's total. That hardly seems insignificant.

So, while Niskanen and I reach the same destination, we travel different routes. My route reveals more concerns about our budget policy and leads me to take Niskanen's conclusions, perhaps, more seriously than he does.

## References

Bernheim, B. Douglas, and Bagwell, Kyle. "Is Everything Neutral?" *Journal of Political Economy* 96 (April 1988): 308–38.

Barro, Robert J. "Are Government Bonds Net Wealth?" *Journal of Political Economy* 82 (November/December 1974): 1095–117.

Kotlikoff, Laurence J. "Intergenerational Transfers and Savings." National Bureau of Economic Research Working Paper no. 2237, May 1987.

Miller, Preston J., and Roberds, William. "The Quantitative Significance of the Lucas Critique." Federal Reserve Bank of Minneapolis Research Department Staff Report no. 109, April 1987.

Miller, Preston J., and Wallace, Neil. "International Coordination of Macroeconomic Policies: A Welfare Analysis." Federal Reserve Bank of Minneapolis *Quarterly Review* 9 (Spring 1985): 14–32.

Poterba, James M., and Summers, Lawrence H. "Finite Lifetimes and the Effects of Budget Deficits on National Saving." *Journal of Monetary Economics* 20 (September 1987): 369–91.

Samuelson, Paul A. "An Exact Consumption-loan Model of Interest with or without the Social Contrivance of Money." *Journal of Political Economy* 66 (December 1958): 467–82.

Stern, Gary H. "The Unpleasant Arithmetic of Budget and Trade Deficits." Federal Reserve Bank of Minneapolis *Annual Report* (1986): 3–16.

Stern, Gary H. "The Federal Budget's Effects on Intergenerational Equity: Undone or Not Undone?" Federal Reserve Bank of Minneapolis *Quarterly Review* 11 (Winter 1987): 2–6.

# Comment

# Conflicting Views of the Twin Deficits*

*John Williamson*

William Niskanen would have us believe that a series of mysteries surrounds the relation, or lack thereof, between the twin deficits. The truth seems to me altogether more boring: Economists actually do understand the relations tolerably well.

## Niskanen's Challenge to the Conventional View

The conventional view is that an *exogenous* increase in the structural budget deficit can be expected to result in a (smaller) increase in the current account deficit. This view does not rest on two separate "pillars," one an identity and the other a plausible causal chain, but rather emerges from a wide class of models that embody *both* the identity

$$F = G + (I - S)$$

where $F$ = current account deficit, $G$ = the budget deficit, and $(I - S)$ is the private sector financial deficit, *and* the so-called "Feldstein chain." (As I am sure Martin Feldstein would be the first to admit, he did have some intellectual antecedents!)

In certain special cases, these models generate extreme results. For example, with the Ricardo-Barro effect equal to $-1$, or complete crowding out, an exogenous change in the budget deficit will have no impact on the trade balance.[1] Or with perfect goods arbitrage, as Ronald McKinnon nowadays assumes, the impact will be one-for-one. But with conventional parameter values the impact is partial.

Niskanen argues that the identity implies that protection by itself cannot change the trade balance. This is erroneous. In an underemployed economy, protection shifts purchases to domestic goods and thus raises income, which generates endogenously the increased

---

*Reprinted from *Cato Journal* 8 (Fall 1988): 529–32.

The author is a Senior Fellow at the Institute for International Economics.

[1] I thought it was a stylized fact that the Ricardo-Barro effect was about $-0.5$. Are the results in Masson and Knight (1986) atypical?

savings that preserve the identity.[2] The case for free trade is overwhelming, but we weaken it by deploying patently specious arguments in its support.

It had never before occurred to me that absence of a close historical relationship between fiscal deficits and current account deficits, either intertemporally in U.S. experience (Niskanen's Figure 1) or internationally[3] (his Figure 2), would be taken to constitute evidence against the conventional view. Perhaps McKinnon should feel uncomfortable with this evidence, but most of us have little difficulty conceiving of explanations. For example, an investment boom tends both to reduce the budget deficit and to increase the trade deficit. So if the range of variation in the strength of investment has been comparable to exogenous variations in the budget deficit, it is entirely possible that no systematic positive relationship between trade and fiscal deficits will show up in the raw data.[4]

Let me move on to discuss Niskanen's "plausible hypothesis": Increased budget deficits increase real interest rates, which appreciate the real exchange rate, which increases the real trade deficit. This "Feldstein chain" is not valid always and everywhere. For example, the market expected the increased fiscal deficits in the early years of Mitterrand's government to be monetized, which naturally depreciated rather than appreciated the French franc. Neither is it the unique channel from budget to trade deficits. A second relation is important as long as the economy is below full employment: An increased budget deficit increases real income, which increases the trade deficit as more imports are bought due to income effects. This second relation would seem to rest upon some of the most secure links known to econometrics, the only possible exception being the Ricardo-Barro challenge to the hypothesis that budget deficits are expansionary. But let us concentrate on the full-employment comparison and whether the links in the Feldstein chain are as tenuous as Niskanen claims.

He cites two papers of Paul Evans (1985, 1987) to question whether bigger budget deficits raise interest rates. The first of the two papers

[2]This result is unambiguous if the exchange rate is fixed, but depends upon capital mobility when it floats. With a floating exchange rate and zero capital mobility it is true that protection does not increase income, but that is still not because of an identity.

[3]Neither had I realized the generality of fiscal virtue before seeing Figure 2: Only 4 of 20 countries are shown as averaging fiscal deficits over the period 1970–84. But then, only 4 countries out of 20 managed to have payments surpluses. Is the world really like this?

[4]The historical interrelationships of private and public savings-investment balances and the current account are extensively analyzed in Marris (1987, ch. 1).

essentially points out that the United States has had large budget deficits on three occasions between 1858 and President Reagan—during the Civil War, World War I, and World War II—and that these were not periods of particularly high real interest rates. (This takes many pages of econometrics.) What the author never asks is whether relevant economic behavior, like savings behavior or portfolio management, might change during total war. Total war is, after all, a rather powerful social experience, as those of us who almost made the "Hope and Glory" generation can testify, and would seem quite capable of shifting the savings propensity a few points (especially as governments try very hard to suppress consumption) or discouraging frivolous activities like calling one's broker.

The other Evans paper is a Friedman-Meiselman (1963) type of reduced form regression of interest rates on variables that include the budget deficit. So far as I can see, Evans' 1987 paper suffers from the same defect that rendered the Friedman-Meiselman paper of no value in discriminating between alternative hypotheses, namely that it neglects the possibility of reverse causation. If fiscal policy tended to become more expansionary when the economy was weak and therefore interest rates were low, this shows up as rejection of the hypothesis that budget deficits raise interest rates.

The two Evans papers are supplemented by assertions that an extra $100 billion of U.S. goverment debt increases the world real interest rate by only 2 basis points on a consol plus a portfolio effect specific to the U.S. government. The empirical basis of the quantitative estimate is not evident.

Niskanen's challenge to the conventional view that an increase in the real interest differential raises the real exchange rate is no more convincing. This relationship does not depend on constancy of the forward rate: That is merely a convenient expositional simplication. It depends on uncovered, and not covered, interest parity. His "evidence" is simply irrelevant.

I would suggest that a more reliable source of evidence for assessing the impact of budget deficits on the trade balance than those cited by Niskanen is to be found in the large econometric models. I do not need to do this link by link, for an authoritative recent study has addressed precisely the issue in hand on the basis of a series of the principal models. Helkie and Hooper (1988) find that on the basis of the average results of nine models the U.S. fiscal expansion over 1980–85 they can explain (through its direct effect on income as well as through the Feldstein chain) some $70 billion of the $143 billion deterioration in the U.S. current account over the years 1980–86. Foreign fiscal contraction accounts for a further $25 billion.

## The Relevant Conclusion

The conclusion seems to be inescapable. The trade deficit as well as the budget deficit results in substantial measure from the fiscal adventures of the early years of the Reagan administration. Even the Council of Economic Advisers (1988, pp. 109–11) accepts this as a fact.

Let us hope that the complacency toward the trade deficit that Niskanen expresses in the final pages of his paper will prove to be better justified than his analysis of its causes, and that the United States will escape the financial crisis that has sooner or later overtaken every other country to have allowed its external financial affairs to get into such an unholy mess. One of the tragedies of the 1980s was that there was no international monetary order capable of offering any defense against the irresponsible rejection of such knowledge as economists actually do possess in the pursuit of ideological whims and populist dreams like not paying taxes. Is it too much to hope that if and when Niskanen's complacency proves unjustified we may be governed by men of vision who grasp the opportunity to recreate a world monetary order that offers such a defense in the future?

## References

Council of Economic Advisers. *Economic Report of the President*. Washington, D.C.: Government Printing Office, 1988.

Evans, Paul. "Do Large Deficits Produce High Interest Rates?" *American Economic Review* 75 (March 1985): 68–87.

Evans, Paul. "Interest Rates and Expected Future Deficits in the United States." *Journal of Political Economy* 95 (February 1987): 34–58.

Friedman, Milton, and Meiselman, David I. "The Relative Stability of Monetary Velocity and the Investment Multiplier in the United States, 1898–1958." In Commission on Money and Credit, *Stabilization Policies*. Englewood Cliffs, N.J.: Prentice Hall, 1963.

Helkie, William L., and Hooper, Peter. "An Empirical Analysis of the External Deficit, 1980–86." In *External Deficits and the Dollar*. Washington, D.C.: Brookings Institution, 1988. Edited by R. C. Bryant, G. Holtham, and P. Hooper.

Marris, Stephen N. *Deficits and the Dollar: The World Economy at Risk*, revised ed. Washington, D.C.: Institute for International Economics, 1987.

Masson, Paul R., and Knight, Malcolm. "International Transmission of Fiscal Policies in Major Industrial Countries." *IMF Staff Papers* 33 (September 1986) 387–438.

# 14

# Dollars and Deficits: Substituting False for Real Problems*

*A. James Meigs*

Today, people are bewitched, bothered, and bewildered by talk about the twin deficits. However, concentration on the budget deficit and the trade deficit diverts attention from more serious problems: The growth in government spending and the rise of protectionism in international trade.

Both problems impose enormous costs on people of the United States and the rest of the world, and both are extremely difficult to resist. They do not confront us with urgent crises; they are more like a drug habit. They depress world economic growth by impairing the allocation of world resources year in and year out. Both problems are peculiarly intractable and insidious because both provide rich opportunities for public officials and legislators to confer large benefits on a few people while imposing small costs on many.[1]

As economists of the public choice school have taught us, the incentives facing legislators are heavily biased toward increasing spending on individual programs. No legislator expects to be rewarded for voting to cut a program that benefits some of his constituents. We can see that, but we have not yet learned what to do about it. That lack of solution is what makes controlling public spending so difficult.

With their opportunities for increasing expenditures now restricted by a dearth of revenues and by public disapproval of deficits, legis-

---

*Reprinted from *Cato Journal* 8 (Fall 1988): 533–53.

The author is an independent analyst in Princeton, New Jersey, and a former Senior Vice President and Chief Economist at the First Interstate Bancorp. This paper grew out of a topic suggested by Milton Friedman. It benefited greatly from his comments on an early draft. Colin D. Campbell, David I. Meiselman, Mickey D. Levy, Phillip E. Vincent, P. Kenneth Ackbarali, Noreen Doyas, A. Lynn Reaser, Nancy Kane, Rod Swanson, and Steven A. Hess also provided helpful suggestions. The usual caveat applies.

[1]Concentrating on the deficits also diverts attention from other serious problems. For example, Roberts (1988, p. 38) notes that overemphasis on reducing the budget deficit, if necessary by tax increases, diverts attention from monetary policy and a U.S. tax system that discourages private saving.

lators and bureaucrats find trade protectionism a fruitful source of benefits to sell. Kenneth Brown (1987, p. 97) argues that rent-seeking officials who formulate and administer trade policies prefer, where possible, to work through country-by-country negotiations and quantitative restraints on individual products rather than to take the wholesale route through the General Agreement on Tariffs and Trade. Jan Tumlir (1984) made similar observations.

Nevertheless, popular discussion continues to regard the key problems as twofold: the U.S. budget deficit, as opposed to the level of government spending; and the U.S. trade deficit, as opposed to the level of restraints on international trade. Those deficits look like crises to some observers.

This substitution of false problems for real problems tends to make a large fraction of public policy discussion largely irrelevant. Moreover, measures proposed for reducing the two deficits would make the other problems worse. Tax increases to reduce the budget deficit would weaken what little discipline there now is over expenditures in the federal government. Reducing the trade deficit by retaliating against "unfair" trade practices of other nations or by curbing imports with direct restraints would, by definition, increase protectionism. Finally, reducing imports and increasing exports by manipulating exchange rates would raise a host of additional problems without appreciably reducing pressures for trade protection.

## Costs of Government

The level of government spending, rather than the budget deficit, is the real problem because that level determines what fraction of the community's resources is allocated by the state. However spending is financed, the resources taken for government spending are no longer available for disposition by individuals in the community. The problem is the size of the fraction of the community's total output that is allocated, supposedly on our behalf, by government officials as opposed to the fraction available for individuals to decide how to use.

It is difficult to measure the benefits of governmental activities to society as a whole, not to mention the benefits to the people who contribute the resources. According to George Stigler (1988, p. 9):

> Our national income accounts value governmental activities at their cost of operation, so every porkbarrel bridge on an untravelled road is valued at cost along with wise and farseeing actions such as NSF grants of money to economists for research designed to eliminate poverty, not least for economists. The growth of functions of government transforms output from goods and services valued by the

market to goods and (mostly) services valued by the legislature, the chosen voice of the people.

Furthermore, budgeted expenditures are only a rough guide to the problem of determining who controls the allocation of resources. Governments have become adept at evading spending limits by requiring individuals and firms to make expenditures for, say, antipollution equipment or other governmentally mandated items that never show up in the official budget. Stigler points out that protectionism permits government agencies to achieve large redistributions of income from consumers to certain favored producers without reporting the transfers in the budget or in any governmental account.

Government is a very poor mechanism for allocating resources. The large deadweight losses in redistributing income can actually exceed the net income being transferred. For example, Stigler (1988, p. 10) found that the total deadweight loss of protecting beet sugar farmers is about 18 cents per pound of sugar, or more than four times the gain received by the farmers. He estimates that these and other efforts to redistribute income—one of the principal activities of modern governments—reduce efficiency of the total economy:

> Over the past half century, the rate of growth of gross national product per unit of capital and labor employed has declined (let us call this measured efficiency). Partly that decline is attributable to the failure to include the returns in social welfare from research, safety, environmental and income redistribution policies. Surely another large part of the decrease in measured efficiency is due to the large and still rising deadweight losses included in carrying out these social welfare programs [Stigler 1988, p. 10].

If we want to facilitate economic growth through fiscal policy, there are two possible courses of action. The first is to improve the government's allocation-decision machinery. Experience and public choice economics indicate that this approach is unlikely to accomplish very much. The second course is to reduce the share of national resources processed through the federal government's creaky machinery. That course was proposed in the 1981 Reagan Economic Recovery Program but was not fully carried through.[2]

Reducing the share of government spending in total gross national product would increase the share of goods and services valued by the market and would reduce the share valued by the legislature and government agencies. The resulting improvement in allocation of

[2]The Reagan administration succeeded in slowing growth of the share of Federal expenditures in gross national product, but the share was still larger in the administration's final year than in its first year.

resources would make it possible for growth rates of total output, consumption, and saving to increase.

## Why Is Spending so Difficult to Control?

Every year, it seems, we witness the pre-Christmas budget charade. Public discussion focuses on the budget deficit as though it were the object of the exercise, while paying little attention to the multitude of decisions allocating a large chunk of the GNP. This charade is an excellent example of how the deficit diverts attention from more important problems.

The year-end frenzy mainly reveals the incapacity of Congress to make rational budget decisions. Congress demonstrates that it does not know how to decide what share of national income should be allocated by the federal government. It further demonstrates that it has no system for allocating total expenditures among the various functions of govenment other than by bargaining among interest groups and by logrolling. No wonder financial markets around the world have displayed a decline in confidence in the U.S. economy and its managers.

The Congressional Budget and Impoundment Control Act of 1974 was supposed to give Congress the tools for managing the budget in a more business-like way. It succeeded only in spreading a layer of intricate machinery over a giant swap meet. Congressional budgeting has not always been such a tawdry business. Something happened during the 1960s and 1970s to break down a disciplined system that had kept the budget roughly in balance for many years.

Allen Schick (1983) and his collaborators argue in their book, *Making Economic Policy in Congress,* that strong committee chairmen from both parties formerly viewed themselves as guardians of the public purse. They oversaw budgets that grew incrementally from year to year as they distributed the annual expected increase in revenue resulting from economic growth among the various departments and functions of the federal government. But they did not attempt to distribute more revenue than they expected the tax system to yield.

Internal discipline began to erode in the Congress during the late 1960s with the opening up of the budget process, the demands for a greater social role for government, the growing independence of individual members of Congress, the proliferation of new committees and subcommittees, and the decline in the influence of party leadership. As Schick (1983, p. 258) says, "Many of the reforms that 'democratized' Congress in the late 1960s and early 1970s opened it to increased pressure for benefits from the federal government." These changes cannot easily be reversed.

In spite of this decay and inefficiency in Congress, the budget's growth rate was reduced during President Reagan's administration. How was this accomplished? I believe the key step was to deprive Congress of revenues for new programs. One consequence was a larger deficit for a while, maybe a long while. Another consequence was a brake on growth of federal spending. In former times, the possibility of running a deficit made government spending larger than it otherwise would have been. Today, the deficit is large enough to embarrass Congress into exerting more restraint on spending than it otherwise would.

No matter how pitifully members of Congress and lobbyists may writhe and wail today, the money for bold new spending programs simply is not in sight, unless other programs are cut or the public can be persuaded to accept tax increases.[3] In his paper, "The Domestic Budget after Gramm-Rudman—and after Reagan," John Weicher (1987, p. 270) says, "The tax reform passed in 1986 will make future tax increases more obvious and, therefore, more difficult politically; the continuing large budget deficits will put downward pressures on federal spending." I would add that indexing personal income tax exemptions and rates to inflation, which was approved in the 1981 tax bill, put further downward pressure on spending by reducing the inflation-revenue dividends produced by bracket creep. This pressure means that the deficit and public resistance to tax increases are now the most effective constraints we have over government spending.

Increasing taxes to reduce the deficit would weaken restraint on spending—a high price to pay. Yet many people in the business community and the economics profession disagree. The editors of *Fortune* (1987, p. 36), for example, say, "It would be wonderful if the budget deficit could be narrowed without raising taxes. Wonderful but impossible. Politicians of both parties demand more taxes as the price for less spending." To say that politicians demand more taxes should not surprise anyone, for politicians of both parties are in the business of providing benefits to specific groups of constituents. Politicians are desperate for new revenues to distribute—not a compelling argument for giving them what they want.

[3]A *Wall Street Journal* story on a congressional vote to override President Reagan's veto of a highway bill said, for example, "While the Democrats had the muscle to save a traditional program like highway spending, it has become almost impossible, politically and economically, to launch big new spending programs." And, later in the same piece, "Democrats feel obliged, along with the President, to continue to bring deficits down" (Birnbaum 1987).

I believe it is much too optimistic to expect Congress to use proceeds from a tax increase to reduce the deficit. Legislators have little or no incentive to do that. Furthermore, as Congress is now organized, there is no way for a president to enforce an agreement with Congress that expenditures would be cut in exchange for presidential approval of a tax increase, other than to shut down government by refusing to sign a year-end, mammoth, continuing resolution. In 1982 President Reagan thought he had an agreement that Congress would reduce spending by three dollars for every dollar of tax increase that he would approve. Therefore, he agreed to one of the largest tax increases in U.S. history (roughly $100 billion), but Congress reneged on the agreement to cut spending (see Niskanen 1988, pp. 77–78). No organized entity in Congress can or will make binding contracts or be held accountable for breaking promises.

A tax increase would only make the federal government bigger, in my opinion, while damaging taxpayers' incentives to work, save, and invest. This dilemma leaves us to consider the costs of tolerating budget deficits, because that is what we may do for some years. I would prefer to see the federal government operate under a balanced-budget rule, but we probably are years away from that. If the deficit is a constraint on growth of federal spending in the meantime, as I believe it is, we must ask whether other costs associated with deficits would offset that one benefit.

## Costs of Budget Deficits

Most public discussion assumes that the costs and dangers of budget deficits are so obvious and so large that deficits must be reduced by any means possible, including tax increases. I disagree. Deficits are bad, but bad compared to what? Some proposed cures could be worse than the disease.

Mickey Levy, David Meiselman, and others have pointed out that the size of the budget deficit tells little about what U.S. fiscal policy is, if the country has a fiscal policy. Levy (1988, p. 58), for example, says, "As residuals of tax revenues and spending, deficits provide only limited and ambiguous information about fiscal policy. Failure to recognize this has tended to oversimplify and mislead fiscal policy analysis, in part by focusing only on the aggregate demand impact of deficit changes." To appraise fiscal policy, therefore, we must examine all component parts on both the expenditure and the revenue sides of the budget.

Meiselman argues that in order to appraise the costs of government programs we must analyze how the programs are financed. In a general equilibrium framework, he says, we must consider the resource costs of expenditure programs, the distortions in resource allocation introduced by the programs, and the additional distortions and costs introduced by the means of financing. Whether taxes, borrowing, or inflation, each method of financing involves costs and distortions that can be evaluated only by comparing them with the alternatives available.[4]

Therefore, a budget deficit is not automatically the most costly method of financing expenditures. A given dollar change in the deficit could make the United States better off or worse off, depending on which tax or expenditure measures caused the change. Some taxes are worse than others and could be worse than the deficit they are supposed to reduce (see Darby 1987, Levy 1988, Roberts 1988).

If taxes are proposed for reducing the deficit, we must consider their effects on incentives to work, save, and invest. These effects are not trivial, as we found when marginal tax rates were reduced after 1980.

The more conventional discussion of deficits focuses on three major alleged dangers: (1) Deficits are inflationary; (2) changes in deficits stimulate or depress rates of economic expansion; and (3) deficits raise interest rates, which in turn reduce private investment and/or attract capital from abroad, ushering in international adjustment problems that we will discuss later. I believe the evidence for all three arguments is very weak.

Regarding the first charge, I do not know of any evidence that the budget deficit's size has an independent effect on the inflation rate at any given rate of monetary expansion. The Federal Reserve is in charge of the money supply and the inflation rate; however, Federal Reserve chairmen traditionally would rather lecture Congress on the evils of deficits than explain monetary policy. Although inflation came down as deficits went up in the 1980s, I believe that U.S. long-term interest rates are now higher than they otherwise would be because international investors and borrowers are afraid future U.S. politicians may decide to inflate their way out of the federal government's domestic and international debts. Those concerns are a respectable argument for controlling the deficit's size.

Regarding the second charge, I would argue that conventional macroeconomic theories explaining the impacts of changes in budget deficits on income are now in too much disarray to serve as bases for policy (see Levy 1988, Meiselman 1981). The coup de grace to the orthodox Keynesian analysis of the effects of deficits that many of us

[4]Conversations with Professor Meiselman. See also Meiselman (1981).

were taught when we were young and impressionable came in the early 1980s. While some economists predicted that the deficit would push the economy into an inflationary boom, others feared the deficit actually would prevent the economy from recovering from the 1981–82 recession. It did neither. Although gallons of ink and buckets of crocodile tears have been expended on the hypothetical dangers of reducing a budget deficit by cutting spending, we need not review those arguments here.

Regarding the third charge, it has been extraordinarily difficult to demonstrate empirically that budget deficits raise interest rates. Many people argue that deficits should raise interest rates, but they have a difficult time proving it. (See Brunner, Levy, Meiselman, Darby, Evans.)

An ingenious recent effort by Paul Wachtel and John Young (1987) demonstrates that announcements of unanticipated changes in projected deficits will affect interest rates in the expected direction on the day of each announcement. Having spent years observing securities dealers and traders at close range, I believe the Wachtel and Young results are consistent with typical dealer reflexes of reacting quickly to new clues about the size of future Treasury auctions. Dealers are preoccupied with flows of funds and securities. However, I need more evidence before concluding that Wachtel and Young have found a clear, dependable relationship between deficits and interest rates, where so many other researchers have failed.

My reason for not expecting to find strong interest-rate effects of changes in budget deficits is based on analyzing the problem in terms of stocks, rather than in terms of flows. Considering demands and supplies of stocks of assets suggests that current and prospective budget deficits have less influence on interest rates than is implied by many popular arguments for reducing the deficit. As Karl Brunner (1986, p. 715) argued:

> The direct link between deficits and interest rates [in conventional flow analysis] . . . suggests a massive effect on nominal and real rates of interest. The stock analysis conveys a very different sense. Deficits modify interest rates only indirectly. They gradually increase the stock of real debt and interest rates respond to this increase in the stock. But this increase in the stock relative to the inherited stock is modest compared to the savings-deficit proportion. We should expect therefore a smaller impact on interest rates by deficits than is typically suggested by a flow approach.

Brunner does not mean that the deficit is irrelevant. What matters most is what happens to the size of the stock of real public debt in comparison with the real stocks of all other assets. Changes in the

U.S. budget deficit have some effects in the expected directions, but the large, predictable, dominant effects on real interest rates that many analysts expect today simply cannot be demonstrated.

## Causes and Costs of Trade Deficits

In reviewing the economic literature and the op-ed pages, I found several main hypotheses used to explain the U.S. trade deficit and to defend various policies for dealing with it. For convenience, I will group them in three general views: the pure trade view, the U.S. capital vacuum cleaner view, and the U.S. investors' paradise view.

In the pure trade view, competitiveness problems, trade barriers abroad, consumer preferences for imported goods, Americans' high propensity to consume both private and public goods, and misaligned exchange rates cause us to import more than we export. Then we are said to borrow abroad to pay for the excess of imports over exports (see Friedman 1987).

In the U.S. capital vacuum cleaner view, which is very popular in other countries, the U.S. budget deficit raises interest rates and pulls in capital from abroad. People in other countries finance the U.S. budget deficit. The United States is then charged with depriving Third World countries and others of the capital they need to develop and work out of their debt problems.[5] The trade deficit appears as the mirror image of capital flows; goods from other countries are exchanged for U.S. securities and other assets.

However, there are serious flaws in this argument. First, it depends on strong, predictable effects on interest rates that I do not believe can be demonstrated. Second, when the dollar was rising between 1980 and 1985, the budget deficit was blamed for attracting foreign capital and thus for causing the dollar to appreciate (Levy 1988, p. 63). Appreciation of the dollar, in turn, was said to increase the current accounts deficit through its effects on prices of U.S. imports and exports. Therefore, some analysts concluded that it would be necessary to reduce the budget deficit in order to reduce the trade deficit. But when the dollar began to fall again, the budget deficit was blamed. To halt the decline in the dollar, therefore, other analysts, or the same ones, decided that it was imperative for the United States to reduce its budget deficit.[6] The same medicine was prescribed for

[5]For a discussion of possible effects of U.S. deficits on the international debt problem, see Michael Mussa (1984).

[6]See Torday (1988) for a typical financial press statement on the twin deficits when the dollar is falling. He writes, "Calls for Washington to boost the dollar through firm action aimed at cutting its budget and trade deficits have been widespread for months but haven't been heeded by the Reagan administration or Congress."

two different problems. Why should budget deficits of roughly the same size cause the dollar to rise at one time and fall at another?

In the U.S. investors' paradise view, the new economic policy regime introduced by the Reagan administration in the 1980s reduced risks and increased the real after-tax return on investment in the United States. Depressing political and economic developments in the rest of the world at the same time increased the relative attractiveness of the United States for investors from other countries and for American investors, especially commercial banks.

In this view, the capital inflows represent a classic response to the situation of a country whose domestic investment opportunities exceed its domestic savings. Japan and Germany, in contrast, are behaving like countries whose domestic savings exceed their domestic investment opportunities. So, capital flows from Japan and Germany to the United States. Investors, entrepreneurs, and the general public on both sides of the oceans benefit from the capital flows (see Darby 1987 and *Economic Report of the President* 1985).

The trade deficit may be mutually determined, as Meiselman argues, by both capital flows and competitiveness factors. There is something to the loss-of-competitiveness argument in the case of the U.S. automobile and steel industries. By the slippery canons of balance-of-payments accounting, a large part of the U.S. trade deficit can be accounted for by net imports of steel and autos. For a long time the managers and unions in these industries did not recognize that they were in a world market. They acted as though they had a secure national market in which all increases in their costs could be passed to their U.S. customers. As in other long-run evolutionary processes, it is difficult now for them to turn back the calendar. U.S. consumers have learned to like, and to trust, imported cars, even in the face of price differentials and trade restraints.

Many U.S. farmers, and the legislators who try to help them with price supports and other subsidies, suffer from a similar lack of realism about the opportunities and problems of participating in a global economy. By pricing U.S. farm products out of world markets, U.S. policymakers have contributed to the decline in our farm exports.

I called the canons of balance-of-payments accounting slippery because changing one or more of the flows is unlikely to change the trade deficit by the same amount. If, as I believe, capital flows are the principal determinant of trade flows, reducing the trade deficit in one area such as autos would not change the overall trade deficit. People in other countries would merely use a different package of goods to pay for the U.S. capital assets they want to buy. Americans could, in effect, get new capital from abroad on better terms if the U.S. auto and steel industries were to improve their performance.

## Costs of Protectionism

Advocates of protection argue that trade deficits injure U.S. producers of internationally traded goods. But what is there about the XYZ industry that would justify the cost of special protection in a highly developed economy like the United States? Unfortunately, people who advocate protection for the XYZ industry are not required to answer that question; the political system now permits an industry to extract costs of protection from the whole population without weighing the costs and benefits to everybody else. This is where the problems of controlling spending and resisting protectionism are similar.

We are all familiar with studies of the costs to consumers and others for protecting particular industries. Tumlir, however, stressed what I believe is an even more important cost, and one that is little recognized: the cost of interfering with the international price system through quantitative restrictions on trade. According to Tumlir (1984, p. 357):

> I find it difficult to work up much interest in tariffs, which both history and theory show to be quite innocuous protective devices, at least when stabilized. Once in place, they do not interfere with changes in relative prices. My main concern is with quantitative restrictions, which have the effect of paralyzing the price system in their area of application.

Unfortunately, quantitative restrictions are the ones that are most in vogue today among politicians, officials, and representatives of producer groups. Politicians and producer groups prefer such restrictions because their costs cannot be measured easily. And, as Kenneth Brown (1987) argues, officials charged with formulating and carrying out trade policy prefer quantitative restrictions because they are labor intensive; these restrictions require endless negotiations and renegotiations with numerous countries to establish and to police quotas on individual products.[7]

Other advocates of protectionism argue that large trade deficits cause intolerable changes in U.S. industrial structure. Between 1980 and 1985 some advocates feared that the United States was in danger of losing its industrial base and that we were becoming a nation of

[7]See Lardner (1988a, 1988b) for a fascinating account of using quota agreements in a long, costly, futile campaign to protect the U.S. textile and apparel industries from competition with producers in third world and newly industrialized countries.

short-order cooks and sales clerks. It is now clear that these arguments were grossly overstated. The United States is not being deindustrialized.

However, worldwide changes in industrial structure, or in the location of economic activities, are taking place with the inexorable force of geologic processes, but more rapidly. Exchange rate manipulation and the whole panoply of other protective devices are puny defenses against fast-forward continental drift. In the case of the textile industry, Nancy Kane (1988) argues that we are now seeing shifts in global location in response to technological and other influences that are similar to the regional shifts that occurred within the continental United States much earlier.[8]

In the economic expansion following the 1981–82 recession, U.S. domestic demand grew faster than output. Imports made up the difference. Imports were then blamed for holding down GNP growth. To Americans who were not accustomed to viewing international trade as more than a minor blessing, or annoyance, the surge of imports was unsettling. The times seemed out of joint. Perhaps most mystifying of all was the rise of the dollar on exchange markets. It was easy to consider the "overvalued dollar" as the cause of domestic ills ranging from farm mortgage foreclosures in the Corn Belt to layoffs in the Rust Belt.[9] The effort to devalue the dollar, which began in 1985 with the Plaza Agreement, was one of the regrettable consequences of overemphasizing the trade deficit.

## Attempting to Devalue the Dollar

Karl Brunner (1986, p. 709) tied exchange rates to the twin deficits in a description of European reactions to U.S. policies:

> The [budget] deficit seems to be the cause of double-digit nominal interest rates and the highest real rates since the 1930s. Such interest rates produce apparently an "overvalued dollar" encouraging imports and lowering our exports. This pattern reduces, so we hear, our welfare, as it lowers domestic employment and output below the otherwise achievable level. And the close interdependence of national capital markets transmits the effects of the "high interest policy" pursued by the U.S. government, represented by a "loose" fiscal and "tight" monetary policy, to all major nations. This vision offers European officials an excellent opportunity to blame U.S. policy for their economic troubles.

[8]See also Brown (1987), Kane (1987), McKenzie (1987), and Tatom (1986).

[9]In 1987 and 1988 the relative rates of growth of U.S. domestic final demand and imports reversed. Although imports remained high by past standards, domestic demand started to grow faster than imports, contributing to a recovery in U.S. manufacturing.

Although Brunner thought these ideas deserved sarcastic treatment, they apparently were being treated as a serious diagnosis by some members of Congress and inside the Department of Treasury. A blizzard of complaints from U.S. manufacturers and farmers convinced legislators and officials that something must be done about exchange rates—and quickly.

Until concerns about the domestic economy and fears that the trade deficit would lead to more protectionism caused the Reagan administration to begin nudging the dollar down in 1985, the administration had faithfully observed a policy of not intervening in exchange markets. The nonintervention policy had been announced in the 1981 Reagan Economic Recovery Program. James Baker, secretary of the treasury, announced the reversal of the administration's exchange market policy at the Hotel Plaza in New York City in September 1985. Although the Plaza Agreement met loud world applause, it reminds me of another fateful turn in U.S. policy: the broadening of the U.S. role in Vietnam in 1963.

After American officials encouraged the generals' coup that deposed President Diem in November 1963, the United States effectively took over responsibility for conduct of the war. Richard Holbrooke, who was in Vietnam at the time, later argued that history would hold the United States accountable in one way or another, even for things beyond U.S. control. He said, "Washington, in short, had found the worst possible level of involvement—deep enough to be held responsible, not skillful enough to find a government that could be effective in the war against the Viet Cong" (Holbrooke 1987, p. 46).

In the Plaza Agreement and subsequent agreements, I believe Washington again found the worst possible level of involvement—deep enough to be held responsible, not skillful enough to achieve its objectives in exchange markets. Ever since, the United States and its hapless partners have been lurching from one misadventure in exchange markets to another. Agreement has been piled on agreement as the dollar alternately appears too high or too low to satisfy the officials of the Group of Seven and their critics. Of course, this is not a question of skill alone. The U.S. government is being held accountable for things that are beyond Washington's control, or beyond the control of any government.

The decision to deal with the threat of protectionism by attempting to devalue the dollar is ironic because devaluation could be called "instant protection" itself. Devaluation was intended to discourage imports by increasing the dollar prices of imports and to encourage exports by reducing their prices in foreign currencies. Called "beggar-thy-neighbor" policies during the 1930s, devaluations intended to influence a nation's trade balance were disavowed in the Bretton Woods Agreement at the end of World War II.

Unfortunately, devaluing a currency is not like pulling a master switch that immediately changes prices of imports and exports by the same amounts and in the desired directions. Price effects vary in amounts and timing from product to product, raising new adjustment problems in many markets. Effects on the U.S. trade deficits have been so slow and difficult to see that pressure for protectionism has not diminished.

Exchange rate manipulation, as an alleged substitute for protectionism, has been costly. One cost has been an increase in market uncertainty as exchange traders agonize over each rumor about central bank actions and secret agreements among the Group of Seven. And information about international relative prices that people the world over need for allocating resources is frequently distorted, as it also is distorted by the trade restraints that troubled Tumlir (Meigs 1977, 1987; Tumlir 1984).

If the exchange interventions by the United States and its collaborators had been fully sterilized (that is, if they had been offset by central-bank sales and purchases of domestic assets), they should not have resulted in perceptible changes in domestic monetary policies. But what do we see?

There have been large changes in rates of monetary growth in Japan, Germany, and the United States since the resumption of exchange market intervention in 1985. We probably will never know how much exchange rate management caused monetary policies to differ from what domestic conditions in each country would have indicated. When the authorities tried to halt the dollar's decline in early 1987, for example, monetary expansion accelerated in Japan and Germany and decelerated in the United States. If these relative trends were to persist, the dollar probably, but not certainly, would eventually rise against the yen and the Deutsche mark. The U.S. authorities might call this rise the result of policy coordination. They have wanted the governments of Japan and West Germany to stimulate their economies while the others have wanted the United States to cool its economy. The tentative evidence indicates that the United States and its partners risk at least some damage to domestic stability in exchange for elusive effects on exchange rates and a reduction in the U.S. trade deficit.

## Should We Reduce the Capital Inflow?

Advocates of reducing the U.S. trade deficit should realize that doing so would also reduce the inflow of capital from abroad. Do we really want to do that? If so, why? U.S. governors and mayors who now go to Europe and Japan with delegations of boosters to attract investors may not have heard that they might be boosting the trade deficit by encouraging capital inflows.

Some analysts see the capital inflow as building a debt burden that will depress the living standards for future generations of U.S. citizens. C. Fred Bergsten, for example, was quoted in the *Wall Street Journal* on December 16, 1987, as saying, "The borrowing binge of the '80s leaves a legacy in terms of annual debt service to foreigners equivalent to about 1.5% to 2% of the whole gross national product. That's a permanent cost that will be levied on ourselves, our children and our grandchildren." I disagree. I believe instead that capital inflows from abroad will make future incomes of U.S. residents *larger* than they would otherwise be.

Benjamin Friedman and others say that much of the foreign capital is used for consumption rather than for investment in productive facilities, leaving Americans with more debt and fewer assets. But this merely reflects the U.S. saving rate, which is lower than saving rates in other countries. If the foreign capital had not come in, would Americans have consumed less, or would they have invested less? The answers are not obvious.

The total capital stock available to U.S. workers and businesses, for any given U.S. saving rate, surely must grow more rapidly with an inflow of capital from abroad than it would without that inflow, even though some imported capital may be consumed instead of being invested in productive facilities. The greater growth of capital stock, therefore, must be reflected in greater growth of total U.S. product (and consumption) than we otherwise would have. So the "burden of debt service" can be paid out of the greater product. How would this be different from the burden of domestic debts? Why does it matter who holds the debt (or equity)?

Foreign owners of businesses in the United States receive the marginal product of their capital, but American workers and various state, local, and federal tax authorities get the rest of the product of the enterprises in which the capital is employed. The total product is certainly greater than it would be without the capital. Moreover, Japanese and European plant managers are now bringing improved management techniques to our country, just as American managers took improved management techniques to other developing countries in the past.[10]

[10]See Stein (1987) for a similar view of the effects of capital inflows.

We may wish that Americans saved more. But the savings rate is not a policy variable to be managed by the federal government. Who knows what is the right level of saving? For believers in free markets the "correct" level of saving is the level resulting from the free exercise of individual preferences in a world in which incentives to save or consume are not distorted by governmental taxing and other activities. This suggests that to minimize such distortions we should examine how our system of taxes and income transfers influences national saving. Some public tax and other policies clearly bias peoples' choices toward consumption and away from saving. This bias is part of the problem of financing public expenditures in the least damaging way.

The growth of consumption reflects the free choices of millions of U.S. residents. Should they be prevented from consuming so much? Should they be forced to save more? Some analysts are so worried about the low U.S. saving rate that they recommend an element of compulsion to increase it. Brian Motley and Marc Charney (1988), for instance, recommend that growth of domestic demand should be slowed to increase domestic saving. Although they believe a decrease in federal expenditures would help, they think that would be difficult to do. "Alternatively," they say, "an increase in taxes or some cutback in federal transfers would reverse the rise in the share of national income accruing to the private sector." It is difficult for me to understand why a rise in the share of national income accruing to the private sector should be deplored. The reasoning of Motley and Charney indicates how preoccupation with deficits could lead to an increase in government spending (assuming I am correct in expecting that a revenue gain would be used for increasing expenditures rather than reducing the deficit).

We could say that Americans are consuming a larger share of current income now than in the past because they have built up vast stocks of human capital and consumer durable goods and because they have great confidence in their prospects. After all, the U.S. economy has provided 19 million new jobs since 1982, while employment in Europe and Japan has been nearly static. The family that borrows to pay for current consumption or for investment in housing, education, or durable goods does take on a burden for the future. But why should this burden be considered irrational?

There is one further argument for discouraging capital inflows or rather for discouraging growth of U.S. indebtedness to people in other countries. The argument, developed forcefully by Benjamin Friedman (1986, 1987), is that increasing indebtedness to foreigners has worrisome implications for the independence of U.S. economic policy and for the nation's ability to achieve a rising standard of living. According to Friedman (1986, p. 146) "At the most obvious level, net debtor status implies the need not just to service debt obligations owed abroad but to nurture foreign leaders' confidence in the nation's ability to meet its obligations, and hence their willingness to hold them."

Finally, Friedman (1986) is afraid that foreigners' portfolio preferences will differ from those of American investors and thus will influence asset returns here. In particular, he expects that growing participation of foreign investors in U.S. financial markets will require a greater premium of expected returns on long-term debts over expected returns on short-term debts than has been true in the past.

Friedman's analysis of capital-market effects of foreign investment in the United States does not suggest to me that investors in other countries will impose damaging requirements on the U.S. government or on private borrowers in this country. Foreign investors want the same market conditions that American investors want: stability and predictability in economic policies, and protection of property rights. Foreign investors in U.S. assets must also consider exchange risk, which behooves U.S. policymakers to avoid actions or statements that would undermine confidence in the domestic and international purchasing power of the dollar.

People in financial markets worry more about what governments and central banks may do about a change in a budget deficit or a trade deficit than they do about direct effects of either deficit on corporate earnings or interest rates. Therefore, policymakers should be careful about what they do or say regarding policy changes that could affect the prices of assets held by investors, either domestic or foreign. A sudden loss of investor confidence in the U.S. economy and in its managers could have painful consequences.

A diligent observer of economic policies and financial markets, Michael Keran (1988), argues that three major actions by the U.S. government could, as many analysts fear, trigger the loss of foreign confidence in U.S. economic policy. The first would be any actions that would increase budget deficits. (Investors have already discounted lack of progress in reducing deficits, he says.) This argument would be all to the good if it makes future congresses more cautious about increasing spending. However, I do not believe policymakers should assume that any or all tax increases that are advertised as intended to reduce budget deficits would sit well with foreign investors. The second policy error that Keran says would shake foreign investors' confidence would be the passage of strongly protectionist trade legislation and a threat to impose capital controls. That policy would be devastating. The third error would be a perception that the Federal Reserve was following an inflationary monetary policy. That policy too would be devastating to investor confidence, not only abroad but also at home.

There is nothing on Keran's list of confidence-shaking policies that should not also apply to American investors. Financial markets at home and abroad are acutely sensitive to real or rumored policy changes that would affect asset values. Policymakers who fail to consider the financial effects of their actions or statements, therefore, will be promptly embarrassed.

## Conclusions

Misplaced concern over budget deficits and trade deficits tempts the government and its official and unofficial advisers to let down their guard against more important problems, especially the growth of government spending and the rise of protectionism in international trade. This same concern tempts them to adopt policies to deal with the deficits that would do more harm than good. Among these harmful policies are proposed tax increases, which would merely increase the size of government and have damaging effects on incentives. Other harmful policies, such as trade restraints and manipulation of exchange rates, would damage U.S. consumers and other members of the global economy.

Controlling the growth in federal spending and the rise of protectionism is difficult because our political system makes it possible for legislators and officials to confer large benefits on well-organized interest groups while imposing small costs on the unorganized majority. As Stigler (1988, p. 11) writes, "It is a small, diffused and unenterprising special interest group that does not find some accommodation in the political scene." Perhaps that is the price of democracy. I hope not.

Exchange rate manipulation is especially damaging, because it increases risks in financial markets and in markets for goods and services by impairing information on international relative prices. It injects whole new realms of uncertainty in financial markets. A currency that is subject to direct, arbitrary, unpredictable interventions by governments is less desirable to hold as a store of international purchasing power than it would be if its exchange value were determined solely by market forces. The uncertainty engendered by attempts to manipulate exchange rates may have pushed the dollar below its long-run equilibrium value, giving foreign investors an opportunity to acquire U.S. equities, land, and other direct investments at bargain prices. Thus, U.S. exchange rate policy may actually be contributing to the trade deficit by encouraging the large capital inflow.

## References

Anderson, Gerald H., and Carson, John B. "U.S. Dependence on Foreign Saving." Federal Reserve Bank of Cleveland *Economic Commentary*, 1 September 1987.

Birnbaum, Jeffrey H. "Democrats Know Spending Pie Won't Get Bigger But Are Determined to Control How It's Sliced." *Wall Street Journal*, 9 April 1987.

Brown, Kenneth M. "Changes in Industrial Structure and Foreign Competition—The Policy Arguments." In *Deficits, Taxes, and Economic Adjustments*, pp. 97–128. Edited by Phillip Cagan. Washington, D.C.: American Enterprise Institute, 1987.

Brunner, Karl. "Deficits, Interest Rates, and Monetary Policy." *Cato Journal* 5 (Winter 1986): 709–26.

Caiden, Naomi. "The Politics of Subtraction." In *Making Economic Policy in Congress*, pp. 100–30. Edited by Allen Schick. Washington, D.C.: American Enterprise Institute, 1983.

Darby, Michael R. "The Shaky Foundations of the Twin Towers." Remarks at Dartmouth College, 2 October 1987.

Dornbusch, Rudiger W. "The Dollar: How Much Further Depreciation Do We Need?" Federal Reserve Bank of Atlanta *Economic Review*, 72 (September/October 1987): 2–13.

Dreyer, Jacob S. "The Behavior of the Dollar: Causes and Consequences." In *Deficits, Taxes, and Economic Adjustments*, pp. 5–62. Edited by Phillip Cagan. Washington, D.C.: American Enterprise Institute, 1987.

*Economic Report of the President*. Washington, D.C.: Government Printing Office, various years.

Ellwood, John W. "Budget Control in a Redistributive Environment." In *Making Economic Policy in Congress*, pp. 69–99. Edited by Allen Schick. Washington, D.C.: American Enterprise Institute, 1983.

Evans, Paul. "Do Large Deficits Produce High Interest Rates?" *American Economic Review* 75 (March 1985): 68–87.

Evans, Paul. "Interest Rates and Expected Future Deficits in the United States." *Journal of Political Economy* 95 (February 1987): 34–58.

*Fortune*. "The Budget Deficit: What to Do," 7 December 1987, pp. 36–37.

Friedman, Benjamin M. *Implications of the U.S. Net Capital Inflow*. NBER Reprint no. 878. Reprinted from *How Open Is the U.S. Economy?* pp. 137–61. Edited by R. W. Hafer. Lexington: D.C. Heath and Company, 1986.

Friedman, Benjamin M. "Long-Run Costs of U.S. Fiscal Policy: The International Dimension." Paper prepared for the conference on Ties that Bind: Debts, Deficits, Demography, sponsored by Americans for Generational Equity, Washington, D.C., 10–11 September 1987.

Haberler, Gottfried. "The International Monetary System and Proposals for International Policy Coordination." In *Deficits, Taxes, and Economic*

*Adjustments*, pp. 63–96. Edited by Phillip Cagan. Washington, D.C.: American Enterprise Institute, 1987.

Holbrooke, Richard. Review of *A Death in November*, by Ellen J. Hammer. *The New Republic*, 14 December 1987, pp. 44–47.

Kane, Nancy. "The Myth of Deindustrialization." First Interstate Bancorp *Managers' Economic Letter* 6, no. 20 (5 October 1987).

Kane, Nancy. *Textiles in Transition: Technology, Wages and Industry Relocations in the U.S. Textile Industry, 1880–1930*. Westport, Conn.: Greenwood Press, 1988.

Keran, Michael W. "Foreign Influences on the U.S. Economy." The Prudential *Economic Review* (January 1988).

Lardner, James. "Annals of Business (Global Clothing Industry—Part I)." *The New Yorker*, 11 January 1988a, pp. 39–73.

Lardner, James. "Annals of Business (Global Clothing Industry—Part II)." *The New Yorker*, 18 January 1988b, pp. 57–73.

Levy, Mickey D. "Origins and Effects of the Deficit." In *Assessing the Reagan Years*, pp. 45–69. Edited by David Boaz. Washington, D.C.: Cato Institute, 1988.

McKenzie, Richard B. "The Emergence of the Service Economy: Fact or Artifact?" Cato Institute Policy Analysis no. 93, 27 October 1987.

Meigs, A. James. "The Role of Information Disclosure in International Monetary Policy." In *Federal Reserve Policies and Public Disclosure*, pp. 49–71. Edited by Richard D. Erb. Washington, D.C.: The American Enterprise Institute, 1977.

Meigs, A. James. "The Rise and Fall of the Almighty Dollar: Lobotomy by Committee." *The Chapman College Economic & Business Review*, June 1987.

Meiselman, David I. "Tax Cuts, Inflation, and Interest Rates." Statement for Hearings before the Joint Economic Committee, U.S. Congress, on "Tax Policy: Are Tax Cuts Inflationary?" 23 February 1981.

Motley, Brian, and Charney, Marc. "The Saving Shortfall." *FRBSF Weekly Letter*, 1 January 1988.

Mussa, Michael. "U.S. Macroeconomic Policy and Third World Debt." *Cato Journal* 4 (Spring/Summer 1984): 81–95.

Niskanen, William A. *Reaganomics: An Insider's Account of the Policies and the People*. New York: Oxford University Press, 1988.

Roberts, Paul Craig. "Reaganomics and the Crash: The Fallacious Attack on the Twin Towers of Debt." *Policy Review*, no. 43 (Winter 1988): 38–42.

Schick, Allen. "The Distributive Congress." In *Making Economic Policy in Congress*, pp. 257–73. Edited by Allen Schick. Washington, D.C.: American Enterprise Institute, 1983.

Stein, Herbert. "World Economy Doesn't Hang in the Imbalance." *Wall Street Journal*, 30 December 1987.

Stigler, George J. "The Adam Smith Lecture: The Effect of Government on Economic Efficiency." *Business Economics* 23 (January 1988):7–13.

Tatom, John A. "Why Has Manufacturing Employment Declined?" Federal Reserve Bank of St. Louis *Review* 68 (December 1986):15–25.

Torday, Peter. "Central Banks Set to Counter Dollar Assault." *Wall Street Journal*, 4 January 1988.

Tumlir, Jan. "Economic Policy for a Stable World Order." *Cato Journal* 4 (Spring/Summer 1984):355–64.

Wachtel, Paul, and Young, John. "Deficit Announcements and Interest Rates." *American Economic Review* 77 (December 1987):1007–12.

Weicher, John C. "The Domestic Budget after Gramm-Rudman—and after Reagan." In *Deficits, Taxes, and Economic Adjustments*, pp. 243–73. Edited by Phillip Cagan. Washington, D.C.: American Enterprise Institute, 1987.

# 15

# DO TRADE DEFICITS MATTER?*

*Paul Heyne*

## Introduction

Some things matter whether or not they exist. The Loch Ness monster is one. National trade deficits are another. Trade deficits obviously matter to many people, because (whatever they are) they seem to have significant consequences. They cause problems or create undesirable constraints or compel government policy changes.

It is often extraordinarily difficult, however, to determine the precise consequences of trade deficits, real or alleged. The current U.S. trade deficit provides a good example. Are the problems supposedly associated with it the *causes* of the deficit or its *effects*? Has the United States been running a continual trade deficit since 1975, as some reports would have it? Or are we only on the way toward a deficit, as a consequence of our current economic recovery and the lagging recovery of our principal trading partners?

Both claims are made and published. Those who report to alarmed readers that the United States has run a trade deficit in every single month over the past seven years almost never stop to reconcile this "fact" with the equally well-established "fact" that U.S. exports of goods and services exceeded imports from 1976 through 1982 by an annual average of almost $13 billion.[1] How can a $90 billion surplus be accumulated by running deficits each and every month?

The explanation, of course, is that the monthly "deficits" are the difference between merchandise exports and imports, while the annual "surpluses" are the difference between exports and imports of merchandise plus services. Now it is essential that the phrase "of course" appear in the above explanation, to avoid any implication that I think I am saying something new or profound by calling attention to the

*Reprinted from *Cato Journal* 3 (Winter 1983/84): 705–16, with revisions.

The author is a Lecturer in Economics at the University of Washington.

[1]In this paper all data on U.S. international transactions are based on the standard Department of Commerce calculations, as reported in numerous official publications. See, for example, the International Statistics section in the monthly issues of *Economic Indicators*.

difference between the merchandise trade balance and the balance on goods and services. After careful reflection, however, I want to withdraw the phrase. Let the first sentence of this paragraph stand unblushingly stripped of its fig leaf.

It is quite possible that nothing at all in this paper is new or profound. That in fact is exactly how it appears to me. The entire essay seems to me to be a series of fairly obvious assertions. If I am going to start saying "of course," therefore, I will have to do an awful lot of it, and that would quickly grow tiresome. More importantly, it would disguise the essential point I want to make, which is that we are not thinking carefully or communicating responsibly when we talk about trade deficits. I am therefore going to omit the defensive "of course" in everything that follows, and try instead to be clear. It might even happen that, if I make my position unmistakably clear, some critic will be able to rescue me from error, and show me why those who speak of trade deficits are in fact making sense, not wandering in darkness and confusion.

It is not only backwoods editors or small-town journalists who treat deficits in merchandise trade as if they were more than they are. The *Wall Street Journal* and the *New York Times* frequently report the Commerce Department's monthly merchandise trade figures in a language of alarm, offering no hint to the reader that the deficits result from a partial accounting.[2] The government's forecast of a more than $100 billion merchandise trade deficit for 1984, for example, was referred to by the *Journal* as "a red-ink total." If they do these things in a green tree, what shall be done in the dry? So let us return to fundamentals to see if we can first agree what it is we are talking about.

We should all be able to agree that any report of a deficit or surplus in a nation's total international transactions is necessarily based on a partial accounting of some sort, for the simple reason that all international economic transactions are treated as exchanges, in which, for accounting purposes, the value of whatever is given up is exactly equal to the value of what is obtained in return. Consequently, the balance of payments always and necessarily balances. If the flow of measured exports exceeds or falls short of the total of measured imports, measuring errors must have occurred—as they are bound to do in any attempt to keep track of the international transactions of 230 million people. The record keepers consequently add the dif-

[2]Readers who want to sample these reports should see the newspapers on the 29th day of any month.

ference to the smaller of the two flows and label it "statistical discrepancy."

It follows from this that any announcement of a deficit or surplus in a nation's foreign transactions results from a decision ***not to count certain transactions.*** Which ones? And why are they excluded? In order to see what might be going on here, we must first turn our attention to one of the most useful and simultaneously most misleading concepts in economics, the concept of ***equilibrium.***

## The Concept of Equilibrium

In economic theory, an equilibrium situation is a situation of balance among contending forces. It is a stable situation, in the sense that it can be expected to persist as long as all the contending forces retain their present form. The crucial point to be noticed is that ***equilibrium is a concept,*** not something that can be observed empirically. Any and every constellation of economic variables is an equilibrium constellation *from some point of view.* After all, any actual situation must be the result of a balance among contending forces, however momentary that balance may be. And every imaginable situation will be an "equilibrium" if we imagine the appropriate circumstances.

The point is much easier to make with concrete examples.[3] Let's take the common textbook case of government price supports and an equilibrium price for corn. Although economists frequently characterize the equilibrium price as "the price that clears the market," this cannot be a correct definition since ***the market clears at every price.*** The quantity of corn purchased is always equal to the quantity sold, whatever the price, because purchases and sales are opposite sides of the same coin.

"Wait a moment," an economic theorist will object: "The quantities purchased and sold are not the same thing as the quantities demanded and supplied. It is quite true that purchases will exactly match sales; but sellers might *want* to sell more than purchasers are willing to buy. The quantity supplied at the going price, in other words, might be greater than the quantity demanded at that price—which is what we mean by a disequilibrium. The market only clears when the quantity that demanders *want* to purchase matches the quantity that suppliers *want* to sell."

But notice what this argument implies. It tells us that some demanders or suppliers are behaving differently from the way they want to

[3]My argument in this section has been extensively influenced by the perceptive analysis in Cheung (1974).

behave. Is that not rather odd? If the suppliers of corn want to sell more than they are actually selling, why do they not do so?

"They cannot," our hypothetical theorist replies, "because the price is too high."

Then why do some corn suppliers not offer to sell at a slightly lower price, which is what we would predict if the corn suppliers really do want to sell more corn than buyers want to purchase?

"Suppliers do not have any incentive to lower their price," is the rejoinder, "as long as the government stands willing to purchase at the support price all the corn suppliers want to sell at that price."

End of the argument. An equilibrium price for corn, it now emerges, is the price that would clear the market in the absence of a government price support program. It is the price that equates the quantity supplied with the quantity demanded when we exclude from consideration the demand stemming from the Commodity Credit Corporation.

If every situation is taken to be an equilibrium situation, the concept of equilibrium is useless. The usefulness of the concept hinges, therefore, on our ability to specify and distinguish disequilibrium situations. We do this by isolating and excluding some of the forces supposedly at work in the situation under analysis. In the case just argued, the government's demand was excluded in order to focus attention on the factors causing the amount of corn in storage to rise or fall. The exclusion is justified by the purpose it serves. The danger is we may forget about the purpose that led to the exclusion which defined the disequilibrium, and we may start pretending that the government-supported price is "really" a disequilibrium price. That approach is simply nonsense.

Consider another example. Economists frequently claim (I have done it myself) that legislated price controls create shortages by preventing prices from moving to their equilibrium levels. But what do we mean by a shortage? We do not mean a situation in which there is not enough for all buyers to have as much as they want, because that describes just about every situation. We live in a world where scarcity is the general rule. When economists speak of shortages, they usually mean situations in which demanders are unable to purchase all that they want to purchase *at the prevailing price.*

But that is not really accurate, either. If demanders cannot purchase as much as they would like to purchase, would they not search for ways to accommodate their preferences more satisfactorily? And would these efforts not raise the price that purchasers must pay, until the quantity demanded comes into line with the quantity supplied? In the presence of effective legal controls on the *monetary* price, the adjustment in response to competition among purchasers will have to occur entirely in the nonmonetary components of the buyers' opportunity cost. But those components affect the quantity demanded just as surely as the monetary price affects it. When we speak of "the quantity demanded at the prevailing price," we are really talking about the quantity demanded at the prevailing cost of acquisition, which includes all kinds of nonmonetary costs.

The economist's claim that price controls create shortages turns out, therefore, to be the claim that price controls lead to increases in nonmonetary costs of acquisition. The "disequilibrium" prices produced by price controls are disequilibrium prices only if we exclude from consideration *changes* in nonmonetary components of the purchase price. This exclusion is justified by the economist's desire to isolate these changes and to examine their effectiveness, relative to changes in monetary price, in securing mutual accommodation between suppliers and demanders. We see once again that an analytical intention suggested the exclusion that gave meaning to the notion of a disequilibrium.

*Every claim of a disequilibrium rests upon an analytical exclusion.* It is sometimes important to insist on this fact, in order to avoid giving the impression that the "problem" with a "disequilibrium" is independent of human purposes. A playground seesaw is in physical equilibrium when a 50–pound person sits on one end and a 200–pound person on the other. Only when we take account of the parties' desire to move up and down can we correctly say that the seesaw is in disequilibrium when the heavy person is on the far end rather than up toward the middle.

With only two parties, intentions or purposes are relatively easy to ascertain; we can therefore usually decide quickly whether or not a seesaw is in disequilibrium and start looking for an equilibrium solution. Can we do the same in the case of an alleged disequilibrium in the balance of international payments?

## Disequilibrium in the Balance of Payments

I think we would be far more suspicious when confronted by any alleged trade deficit if we stopped to realize how much is concealed in such disequilibrium claims. They are often, as Fritz Machlup ([1958] 1963) has argued, disguised political judgments. I happen not to share the horror of political or ethical judgments that is conventionally professed among economists. But *disguised* political judgments are another matter. They violate the imperative of clarity. And lack of clarity in an area where conflicting political interests abound is an invitation to trouble. That is certainly the case when we start talking about trade deficits.

Any claim of deficit or surplus in a nation's trade balance, I have argued, necessarily rests upon a decision to exclude some items when calculating the balance. Which ones? And why are they excluded? We are ready now, after our digression on the equilibrium concept, to suggest an answer. The items excluded will be those that enable the persons alleging a trade deficit (or surplus) to call attention to the problems that concern them.

It must be granted at the outset that most people who talk or write about trade deficits are simply taking over uncritically someone else's definition. They may not know what has been excluded in order to create the deficit; and if they do know, they may have no idea of how the exclusion can be justified. I certainly do not want to be understood as arguing that every journalist, academician, or economist in the Commerce Department is concerned about some particular problem when referring to trade deficits. I am more interested in maintaining that all concepts of a trade deficit harbor concealed concerns and disguised political judgments—concealed and disguised, more often than not, from the very people wielding the concepts.

The deficit most often discussed by the news media is the merchandise trade deficit. Recorded data indicate that the United States has imported a greater dollar value of merchandise than it has exported in every single month since the end of 1975. But why is that called a deficit? What is significant about the relationship between merchandise exports and imports, taken by itself? I do not know how to answer that question, because I do not think that it has any significance, and I do not recall ever encountering an explanation that went beyond vague rhetorical alarms.

It is often suggested or implied that the growing merchandise trade deficit reveals this country's increasing inability to compete internationally with goods manufactured in other countries. But what does this really mean? The inability of General Motors to persuade motorists to buy its automobiles rather than, let us say, Japanese automobiles, probably constitutes a problem for GM's managers, employees, shareholders, and franchised dealers. But how do we know that this demonstrates an increasing inability of "this country" to compete, rather than the ongoing operation of the principle of comparative advantage?

I have learned from experience how difficult it is to persist in this line of argument and be taken seriously. It is simply "obvious" to many people that the United States cannot prosper if our imports of manufactured goods regularly exceed our exports of manufactured goods—as has supposedly been the case for the past seven years and more. I shall pass by the fact that merchandise is not the same as manufactured goods, that the growth of petroleum imports has had far more effect on our merchandise trade balance over the past decade than the dreaded Japanese have had, and that the United States actually exported a greater value of manufactured goods than it imported in both 1980 and 1981, as well as in 1977 and 1979 if we use customs valuations in our calculations. I shall pass by these facts quickly because I fail to see that anything of inherent significance would have been established even if it were true that U.S. exports of manufactured goods had been below imports for each of the past 10 years.

This is not to deny that U.S. firms have often performed poorly in recent years, or that sizeable sectors of the economy are going to diminish dramatically or disappear if major adjustments do not occur in response to foreign competition. What I deny is that comparisons of aggregate merchandise exports with imports provide any kind of help in describing, diagnosing, or prescribing for this situation.

They do, however, provide political arguments that can be used by people who want protection from foreign competitors or subsidies for their efforts to sell abroad. For the existence of a trade deficit implies that the ratio of imports to exports *must eventually decline,* since no deficit can continue forever. So we might as well get on with it now: Fund the Export-Import Bank, restrict imports from nations that interfere with our exports, slap penalties on foreign firms that are "dumping" in our markets, and face up in general to the fact that free trade is good trade only if it is "fair trade."

Trade deficits are politically potent weapons because "everyone knows" that "deficits cannot continue indefinitely." Even the federal government must eventually stop running deficits, or else . . . something fearful will happen. What? Popular opinion is vague about the consequences, but fairly firm in the underlying conviction that "you cannot go on running deficits forever."

The truth is that the federal government can indeed go on adding indefinitely to its indebtedness, with no assignable limit. It can spend more than it collects in taxes, even without expanding the money stock, so long as it can collect the difference in loans. And it will be able to borrow just so long as and to the extent that people are willing to loan to it. People will be willing to buy and hold government bonds insofar as they think they will be better off owning government bonds than they would be with alternative assets. When the public displays reluctance to hold all the debt that the federal government must issue in order to finance a current deficit, a slight decline in the purchase price of government bonds quickly secures their cooperation. Consequently, the federal government never does operate "in the red": Total outlays are always matched exactly by total receipts, as long as receipts are defined to include funds raised by borrowing. The concept of a government budget deficit has meaning only insofar as we exclude borrowed funds from the total of government receipts. We might well want to do that, for various analytical purposes. But once again it is the analytical intention that creates the deficit, by specifying what will be excluded from total receipts—which would otherwise necessarily equal total outlays.

For reasons that are unclear to me, this line of argument does not seem to be generally accepted when it comes to discussions about the balance of payments.[4] The data-tenders calculate deficits or surpluses of various kinds with an astonishing lack of attention to what has been excluded in the process. It is no doubt obvious, at least in the Department of Commerce, that the merchandise trade deficit omits services. But to whom is it obvious that something has also been omitted when the data-keepers calculate the balance of trade on goods *and* services? It is not at all obvious, I submit, to some knowledgeable writers for the *Wall Street Journal*, to take just one example.

The headline on a *Journal* back-page story by Alfred L. Malabre, Jr. (9 August 1983) declared: "As Economy Continues to Revive from Slump, Country's Balance of Trade Grows Sicklier." An accompanying chart, drawn from Commerce Department data, showed net exports of goods and services declining steeply from over $50 billion on an annual basis in the fourth quarter of 1980 to about $10 billion at an annual rate in the first quarter of 1983, and still headed downward.

It is all quite puzzling. To begin with, why is this called "sicklier"? If surpluses are evidence of health and deficits are signs of sickness, should the correct description not at least have been "less healthy"? But that still is not the basic question. Why should a deficit be regarded in the first place as evidence of economic ill health? We could probably all agree that some events that produce deficits are

[4]The *Survey of Current Business* celebrated its 50th anniversary in 1971 with a special issue devoted to a review of the programs of the Bureau of Economic Analysis (then the Office of Business Economics) in the Department of Commerce. Several of the distinguished scholars who were invited to contribute focused on balance-of-payments accounting. Their comments are illuminating, but they leave the reader—this reader, at least—wondering why the bureau continued afterward to gather, publish, *and publicize* balance-of-payments data. See *Survey of Current Business* (1971, pp. 1–22, 33–35, 105–7, and the concluding comments of Bureau Director George Jaszi in his brilliant and witty review of the symposium, pp. 212–13).

evidence of matters gone wrong. Short-term borrowing to finance grain imports made necessary by a harvest failure, for example, would push a nation's balance of trade toward deficit as conventionally defined. But the problem here is the harvest failure, not the deficit in the trade balance, and obsession with the deficit that results from the harvest failure obscures the problem.

Not only is the deficit a mere symptom of the problem, it is also a symptom of the problem's resolution. And that is extremely important to keep in mind. The deficit is evidence that funds were made available with which to purchase grain after the harvest failure, and thus to ward off starvation. Is not the deficit, viewed in this larger perspective, something to welcome rather than to lament? Lamentation is appropriate with regard to the harvest failure; but the deficit is something for which the nation's citizens could properly be grateful.

We are still talking about deficits, however, without deciding what they are. An actual deficit cannot exist in an accounting system that *defines* credits and debits so that they are necessarily equal. Trade deficits must therefore be conceptual phenomena. A trade deficit must be a disequilibrium, not an actual inequality between purchases and sales. And a disequilibrium, we have argued, entails the isolation and exclusion of some factors for purposes of analysis. What do the keepers of the trade balance exclude in order to calculate a deficit or surplus? And why?

They do not offer us an unambiguous answer. Let me therefore suggest that they intend to exclude what we may call "involuntary" transactions. They assume that international exchange includes two distinguishable kinds of transactions. Some are undertaken for the sake of prospective advantage; people initiate such transactions because they hope to gain something from them. These "autonomous" transactions will ordinarily tend to balance each other off; a nation's imports will be financed basically by means of its export earnings. Imports and exports, it must be remembered, include services as well as merchandise, and services include both the loan of capital and payments for the use of capital.

Almost inevitably, however, on this view of the matter, the "autonomous" transactions initiated by households, business firms, governments, and other agencies will fail to produce a precise match between debits and credits in each trading nation. The difference will have to be made up by compensating transactions, or what we are calling "involuntary" transactions to indicate that the parties initiating them do not undertake them for the sake of prospective advantage to themselves, but rather to accommodate the actions of others. Thus, if a nation's financial institutions increase their holdings of deposits denominated in a foreign currency, *not* for the sake of the interest return on those deposits, but rather to compensate for a merchandise net export surplus, that increase in deposits represents a surplus in the nation's balance of trade (and a deficit for the nation whose liabilities have increased). Deficits and surpluses are calculated, then, by excluding from the totals of export and import transactions all such "involuntary" or merely compensating transactions.

## Some Caveats

This use of the equilibrium concept strikes me as thoroughly illegitimate. To begin with, a distinction between "autonomous" and "involuntary" transactions is hard to draw without abandoning the basic premise of economic theory: that actions represent rational choices under constraint. Moreover, commercial banks clearly do not hold foreign assets in order to square the national trade balance. Nor do central banks! Just what does make central bankers tick is a mystery to many, of whom I am one; but I am confident that no central bank anywhere adjusts the composition of its asset portfolio in order to equate the balance of payments, if for no other reason than that it cannot possibly acquire the information it would need to do so.

The managers of financial institutions, whether private or official, national or international, affect the balance of payments in the same way that ordinary exporters and importers do it: as the consequence of pursuing their own interests in a situation with diverse but limited options. This is not to say that central bankers do not pursue what they regard as the national interest. They well may. But when they do so, they do *not* do it by aiming at a balance in the balance of international payments. We know this is not their target because we know this is a target they cannot see. They are necessarily aiming at something else if they are "aiming" at anything at all.

Their actual target might be some particular foreign exchange rate, or some rate of growth in a domestic monetary aggregate, or some desired interest rate, or improved relations with influential parties who want central bank intervention in foreign exchange markets, or even the election of a particular presidential candidate.[5] There are many possibilities. And that is the problem. The allegation of a trade deficit amounts to a vague claim that international exchange transactions are out of order and must be set right. The fundamental issues of exactly what is out of order and how it got that way do not have to

[5]In support of the last possibility, see Lindley H. Clark (1983, p. 33).

be addressed. With the problem undefined, the solution is necessarily undefined. A wide variety of actions might be appropriate. Since even experts disagree extensively on just how any particular policy move is likely to affect the long list of important variables in the world of domestic finance and international exchange, the declaration of a trade deficit amounts in practice to a kind of declaration of martial law. What is most dangerous about such a declaration is that it gives government officials a license to subordinate the rule of law and respect for established rights to considerations of political advantage.

I do not want to be misunderstood. I am not now claiming, whatever I might believe, that we would be better off if central banks stayed out of the foreign exchange markets. Nor am I trying to construct an argument for unrestricted international trade. My claim is a much more limited one. It is that whatever the proper role of government might be in affecting the course of international trade, the concept of trade deficits and surpluses or disequilibrium in the balance of payments darkens counsel. It has no agreed-upon meaning. The concept ought to be abandoned, so that the way can be cleared for more responsible and effective discussion of the issues that concern us.

I have never encountered a case in which the concept of a balance-of-payments disequilibrium was used to interpret an economic problem where the problem could not have been more clearly explicated, in my judgment, by abandoning the concept. What would we substitute for it? We could use whatever assertion the balance-of-payments concept is concealing in each particular case. Every claim of a balance-of-payments disequilibrium can be more accurately and adequately expressed as a prediction, such as "The dollar will depreciate relative to certain other currencies," or "Certain desired imports will not be available unless foreign lenders can be persuaded to extend credit," or "It is going to be increasingly difficult for producer A to sell in market Y," or "Important political support will be secured by imposing quotas on the importation of goods M and N."[6]

[6]At a time when macroeconomic theory is in such unsettled shape, it seems to me more than ever imperative to strive for clarity in our assertions in this area. We all use theory as a shorthand in making empirical assertions, as when we say that "the outfielder missed the fly ball because of the sun." This practice begins to create confusion as soon as relationships "settled" by theory start behaving in ways inconsistent with the theory (or consistent with only *some versions* of the theory). Relevant examples include relationships at the present time between money stock growth rates and interest rates and between foreign exchange rates and relative rates of inflation.

## Conclusion

I am uncomfortably aware of the violence that this recommendation does to long-established tradition. The concept of a balance of international payments has been called, by economists far more reputable than I, a significant analytical achievement.[7] I am claiming that it was in fact and from the beginning a conceptual device that concealed more than it revealed. And the trouble with such concepts in the social sciences is that they facilitate the presentation of political arguments in the garb of empirical assertions.

I think Adam Smith was right. "Nothing . . . can be more absurd than this whole doctrine of the balance of trade."[8] It is a concept originally devised and promulgated by merchants in order to promote their special interests under the pretense of protecting the national interest. A government that tries to watch over the balance of trade has embarked upon a task that is intricate, embarrassing, and fruitless.[9]

## References

Cheung, Steven N. S. "A Theory of Price Control." *Journal of Law and Economics* 17 (April 1974): 53–71.

Clark, Lindley H. "The Odd Couple: Treasury and Fed Try to Reelect Reagan." *Wall Street Journal,* 16 August 1983, p. 33.

Machlup, Fritz. "Equilibrium and Disequilibrium: Misplaced Concreteness and Disguised Politics." *Economic Journal* 68 (March 1958). Reprinted in Machlup, *Essays on Economic Semantics*, pp. 43–72. Englewood Cliffs, N.J.: Prentice-Hall, 1963.

Malabre, Alfred L., Jr. "As Economy Continues to Revive from Slump, Country's Balance of Trade Grows Sicklier." *Wall Street Journal*, 9 August 1983, p. 56.

Schumpeter, Joseph A. *History of Economic Analysis*. New York: Oxford University Press, 1954.

Smith, Adam. *The Wealth of Nations*. 1776. Reprint. New York: The Modern Library, Random House, 1937.

*Survey of Current Business* 51, no. 7, pt. 2 (July 1971).

[7]In his *History of Economic Analysis,* Joseph Schumpeter (1954, pp. 352–53) calls the balance of payments "an important datum in the diagnosis of the economic condition of a country and an important factor in its business processes." Against his explicit claim that development of the concept represented a significant analytical advance. I would adduce his own discussion on pages 352–53, including the long footnote 6. Schumpeter's actual discussion seems to me to demonstrate the inherent ambiguity of the concept and its vast potential for buttressing question-begging arguments.

[8]Smith, *The Wealth of Nations* (1776), bk. IV, chap. III, pt. 2, par. 2; in Modern Library edition (1937, p. 456).

[9]See Smith ([1776] 1937, pp. 376–77).

# 16

# The U.S. Net International Investment Position: Misstated and Misunderstood

*Michael Ulan and William G. Dewald*

## Introduction

According to official figures, the United States in the 1980s has experienced persistently large and unprecedented deficits in its current account in the balance of international payments and a depletion of its Net International Investment Position (NIIP).

The current account balance is the value of the net flow of trade in goods and services and unrequited transfers. One of the components of trade in services is investment income, including such items as accrued interest and capital gains and losses. In 1987, U.S. income on foreign investments was $103.8 billion while foreign income on investments in the United States was $83.4 billion. For comparison, merchandise exports were $249.6 billion, and the overall current account deficit $154.0 billion. The investment income elements of the nominal current account are obviously important. Evidence presented in this paper reveals that the official figures may be substantially misstated because they do not reflect effects of market prices on important components of our investments abroad and foreign investments here. When inflation-adjusted estimates of market values of international investments are taken into account, the U.S. NIIP tends to be larger and our current account deficit smaller than the official measures.

Figure 1 shows the official NIIP between 1970 and 1987. The argument is frequently made in the press that the nation will soon face a substantial net outflow of foreign investment earnings and a corresponding cut in our standard of living because we must service

---

The authors are economists with the Planning and Economic Analysis Staff at the U.S. Department of State. They wish to thank Russell B. Scholl and others at the Bureau of Economic Analysis of the Department of Commerce, Robert E. Lipsey, J. Hayden Boyd, William A. Niskanen, and Allan H. Meltzer for their helpful comments on earlier versions of the paper. The usual caveat applies. The views expressed in the paper are those of the authors and not necessarily those of the Department of State or the federal government.

*FIGURE 1*

OFFICIAL U.S. NET INTERNATIONAL INVESTMENT POSITION AT YEAR-END

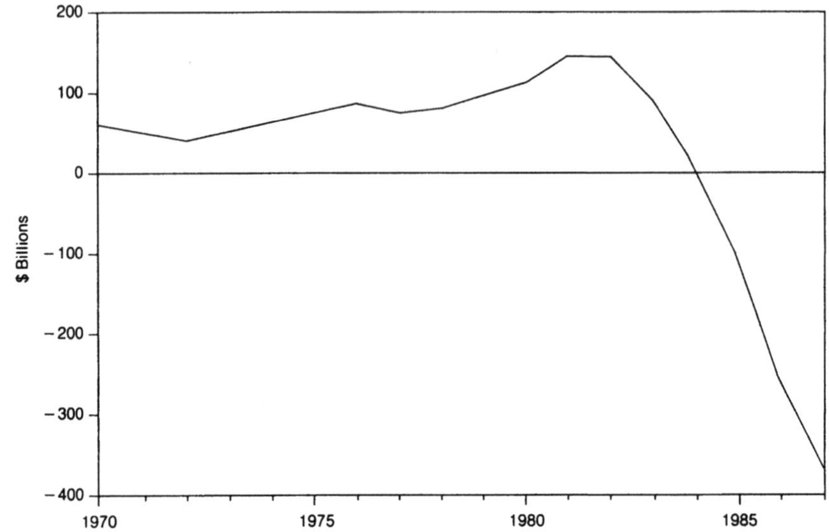


the rapidly growing net investment position of foreigners in the United States. Until 1985, the official U.S. NIIP had not been negative for more than 70 years.

Furthermore, net international investment income as officially measured in the current account added to our foreign exchange receipts and our potential to acquire not only foreign goods and services but also foreign investments. In fact, we continued to earn a positive net return on our net international investment position even in 1986 and 1987 despite the negative official NIIP.

According to many commentators, eliminating the current account deficit and the depletion of the NIIP as officially measured is the number one economic policy priority, justifying proposals for not only increased trade restrictions but also regulations limiting foreign investment in the United States. And, as the story goes, should policies prove inadequate in eliminating the imbalance in our current account and the resulting deterioration in our NIIP, the nation faces soaring interest rates, a plunging dollar, and a serious recession when the flow of foreign funds to the United States ultimately dries up.[1]

[1]See, for example, Aho and Levinson (1988).

So much hinges on the underlying statistics measuring the NIIP and current account that it is compelling to examine the official figures carefully.[2] The close correspondence between the nominal current account balance and the change in the NIIP since 1971 is shown in Figure 2. Some indication that even those who compile the figures are concerned about the accuracy of the NIIP is that they have labeled it only a "rough indicator" and not a precise measure in their articles that are regularly published in the *Survey of Current Business (SCB).* Nonetheless, the published NIIP is not only frequently cited in the financial press but is used as an input in both private and government studies.[3]

The published figures have some obvious shortcomings:

- They are a mixture of not only cross-country debt positions but also equity positions and gold holdings, the latter valued at the official price of $42.22 an ounce, which is far below today's market price.

*FIGURE 2*

CURRENT ACCOUNT AND CHANGE IN NIIP RELATIVE TO GNP

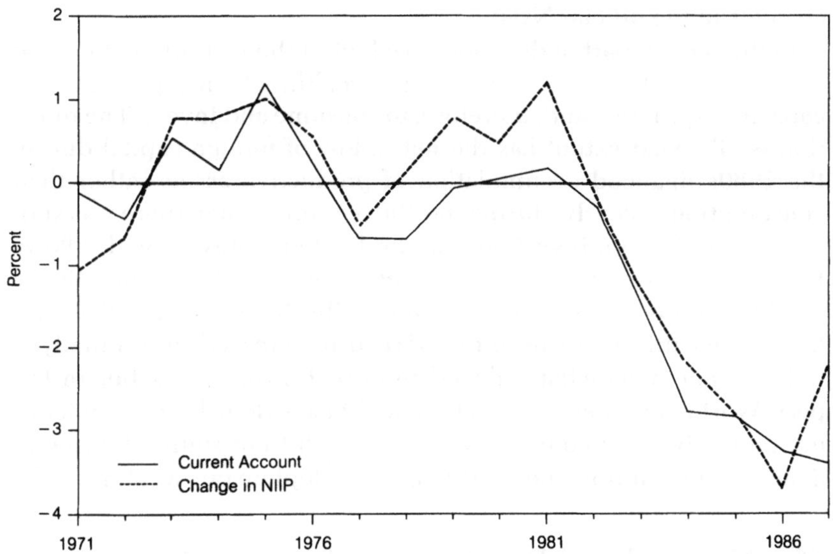


[2]In recent years, the international investment position tables have been published in June issues of the *Survey of Current Business.*

[3]See, for example, Islam (1988) and U.S. Department of Commerce, International Trade Administration (1988).

- The official data measure some assets and claims at market value but others at book value. Among the latter are bank loans as well as both inward and outward direct investment. Though portfolio investment is generally valued at market prices, it is reclassified as direct investment when equity holdings in a foreign firm rise to 10 percent of its outstanding shares.
- The official NIIP is not adjusted for inflation. The real value of financial instruments and international monetary reserves is affected by changes in price levels.

In the first part of this paper, we present several rough revaluations to market of U.S. direct investment abroad and foreign direct investment here. Regardless of the procedure, we find that revaluation increases the value of U.S. holdings abroad more than it increases the value of foreign direct investment in the United States, thereby substantially reducing, or perhaps eliminating, the negative U.S. NIIP. We also compare *changes* in the NIIP, official and revalued, with the official current account balance. We find that current account deficits, based on changes in the NIIP with direct investment valued to market, tend to be smaller in the 1980s in both real and nominal terms than current account deficits or the generally closely related changes in the official NIIP.

In the second part of the paper, we look at the measurement of the U.S. NIIP in the context of national wealth, which represents our capacity to produce and, therefore, to consume and invest. The question is: To what extent has the net inflow of foreign capital during the 1980s financed accumulation of productive assets rather than consumption? Clearly, during the 19th century, when there was substantial net foreign investment in the United States, capital inflows financed our growing productive power, and both the United States and foreign investors benefited. During the 1980s, we find that U.S. tangible wealth *inclusive* of the NIIP also increased substantially—but at a rate somewhat reduced from that observed earlier in the post–World War II era. The nation might have done better, but it did not do badly. As a country, we certainly did not simply borrow to finance consumption and, in the process, deplete our wealth.

## The Nominal and Real Current Account Deficit

The current account of the balance of payments incorporates exports and imports of goods and services and transfers. Exports and imports do not have to balance. When a nation exports more than it imports, it accumulates foreign exchange that is invested in foreign assets—

financial instruments such as deposits and securities, land and owner-occupied housing, or direct ownership of 10 percent or more of business firms.

Investors who acquire foreign deposits, securities, and businesses do so with the expectation of earning a profitable return. As mentioned, an important component of exports and imports of services is the return on foreign investments, including, in principle, not only realized returns in the form of interest and dividends but also unrealized returns in the form of appreciation in the value of investments. The appreciation might result from changes in either exchange rates or market prices denominated in foreign currency. One problem with the official current account and NIIP figures is that they are not based on market prices of important components of both the foreign investments that we hold in other countries and investments here that are held by foreigners.

A second problem is that the official figures are expressed solely in nominal terms. After living through the 1970s, most of us know that unexpected inflation cuts the real value of the return that a lender earns, thereby benefiting borrowers and injuring lenders. Comparable real wealth transfers can occur when credit is extended across national boundaries. Such changes in real values would appropriately be reflected in deflated NIIP and current account statistics. The question is how to make such calculations. Simply dividing the current account by the price level is not enough since that procedure does not take into account the effects of inflation on the real values of the outstanding stocks of assets and claims. We have developed a real current account deficit analogous to the real budget deficit.

Robert Barro (1984) and Robert Eisner (1986), among others, have used the concept of a government real budget position, which is defined as the change in the real value of its outstanding net asset position. In calculating a real deficit, a nominal deficit is adjusted for changes in the real purchasing power of the outstanding stock of government debt and assets that result from changes in market interest rates and the general level of prices. According to this concept, when the government has a negative net financial position, a nominal deficit may well amount to a real surplus during a period of substantial inflation. Inflation directly reduces the real value of the outstanding government debt. In addition, higher market interest rates resulting from inflation reduce the market prices of outstanding government debt so that the rate of return to investors matches that available elsewhere in the market. In a nutshell, a nominal deficit is a real surplus if it is smaller than the reduction in the real value of government net liabilities brought about by inflation and changes in market prices of government debt and assets. Correspondingly, any nominal flow, including the current account balance on international transactions, is appropriately converted into real terms.

In our calculation of a real current account balance for the United States, we began with the U.S. NIIP, changes in which should match, in principle, the balance in the capital account of the balance of payments. The capital account balance is equal to the negative of the current account balance since, by construction, the balance of payments sums to zero.[4]

In order to convert nominal current account data into real terms, it is necessary to have data on the outstanding stock of U.S. international assets and foreign claims on the United States. There is no published balance sheet associated with the U.S. capital account as such. Nevertheless, conceptually, the foreign assets and foreign claims data that compose the U.S. NIIP are analogous to the stocks of assets and claims associated with accumulated capital outflows from and inflows to this country. Furthermore, despite the differences in valuation between the published capital flow or current account balance data and changes in the NIIP, Figure 2 demonstrates that major movements in the series are much the same. Accordingly, in this study, we have used the NIIP data to represent the stock of U.S. foreign assets and the stock of foreign claims on the United States, and changes in the NIIP in nominal and real terms respectively as proxies for the U.S. current account in nominal and real terms.

## The Official Net International Investment Position

The net of outstanding U.S. assets abroad and foreign assets in the United States as published by the Bureau of Economic Analysis (BEA) is often termed the U.S. "net debt" position. But this is a misstatement, since it includes equity, gold, and foreign-exchange holdings in addition to debt. The official figures for U.S. assets abroad, foreign assets in the United States, and the official NIIP are reproduced in Table 1.

[4]In practice, there is a discrepancy between capital and current account balances. It is possible that a significant portion of the statistical discrepancy, which amounted to more than $200 billion over the last 10 years, reflects unreported capital inflows. To that extent, the official data may understate foreign claims on the United States and overstate the U.S. NIIP. Furthermore, although during the 1970s and 1980s U.S. current account balances and changes in the U.S. NIIP have exhibited similar trends, there occasionally have been substantial year-to-year differences between the two series, for example, $55 billion in 1987. One source of that difference arises from the failure to measure all transactions. Another is that the BEA does not use consistent asset valuation adjustments for the current account and the NIIP.

Under the heading of "U.S. Assets Abroad," the BEA includes

- U.S. government assets—official reserve assets (gold, special drawing rights, International Monetary Fund reserve position, and foreign currency holdings); non-official-reserve government assets (loans to foreigners and other long-term assets, such as paid in capital subscriptions to international organizations); and nonreserve holdings of foreign currencies and other short-term assets; and
- U.S. private assets—direct investment abroad, foreign securities, claims on unaffiliated foreigners reported by U.S. nonbanking concerns, and claims reported by U.S. banks not reported elsewhere.

Under the heading of "Foreign Assets in the United States," the BEA includes

- Foreign official assets in the United States—U.S. government securities, other federal liabilities (primarily liabilities associated with military sales contracts and other transactions arranged with or through foreign official agencies), U.S. liabilities reported by U.S. banks not included elsewhere, and other foreign official assets; and
- Other foreign assets in the United States—direct investment in the United States, U.S. Treasury securities, corporate and other securities, liabilities to unaffiliated foreigners reported by U.S. nonbanking concerns, and U.S. liabilities reported by U.S. banks not included elsewhere.

As noted, the BEA values gold at its official price, nonsecuritized loans and direct investment at book value, but all other assets at year-end market value, adjusting for changes in asset prices and exchange rates.

## Derivation of Direct Foreign Investment at Market Values

We make two major modifications to the BEA's net international investment data. First, we exclude gold. If we valued gold at the current market price, which is roughly 10 times the official price of $42.22 an ounce, national wealth would increase by about $100 billion, but the gold stock is no more an international monetary asset than is our stock of wheat, in fact less. Since 1971, the United States, with minor exceptions, has not bought or sold gold.

Second, we revalue direct foreign investment to market. The BEA values U.S. direct investment abroad and foreign direct investment here at original cost, so the change in direct investment during any

*TABLE 1*

U.S. NET INTERNATIONAL INVESTMENT POSITION AT YEAR-END, 1987
(MILLIONS OF DOLLARS)

| | | | |
|---|---|---|---|
| **U.S. Assets Abroad** | | | |
| U.S. Official Reserve Assets | | | |
| Gold | 11,078 | | |
| Special drawing rights | 10,283 | | |
| Reserve position in the International Monetary Fund | 11,349 | | |
| Foreign currencies | 13,090 | | |
| Total | | 45,800 | |
| U.S. Government Assets, Other Than Official Reserve Assets | | | |
| U.S. loans and other long-term assets | | | |
| Repayable in dollars | 85,995 | | |
| Other | 1,614 | | |
| U.S. foreign currency holdings and U.S. short-term assets | 775 | | |
| Total | | 88,384 | |
| U.S. Private Assets | | | |
| Direct investment abroad | 308,880 | | |
| Foreign securities: | | | |
| Bonds | 91,016 | | |
| Corporate stocks | 55,732 | | |
| U.S. claims on unaffiliated foreign reported by U.S. nonbanking concerns | 30,125 | | |
| U.S. claims reported by U.S. banks, not included elsewhere | 547,868 | | |
| Total | | 1,033,622 | |
| Total U.S. Assets Abroad | | | 1,167,807 |

| | | | |
|---|---|---|---|
| **Foreign Assets in the United States** | | | |
| Foreign Official Assets in the United States | | | |
| U.S. government securities | 219,056 | | |
| Other U.S. government liabilities | 14,967 | | |
| U.S. liabilities reported by U.S. banks, not included elsewhere | 31,821 | | |
| Other foreign official assets | 17,288 | | |
| Total | | 283,132 | |
| Other Foreign Assets in the United States | | | |
| Direct investment in the United States | 261,927 | | |
| U.S. Treasury securities | 78,390 | | |
| U.S. securities other than U.S. Treasury securities | | | |
| Corporate and other bonds | 170,989 | | |
| Corporate stocks | 173,374 | | |
| U.S. liabilities to unaffiliated foreigners reported by U.S. nonbanking concerns | 28,837 | | |
| U.S. liabilities reported by U.S. banks, not included elsewhere | 539,391 | | |
| Total | | 1,252,908 | |
| Total Foreign Assets in the United States | | | 1,536,040 |
| **Net International Investment Position** | | | −368,233 |

NOTE: Totals may differ slightly from sums of component parts because of rounding.
SOURCE: U.S. Department of Commerce, *Survey of Current Business*, June 1988, p. 78.

given year is essentially the sum of unrepatriated earnings on investment in place at the beginning of the year—including, for U.S. investment abroad, capital gains and losses accruing from changes in the foreign-exchange value of the dollar—and the flow of new direct investment during the year.

For portfolio investment, the BEA shows the change in the value of holdings attributable to dollar appreciation and depreciation explicitly in a table. The space for changes in holdings of U.S. direct investment abroad attributable to exchange rate changes is blank. What the BEA does is to subsume the effects of exchange rate changes on the book value of U.S. direct investment abroad under the heading of reinvested earnings. That is, the BEA adjusts the outstanding book values of direct investment for changes in exchange rates. The BEA does not, however, adjust direct investment for changes in market values in terms of local currencies.

Under the BEA's accounting procedures, all income on foreign investment—unrepatriated as well as repatriated—is counted as investment income in the current account. Unrepatriated earnings are considered to be new foreign investment in the capital account of the U.S. balance of payments.

How far off is the BEA's valuation of direct foreign investment? Potentially a lot. Not only have company values tended to increase in real terms as the real world product has grown, but there have also been substantial changes in the general levels of prices affecting the nominal values of direct investments along with everything else. As we shall show, the market values of accumulated direct foreign investment—both U.S. holdings abroad and foreign investment here—are estimated to be far greater than the official BEA figures indicate.

We present three approximations of the market value of direct foreign investment based on stock market indices here and abroad, capitalized earnings generated by direct investments, and deflators for fixed investment. Each of the three revaluation measures, which are discussed in the following sections, yields a substantially larger U.S. net direct foreign investment position than the official figures. Table 2 and Figure 3 present the official book value and the three revalued measures of foreign direct investment. Others such as Hooker (1988), Eisner and Pieper (1988), and Islam (1988) have also recognized that the official book valuation of foreign direct investment substantially understates the U.S. NIIP.

## Stock Market Revaluation of Direct Investment

We assume the market value of U.S. direct foreign investment in any foreign country varies directly with the local currency denomi-

*TABLE 2*

FOREIGN DIRECT INVESTMENT: BOOK AND MARKET VALUES
(BILLIONS OF DOLLARS)

| End of Year | Book Value | | | Stock Market Prices | | | Earnings | | | Investment Deflators | | |
|---|---|---|---|---|---|---|---|---|---|---|---|---|
| | U.S. Assets | Foreign Assets | Balance | U.S. Assets | Foreign Assets | Balance | U.S. Assets | Foreign Assets | Balance | U.S. Assets | Foreign Assets | Balance |
| 1950 | 11.8 | 3.4 | 8.4 | 11.8 | 3.4 | 8.4 | n.a. | n.a. | n.a. | 11.8 | 3.4 | 8.4 |
| 1951 | 13.0 | 3.7 | 9.3 | 14.5 | 4.4 | 10.1 | 16.4 | 1.4 | 15.0 | 13.8 | 3.7 | 10.0 |
| 1952 | 14.7 | 3.9 | 10.8 | 16.5 | 5.0 | 11.5 | 20.4 | 1.4 | 19.1 | 16.1 | 4.1 | 12.1 |
| 1953 | 16.3 | 4.3 | 12.0 | 18.3 | 5.3 | 13.0 | 21.7 | 1.8 | 19.9 | 17.8 | 4.5 | 13.3 |
| 1954 | 17.6 | 4.6 | 13.0 | 22.8 | 6.8 | 16.0 | 25.8 | 2.0 | 23.8 | 19.2 | 4.8 | 14.4 |
| 1955 | 19.4 | 5.1 | 14.3 | 30.0 | 10.0 | 20.0 | 32.4 | 2.5 | 30.0 | 21.3 | 5.4 | 15.9 |
| 1956 | 22.5 | 5.5 | 17.0 | 34.5 | 12.1 | 22.3 | 41.8 | 2.6 | 39.2 | 25.7 | 6.3 | 19.4 |
| 1957 | 25.3 | 5.7 | 19.7 | 36.0 | 10.8 | 25.2 | 46.3 | 2.5 | 43.9 | 29.4 | 6.8 | 22.7 |
| 1958 | 27.4 | 6.1 | 21.3 | 39.9 | 14.6 | 25.2 | 42.7 | 2.6 | 40.0 | 31.8 | 7.1 | 24.7 |
| 1959 | 29.8 | 6.6 | 23.2 | 54.7 | 16.8 | 37.9 | 50.5 | 4.0 | 46.4 | 34.6 | 7.7 | 26.9 |
| 1960 | 31.9 | 6.9 | 25.0 | 62.5 | 16.2 | 46.3 | 60.7 | 6.6 | 54.1 | 37.5 | 8.0 | 29.5 |
| 1961 | 34.7 | 7.4 | 27.3 | 72.6 | 20.9 | 51.7 | 70.0 | 8.0 | 62.8 | 40.4 | 8.4 | 32.0 |
| 1962 | 37.3 | 7.6 | 29.7 | 67.9 | 18.3 | 49.6 | 78.3 | 7.4 | 71.0 | 43.5 | 8.9 | 34.6 |
| 1963 | 40.7 | 7.9 | 32.8 | 76.1 | 22.2 | 53.9 | 87.7 | 8.7 | 79.0 | 48.6 | 9.2 | 39.4 |
| 1964 | 44.5 | 8.4 | 36.1 | 82.4 | 25.6 | 56.9 | 92.1 | 9.5 | 82.6 | 51.7 | 9.6 | 42.1 |
| 1965 | 49.5 | 8.7 | 40.7 | 85.3 | 28.5 | 56.8 | 100.7 | 12.0 | 88.7 | 58.9 | 10.3 | 48.6 |
| 1966 | 51.8 | 9.0 | 42.7 | 81.1 | 25.5 | 55.5 | 90.4 | 12.2 | 78.2 | 66.0 | 11.2 | 54.8 |
| 1967 | 56.6 | 9.9 | 46.6 | 98.3 | 31.5 | 66.9 | 93.9 | 13.8 | 80.2 | 71.3 | 12.2 | 59.1 |
| 1968 | 61.9 | 10.8 | 51.1 | 126.4 | 36.1 | 90.3 | 110.0 | 14.6 | 95.3 | 78.9 | 13.7 | 65.2 |

*TABLE 2 (cont.)*

FOREIGN DIRECT INVESTMENT: BOOK AND MARKET VALUES
(BILLIONS OF DOLLARS)

| End | Book Value | | | Stock Market Prices | | | Earnings | | | Investment Deflators | | |
|---|---|---|---|---|---|---|---|---|---|---|---|---|
| of Year | U.S. Assets | Foreign Assets | Balance | U.S. Assets | Foreign Assets | Balance | U.S. Assets | Foreign Assets | Balance | U.S. Assets | Foreign Assets | Balance |
| 1969 | 68.0 | 11.8 | 56.2 | 134.4 | 32.3 | 102.1 | 131.3 | 14.6 | 116.8 | 89.5 | 15.8 | 73.8 |
| 1970 | 75.5 | 13.3 | 62.2 | 128.1 | 33.2 | 94.9 | 134.8 | 14.4 | 120.4 | 104.7 | 18.0 | 86.7 |
| 1971 | 82.8 | 13.9 | 68.8 | 148.8 | 37.5 | 111.3 | 153.6 | 19.5 | 134.1 | 123.6 | 19.6 | 104.0 |
| 1972 | 89.9 | 14.8 | 75.0 | 195.4 | 45.8 | 149.7 | 189.8 | 22.3 | 167.6 | 142.5 | 21.1 | 121.4 |
| 1973 | 101.3 | 20.6 | 80.8 | 182.3 | 42.7 | 144.5 | 277.5 | 27.0 | 250.5 | 184.0 | 25.1 | 158.9 |
| 1974 | 110.1 | 25.1 | 84.9 | 149.9 | 34.7 | 115.1 | 249.3 | 17.3 | 232.0 | 227.2 | 34.5 | 192.7 |
| 1975 | 124.0 | 27.7 | 96.4 | 186.6 | 48.6 | 138.0 | 182.2 | 24.5 | 157.7 | 253.7 | 40.2 | 213.5 |
| 1976 | 136.8 | 30.8 | 106.0 | 188.9 | 60.1 | 128.8 | 193.7 | 31.7 | 162.0 | 280.0 | 47.3 | 232.6 |
| 1977 | 146.0 | 34.6 | 111.4 | 209.9 | 57.1 | 152.8 | 205.4 | 29.6 | 175.8 | 320.0 | 54.8 | 265.3 |
| 1978 | 162.7 | 42.5 | 120.3 | 260.2 | 67.0 | 193.2 | 242.6 | 40.1 | 202.5 | 379.6 | 67.6 | 311.9 |
| 1979 | 187.9 | 54.4 | 133.4 | 328.9 | 87.7 | 241.2 | 317.0 | 52.8 | 264.2 | 452.8 | 86.0 | 366.8 |
| 1980 | 215.4 | 83.0 | 132.3 | 402.9 | 139.1 | 263.8 | 292.4 | 68.0 | 224.4 | 520.4 | 112.2 | 408.2 |
| 1981 | 228.3 | 108.7 | 119.6 | 384.9 | 152.1 | 232.9 | 256.7 | 54.4 | 202.3 | 522.2 | 149.5 | 372.7 |
| 1982 | 207.8 | 124.7 | 83.1 | 374.4 | 187.6 | 186.8 | 177.2 | 26.1 | 151.1 | 490.8 | 167.1 | 323.7 |
| 1983 | 207.2 | 137.1 | 70.1 | 474.2 | 234.9 | 239.4 | 197.7 | 54.0 | 143.7 | 462.2 | 175.8 | 286.3 |
| 1984 | 211.5 | 164.6 | 46.9 | 479.9 | 260.5 | 219.4 | 217.1 | 94.4 | 122.7 | 432.0 | 202.9 | 229.1 |
| 1985 | 229.7 | 184.6 | 45.1 | 702.7 | 346.8 | 356.0 | 382.6 | 70.1 | 312.6 | 491.4 | 223.3 | 268.1 |
| 1986 | 259.9 | 220.4 | 39.5 | 949.4 | 452.4 | 497.0 | 485.5 | 68.0 | 417.5 | 564.5 | 251.5 | 313.0 |
| 1987 | 308.8 | 261.9 | 46.9 | 1,016.0 | 495.5 | 520.6 | 807.8 | 162.2 | 645.6 | 714.5 | 299.4 | 415.1 |

NOTE: n.a., not available. Balances may not equal differences between U.S. and foreign assets because of rounding.

*FIGURE 3*

UNITED STATES DIRECT INVESTMENT ABROAD

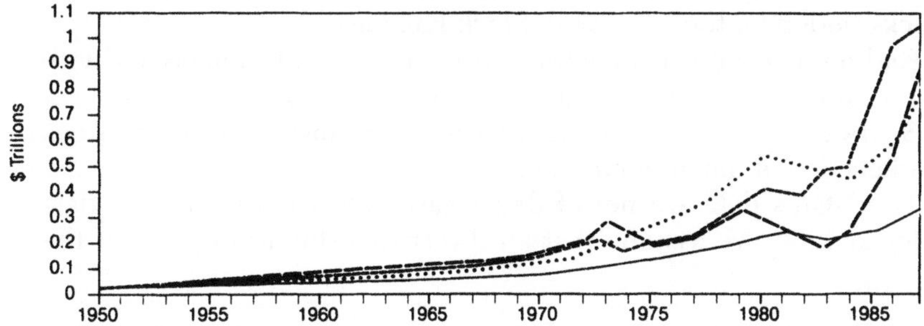


FOREIGN DIRECT INVESTMENT IN THE UNITED STATES

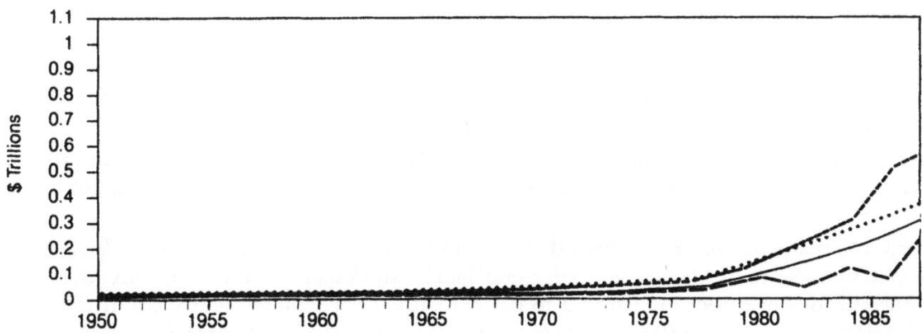


U.S. NET DIRECT FOREIGN INVESTMENT

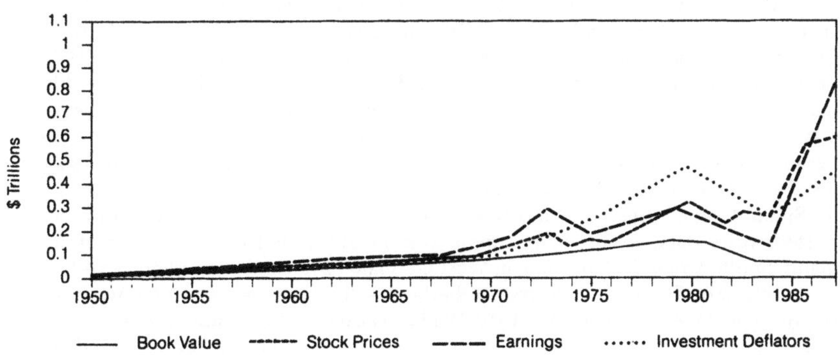

nated stock market index of industrial share prices in that country. Similarly, we assume that the market value of foreign direct investment in the United States varies directly with the prices of industrial stocks traded on the New York Stock Exchange.[5]

End-of-year positions for U.S. direct investment in many individual countries are available through 1987.[6] The country breakdown of U.S. investment abroad is of interest since prices on major stock markets do not move in tandem.[7]

The BEA's data are net of depreciation. Since we have no data prior to 1950, we assume that all direct investment in place at the

[5]In principle, it would be desirable to adjust the foreign assets of U.S. banks to reflect the discounts at which outstanding loans to some countries are trading in the secondary market. Prices for such transactions have been published biweekly by Salomon Brothers since the fall of 1987; currently, similar data are also published by Shearson-Lehman Brothers. This secondary market is very thin, and there are no good price data for earlier periods. Consequently, we have not discounted U.S. bank loans to developing countries though we recognize this omission might result in a substantial overstatement of U.S. foreign assets. According to Federal Reserve data on exposure of U.S. banks in the Third World and Shearson-Lehman Brothers data on secondary market prices, the adjustment to bank portfolios as of March 1988 would be about $40–$45 billion, equal to about 8 percent of the year-end 1987 total of foreign assets of private U.S. banks reported in the March 1988 *SCB* (Bach 1988; *Euromoney* 1988).

[6]See U.S. Department of Commerce, BEA (1982, 1986); the BEA's *U.S. Direct Investment Abroad* (various issues); *SCB* (August 1986, pp. 40–73); and *SCB* (August 1987, pp. 85–99).

[7]In order to make our market-valued direct investment data consistent with the BEA's year-end figures, we used as close to year-end data for stock market indices in converting the book values of direct investment to market value as we conveniently could. The stock-price indices are available on *International Financial Statistics (IFS)* data tapes and in the August 1988 issue of the *IFS*; however, the stock-price indices from this source are available only as monthly, quarterly, and annual averages.

Among the countries for which BEA reports U.S. investment positions, the *IFS* tapes contain local currency annual average stock market indices over the entire 1950–87 period for the United Kingdom, South Africa, Denmark, Italy, Ireland, Japan, West Germany, France, Switzerland, Sweden, Belgium, Norway, and the Netherlands. Indices for Spain, Canada, Australia, and New Zealand begin in 1952, 1956, 1957, and 1960 respectively. For all the countries except Canada, Spain, and New Zealand, monthly average data are available beginning in 1957. For these countries, monthly data begin in 1959, 1961, and 1961 respectively. We used December average stock prices to represent year-end data where the monthly data are available. For years before 1957, we used annual averages where available.

For Spain, Canada, Australia, and New Zealand in years prior to the availability of their stock price data, we used the simple average of the indices for the markets in England, South Africa, Ireland, Japan, West Germany, France, Switzerland, Sweden, Belgium, Norway, Denmark, and the Netherlands—the countries for which we have stock price data for every year since 1950. We have also used this simple average index to represent the yearly values of U.S. direct investment in all countries for which we lack stock price data. For the end 1987 value of stocks in New Zealand, we used the price index for July 1987.

end of 1950 occurred that year. To obtain the market value of direct investment at the end of 1951, we added to the 1950 investment position the net new investment and the change in the market value of the 1950 stock of capital during 1951.[8]

Summing across countries yields a market value of $14.5 billion for U.S. direct foreign investment at year-end 1951. We estimated subsequent market values analogously. By year-end 1987, U.S. direct investment abroad had mushroomed to $1,016 billion by our calculations, more than triple the book value. A similar procedure was used to estimate the market value of foreign direct investment here.[9] It was estimated to be $4.4 billion at year-end 1951, equal to about a third of U.S. direct investment abroad. By year-end 1987, the estimated market value of foreign direct investment here was $495.5 billion, nearly twice the BEA's book value, and, as revalued on the basis of stock indices, equaled less than half of U.S. direct investment in other countries. Our calculations have also taken into account the effect of foreign exchange rate changes on the estimated excess of the market value of direct investment over book value. The BEA figures already incorporate the effect of exchange rate changes on the book values of U.S. direct investment.

Share prices presumably reflect productivity growth in individual countries and are particularly relevant in valuing direct investment that takes the form of portfolio investments of 10 percent or more of the stock of an existing firm. However, the indices for U.S. and foreign stock markets may not represent the industries in which direct investment has occurred. Stock indices often do not include new and rapidly growing firms that may be more representative of new direct investment than are the established firms included in a stock price index.

Another problem results because U.S. firms retain a larger percentage of earnings than do foreign firms. Presumably, stock markets value firms according to earnings and dividend practices, with share prices reflecting retained earnings. Hence, counting all retained

[8]Algebraically, in each country *i* at the end of year *t*, the market value in dollars of the stock of U.S. foreign investment is

$$K_{i,t} = K_{i,t-1}*(S_{i,t}/S_{i,t-1}) + I_{i,t} + (-F_{i,t})*[K_{i,t-1}*(S_{i,t}/S_{i,t-1}) - B_{i,t-1}]$$

where $K$ = market value of the stock of U.S. direct investment;
$F$ = percent change, foreign currency units per dollar;
$B$ = accumulated book value of U.S. direct investment including exchange rate adjustment of book value;
$S$ = stock price index; and
$I$ = book value of the flow of net U.S. direct investment in year $t$.

[9]See Scholl (1988) and U.S. Department of Commerce, BEA (1984).

earnings as new investment and using a stock market adjustment of the value of the stock of outstanding capital involves some double counting. This effect is at least partly offset since U.S. firms tend to return a smaller fraction of total earnings to stockholders as dividends than do foreign firms. Consequently, share prices of U.S. firms abroad would tend to be higher than those of foreign firms with similar earnings. The extent to which these errors are offsetting is an empirical matter, which, unfortunately, we lack the data to evaluate.

## Capitalized Earnings Revaluation of Direct Investment

We also revalued direct foreign investment by capitalizing the income flows generated by the stock of outstanding investment. Capitalized earnings have appeal as a means of valuing investment assets, but there is considerable noise in the data and, further, a problem in choosing an appropriate discount rate.

Risk factors may differ widely across countries and industries, and over time. One example is the very different pattern of holdings of government securities by U.S. and foreign investors. At the end of 1987, according to Table 1, U.S. government securities, which are low-risk and low-return investments, compose 19 percent of foreign assets in the United States. In contrast, U.S. official assets, excluding gold, account for only 3 percent of U.S. foreign assets. Hence, the portfolio of U.S. foreign assets may have tended to be riskier than foreign holdings in the United States and, in the aggregate, yield a higher return than earned by foreigners here. Income on foreign direct investment in the United States is also very low compared to the return on U.S. direct investment abroad.

We used only a very rough approximation of the discount rate to capitalize direct investment flows to both U.S. and foreign holders.[10]

[10]The choice of a three-year period for averaging represents a compromise between the desire to expand the period over which the earnings rate is calculated and the desire not to lose observations. From 1960, we used earnings data published in the *SCB*. For the earlier period, *SCB* earnings data pertain to only repatriated earnings; hence, we added retained earnings derived from sources cited at the end of the paper. We calculated capitalized values for the earnings on U.S. direct investment abroad and for the earnings on foreign direct investment here separately.

Algebraically, the capitalized value of earnings is

$$V_t = Y_t/[(E/P)_t*(E/P)_{t-1}*(E/P)_{t-2}]^{1/3}$$

where $Y$ = earnings on foreign direct investment; and
$E/P$ = the aggregate earnings/price ratio for the S&P 500 stocks.

## Fixed Investment Deflator Revaluation of Direct Investment

Our third alternative uses the U.S. and foreign deflators for fixed investment goods to revalue stocks of direct investment. Such an approach was used by Hooker (1988), though with the overall U.S. GNP deflator rather than the fixed investment deflators. The figures that we present for this approximation are those of Eisner and Pieper (1988), who take account of both exchange rate effects and differences in foreign and domestic capital goods prices. We have some qualms about such revaluations because the U.S. deflator for fixed investment goods, for example, has not reflected even major movements in stock prices very closely, a fact that tends to confirm that market values of firms depend on far more than the cost of capital equipment. A decrease in the supply price of capital goods could well enhance earnings and market valuation of a firm.

## Official and Market-Valued Direct Foreign Investment

Table 2 shows that, on balance, each of the market valuation approximations yields substantially larger U.S. net foreign direct investment positions than do the official book value figures. At year-end 1987, the official figures value net U.S. direct foreign investment at $46.9 billion; the investment deflator approximation raises the net to $415.1 billion; the stock price approximation, to $520.6 billion; and the earnings capitalization approximation, to $645.6 billion.

Figure 3 depicts the alternative direct investment values. Each reflects a strong uptrend over the entire 1950–87 period but wide differences over shorter periods. Between 1980 and 1987, the book value of U.S. direct investment abroad and foreign direct investment here increased by $93.4 billion and $178.9 billion respectively, a decrease in the net U.S. position of $85.5 billion. At the other extreme, based on capitalized earnings, $515.4 billion was added to U.S. direct foreign investments over this period but only $94.2 billion to foreign direct investments here, a net increase of $421.2 billion. Based on stock prices, $613.1 billion was added to U.S. direct investments abroad and $356.4 billion to foreign direct investments in the United States, a net increase of $256.8 billion. Though the U.S. net direct investment position based on deflators was considerably eroded over the intervening period, it was essentially the same in 1987 as 1980.

## Official and Market-Valued Net International Investment Positions

Table 3 presents the official and revalued NIIPs in total, incorporating both direct and portfolio investment, but excluding gold.

*TABLE 3*

NOMINAL U.S. NET INTERNATIONAL INVESTMENT POSITION
EXCLUDING GOLD
(BILLIONS OF DOLLARS)

| End of Year | *SCB* | Valued to Market via Stock Prices | Earnings | Investments Deflators |
|---|---|---|---|---|
| 1970 | 47.4 | 80.1 | 105.6 | 71.9 |
| 1971 | 35.3 | 77.7 | 100.5 | 70.4 |
| 1972 | 26.5 | 101.2 | 119.1 | 72.9 |
| 1973 | 36.2 | 100.0 | 206.0 | 114.4 |
| 1974 | 47.1 | 77.3 | 194.1 | 154.8 |
| 1975 | 62.6 | 104.3 | 124.0 | 179.8 |
| 1976 | 72.0 | 94.8 | 127.9 | 198.6 |
| 1977 | 61.0 | 102.4 | 125.4 | 214.9 |
| 1978 | 64.4 | 137.4 | 146.7 | 256.1 |
| 1979 | 83.3 | 191.1 | 214.1 | 316.7 |
| 1980 | 95.1 | 226.6 | 187.2 | 371.0 |
| 1981 | 130.0 | 243.2 | 212.7 | 383.1 |
| 1982 | 125.8 | 229.5 | 193.8 | 366.4 |
| 1983 | 78.4 | 247.5 | 152.1 | 294.5 |
| 1984 | −7.5 | 164.9 | 68.3 | 174.6 |
| 1985 | −121.7 | 188.6 | 144.5 | 100.7 |
| 1986 | −280.3 | 177.5 | 103.7 | −6.4 |
| 1987 | −379.3 | 94.3 | 219.4 | −11.2 |

Whereas the official book values show a negative $379 billion U.S. net investment position at the end of 1987, two of the three revaluations show continued positive positions.

While the *SCB* series declined each year after 1981 and turned negative in 1984, not so the revalued series. The stock-price-based series peaked at about $250 billion in 1983 but then declined to about $100 billion in 1987. The earnings balance hit a bottom in 1984 but then recovered to a record level by the end of 1987 as a result of the combination of movements in earnings here and abroad, dollar depreciation, and the fall in yields that accompanied disinflation. The deflator-based series persistently declined after 1981 from a peak of over $380 billion in 1981 to about zero in 1986 and 1987.

## Revaluation of the Current Account Balance

Table 4 presents alternative U.S. current account balances: (1) the series bearing that label released by the BEA, which is the sum of

*TABLE 4*

NOMINAL U.S. CURRENT ACCOUNT BALANCE
(BILLIONS OF DOLLARS)

| | | Change in Net International Investment Position | | | |
|---|---|---|---|---|---|
| | | | Valued to Market via | | |
| Year | Current Account | *SCB* | Stocks | Earnings | Investment Deflators |
| 1971 | -1.4 | -12.1 | -2.4 | -5.1 | -1.5 |
| 1972 | -5.8 | -8.8 | 23.5 | 18.6 | 2.5 |
| 1973 | 7.1 | 9.7 | -1.2 | 86.7 | 41.4 |
| 1974 | 2.0 | 10.9 | -22.7 | -11.9 | 40.5 |
| 1975 | 18.1 | 15.6 | 27.0 | -70.1 | 24.9 |
| 1976 | 4.2 | 9.3 | -9.5 | 4.0 | 18.8 |
| 1977 | -14.5 | -11.0 | 7.6 | -2.5 | 16.3 |
| 1978 | -15.4 | 3.4 | 35.0 | 21.2 | 41.2 |
| 1979 | -0.9 | 18.8 | 53.7 | 67.5 | 60.5 |
| 1980 | 1.9 | 11.8 | 35.5 | -26.9 | 54.3 |
| 1981 | 6.9 | 34.9 | 16.6 | 25.5 | 12.1 |
| 1982 | -8.7 | -4.2 | -13.7 | -19.0 | -16.7 |
| 1983 | -46.2 | -47.5 | 18.1 | -41.8 | -71.9 |
| 1984 | -107.1 | -86.1 | -82.6 | -83.7 | -119.9 |
| 1985 | -115.1 | -114.2 | 23.7 | 76.9 | -74.0 |
| 1986 | -138.8 | -158.5 | -11.0 | -47.1 | -107.1 |
| 1987 | -154.0 | -99.0 | -83.2 | 121.3 | -4.7 |

exports, imports, and unrequited transfers; (2) the generally closely related change in the U.S. NIIP excluding gold as published in the *SCB*; and (3) our three series based on changes in our revalued U.S. NIIP excluding gold.[11]

[11]The differences between the series published by the BEA under the title of "Current Account Balance" and the changes in the U.S. NIIP excluding gold as presented in the *SCB* are frequently substantial, for example, $55 billion in 1987. The 1987 revision of several years of data on U.S. merchandise exports to Canada reveals that major transactions may not be recorded in U.S. trade data. The adjustment amounted to more than $10 billion for 1986. If the pattern of missed transactions changes over time, movements in external balances will also be affected. Some of the data in the investment position table are generated from sample surveys and are subject to year-to-year differences in the reliability of the sample.

Balance-of-payments accounting is far from exact. The failure to capture all legal transactions in trade and investment data and differences in valuation procedures account for differences among the official current account balance, the capital account balance, and the change in the official NIIP excluding gold as shown in Table 4. Over the 1970s and 1980s there are significant differences from year to year in these series, but generally there is the same underlying trend.

Failure to account for changes in the market values of U.S. direct foreign investment and foreign direct investment here in the official measurements contributes to large differences between the official figures and our estimated measures of U.S. international investment balances. If the revalued measures are correct, the official figures substantially misstate the U.S. current account balance.

## Inflation Adjustment of the Current Account Balance

The next step is to adjust nominal current account balances for inflation. For each year 1971–87, we calculate the changes in U.S. assets abroad and foreign claims on the United States in real terms and take the difference between the two as an estimate of the real current account balance. We perform these adjustments for total assets and claims both as they appear in the *SCB* and incorporating our revaluations of direct investment to market.

Our measure of inflation is the deflator for net fixed reproducible wealth in the United States which we derived from the *SCB*. Since a major objective of this study is to examine the U.S. NIIP and the changes in that position in the context of national wealth and its growth, we use a measure of inflation closely related to wealth. We chose the deflator associated with the net—rather than the gross—stock of fixed reproducible wealth, since investment is considered net of depreciation. Table 5 presents data on real U.S. net foreign assets from which the real current account estimates were derived. Table 6 provides data on real U.S. current account balances. Figure 4 presents the nominal and revalued real current accounts relative to nominal and real GNP respectively.

## The Net International Investment Position and U.S. Wealth

The Federal Reserve publishes annual data in its *Balance Sheets for the U.S. Economy* (1988) on tangible assets for the private sector of the U.S. economy with assets valued at replacement cost. The Fed uses procedures such as are employed by the BEA to value reproducible assets, but the Fed differs in its treatment of land and financial assets.[12]

Table 7 presents total U.S. private and government tangible assets for the period 1970–87 plus the various NIIPs, all figures deflated by the reproducible capital stock deflator. At year-end 1987, domestic

[12]Major differences in the treatment of U.S. external assets and claims by the Fed and BEA are identified in Appendix A.

*TABLE 5*

REAL U.S. NET FOREIGN ASSETS
(BILLIONS OF 1982 DOLLARS)

| | | Valued to Market via | | | Deflator for Net Fixed Reproducible Tangible Wealth |
|---|---|---|---|---|---|
| Year | *SCB* | Stocks | Earnings | Investment Deflators | |
| 1970 | 117.9 | 199.3 | 262.7 | 178.8 | 0.402 |
| 1971 | 83.1 | 182.9 | 236.5 | 165.7 | 0.425 |
| 1972 | 59.3 | 226.0 | 265.8 | 162.8 | 0.448 |
| 1973 | 74.7 | 206.2 | 424.7 | 235.8 | 0.485 |
| 1974 | 83.9 | 137.7 | 346.0 | 276.1 | 0.561 |
| 1975 | 105.5 | 175.6 | 208.7 | 302.6 | 0.594 |
| 1976 | 113.9 | 150.0 | 202.4 | 314.2 | 0.632 |
| 1977 | 88.7 | 148.8 | 182.3 | 312.4 | 0.688 |
| 1978 | 83.2 | 177.3 | 189.3 | 330.5 | 0.775 |
| 1979 | 98.1 | 225.1 | 252.2 | 373.0 | 0.849 |
| 1980 | 102.7 | 244.7 | 202.2 | 400.7 | 0.926 |
| 1981 | 131.0 | 245.2 | 214.4 | 386.2 | 0.992 |
| 1982 | 125.7 | 229.3 | 193.6 | 366.0 | 1.000 |
| 1983 | 75.9 | 239.9 | 147.2 | 285.4 | 1.032 |
| 1984 | −7.2 | 155.7 | 64.4 | 164.9 | 1.059 |
| 1985 | −112.4 | 174.1 | 134.0 | 92.9 | 1.083 |
| 1986 | −254.8 | 161.4 | 89.1 | −5.9 | 1.100 |
| 1987 | −334.8 | 83.2 | 193.6 | −9.8 | 1.133 |

private holdings of tangible assets totaled $12.5 trillion and government tangible assets $3.3 trillion, up at 2.7 and 2.0 percent annual rates since 1980. Growth of private sector and total wealth in the period 1980–87 was somewhat slower than over the period 1948–87. Table 7 also presents the tangible wealth figures incorporating the various U.S. NIIP measures. According to these figures, real U.S. wealth continued to grow in the 1980s at 2.1 to 2.5 percent a year, in each case down from the rates experienced in the 1970s but faster than indicated by the wealth measure based on the official NIIP.

Table 8 and Figure 5 reveal that the U.S. NIIP trended down relative to total net wealth in the 1980s according to both official and revalued figures. The official data indicate that net foreign claims were equal to 2.2 percent of U.S. national wealth at the end of 1987 whereas, based on the deflators revaluation, the U.S. NIIP was close to balance. With direct investment revalued to market on the basis

*TABLE 6*

REAL U.S. CURRENT ACCOUNT BALANCES
(BILLIONS OF 1982 DOLLARS)

| | | Valued to Market via | | |
|---|---|---|---|---|
| Year | *SCB* | Stocks | Earnings | Investment Deflators |
| 1971 | -34.8 | -16.4 | -26.1 | -13.1 |
| 1972 | -23.8 | 43.0 | 29.3 | -2.9 |
| 1973 | 15.5 | -19.8 | 158.8 | 73.0 |
| 1974 | 9.2 | -68.4 | -78.7 | 40.3 |
| 1975 | 21.5 | 37.8 | -137.3 | 26.6 |
| 1976 | 8.4 | -25.6 | -6.3 | 11.6 |
| 1977 | -25.2 | -1.1 | -20.1 | -1.8 |
| 1978 | -5.5 | 28.4 | 6.9 | 18.1 |
| 1979 | 14.9 | 47.8 | 63.0 | 42.5 |
| 1980 | 4.6 | 19.6 | -50.0 | 27.6 |
| 1981 | 28.3 | 0.5 | 12.2 | -14.5 |
| 1982 | -5.4 | -15.9 | -20.9 | -20.2 |
| 1983 | -49.7 | 10.6 | -46.3 | -80.6 |
| 1984 | -83.0 | -84.2 | -82.8 | -120.5 |
| 1985 | -105.3 | 18.4 | 69.7 | -72.0 |
| 1986 | -142.4 | -12.7 | -44.9 | -98.8 |
| 1987 | -80.0 | -78.2 | 104.5 | -4.0 |

of stock indices or capitalized income, the U.S. net international investment position remained positive though smaller than in 1980.[13]

## Conclusion

When direct investment is revalued to market, we estimate that the U.S. NIIP as about $400 billion to $600 billion more than the official NIIP indicates through the end of 1987, though, by all but the earnings measure, the NIIP is below its peak values of 1980 or 1981.

Whatever the cause, the bottom line indicates that the rate of accumulation of U.S. tangible wealth, *adjusted for net foreign claims,*

[13]Domestic assets are valued at current cost, which is akin to market value. Hence, for purposes of comparing the U.S. net external asset position to national wealth, the authors' estimates, which are based on market values of the assets and claims in the NIIP table, are preferable to official figures, which include direct investment at book instead of market value. The domestic and international data series are not fully comparable since international investments include financial assets and claims while the domestic wealth measure pertains only to tangible assets.

*FIGURE 4*

NOMINAL AND REVALUED REAL CURRENT ACCOUNT BALANCES RELATIVE TO GNP

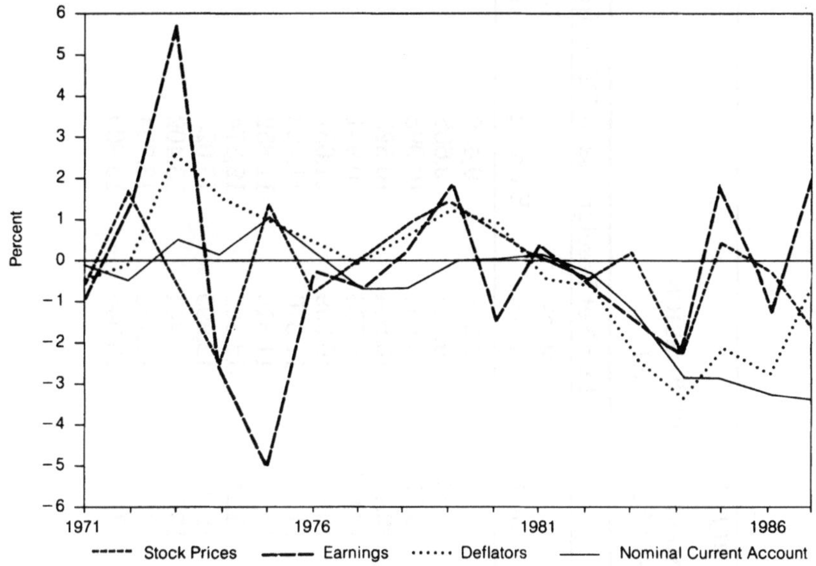


even as estimated on the basis of official data, has been positive but somewhat lower during 1980–87 than earlier in the post–World War II period. Overall U.S. wealth, *inclusive of net foreign assets,* increased by 16 percent in real terms over this period based on the official figures. When direct investment is valued at market by any of the revaluations presented in the paper, the estimated gain ranges upward from 16 percent to 19 percent.

The change in the official U.S. NIIP over the 1980–87 period was equal in magnitude to 20.4 percent of the increase in U.S. wealth inclusive of net foreign assets. The comparable figure derived from the deflator-based revaluation of direct foreign investment was much the same—18.9 percent—but was only 6.7 and 0.3 percent of the increase in total U.S. wealth when direct investment was revalued to market according to the stock-price and earnings-capitalization procedures respectively. By any of these measures, both Americans and foreigners have invested in the United States since 1980 and both are the richer for it.

These figures show that the expansion of our productive capacity during this period was not solely attributable to the investment of

*TABLE 7*

U.S. WEALTH: DOMESTIC PLUS FOREIGN
(BILLIONS OF 1982 DOLLARS)

| End of Year | Net Domestic Tangible Wealth | | | Including Net Foreign Assets Taken from | | | |
|---|---|---|---|---|---|---|---|
| | Private Sector | Public Sector | Total | *SCB* | Stock Prices | Earnings | Investment Deflators |
| 1970 | 7,035 | 2,134 | 9,169 | 9,287 | 9,368 | 9,432 | 9,348 |
| 1971 | 7,245 | 2,184 | 9,428 | 9,511 | 9,611 | 9,665 | 9,594 |
| 1972 | 7,580 | 2,250 | 9,830 | 9,890 | 10,056 | 10,096 | 9,993 |
| 1973 | 8,056 | 2,342 | 10,398 | 10,473 | 10,604 | 10,823 | 10,634 |
| 1974 | 8,164 | 2,431 | 10,595 | 10,679 | 10,733 | 10,941 | 10,871 |
| 1975 | 8,387 | 2,436 | 10,823 | 10,929 | 10,999 | 11,032 | 11,126 |
| 1976 | 8,793 | 2,427 | 11,220 | 11,334 | 11,370 | 11,422 | 11,534 |
| 1977 | 9,183 | 2,487 | 11,670 | 11,759 | 11,819 | 11,852 | 11,982 |
| 1978 | 9,555 | 2,630 | 12,184 | 12,268 | 12,362 | 12,374 | 12,515 |
| 1979 | 10,009 | 2,761 | 12,770 | 12,868 | 12,995 | 13,023 | 13,143 |
| 1980 | 10,346 | 2,854 | 13,200 | 13,302 | 13,444 | 13,402 | 13,600 |
| 1981 | 10,691 | 2,850 | 13,540 | 13,671 | 13,785 | 13,754 | 13,926 |
| 1982 | 10,814 | 2,901 | 13,715 | 13,841 | 13,945 | 13,909 | 14,081 |

| | | | | | | | |
|---|---|---|---|---|---|---|---|
| 1983 | 11,042 | 2,952 | 13,994 | 14,070 | 14,234 | 14,142 | 14,280 |
| 1984 | 11,312 | 3,007 | 14,319 | 14,312 | 14,475 | 14,384 | 14,484 |
| 1985 | 11,517 | 3,125 | 14,641 | 14,528 | 14,816 | 14,775 | 14,735 |
| 1986 | 12,041 | 3,179 | 15,220 | 14,970 | 15,381 | 15,314 | 15,214 |
| 1987 | 12,501 | 3,275 | 15,777 | 15,442 | 15,860 | 15,970 | 15,767 |
| Average Growth Rates (Percent): | | | | | | | |
| 1948–87 | 3.5 | 2.2 | 3.1 | n.a. | n.a. | n.a. | n.a. |
| 1970–80 | 3.9 | 2.9 | 3.7 | 3.7 | 3.7 | 3.6 | 3.8 |
| 1980–87 | 2.7 | 2.0 | 2.6 | 2.2 | 2.4 | 2.5 | 2.1 |

SOURCES: *SCB* (March 1980, pp. 33–43); Musgrave (1986, 1987, 1988); U.S. Department of Commerce, BEA (1987, 1988).

*TABLE 8*

| U.S. FOREIGN ASSETS RELATIVE TO NATIONAL WEALTH (PERCENT) | | | | | FOREIGN CLAIMS ON THE UNITED STATES RELATIVE TO NATIONAL WEALTH (PERCENT) | | | | | U.S. NET FOREIGN ASSETS RELATIVE TO NATIONAL WEALTH (PERCENT) | | | | |
|---|---|---|---|---|---|---|---|---|---|---|---|---|---|---|
| | | Valued to Market via | | | | | Valued to Market via | | | | | Valued to Market via | | |
| Year | *SCB* | Stocks | Earnings | Deflators | Year | *SCB* | Stocks | Earnings | Deflators | Year | *SCB* | Stocks | Earnings | Deflators |
| 1970 | 4.2 | 5.6 | 5.8 | 5.0 | 1970 | 2.9 | 3.4 | 2.9 | 3.0 | 1970 | 1.3 | 2.1 | 2.8 | 1.9 |
| 1971 | 4.2 | 5.9 | 6.0 | 5.2 | 1971 | 3.3 | 3.9 | 3.5 | 3.5 | 1971 | 0.9 | 1.9 | 2.4 | 1.7 |
| 1972 | 4.3 | 6.7 | 6.5 | 5.5 | 1972 | 3.7 | 4.4 | 3.8 | 3.8 | 1972 | 0.6 | 2.2 | 2.6 | 1.6 |
| 1973 | 4.2 | 5.9 | 7.7 | 5.8 | 1973 | 3.5 | 3.9 | 3.6 | 3.6 | 1973 | 0.7 | 1.9 | 3.9 | 2.2 |
| 1974 | 4.1 | 4.8 | 6.4 | 6.1 | 1974 | 3.3 | 3.5 | 3.2 | 3.5 | 1974 | 0.8 | 1.3 | 3.2 | 2.5 |
| 1975 | 4.4 | 5.4 | 5.3 | 6.4 | 1975 | 3.4 | 3.8 | 3.4 | 3.6 | 1975 | 1.0 | 1.6 | 1.9 | 2.7 |
| 1976 | 4.7 | 5.5 | 5.5 | 6.8 | 1976 | 3.7 | 4.1 | 3.7 | 4.0 | 1976 | 1.0 | 1.3 | 1.8 | 2.7 |
| 1977 | 4.6 | 5.4 | 5.3 | 6.7 | 1977 | 3.8 | 4.1 | 3.8 | 4.1 | 1977 | 0.8 | 1.3 | 1.5 | 2.6 |
| 1978 | 4.6 | 5.7 | 5.5 | 6.9 | 1978 | 3.9 | 4.2 | 3.9 | 4.2 | 1978 | 0.7 | 1.4 | 1.5 | 2.6 |
| 1979 | 4.6 | 5.9 | 5.8 | 7.0 | 1979 | 3.8 | 4.1 | 3.8 | 4.1 | 1979 | 0.8 | 1.7 | 1.9 | 2.8 |
| 1980 | 4.9 | 6.4 | 5.5 | 7.4 | 1980 | 4.1 | 4.6 | 4.0 | 4.3 | 1980 | 0.8 | 1.8 | 1.5 | 2.9 |
| 1981 | 5.3 | 6.4 | 5.5 | 7.5 | 1981 | 4.3 | 4.6 | 3.9 | 4.6 | 1981 | 1.0 | 1.8 | 1.6 | 2.8 |
| 1982 | 5.9 | 7.1 | 5.7 | 8.0 | 1982 | 5.0 | 5.5 | 4.3 | 5.3 | 1982 | 0.9 | 1.6 | 1.4 | 2.6 |
| 1983 | 6.0 | 7.8 | 5.9 | 7.7 | 1983 | 5.4 | 6.1 | 4.9 | 5.7 | 1983 | 0.5 | 1.7 | 1.0 | 2.0 |
| 1984 | 5.8 | 7.6 | 5.9 | 7.3 | 1984 | 5.9 | 6.5 | 5.4 | 6.1 | 1984 | −0.0 | 1.1 | 0.4 | 1.1 |
| 1985 | 5.9 | 8.9 | 6.9 | 7.6 | 1985 | 6.7 | 7.7 | 6.0 | 6.9 | 1985 | −0.8 | 1.2 | 0.9 | 0.6 |
| 1986 | 6.3 | 10.5 | 7.7 | 8.2 | 1986 | 8.0 | 9.4 | 7.1 | 8.2 | 1986 | −1.7 | 1.0 | 0.6 | −0.0 |
| 1987 | 6.5 | 10.4 | 9.3 | 8.7 | 1987 | 8.6 | 9.9 | 8.0 | 8.8 | 1987 | −2.2 | 0.5 | 1.2 | −0.1 |

*FIGURE 5*

U.S. NET INTERNATIONAL INVESTMENTS RELATIVE TO NATIONAL WEALTH

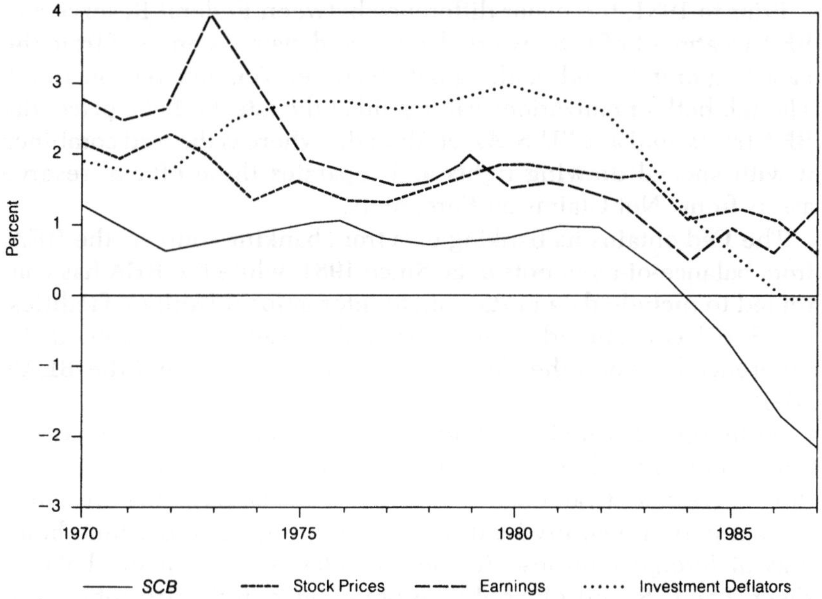


foreigners in the United States. Furthermore, based on our growing wealth, continued increases in our standard of living are not threatened by the necessity to service net claims of foreigners on our productive capacity. It is certainly true that we could grow richer still if we saved and invested even more than we do, but it is certainly not true, as is frequently asserted, that we have simply borrowed abroad to consume and not to invest.

It is important to take note that these data on wealth omit mineral wealth and such nontangibles as investments in human capital and research and development. All told, the change in the U.S. NIIP, in both the official and revalued figures, remains very small relative to the level of and the increase in U.S. wealth in the 1980s and, in any case, is not a reason for panic. The U.S. standard of living may well be threatened by proposals to increase trade or foreign investment restrictions justified by the depleted NIIP and current account deficit *as officially measured.* It is not threatened by what appear to be at the most only comparatively small net foreign claims on our growing national assets.

## Appendix A: Federal Reserve and Bureau of Economic Analysis Treatment of U.S. External Assets and Claims

Prior to 1981, the major difference between Federal Reserve and BEA treatment of U.S. external assets and claims stemmed from the handling of gold and banking data (van der Ven and Wilson 1986). Though both organizations value gold at the latest official price, the BEA treats gold as a "U.S. Asset Abroad," whereas the Fed combines it with special drawing rights and separates these official reserve assets from "Net Claims on Foreigners."

The Fed obtains its banking data from banking sources; the BEA, from balance-of-payments data. Since 1981, while the BEA has continued to include data pertaining to international banking facilities, the Fed has excluded them. This shift in definition widened the difference between the Fed's "net-claims" concept and the BEA's NIIP.

While the BEA includes both U.S. equity investment abroad and foreign equity holdings here—portfolio and direct—in the NIIP (with direct investment valued at book rather than market), the Fed counts foreign portfolio equity holdings here—but not U.S. portfolio holdings of foreign equities—in the "net-claims" line of the balance sheet. The U.S. portfolio holdings of foreign equities are not considered by the Fed because they are not a foreign liability.

The Fed treats bonds sold by Netherlands Antilles affiliates of U.S. corporations as foreign bond holdings while the BEA nets the intracompany debt represented by these bonds against U.S. foreign direct investment. The Fed balance sheets exclude all tangible government assets except gold and special drawing rights. In the national income and product accounts (NIPA), all government expenditures are considered to be current consumption. Moreover, private as well as public investment in such areas as human capital and research and development are omitted from both the NIPA investment data and the Fed's capital stock figures. Ignoring government investment—civilian or military—plus mineral rights, human capital, and research and development (R&D) certainly understates the stock of national wealth.

Since the BEA publishes the value of the stock of government fixed reproducible assets, it would be easy to incorporate these capital assets in the Fed's balance sheets. Data on stocks of government inventories, though unpublished, are also available from the BEA and could also be included in calculating national wealth. R&D expenditures are treated as a cost in the NIPA. It would be simple to count R&D spending as investment though difficult to depreciate the resulting stock appropriately in order to derive a value for the net stock of R&D capital.

Furthermore, in failing to consider tangible public sector assets, the Fed ignores a substantial segment of national wealth. Governments own roads, schools, offices, both civilian and military equipment, inventories, and land. All told, governments—federal, state, and local—own roughly 20 percent of U.S. wealth (reproducible tangibles plus land). Our estimates of the value of government land in 1986 and 1987 are extrapolations of the figures given by Eisner (1986) derived by applying the rate of increase in private-sector land values found in the Fed data to government land.

In the calculations of national wealth, land is valued at farmland equivalent prices; subsurface assets are not included. According to U.S. Bureau of Mines personnel (Biviano 1988), there are no recent estimates of the aggregate value of mineral reserves owned either privately or publicly in the United States. In a recent article and National Bureau of Economic Research working paper, however, Boskin and co-authors (1985, 1987) estimate the value of government land by including estimates of oil and gas mineral rights beneath federal lands and an adjustment for that portion of government land that is urban rather than rural. The figures are somewhat shaky (see Rosenthal, Rose, and Slaski [forthcoming]) but may be indicative of the extent of undervaluation of land in the Fed's data for the private sector and others' estimates (e.g., those of Eisner 1986) for the public sector.

## Appendix B: Data Sources

The data used in this study were those pertaining to

- U.S. assets abroad and foreign assets in the United States found in *SCB* (August 1984) and Scholl (1986, 1987, 1988).
- Nominal U.S. current account balances and earnings/price ratios found in the 1988 and 1989 *Economic Report of the President and Annual Report of the Council of Economic Advisers*.
- Book value of U.S. direct investment abroad by country since 1950, found in U.S. Department of Commerce, BEA (1982, 1986); *SCB* (August 1986); Scholl (1987); and Bach (1988).
- Price indices for stocks traded on the New York Stock Exchange and major stock exchanges in other industrial countries for which country-specific data on U.S. direct investment are found in the publications cited above, taken from *International Financial*

*Statistics* data tapes for 11 and 31 March and 13 May 1988, and the August 1988 *International Financial Statistics.*

- Year-end exchange rates for the dollar taken from *International Financial Statistics* data tapes, 31 January 1989.
- Deflator for fixed reproducible tangible wealth derived on the basis of data found in Musgrave (1986, 1987, 1988).
- Earnings on foreign direct investment found in *SCB* (March 1953, p. 8; June 1956, p. 24; June 1960, p. 14; June 1961, p. 12; and June 1988, pp. 40–41). Since data for years prior to 1960 refer to repatriated earnings only, for prior years, reinvested earnings found in U.S. Department of Commerce, BEA (1982, pp. 55–64; 1984, p. 8) were added to the *SCB* earnings data.
- Book values of foreign direct investment in the United States found in U.S. Department of Commerce, BEA (1984, pp. 2–3) and Scholl (1988, p. 78).
- Year-end stocks of residential structures and nonresidential plant and equipment at current cost, taken from the April 1988 *Balance Sheets for the U.S. Economy, 1948–87,* published by the Board of Governors of the Federal Reserve System.
- Nominal and real reproducible tangible wealth in the United States, found in Musgrave (1987, 1988).
- Data on investment deflator-adjusted values of U.S. investment abroad, and foreign investment in the United States taken from Eisner and Pieper.
- Government asset figures taken from Eisner (1986); updated and revised data relating to federal financial assets and liabilities furnished to the authors by Pieper; and updated and revised data relating to federal, state and local inventories furnished to the authors by Musgrave.
- Shearson-Lehman Brothers bank-loan secondary-market-price data from *Euromoney,* 21 March 1988.
- Outstanding U.S. bank-loan data from Federal Reserve Board Statistical Release, April 1988.

Requests for the data should include a high-density diskette and return mailer sent to the authors at the following address: EB/PAS, Room 3425, U.S. Department of State, Washington, DC 20520.

## References

Aho, C. Michael, and Levinson, Marc. *After Reagan: Confronting the Changed World Economy.* New York: Council on Foreign Relations, 1988.

Bach, Christopher L. "U.S. International Transactions, Fourth Quarter and Year 1987." *Survey of Current Business* (March 1988): 27–59.

*Balance Sheets for the U.S. Economy, 1948–1987*, Washington; Board of Governors of the Federal Reserve System, 1988.

Barro, Robert J. *Macroeconomics*. New York: John Wiley and Sons, 1984.

Biviano, Marilyn. U.S. Bureau of Mines, telephone conversation with author, 25 May 1988.

Boskin, Michael J.; Robinson, Marc S.; O'Reilly, Terrence; and Kumar, Pnaveen. "New Estimates of the Value of Federal Mineral Rights and Land," *American Economic Review* 75 (December 1985): 923–36.

Boskin, Michael J.; Robinson, Marc S.; and Huber, Alan M. "Government Saving, Capital Formation, and Wealth in the United States, 1947–1985." Cambridge, Mass.: National Bureau of Economic Research, 1987.

Eisner, Robert. *How Real Is the Federal Deficit?* New York: The Free Press, 1986.

Eisner, Robert, and Pieper, Paul J. "The World's Greatest Debtor Nation?" Paper presented to joint session of North American Economics and Finance Association and American Economic Association, New York, 30 December 1988.

*Euromoney*, 21 March 1988.

Hooker, Sarah A. *The International Investment Position of the United States*. Santa Monica, Calif.: The Rand Corporation, October 1988.

Islam, Shafiqul. "America's Foreign Debt: Fear, Fantasy, Fiction, and Facts." Paper presented to Congressional Research Service Workshop, Washington, D.C., 1 April 1988.

Musgrave, John C., "Fixed Reproducible Tangible Wealth in the U.S.: Revised Estimates." *Survey of Current Business* (January 1986): 51–70.

Musgrave, John C. "Summary Fixed Tangible Wealth Series, 1929–1986." *Survey of Current Business* (November 1987): 36–37.

Musgrave, John C., "Fixed Reproducible Tangible Wealth in the United States, 1984–87." *Survey of Current Business* (August 1988): 84–87.

Rosenthal, Donald H.; Rose, Marshall B.; and Slaski, Lawrence J. "The Economic Value of the Oil and Gas Resources on the Outer Continental Shelf." *Marine Resources Economics*, forthcoming.

Scholl, Russell B. "The International Investment Position of the United States in 1985." *Survey of Current Business* (June 1986): 26–35.

Scholl, Russell B. "The International Investment Position of the United States in 1986." *Survey of Current Business* (June 1987): 38–45.

Scholl, Russell B. "The International Investment Position of the United States in 1987." *Survey of Current Business* (June 1988): 76–84.

*SCB* "Government-Owned Fixed Capital in the United States, 1925–1979." *Survey of Current Business* (March 1980): 33–43.

*SCB* "U.S. Direct Investment Abroad: Detail for Position and Balance-of-Payments Flows, 1986." *Survey of Current Business* (August 1987): 85–99.

U.S. Department of Commerce. Bureau of Economic Analysis. *Selected Data on U.S. Direct Investment Abroad, 1950–1976*. Washington, D.C.: Government Printing Office, 1982.

U.S. Department of Commerce. Bureau of Economic Analysis. *Selected Data on Foreign Direct Investment in the United States, 1950–1979*. Washington, D.C.: Government Printing Office, 1984.

U.S. Department of Commerce. Bureau of Economic Analysis. *U.S. Direct Investment Abroad: Balance of Payments and Direct Investment Positions Estimates, 1977–1981*. Washington, D.C.: Government Printing Office, 1986.

U.S. Department of Commerce. Bureau of Economic Analysis. *Fixed Reproducible Tangible Wealth in the United States, 1925–1985*. Washington, D.C.: Government Printing Office, 1987.

U.S. Department of Commerce. Bureau of Economic Analysis. "Government Inventories," unpublished print-out, May 1988.

U.S. Department of Commerce. Bureau of Economic Analysis. *U.S. Direct Investment Abroad*. Washington, D.C.: Government Printing Office, various issues.

U.S. Department of Commerce. International Trade Administration. *International Direct Investment*. Washington, D.C.: Government Printing Office, November 1988.

van der Ven, Guido, and Wilson, John F. "The United States International Asset and Liability Position: A Comparison of Flow of Funds and Commerce Department Presentations." *International Finance Discussion Papers*, Washington, D.C.: Board of Governors, Federal Reserve System, 1986.

# Part V

# Toward a Stable International Order

# 17

# How Strong Is the Case for International Coordination?*

*Joachim Scheide and Stefan Sinn*

## International Economic Coordination: In What Form and in Which Areas?

There seems to be a consensus among politicians and economists that economic problems such as high unemployment and inflation can be solved only if economic policies are coordinated on an international scale. The 1987 economic summit at Venice viewed international coordination as essential "to achieving stronger and sustained global growth, reduced external imbalances, and more stable exchange rate relationships."[1] In a similar vein, Helmut Schmidt (1983, p. 24) argued that "the major industrial countries' policy mix must be coordinated." The European Community Commission (1986), as well as the Organization for Economic Cooperation and Development (1987a), has recently urged policymakers to implement a cooperative policy action to restore satisfactory macroeconomic performance of the major industrial countries. These calls for more international coordination receive their theoretical underpinnings from the work of a number of economists who argue that by coordinating their policies individual countries can avoid negative spillover effects of uncoordinated sovereign policymaking and take advantage of positive spillover effects. Coordination would allow each country to achieve its economic targets to a greater degree than if it pursued an independent policy stance.[2]

Three different *forms* of international economic policy coordination can be distinguished (see Putnam and Bayne 1984; Cooper 1987, p. 183): (1) exchange of information on the current and future stance

---

*This article is based on Scheide and Sinn (1987).

The authors are economists at the Kiel Institute of World Economics in the Federal Republic of Germany.

[1]Venice Economic Declaration, par. 3.

[2]The main proponents of this view are Richard N. Cooper, Koichi Hamada, Matthew Canzoneri, Gilles Oudiz, and Jeffrey Sachs. Cooper (1985a) provides a useful summary.

of economic policy to provide a basis for the formulation of economic policies in other countries; (2) agreement on individual policy targets to avoid the pursuit of futile targets; and (3) coordinated use of economic policy instruments to achieve agreed values of macroeconomic targets.[3] The demands for giving up national autonomy become increasingly greater as countries move from the first to the third form of international coordination. It is not surprising that historic examples for the different forms of policy coordination become increasingly rare as they impinge more and more on national sovereignty.[4]

As far as the *areas* of international coordination are concerned, there is a consensus among most economists that international public goods are best provided by coordinated measures of all the governments involved. Examples of such international public goods are an international legal order and the worldwide reduction of trade barriers. There is considerably less consensus on whether the international coordination of monetary and fiscal policies should be used to and can in fact achieve the common targets of high employment, stability of the price level and the exchange rate, and a reduction of current account "imbalances." In order to judge the merits and demerits of international policy coordination, at least four questions have to be addressed:

- On what theoretical grounds can a case be established in favor of explicitly coordinating the economic policies of different countries?
- What are important prerequisites for successful international policy coordination?
- What can we learn from past attempts to coordinate policies?
- What alternatives to explicit policy coordination exist?

These and other issues will be discussed in the remainder of this paper.

[3]These forms of policy coordination pertain to the continued use of policy instruments to achieve certain targets (fine tuning). Coordination may also be used to establish a trade or exchange rate regime, a subject not dealt with here.

[4]The most frequently cited instance of a successful example of the third type of policy coordination is the Bonn summit 1978 (Frenkel 1987, p. 208; Cooper 1985b, p. 370). The Bonn summit is not, however, without critics. According to Jocelyn Horne and Paul Masson (1987, p. 30), "the expansionary measures decided upon at Bonn were soon revised, and the Bonn summit is widely considered to be an example of the pitfalls of international 'fine-tuning.' " Likewise, Roland Vaubel (1985, p. 235) contends that the fiscal stimulus that was the West German government's contribution to the policy package was "ill-timed from a cyclical point of view and contributed to the severe budgetary problems of the early eighties."

## The Game-Theoretic Case for Policy Coordination

One of the cornerstones on which the case for international policy coordination rests is Franco Modigliani's famous observation that "a private enterprise economy using an intangible money needs to be stabilized, can be stabilized, and therefore should be stabilized" (Modigliani 1977, p. 1). Proponents of international policy coordination firmly adhere to Modigliani's credo; it is not surprising that monetarist or new-classical economists either ignore the debate on policy coordination or are highly critical of such proposals.[5]

The other cornerstone on which the case for international policy coordination rests denies Modigliani's second hypothesis on stabilization policies: In interdependent countries where the actions of one policymaker impinge on the targets of other policymakers, sovereign policymaking by itself *cannot* stabilize the economy. In fact, attempts to do so will lead to a situation that is worse than the situation that would have prevailed if there had been no attempts to stabilize the economy. But all is not lost for the cause of fine-tuning: The solution to the problem lies in the international coordination of national policies. As such, Modigliani's second hypothesis is therefore vindicated via the route of international fine-tuning. It follows that the task of proponents of international policy coordination is two-fold: Demonstrate that sovereign policymaking is suboptimal, and show that international policy coordination can improve sovereign policymaking.

The analytical demonstration that sovereign policymaking is suboptimal is by now familiar. We will therefore restrict ourselves to a verbal presentation of its main assumptions and results.[6] At the outset the well-known point is made that macroeconomic policy measures are transmitted to other countries thereby affecting their macroeconomic performance. Various channels for these spillover effects have been considered in the literature,[7] among them are real exchange rate changes and income changes that affect international trade flows. The fact that domestic macroeconomic variables such as output and inflation are affected by policy decisions abroad estab-

[5]Early on Milton Friedman (1964, p. 8) warned: "In recent years, the concern with the international balance of payments has given rise to greater co-operation among central banks. . . . I must confess that I regard the tendency as an exceedingly dangerous one." More recently, an outspoken critic of international policy coordination has been Roland Vaubel (1980, 1983, 1985).

[6]See Cooper (1985a, pp. 1213–17) for a useful introduction to the analytical framework. He also provides a survey of the literature.

[7]See, for example, Canzoneri and Gray (1985, pp. 525–26).

lishes a strategic interdependence among policymakers that can be analyzed using the tools of game theory.

Three basic assumptions are made in order to arrive at the suboptimality of sovereign policymaking:

1. The best course of action for domestic policymakers depends on the policy choices made abroad. It is assumed that policymakers behave myopically when optimizing their response to foreign-policy disturbances: They ignore possible measures of their counterparts caused by their own decisions. This assumption is familiar from models of firms' behavior in oligopoly theory.
2. There is a scarcity of policy instruments and therefore policymakers have to trade off different targets when deciding on the use of their policy instruments. Analytically such trade-offs are modeled using policymakers' utility functions.[8] Optimality then requires that policy instruments be employed until policymakers are indifferent between, for example, a further decline in unemployment and a further rise in inflation.[9]
3. Uncoordinated attempts at fine tuning are initiated by a global shock that affects all countries alike.[10] In the absence of corrective policy measures, a negative supply shock would leave output below and inflation above their target values. Policymakers in each country therefore attempt to reattain the output and inflation levels they had desired before the shock occurred. An alternative that is not considered would be an adjustment of targets to levels that are more appropriate to worldwide economic conditions after the shock has occurred.

Given these assumptions, it can be shown that individually rational behavior of each policymaker leads to a globally suboptimal situation, a result that is demonstrated using two scenarios.

In *scenario 1* it is assumed that foreign expansionary policy is transmitted positively to the home country, causing a rise in output. Matthew Canzoneri and Jo Anna Gray (1985) have called this scenario "locomotive world."[11] The suboptimality arises in this case because uncoordinated policy measures to combat the negative out-

[8]Gilles Oudiz and Jeffrey Sachs (1984, pp. 37–38) attempt to quantify (or reveal) the preferences of policymakers. Their analytical framework is rejected in Martinez-Oliva (1987).

[9]Not surprisingly, all models imply a positive trade-off between output and inflation.

[10]Cf. Canzoneri and Gray (1985, p. 549): "By assumption, all games are initiated by a global shock that will, in the absence of corrective policy, cause output levels in both countries to deviate from their full employment values."

[11]The analysis in Drèze et al. (1987) is based on scenario 1.

put effects of the external shock do not go far enough. Individual optimizing implies that expansionary measures continue until the marginal utility gain from a further increase in employment is just matched by the marginal utility loss from a further increase in inflation. From a global point of view, however, welfare would increase at this point if the home country undertook further expansionary measures because output abroad would rise. Since these positive spillover effects do not enter the welfare calculations of policymakers, additional expansionary measures are not undertaken.[12] Since every policymaker behaves in this way, a contractionary (less expansionary) bias characterizes economic policies throughout the world. Scenario 1 is occasionally said to characterize the period after the rise in oil prices at the end of the 1970s. It is claimed that the worldwide recession in the wake of the second oil price rise would have been less severe if countries had coordinated their macroeconomic policies.

A "beggar-thy-neighbor" world is depicted in *scenario* 2. In this case policy measures cause negative spillovers in the other country. Usually it is assumed that policymakers try to "import" price stability via a real appreciation of their currency caused by a monetary policy that is more restrictive than abroad.[13] If all policymakers act in this manner, they can never for long achieve their aim because of the reaction from abroad that they myopically fail to take into consideration. Thus the wish of every policymaker to "import" price stability results in a dynamic adjustment process familiar from duopoly theory as the zig-zag movement between two reaction functions. As policymakers continue to react to disturbances from abroad, their policy stance becomes progressively more restrictive. It is only at the intersection of the reaction functions of both policymakers that this process ceases. The equilibrium thus attained is usually referred to as a noncooperative Nash-equilibrium.

This type of equilibrium is characterized by the fact that both countries choose the *same* (low) rate of monetary expansion with the exchange rate remaining constant and the inflation target abroad no

[12]Canzoneri and Gray (1985, p. 560) write: "While both players respond to an oil price increase by increasing their money growth rates, they do not increase them enough." The reasons why countries prefer not to contribute to further increases in monetary growth is similar to the incentive problems of the provision of public goods: It is optimal for everyone to speculate on a free ride on the locomotive of expansionary policy abroad.

[13]The analyses of Cooper (1985a, pp. 1214–18) and Oudiz and Sachs (1984, p. 50 ff.) are based on scenario 2.

longer affected by domestic monetary policy. But the noncooperative Nash-equilibrium is suboptimal from a global point of view: Since monetary policy is more restrictive than originally planned, unemployment is needlessly high. Empirically scenario 2 is said to characterize worldwide economic policies in the early 1980s, when monetary policies in Western Europe were quite restrictive in order to avoid an even greater depreciation of their currencies against the dollar.

Having demonstrated that uncoordinated attempts at fine-tuning lead to global inefficiencies, it is fairly straightforward to demonstrate that international policy coordination leads to an improvement. Whereas under a system of competitive policies "spillover effects" were ignored in each policymaker's welfare calculus, they are now taken into consideration. By explicitly trading expansionary measures in scenario 1, the coordinating countries remove the "checks and balances" that the international monetary regime impose on a country that seeks to expand on its own—namely, a devaluation of the currency or a loss in reserves. Indeed as most models assume that inflation is caused by a rise in the price of imported goods, there is no theoretical limit to how far countries could jointly expand their money supplies as long as they do so at the same rate.[14]

In scenario 2, coordination consists of the mutual commitment to refrain from competitive beggar-thy-neighbor policies, be they aimed at "importing" employment—the classic worry of Keynesians—or price stability. In both cases coordination leads to a Pareto improvement: Every country is at least as well off in a coordinated regime, and some are even better off. Therefore every country has an incentive to participate in policy coordination.[15] A comparison of the coordinated policy measures in both scenarios shows that coordination may either consist of the joint decision to embark on fine-tuning (scenario 1) or the agreement to refrain from doing so in an uncoordinated way (scenario 2).

[14]Most elementary models on international policy coordination assume that countries are identical in every aspect. In this special case coordination always results in identical measures. Once more complicated models with asymmetries are used, coordination may imply different policy stances in different countries. Thus it is not generally true that policy coordination implies a synchronization of policies in one direction.

[15]Oudiz and Sachs (1984, pp. 3–4) note that this demonstration is an improvement to earlier empirical exercises, which merely demonstrated that a coordinated expansion had a greater impact on worldwide output than an uncoordinated expansion. For this result to hold, however, it had to be assumed that some countries act altruistically. See also Vaubel (1988).

## A Critique of the Game-Theoretic Approach

Supporters of international policy coordination who base their arguments on the game-theoretic approach may wonder at the stupidity of politicians who do not seize this opportunity for welfare gains. Is the widespread absence of coordinated macropolicies a sign of "policy failure" on an international scale, or might there be reasons that explain why the prescription of the game-theoretic approach does not lend itself to an application in the real world? We proceed in two steps. At first the question is addressed whether the game-theoretic characterization of an uncoordinated or competitive international economic system fits the present situation in the world economy. Our main conclusion is that characterizing present worldwide relations among policymakers as a noncooperative Nash-equilibrium is unduely pessimistic. If we are in fact not in as bad a situation as proponents of international policymaking would like to make us believe, a close look at the actual working of international coordination seems called for. This is followed by our second step where we focus on possible costs of international policy coordination.

*Are Policymakers Myopic and Adamant?*

Whether policy coordination can in fact lead to welfare gains depends on initial conditions. Proponents of policy coordination claim that the present international "non-system" is inefficient; we question their assumptions about the behavior of policymakers.

One of the crucial assumptions holds that policymakers do not adjust their macroeconomic targets in the face of adverse external shocks. In fact all games are initiated by this discrepancy between the desired value and the realized value of the policy target and continue until this gap has disappeared. Why would it be more realistic to assume that politicans adjust their targets to more reasonable values in the face of adverse developments?

An adverse external shock carries the simple message for domestic policymakers that their range of attainable targets has become smaller. The result of attempts to deny this are nicely summarized by a Swedish policymaker: "We attempted to build a bridge but ended up with a pier."[16] If policymakers adjusted their targets instead of trying to build bridges, policy coordination would become superfluous because there would no longer be any need for policy measures, be they coordinated or not.[17]

[16]Reported by Oudiz and Sachs (1984, p. 3).

[17]See Martinez-Oliva and Sinn (1988). The conclusion does not change if, instead of building a bridge single-handedly (uncoordinated policies), one tries to do so with the help of others (policy coordination). As will become clear in the course of this essay, the latter amounts to trying to build a bridge and ending up with two piers.

It is well known from duopoly theory that the behavioral assumptions underlying a noncooperative Nash-equilibrium are highly unrealistic. As Michael Bacharach (1977, p. 71) notes, the model of man underlying the Nash equilibrium is "not of rational economic agents but of imbeciles. They learn nothing, clinging in spite of overwhelming counter-evidence to zero reactions." Current international policymaking—while not presenting the textbook case of the coordinated use of policy instruments—does not seem to be conducted by politicians who myopically fail to take into account the reaction of other politicians to their own decisions. In the view of David Mulford (1987, p. 9), "The coordination process . . . is an ongoing process involving regular consultations among the participants on their economic objectives and projections, current policies and performance, and the possible need for remedial action." Consequently, we most probably are not in a noncooperative Nash-equilibrium, and the potential gains from coordination are not as considerable as implied by the game-theoretic approach.

The game-theoretic approach further assumes that in each country there is a scarcity of instruments relative to targets. One reason is that policymakers are assumed to try to achieve not only domestic but also external targets such as a particular balance on the current account or a particular exchange rate. At first sight coordination seems indeed to be necessary for such targets to avoid conflicts. After all, not every country can have a current account surplus, and between any two countries there can be only one exchange rate. Yet one may wonder whether current account balances are meaningful targets of economic policy at all.

Two conjectures are often brought forward in discussions about external account balances. First, there seems to be a tendency in international fora to associate a current account balance of zero with an equilibrium, while positive or negative current account balances are often referred to as imbalances.[18] Second, surpluses carry the odium of beggar-thy-neighbor policies: Germany's and Japan's surpluses are said to lead to an import of employment while the deficit countries deplore a loss of employment. Both conjectures are wrong.[19] Any deficit on the trade account is financed by a surplus on the capital account. As long as the foreign investor earns a good return by invest-

[18]The European Community Commission (1986), as well as the Organization for Economic Cooperation and Development (1987a, pp. ix–x), refers to the presently observed balances as disequilibria. Countries with a deficit are urged to curb spending, while those with a surplus are encouraged to stimulate domestic spending.

[19]One may wonder why economists have not stressed this point more.

ing abroad, there is no reason why the deficit could not continue. Imbalances in the sense of unsustainable situations need not occur.[20] The same is true for a trade account surplus, although there the stability is rarely questioned.

The second conjecture concerns the employment effects of trade account balances. No new jobs are created by the presence of a trade account surplus alone. On the contrary, the concomitant capital export increases employment abroad, in the recipient country. The employment experience of the United States in the first half of the 1980s as a major recipient of capital compared with that of major capital exporting countries supports this view. The balance on the external account of a country is devoid of any normative implications. Its size and its sign cannot be associated with the welfare of a country in the same way as, for example, a stable consumer price index or steady economic growth. The same can be said for the exchange rate. Like any other relative price, the exchange rate serves as an indicator of relative scarcities and cannot be a meaningful target of economic policy.

If exchange rates and external accounts balances cease to serve as targets for economic policy, there may no longer be a scarcity of instruments to attain the targets of policymakers. Instead of searching for new instruments,[21] an equality of the number of targets and instruments can also be achieved by making external targets redundant.[22] This conclusion will not be accepted by those who view the targets of policymakers as sacrosanct and argue that the pursuit of external targets by politicians requires the economist to calculate how these targets can be reached by implementing an internationally coordinated policy package. The package (and the economist's calculations) become superfluous if governments renounce all their external targets. However, such disinterestedness on behalf of the economic profession is currently lacking.

Is the present international monetary system as inefficient as has been claimed and does it therefore warrant an internationally coordinated effort to restore growth and employment? A closer look at present international economic arrangements has shown that they are in fact neither characterized by the inefficient noncooperative Nash-equilibrium nor by a continuous effort at coordination. The

[20]Cf. Samuelson (1972, p. 661): "Thus, there is no necessary reason why a country should ever be paid off for its past lending, unless it has become relatively poorer." The same point is made by David Gale (1974).

[21]See Cooper (1985, pp. 1230–31).

[22]Oudiz (1985, p. ii) describes the scarcity of policy instruments in Europe. Since governments,' policies concentrate on fighting inflation and correcting current account imbalances, no instrument is left for curing unemployment.

true description would probably be that of a system where occasional coordination of economic policy is taking place, mainly in the realm of exchange rate stabilization. In all other areas it is still true what Max Corden observed some years ago: "The current laissez-faire international monetary system is simply a market system which coordinates the decentralized decisions reached by private and public actors and is likely to be as efficient in this as the market system is within the domestic economy" (Corden 1983, p. 71). As a result, the likely gains from coordination are going to be small or zero. As a consequence, possible costs and efficiency losses due to international coordination become more important.

*Efficiency Losses Due to International Policy Coordination*

In many studies international coordination of policies is presented as a panacea to important worldwide economic problems. It is invoked time and again as an unexamined alternative. The proof that existing arrangements are deficient in one aspect or the other is a necessary and sufficient condition to justify the call for coordination. What such Nirvana economics (Demsetz 1969) fails to take into consideration is that policy coordination itself may fail, primarily for two reasons: (1) Policymakers' lack of knowledge about the structure of their economies may prevent an implementation of the optimal plan; and (2) the coordination process changes the incentives for third parties in such a way that their reaction may militate against the success of the coordination package.

The gains from coordination can be realized only if policymakers agree on and know the structure of the world economy and the size of the "spillover effects" of their own policy measures.[23] At present these prerequisites for successful policy coordination are certainly not met.

Table 1 reports the results of a simulation exercise where different econometric models were used to predict the effect of an expansion of U.S. government spending on output and inflation in the United States and the rest of the OECD countries as well as on the dollar exchange rate. While there is some agreement on the sign of the impact multipliers, there is little agreement on the size of the effect.

Even if policymakers are uncertain about the true model of the world and therefore disagree, they will still be able to coordinate policies on the basis of their divergent views as long as each of them *believes* that the agreed-upon measures make his country better off. It is not certain, however, that the agreed-upon policy package does

[23]Cf. Vaubel (1985, p. 237).

*TABLE 1*

SIMULATION EFFECT OF AN INCREASE IN GOVERNMENT EXPENDITURE IN THE UNITED STATES BY 1 PERCENT OF GNP (PERCENTAGE CHANGES)[a]

| Model | GNP: United States | Consumer Price Index: United States | External Value of the Dollar[b] | GNP: Rest of OECD Countries | Consumer Price Index: Rest of OECD Countries |
|---|---|---|---|---|---|
| MCM | 1.8 | 0.4 | 2.8 | 0.7 | 0.4 |
| EEC | 1.2 | 0.6 | 0.6 | 0.3 | 0.2 |
| EPA | 1.7 | 0.9 | 1.9 | 0.9 | 0.3 |
| Project LINK | 1.2 | 0.5 | −0.1 | 0.1 | – |
| Liverpool | 0.6 | 0.2 | 1.0 | – | 0.6 |
| MSG | 0.9 | −0.1 | 3.2 | 0.3 | 0.5 |
| MINIMOD | 1.0 | 0.3 | 1.0 | 0.3 | 0.1 |
| OECD | 1.1 | 0.6 | 0.4 | 0.4 | 0.3 |
| Wharton | 1.4 | 0.3 | −2.1 | 0.2 | −0.1 |
| DRI | 2.1 | 0.4 | 3.2 | 0.7 | 0.3 |

[a]Effect in the second year of increase in government expenditure by 1 percent of GNP.
[b]Positive sign: effective appreciation of the dollar.
SOURCE: Frankel and Rockett (1988, p. 333).

indeed lead to a Pareto improvement. This is the main point of a recent paper by Frankel and Rockett (1988). They assume that while the true model of the world is not known to the policymakers, each one of them believes his model to be the correct one.

Agreement on a coordinated policy package will be reached only if each policymaker believes the package will make his country better off in terms of the macroeconomic targets he pursues. Once policymakers have decided on a coordinated policy package on the basis of their beliefs about the workings of the economy, the effects of these measures can be simulated using the "true" model. Frankel and Rockett repeat this exercise with eight different models; in each round of the simulation exercise another model is the "true" one. The upshot of Frankel and Rockett's study is that in 206 out of 512 possible cases U.S. welfare is reduced by coordination in comparison to the initial, uncoordinated situation; in 289 cases welfare improves. For the remaining OECD countries welfare is improved by coordination in 297 cases; in 198 cases it is reduced.

Frankel and Rockett's results can be illustrated by one of the basic scenarios of international policy coordination: a joint monetary expansion. If politicians believe that by coordinating their expansionary monetary policies they can avoid inflation—because there will be no real depreciation—and raise output, they will engage in the coordination effort. If, however, the true model of the economy is one where monetary expansion—whether coordinated or not—leads to inflation and where employment gains are only small and transitory, the coordination effort will make all participants worse off.

Another reason why international policy coordination may be counterproductive is that it creates adverse incentives for those players that are left out of the coordination game. Kenneth Rogoff (1985) considers the credibility problem of central banks vis-à-vis the private sector. He notes that international policy coordination lowers the incentive for the central bank to prevent inflation. In a system of uncoordinated monetary policies the announcement of the central bank not to yield to private sector pressure to accommodate high nominal wage increases by increasing the money supply is credible because if the central bank were to do so, the country would have to undergo an undesirable real depreciation of its exchange rate. But the same announcement is less credible in a system where monetary policies are coordinated because the threat of a real depreciation is not present. This in turn will fuel inflationary expectations, raise nominal wages, and lead to actual higher inflation if the central bank accommodates the rise in wages.[24]

Rogoff's argument may be illustrated with the help of Table 2, which depicts expectations and actual policy in matrix form to derive implications for the achievement of macroeconomic targets. If monetary policy is not coordinated, inflationary expectations are low

*TABLE 2*

MACROECONOMIC TARGETS UNDER COORDINATED AND COMPETITIVE ECONOMIC POLICIES

| Expectations / Actual Policy Stance | Competitive Regime: Inflationary Expectations Low | Coordinated Regime: Inflationary Expectations High |
|---|---|---|
| Maintaining Price Stability | (1) All targets are achieved | (2) Unemployment |
| Expansionary | (3) Inflation | (4) Inflation |

[24]According to Rogoff (1985, p. 211), "A regime in which governments conduct monetary policy independently may produce lower time-consistent inflation rates than a regime in which central banks cooperate; intergovernmental cooperation can exacerbate the central banks' credibility problems vis-à-vis the private sector."

because the central bank is expected to avoid a depreciation of the currency. The probability of inflation rises in a coordinated regime; therefore inflationary expectations are high and higher wages are set. Rogoff demonstrates that in a coordinated regime the probability of missing one's macroeconomic targets rises. If in a coordinated regime the central bank pursues—contrary to expectations—a stable monetary policy, there is an unexpected rise in real wages leading to unemployment (case 2).[25] If, on the other hand, expectations of a loose monetary policy are fulfilled and the central bank does indeed accommodate the steep wage increases, inflation will result (case 4). Only in case 1 are both targets, price level stability and full employment, actually met. In this case inflationary expectations are low and the central bank does not attempt to become more expansionary. This optimal case prevails under a regime of uncoordinated monetary policies.

While the previous arguments against policy coordination have pointed out that well-intentioned attempts to raise national welfare via international policy coordination may have unintended negative implications for the countries involved, other critics of international policy coordination question the assumption that politicians do in fact aim at raising the welfare of their citizens. Instead they assume that international policy coordination increases the opportunities of politicians to further their own aims at the expense of their citizens. By removing the checks and balances of international currency competition (in the form of an unwanted currency depreciation), international policy coordination allows politicians to form a cartel and collude against citizens by raising their price (inflation rate) and lowering their output (real balances) (Vaubel 1980, 1983, 1985).

## Coordination under Fixed and Flexible Exchange Rates

The world financial system can be characterized as an arrangement of managed floating between the three big blocks: the United States, Japan, and Europe. At the same time, the European Monetary System (EMS), effective since 1979, is a regime of fixed but adjustable rates. What is the experience with these two regimes with respect to international policy coordination?

[25]Case 2, however, is unlikely to occur.

*Coordination to Avoid Undesired Exchange Rate Changes?*

Under fixed exchange rates, economic policies are coordinated by definition.[26] If exchange rates are flexible, countries are relatively independent with respect to monetary and fiscal policy, but there may still be repercussions from policies abroad that affect domestic targets. This is especially the case when policy-induced real exchange rate changes are as large and persistent as they were over the past 15 years. Such changes affect the relative competitive position of the import sector vis-à-vis the export sector of the economy as well as competitiveness among countries. This may lead to temporary or permanent effects on employment. The most important argument with respect to coordination seems to be that movements of real exchange rates immediately affect the inflation rate and can thus cause a violation of an economic target.[27]

An often quoted example in the coordination debate is the competitive revaluation. It is argued that—if inflation rates are to be reduced—monetary policies should be coordinated in order to avoid overly restrictive policies that would affect employment negatively. For example, proponents of coordination usually refer to the dollar revaluation that occurred between 1980 and 1984. Countries in Western Europe followed a rather restrictive policy in order to protect their economies from imported inflation.[28] This example may not be the textbook case of competitive revaluation, but the European complaints about the U.S. policy of high interest rates show that Europeans would have preferred a more moderate policy on the part of the United States. They especially argued again and again that the United States should relax the stance of monetary policy.[29]

[26]This is a special form of coordination, namely the synchronization of monetary policy; all countries have to follow the course pursued by the dominant country. This implies that inflation rates more or less have to converge. The proposal of target zones is similar to such a regime; exchange rates would be more or less fixed. However, target zones—although propagated by proponents of coordination—would run counter to the idea of coordination, if, as in the present discussion, it is suggested that monetary policies should be differentiated among countries. For a critical analysis of target zones, see Scheide (1986).

[27]The experience over the past 15 years shows that this can indeed be a substantial problem; the real exchange rates among, for example, the U.S. dollar, the Deutsche mark, and the Japanese yen have changed by 50 percent or more within a short period of time.

[28]Whether the revaluation of the dollar had a negative impact on employment is difficult to judge. If negative impulses resulted from tighter monetary policies, there were expansionary impulses for export industries.

[29]Ironically, the same countries later complained that monetary policy was too loose. In 1986, they tried to prevent a sharp fall of the dollar by following the expansionary course in the United States (especially in Japan and West Germany).

Another example, which is usually quoted to propagate coordination, is the "French experiment" of 1981–82. The French government tried to fight unemployment by expansionary monetary and fiscal policy.[30] However, this strategy had to be given up very soon because of the pressure on the French franc, which had to be devalued several times within the EMS. Proponents of coordination now argue that it would not have been necessary to give up this policy—which they obviously would support—if other countries had only followed a similar policy (cf. scenario 1).

Why did the franc have to be devalued? If market participants had viewed the experiment as sound policy, the franc would have surely remained strong, but agents obviously expected more inflation. If coordination really had implied an expansionary course elsewhere, proponents of coordination often ignore that such a strategy would have also led to more inflation. In the case of the unilateral move of France, the inflationary dangers only became obvious faster. In the case of coordination, inflation would have gone up too, even in France: first, because of higher monetary expansion in this country, and second, because of the higher increase of import prices.[31]

*The EMS: An Example of Successful Coordination?*

The EMS is usually viewed as an example of successful coordination. There was much skepticism in the beginning, but more recently the judgment has become generally positive.[32] In particular, the proponents point to the substantial reduction of inflation rates in the member countries.[33]

Table 3 shows that inflation rates within the EMS went down substantially. Between 1979 and 1986 the average inflation rate declined by some 6 percentage points, and inflation has been very low recently, which is also due to the decline in oil prices, a common factor for all regions. However, these figures by themselves are not indicative; they have to be compared to those of countries within an uncoordinated system of (flexible) exchange rates. In fact, practically all countries have succeeded in bringing down their inflation rates. The decline was even larger for the average of OECD countries

[30]Cf. the critical assessment in Trapp (1982).

[31]In the case of no coordination, there will be a devaluation with constant foreign prices. In the case of coordination, the exchange rate is unchanged, but import prices go up because monetary expansion abroad increases and leads to an upward movement of prices on all markets.

[32]Stanley Fischer (1987) calls the EMS "surprisingly successful."

[33]The European Community Commission (1986) mentions not only the reduction but also the convergence of inflation rates.

*TABLE 3*

INFLATION RATES IN OECD COUNTRIES[a]

| Year | EMS Countries | Total OECD | OECD Europe | OECD without EMS Countries | OECD Europe without EMS Countries |
|---|---|---|---|---|---|
| 1979 | 8.5 | 9.8 | 10.6 | 10.1 | 14.3 |
| 1980 | 11.7 | 12.9 | 14.3 | 13.2 | 18.5 |
| 1981 | 11.5 | 10.5 | 12.2 | 10.3 | 13.2 |
| 1982 | 10.4 | 7.8 | 10.5 | 7.1 | 10.7 |
| 1983 | 8.5 | 5.2 | 8.2 | 4.3 | 7.7 |
| 1984 | 6.6 | 5.2 | 7.4 | 4.7 | 8.6 |
| 1985 | 5.5 | 4.5 | 6.5 | 4.2 | 7.9 |
| 1986 | 2.7 | 2.6 | 4.0 | 2.6 | 5.9 |
| Percentage-point change between 1979 and 1986: | | | | | |
| | −5.8 | −7.2 | −6.6 | −7.5 | −8.4 |
| Percentage-point change between 1979–80 and 1985–86: | | | | | |
| | −6.0 | −7.8 | −7.2 | −8.3 | −9.5 |

[a]Percentage change of consumer prices over previous year (weights according to OECD).
SOURCE: OECD (1987a, 1987b); own calculations.

outside the EMS; and in 1986 the rate there was as low as in EMS countries, while it was higher when the EMS was established. It is true that the inflation rates in non-EMS European countries are relatively high, but these countries have also been successful and show the largest decline in inflation among the regions mentioned.[34]

These facts should not in any way understate the success of stabilization efforts among EMS countries. It is remarkable that such large progress has been made by countries like Italy and France, which had "traditionally" experienced high inflation.[35] There is even the possibility that the EMS contributed to this success in the sense that it enabled Italy and France to follow a course that otherwise might not have been possible due to political resistance within these countries.[36] But when compared to other regions, the same—or even a larger—reduction was achieved in an uncoordinated system. More-

[34]Paul De Grauwe (1985) arrives at a similar result.

[35]Italy's rate in 1980 was higher than 20 percent, and in France inflation was some 13 percent.

[36]This is the interpretation of Eggerstedt and Sinn (1987). See also Fratianni's paper in the present volume.

over, several countries with traditionally high inflation rates, such as the United Kingdom and Portugal, have been as successful as Italy and France. And it also has to be taken into account that countries such as West Germany, which have always been more stability-oriented, probably needed a longer time to bring down their inflation to acceptable levels.

Therefore one cannot accept the argument that the inflation record of EMS–countries demonstrates how successful international coordination can be. The EMS owes its success to a large extent to the general desire of all countries in the early 1980s to bring inflation down. It is by no means clear whether the EMS will work in the future. If some countries once again resort to loose monetary policies in order to fight unemployment, realignments could be avoided only if West Germany acted in the same way. Certainly current international demands that West Germany should reflate the economy suggest that new conflicts may emerge.[37]

## International Coordination: Only a New Version of the Old Locomotive Theory?

Practically all proponents of coordination use a Keynesian model. This is true for empirical studies (for example, Oudiz and Sachs 1984) as well as for numerous publications on a less technical level such as those of the European Community Commission or the OECD. Typically, four arguments are used.

First, it is argued that high unemployment results from a lack of demand. Economic policies have not been expansionary enough in recent years but have had a deflationary bias. Now the time has come, the argument goes, to give up overly restrictive policies.[38] A typical Keynesian element is the use of "output gaps" in those models. Not only is there much controversy about whether such concepts make sense at all, but the order of magnitude calculated for these gaps is far beyond what other institutions estimate. For example, in his baseline scenario, Oudiz (1985) estimates an output gap for West Germany of some 6 percent for 1986. On the other hand, the estimate of the Sachverständigenrat (1986, p. 65) for potential GNP implies

[37]The attitude of some countries is occasionally ambiguous. On the one hand they expect an advantage by following the stability-oriented course of the West German authorities; on the other hand they complain about their policy stance. Apparently they would prefer stable exchange rates but a higher rate of inflation.

[38]The OECD (1987a, p. xi) argues with respect to West Germany and other countries: "Fiscal prudence over recent years has created scope for a larger budgetary contribution to domestic demand."

that the rate of capacity utilization in 1986 was roughly equal to the long-run average of the period 1963–85.

Second, it is generally taken for granted that policymakers can successfully use monetary and fiscal policy to manipulate output, employment, and the current account in the desired way.[39] This assertion totally relies on the assumption that economic policy can indeed be effective (the Lucas critique obviously has not reached those models yet). After the experience of the last 15 years it is dubious whether money illusion can be persistently exploited as suggested by the models. Further, doubts have been raised—not only by the revival of the "Ricardian equivalence"—about whether fiscal policy can really have the effects on employment, interest rates, and exchange rates that the models imply.[40]

Third, the optimism with respect to the manipulation of real variables certainly has to do with the time horizon of the models; they usually refer to the short run only. A Phillips-curve model is used to estimate the real effects of changes in monetary policy. Similarly, with respect to exchange rates, proponents concentrate on the short-run effects of exchange rate changes. However, there the analysis should go beyond the initial effect of overshooting; what happens afterwards? When monetary expansion decelerates, the rate of inflation will fall rather quickly. But this "success" is not permanent. The idea of overshooting implies that after some time the currency will have to be *devalued*. During the adjustment period prices will rise faster than before.

This third argument has important consequences for the desirability of international coordination: If only short-run exchange rate changes are included in the utility function, there is an illusion about the overall effects of a change in monetary policy. Therefore the time horizon for evaluating economic policies is not appropriate. Even proponents of coordination are skeptical and admit that the short-run effects may not always persist.[41] They also concede that the short-run and long-run utility functions may well be different and, most

[39]Typical examples are publications of the European Community Commission as well as the OECD arguing that surplus countries should raise and deficit countries should lower domestic demand.

[40]For a discussion about the meaning and effects of deficits, see Brunner (1986).

[41]In "General Discussion" (1984, p. 75) of the paper by Oudiz and Sachs (1984) we find: "Sachs acknowledged that some effects might be modified or conceivably even reversed when looked at beyond the horizon of the model." Nevertheless, "he did not agree that the short-run welfare results would be overturned." With reference to the Bonn summit of 1978, Horne and Masson (1987, pp. 29–30) argue that "the Bonn measures placed insufficient emphasis on the medium-term consequences of fiscal expansion."

important, that the short run seems to fit the policymaker's time horizon better.[42] Such an attitude certainly sanctions stop-and-go policies and reduces economic advisers to the level of what Vaubel (1988, p. 298) refers to as "your obedient servant."

Fourth, the supply side and the role of relative prices are rarely mentioned in the models, which primarily refer to output gaps that have to be closed by expansionary demand policies. If interest rates are considered too high, proponents of coordination conclude that monetary policy has to become expansionary. However, high interest rates may also reflect capital shortage, that is, a real phenomenon that cannot be made to disappear by printing money. As far as unemployment is concerned, the role of wages is rarely mentioned. But if unemployment is due to the fact that real wages are too high or that wages are not sufficiently differentiated, the comparative advantage of monetary policy rests with fighting inflation and not unemployment. Monetary policy should therefore be assigned to the former target.

These four arguments resemble those of the locomotive approach that was propagated in the second half of the 1970s. In fact, proponents even stress that the measures taken at that time can be considered as a good example for today's desired policies.[43] There is one important difference, however, in that the recent debate focuses more on game-theoretic arguments, and this focus indicates that some progress in understanding has been achieved. Earlier studies stressed that a coordination package would be beneficial for the group of industrial countries as a whole, but game-theoretic arguments demonstrate that each country would be better off with respect to its own targets if it participates in coordination. Thus, the new approach no longer relies on altruistic behavior of some countries.[44]

In the 1970s, too, proponents of coordinated expansion (for example, Solomon 1978) argued that inflationary dangers did not exist. In their view, the underutilization of capacities was substantial since unemployment was very high compared to the early 1970s. But after the recommended policies were pursued, inflation accelerated. Nevertheless, proponents of coordination still hold today that the locomotive experiment was a success, which obviously implies that

[42]See "General Discussion" (1984, p. 75), where it was noted that "Oudiz observed that what arguments were appropriate in the objective function depended on the time period of the analysis. It was possible to conceive of a long-run analysis and objective function. But this lay beyond the scope of present quantitative models and, possibly, beyond the interest of the policymakers."

[43]See, for example, Cooper (1987, p. 184) and Bean (1985).

[44]See Oudiz and Sachs (1984, pp. 3–4) and Oudiz (1988).

they must have a different explanation for the behavior of inflation—for example, one based on cost-push factors. The fact is, however, that inflation started to accelerate well before oil prices were raised. This acceleration can be explained by the global stance of monetary policy that had become expansionary already in the course of 1977. The oil price hike led to a further increase but was not the prime cause of inflation.[45]

## Is Policy Coordination on an International Level Likely to be Successful?

Present economic problems of industrial countries can hardly be explained by a lack of opportunities to coordinate. After all, international organizations have been established exactly for this purpose, and governments and central banks meet regularly in order to inform each other about policy intentions. Did the governments not take advantage of these opportunities, or was coordination simply "bad"?

As far as the economic summits are concerned, the statements and commitments have in general been empty.[46] This result is only to be expected: Summiteers have every reason to promise very little since their annual meetings make it very easy to "punish" those among them that do not keep their part of the bargain. While certain characteristics of the summits—the small number of participants and the annual repetition of the bargaining game—ensure that those bargains that are struck are also kept by all parties,[47] this very fact militates against detailed and far-reaching agreements. Another reason why summiteers do not promise much is that they know that it would be difficult to carry out the measures "at home."

The lack of precise commitments may also be due to the fact that there are substantial differences between countries with respect to their targets and priorities. This is quite normal, and the flexibility of exchange rates has the important function of allowing countries to pursue different policies that reflect different targets. Although international coordination does not require that all countries have the same priorities and follow the same strategy, it does call for perma-

[45]Inflation first started to go up in the United States where monetary policy had become expansionary very early. Already in the course of 1978, that is, *before* the increase of oil prices, inflation accelerated to some 10 percent from 6.5 percent and 5.5 percent in the previous years. Other countries followed a little later.

[46]The Bonn summit of 1978 may be called an exception. Putnam and Bayne (1984) argue that this lack of precise commitments may have to do with the fact that events of general political relevance also played a role in the conferences.

[47]Put differently, the prisoners' dilemma situation is overcome. See Putnam and Bayne (1984).

nent negotiations about policy measures. While the equilibrium of noncoordination (the Nash-equilibrium) is stable, improving on the Nash-equilibrium requires permanent discussions and negotiations about policy measures. Such bargaining about the correct course of policy leads to uncertainty on the markets. There are numerous examples of public statements by various policymakers on the "correct" level of the foreign currency value of the U.S. dollar or the policy measures to be taken by other countries, which were certainly confusing the market.

One may question whether the bargaining process can in fact find the efficient solution calculated by diligent economic advisers. If we accept for a moment the claim that international policy coordination gives rise to net gains for each country, the bargaining process has to distribute these net gains among the participants. It seems likely that the dispute over a "fair" distribution of gains interferes with the smooth fine-tuning that is required when managing the world economy—a fact that even proponents of policy coordination admit (see, for example, Cooper 1987, p. 188).

Coordination can work and be carried out successfully over a long period of time only if precommitments are credible. Such commitments have to be reliable just like those given on a national level. However, the experience with domestic policies in this respect is not very encouraging. As far as fiscal policy is concerned, in many cases the promises concerning future spending cuts or reduction of deficits were not kept. And monetary targets were missed again and again in many countries (see, for example, OECD 1987a, pp. 15–16).

Present attitudes toward international agreements do not make cooperation a likely prospect for the future. This fact is one of the reasons why the Louvre Accord of February 1987 failed. More generally, the U.S. central bank no longer appears to take monetary targeting seriously. It may be true that the various aggregates have undergone severe changes and that monetary targeting has become more difficult. But the new mode of policy is certainly also due to the fact that the Federal Reserve authorities no longer appear to believe that monetary targeting makes much sense. How else can it be explained that they urge other countries to follow suit and completely neglect targets?[48] Even if one agreed that international coordination was desirable, it would be quite unlikely that successful moves could be expected on the basis of present controversies.[49]

[48]For example, the Deutsche Bundesbank is criticized not because it has not hit the monetary target but because it is trying to return to the target path.

[49]At a recent conference at the Kiel Institute, proponents of coordination argued that

## Can the Targets of Economic Policy Also Be Achieved without Coordination?

It seems that the arguments of proponents of international coordination are not valid or miss the point:

- The assumptions of the game-theoretic approach with respect to the behavior and the knowledge of policymakers are unrealistic.
- The selection of targets and instruments does not make much sense, especially as far as international targets—exchange rates and current account balances—are concerned.
- The focus is almost exclusively on the short run, therefore important long-run effects of policy measures—especially concerning inflation—are not taken into account.
- The relevance of relative prices for growth, employment, and the allocation of resources is neglected.
- There are hardly any success stories of coordination.

Policy mistakes are likely because of the choice of the time horizon or the wrong assignment of targets and instruments. Mistakes can be avoided if all countries accept a concept of economic policy that is oriented at the medium run.[50] This strategy includes a steady monetary policy to achieve price-level stability. Also, fiscal policy should avoid discretionary interventions and follow a preannounced path. Such rules or precommitments are desirable because they make policies predictable for all economic agents by creating stable expectations.[51] Given such a course of monetary and fiscal policy, the responsibility for employment rests with employers and unions.

---

governments had regained a lot of credibility in recent years because they succeeded in bringing down inflation. Since then, however, unemployment has become the most pressing problem, and governments should now use their accumulated credibility and increase the money supply one more time—and certainly, for the last time—to reduce unemployment. Proponents argue that credibility per se is of no use if it is not exploited for something. This may not be the state of the present debate about coordination, but obviously these economists were serious about their proposal.

[50]For this concept, see, for example, Gebert and Scheide (1980) and Vaubel (1983). A medium-run policy is designed to lead to steady growth without inflation—a target shared by all countries participating in the economic summits.

[51]In other words, the government should not interfere with the stabilization efforts of economic agents. If agents make mistakes, they will learn quickly—because they will feel the consequences—and can decide about the adjustments. This concept also implies that the government should refrain from intervention if there are real shocks, which would only obscure the problem and make an adjustment more difficult. For example, referring to the oil price increase, Hayek (1980) wrote: "As the price of gasoline goes up, either you have to buy less gasoline or buy less of everything else. If you look to the government for help for the time being, it makes you not see what your real problem is."

In this strategy, policy instruments are assigned in such a way as to ensure that each one has a comparative advantage over the others in achieving its designated target. Since this assignment is unambiguous, there is no need for international coordination. It is also specific with respect to responsibilities and incentives. For example, it would be of no use if the Deutsche Bundesbank were made responsible for unemployment in other countries. Such an assignment would not only be wrong with respect to the comparative advantage of policy instruments, it would also create a problem of "moral hazard." If members of one country could always hold a foreign country responsible for not having contributed to the domestic target, the incentive to change their own behavior would be small.

If pursued by all countries, this strategy would reduce the unpredictability and volatility of policies and make exchange rates more stable. But exchange rates would still have to be flexible enough to adjust to various circumstances—for example, if countries choose different paths to achieve their targets. There is a role for international coordination if it takes the form of a mutual exchange of information on the course of preannounced domestic policies and if it strengthens policymakers in their resolve to avoid strategies of open conflict such as the erection of trade barriers.

Taking such a rules-based approach to coordination differs significantly from the predominant negotiations approach. The former approach places responsibility on national governments to maintain sound monetary and fiscal policies; the latter approach shifts responsibility from domestic policymakers to international fora. The failure of the negotiations approach points to the need for a policy regime where governments and central banks precommit themselves to specific rules for policy. International competition among economic policies can benefit all countries because authorities can learn from their own mistakes and from good or bad examples of other countries.

## References

Bacharach, Michael. *Economics and the Theory of Games.* Boulder, Colo.: Westview Press, 1977.

Barro, Robert J., and Gordon, David B. "A Positive Theory of Monetary Policy in a Natural Rate Model." *Journal of Political Economy* 91 (August 1983): 589–610.

Bean, Charles R. "Macroeconomic Policy Coordination: Theory and Evidence." *Recherches Economiques de Louvain* 51 (1985): 267–83.

Brunner, Karl. "Deficits, Interest Rates, and Monetary Policy." *Cato Journal* 5 (Winter 1986): 709–26.

Canzoneri, Matthew B., and Gray, Jo Anna. "Monetary Policy Games and the Consequences of Non-Cooperative Behavior." *International Economic Review* 26 (1985): 547–64.

Canzoneri, Matthew B., and Minford, Patrick. "When International Policy Coordination Matters: An Empirical Analysis." Centre for Economic Policy Research, Discussion Paper Series, no. 119, London, 1986.

Cooper, Richard N. "Economic Interdependence and Coordination of Economic Policies." In *Handbook of International Economics,* vol. 2, pp. 1195–1234. Edited by Ronald W. Jones and Peter B. Kenen. Amsterdam: North-Holland, 1985a.

Cooper, Richard N. "Panel Discussion: The Prospects for International Economic Policy Coordination." In *International Economic Policy Coordination,* pp. 366–72. Edited by Willem H. Buiter and Richard C. Marston. Cambridge: MIT Press, 1985b.

Cooper, Richard N. "International Economic Cooperation: Overview and a Glimpse of the Future." In *Interdependence and Cooperation in the World of Tomorrow,* pp. 180–94. A Symposium Marking the Twenty-Fifth Anniversary of the OECD. Paris: OECD, 1987.

Corden, Max W. "The Logic of the International Monetary Non-System." In *Reflections on a Troubled World Economy. Essays in Honour of Herbert Giersch,* pp. 59–74. Edited by Fritz Machlup, Gerhard Fels, and Hubertus Müller-Greling. London: Macmillan, for the Trade Policy Research Centre, 1983.

De Grauwe, Paul. "Should the U.K. Join the European Monetary System?" In House of Commons, Treasury and Civil Service Committee, *The Financial and Economic Consequences of U.K. Membership of the European Communities. Memoranda on the European Monetary System,* pp. 5–11. London, 1985.

Demsetz, Harold. "Information and Efficiency: Another Viewpoint." *Journal of Law and Economics* 12 (April 1969): 1–22.

Drèze, Jacques; Wyplosz, Charles; Bean, Charles R.; Giavazzi, Francesco; and Giersch, Herbert. "The Two-Handed Growth Strategy for Europe: Autonomy through Flexible Cooperation." Brussels: Centre for European Policy Studies, 1987.

Eggerstedt, Harald, and Sinn, Stefan. "The EMS, 1979–1986: The Economics of Muddling Through." *Geld und Währung* 3 (1987): 5–23.

European Community Commission. *Annual Report, 1986–87.* Brussels, November 1986.

Fischer, Stanley. "International Macroeconomic Policy Coordination." NBER Working Paper, no. 2244, Cambridge, Mass., 1987.

Frankel, Jeffrey A., and Rockett, Katharine. "International Macroeconomic Policy Coordination When Policymakers Do Not Agree on the True Model." *American Economic Review* 78 (June 1988): 318–40.

Frenkel, Jacob. "The Collapse of Purchasing Parities During the 1970s." *European Economic Review* 16 (1981): 145–95.

Frenkel, Jacob. "The International Monetary System: Should It Be Reformed?" *American Economic Review* 77 (May 1987): 205–10.

Friedman, Milton. "Post-War Trends in Monetary Theory and Policy." *National Banking Review* 2 (1964): 1–9.

Gale, David. "The Trade Imbalance Story." *Journal of International Economics* 4 (1974): 119–37.

Gebert, Dietmar, and Scheide, Joachim. *Die Lokomotiven-Strategie als wirtschaftspolitisches Konzept*. Kiel, 1980.

"General Discussion" of the Paper by Oudiz and Sachs (1984). *Brookings Papers on Economic Activity*, no. 1 (1984): 74–75.

Hayek, Friedrich A. "Gradualism Unacceptable. Stop Inflation Quickly." *International Herald Tribune*, Paris, 2 February 1980, p. 7.

Horne, Jocelyn P., and Masson, Paul R. "International Economic Cooperation and Policy Coordination." *Finance and Development* 24 (June 1987): 27–31.

Institute for International Economics. *Promoting World Recovery*. Washington, D.C.: December 1982.

Martinez-Oliva, Juan Carlos. "Policy Makers' 'Revealed Preferences' and Macroeconomic Policy Coordination: An Appraisal." Kiel Advanced Studies Working Papers No. 84, February 1987.

Martinez Oliva, Juan Carlos, and Sinn, Stefan. "The Game-Theoretic Approach to International Policy Coordination: Assessing the Role of Targets." *Weltwirtschaftliches Archiv* 124 (1988): 252–68.

Modigliani, Franco. "The Monetarist Controversy or, Should We Forsake Stabilization Policies?" *American Economic Review* 67 (May 1977): 1–19.

Mulford, David C. "Economic Policy Coordination and LDC Debt Problems." Statement before the Subcommittee on Domestic Monetary Policy and the Subcommittee on International Finance, Trade, and Monetary Policy, Washington, D.C., 5 November 1987. In Deutsche Bundesbank, *Auszüge aus Presseartikeln*, no. 83, 17 November 1987, pp. 9–10.

Organisation for Economic Cooperation and Development (OECD). *Economic Outlook*. Paris, June 1987a.

Organisation for Economic Cooperation and Development (OECD). *Main Economic Indicators*. Paris, July 1987b.

Oudiz, Gilles. "European Policy Coordination: An Evaluation." Centre for Economic Policy Research, Discussion Paper Series, no. 81, London, 1985.

Oudiz, Gilles. "Macroeconomic Policy Coordination: Where Should We Stand?" In *Macro and Micro Policies for More Growth and Employment*, pp. 278–91. Edited by Herbert Giersch. Tübingen: J.C.B. Mohr/Paul Siebeck, 1988.

Oudiz, Gilles and Sachs, Jeffrey. "Macroeconomic Policy Coordination among the Industrial Economies." *Brookings Papers on Economic Activity*, no. 1 (1984): 1–64.

Putnam, Robert D., and Bayne, Nicholas. *Hanging Together: The Seven Power Summits*. Cambridge, Mass.: Harvard University Press, 1984.

Rogoff, Kenneth. "Can International Monetary Policy Cooperation Be Counterproductive?" *Journal of International Economics* 18 (1985): 199–217.

Sachverständigenrat zur Begutachtung der Gesamtwirtschaftlichen Entwicklung. Jahresgutachten 1986–87. Bundestagsdrucksache 10/6562, Bonn, 25 November 1987.

Samuelson, Paul A. *Economics*. 9th ed. New York: McGraw-Hill, 1972.

Scheide, Joachim. "Mehr Stabilität durch Wechselkurszielzonen?" *Die Weltwirtschaft*, no. 1 (Summer 1986): 38–46.

Scheide, Joachim, and Sinn, Stefan." Internationale Koordination der Wirtschaftspolitik: Pro und Contra." Kiel Discussion Paper No. 135, November 1987.
Schmidt, Helmut. "The World Economy at Stake." *The Economist*, 26 February 1983, pp. 21–32.
Solomon, Robert. "The Locomotive Approach." Paper presented at the American Enterprise Institute seminar on the Locomotive Theory, Washington, D.C., 13 April 1978. (Available from the author at the Brookings Institution.)
Stein, Herbert. "Best Selling Fiction: 3 Million Lost Jobs." *Wall Street Journal*, European Edition, Brussels, 31 July 1985.
Trapp, Peter. "Frankreich: Ausbruch aus der Rezession gescheitert." *Die Weltwirtschaft*, no. 1 (Summer 1982): 48–63.
Vaubel, Roland. *Internationale Absprachen oder Wettbewerb in der Konjunkturpolitik?* Walter Eucken Institut, Vorträge und Aufsätze, 77, Tübingen, 1980.
Vaubel, Roland. "Coordination or Competition among National Macroeconomic Policies?" In *Reflections on a Troubled World Economy. Essays in Honour of Herbert Giersch*, pp. 3–28. Edited by Fritz Machlup, Gerhard Fels, and Hubertus Müller-Groeling. London: Macmillan, for the Trade Policy Research Centre, 1983.
Vaubel, Roland. "International Collusion or Competition for Macroeconomic Policy Coordination? A Restatement." *Recherches Economiques de Louvain* 51 (1985): 223–40.
Vaubel, Roland. "Comment" on Gilles Oudiz, "Macroeconomic Policy Coordination: Where Should We Stand?" In *Macro and Micro Policies for More Growth and Employment*, pp. 296–300. Edited by Herbert Giersch. Tübingen: J.C.B. Mohr (Paul Siebeck), 1988.

# 18

# Economic Policy for a Stable World Order*

*Jan Tumlir*

## Erosion of the World Market Order

From an institutional perspective, an international economic order consists of little more than two sets of arrangements—or better, commitments exchanged among governments—concerning the national conduct of monetary and trade policies. These two national economic policies have direct and obvious repercussions abroad. They are also the two policies that governments will find it most difficult to pursue in the interest of their societies at large; since governments will be continuously pressed and tempted to act on behalf of organized special interest groups. The monetary commitments and rules focus on maintaining currency convertibility, while trade policy rules typically aim at ensuring stability of trading conditions. Their main task is to limit protection to tariffs that can be bound against unilateral (unnegotiated) increases. The two sets of policy rules must be carefully dovetailed, because over a broad range of situations restrictions on payments and on trade are close substitutes.

When rules of this kind are in force and observed in at least several of the large economies—so that currency convertibility coexists with

---

*Reprinted from *Cato Journal* 4 (Spring/Summer 1984): 355–64, with minor revisions by the editors.

The author was Director of Economic Research and Analysis at the GATT Secretariat in Geneva from 1967 until his retirement in February 1985. Tumlir was a pioneer in the field of constitutional economics, and his death in June 1985 was a great loss to his friends and colleagues. In a memorial volume, Heinz Hauser (1986, p. 8) rightly described Tumlir as "a man of science and policy who repeatedly stressed the great importance of good domestic economic order as a precondition for a viable international economic order at a time when 'Ordnungspolitik,' or constitutional economics, was not yet a fashionable topic within the economic profession."

This paper is based on the author's banquet address given at the Cato Institute's Second Annual Monetary Conference in Washington, D.C., January 20, 1984. Tumlir prepared the paper while he was a Visiting Professor of Economics at UCLA. The views expressed herein are those of the author and should not be attributed to the GATT Secretariat.

price level stability in these economies, and exporters in all countries have equal and stable access to at least these few large national markets—an efficient world market (an international price system) can be said to exist. The relative prices formed in this market will promptly transmit information about incipient scarcities and surpluses anywhere in the world economy. This information is indispensable for timely adjustments in the structure of national economies. The world price system thus allows major economic changes to be anticipated in all societies. The future does not have to arrive in the form of surprises and upheavals.

It is the erosion of this world market order, in its most fundamental functions, that I want to emphasize. The difficulties experienced on the monetary side of it—inflation and highly variable interest and exchange rates—deserve close examination. Clearly, the origin of the debt problem lies in this nexus of inflation, interest, and exchange rates. The story can be told in different ways depending on the predilections of the teller. I personally side with those who emphasize the recent history of the dollar exchange rate. But the picture is incomplete without bringing trade into it, the "real" side, as economists call it, of the world economy.

It is not a reproach to my colleagues specializing in monetary analysis to note that the theorizing about inflation, interest, and exchange rates proceeds, and cannot but proceed, on the assumption of a reasonably competitive world economy in which disturbance and uncertainty arise mainly from monetary policy. If such a competitive system did exist, I am convinced that real exchange rates would be, not perhaps perfectly stable, but certainly much more so than they have been in the last decade. To explain their observed instability, we have to take into account the systemic impairments on the real side of the economy—the great *recent* deviation of reality from our competitive model.

## What Remains of the Price System?

It is trade that connects the national price systems into an international one. The most important information processed by the national price systems is about developments abroad. When, therefore, I talk about protection and the growing inhibition of trade, I am only secondarily concerned with the direct contribution of trade to GNP (for example, the employment effect of exports, specialization, productivity, etc.). Primarily I have in mind the essential role of trade in creating and maintaining an international price system. For that reason, too, I find it difficult to work up much interest in tariffs, which both history and theory show to be quite innocuous protective devices, at least when stabilized. Once in place, they do not interfere with changes in relative prices. My main concern is with quantitative restrictions, which have the effect of paralyzing the price system in their area of application.

Most of you are aware of, and I dare say worried about, the recent growth of protectionism. But I dare say, too, that most of you still consider protection to be more of an exception than the rule. To be sure, it is very difficult to come up with any reliable quantitative indications in this area.[1] Nonetheless, there exist several independent estimates of the proportion of world trade that encounters obstacles of a more severe kind than just tariffs. François David (1983, p. 225), a senior official of the French Ministry of Trade, estimates that between 55 and 60 percent of world trade is subject to nontariff restrictions. Sheila A. B. Page (1981, p. 29), of the National Institute for Economic and Social Research in London, has come up with a figure of 48 percent. My own research indicates between 40 and 45 percent of total trade, and between 20 and 25 percent of world trade in manufactured products, to be similarly restrained in 1982.

Trying to estimate the extent of protection leads to endless disputes, methodological as well as political. We can avoid them by pointing out that, in the present context, we are interested not in protection as such, but in the degree to which it impairs the price system, that is, the degree to which it reduces the amount and value of the information that the international price system is allowed to transmit. In this respect, it can be shown that the above estimates substantially *underestimate* the damage. First, all of the above estimates of protection disregard subsidies. Subsidization, however, has become in the last decade another major cause of distortion in international prices. Second, it is seldom that all trade in a particular product will be controlled by quantitative restrictions. But even if only the trade flows from the lowest-cost sources are so controlled, the rest of international trade in that product, which is not included in the estimates (and which may be by far the larger part of interna-

[1]The main obstacle is posed by the unavoidable task of averaging. There is a large number of protective devices in use, secret bilateral agreements being increasingly preferred. But even if we had information on all the restrictive devices in use, for a meaningful average we would also have to know their *degree of restrictiveness*. Thus in averaging, each item in the array of devices would have to be weighted by the amount of imports *it keeps out*, an unobtainable measure. Furthermore, indicating the extent of protection by the proportion of world trade under restrictions more severe than tariffs is a misleading measure because when world trade grows and the restrictions measured are indeed restrictive, the proportion of trade under them will be declining from year to year.

tional exchanges in that product category), will be transacted at distorted prices.

If the magnitude of the estimates of nontariff restrictions seems fantastic to you—and I would not be surprised by that reaction—try a mental experiment. Try to enumerate all the industries in which pricing is determined or at least strongly influenced by deliberate policy rather than by the market. The list would begin with crude oil, the price of which is the main determinant of all energy prices. It would include almost all of the temperate zone's agricultural products, and those products of tropical agriculture that are subject to commodity agreements. It would include textiles and clothing, an industry that is fiercely competitive in every nation but in which prices in the industrial countries are effectively shielded from the competition of low-cost producers in developing countries. And it would include iron and steel, an industry that is highly concentrated on national levels and, for the time being, also effectively cartelized internationally. In automobiles, Western industries are securely protected by quantitative restrictions against the world's most efficient producer, Japan. Large segments of the petrochemical industry are cartelized, and quantitative restrictions also proliferate in such minor areas as TV sets and tubes, ball bearings, batteries, and computer hardware. In addition, acrimonious negotiations and outright power plays continue as to where the most promising new products are to be manufactured. One is thus justified in asking: What remains of the price system?

When the price system is paralyzed or distorted to this extent, when so many prices are prevented from finding their own proper levels but the exchange rates are free, is it surprising that the latter move erratically? With the price system so extensively impaired, there simply is not enough information to make possible a smooth adjustment of exchange rates to purchasing power parities.

Indeed the difficulty for the economist may now lie in explaining why the world economy still functions at all, however dissatisfied we may be with its functioning. The answer is, of course, that there is a lot of ruin in any economy with a modicum of freedom. I am sometimes unsure whether it is actually an advantage of the capitalist system that it can take such an enormous amount of beating. If it were in the habit of collapsing more frequently, we would perhaps govern ourselves more prudently (and more cheaply to boot). But that is neither here nor there. We want to see how the guardians of the system, the governments of the large countries, react to its deepening crisis.

## Pitfalls of the Negotiations Approach to Trade Liberalization

Important statesmen are issuing calls for a "new Bretton Woods" conference and for a new round of multilateral trade negotiations, which suggests that they are aware of the existence of a crisis. Do they really imagine that it can be resolved by a negotiated agreement, some 90 to 120 governments achieving unanimity in some vast conference room in New York or Geneva on what has been wrong with the world? Perceptions of national interest now differ so much that the conclusion most likely to be agreed upon would be, in the words of Henry Simons, that "nothing should be done about anything until everything has been done about everything else" (1948, p. 325).

A very small number of large countries accounts for the bulk of international trade and a smaller number still for the bulk of international lending. True, there are benefits from expanding the number of countries willing to abide by agreed policy rules, but these benefits decline at the margin and beyond perhaps 10 or 15 countries they begin to fall off sharply. You get to the very small countries rather quickly. At the same time, the costs of expanding membership rise no less steeply. These costs are counted in terms of the growing difficulty of agreement and the growing vacuousness of the rules, as they are eroded by diplomacy. Universal membership systems invariably tend either toward the lowest common denominator in matters of principles and rules or to an untenable arrangement between groups of countries with different rights and obligations, some having more rights than obligations and conversely for others. In particular, the tendency will be strong to build into universal membership systems mechanisms for international redistribution of income and wealth, and this is certain to interfere with the regular exercise of rights and the performance of duties required by a stable international order.

It is therefore difficult to consider these calls for reforming the world by a common effort to be an exercise of international responsibility. I am rather inclined to consider them a flight from responsibility. "Let us call a world reform conference and if it fails, as it most likely will, we shall have demonstrated not only our concern and our will to reform, but also that a real reform is impossible." Take the debt crisis as an example. The creditor countries are hiding behind the International Monetary Fund and are urging the Fund to use its leverage to press the debtor countries to liberalize their imports, or at least to restrain them from imposing further import restrictions. This is not a bad idea in itself, but I fear that the Fund will not be able to support the overload of hopes placed upon it. For what is expected from it is, in short, that it will make good debtors out of bad ones singlehandedly—without the creditors having to change their own policies one bit (except, perhaps, for creating more money through enlarged IMF quotas, as if they did not have enough of an inflation problem).

There is no doubt in my mind that the debtor countries should, for their own good, liberalize their import policy along with other domestic policies. What astonishes me is the political naiveté, and the short-sighted selfishness, of putting this advice in the form of a demand or a condition. To state my thoughts on the issue more precisely, a resolution of the debt problem that is satisfactory to both sides—or at least minimizes the risk of some form of an open crisis—requires some combination of two general policy approaches on the part of the debtor countries: macroeconomic tightening and microeconomic liberalization.

## Policy Requirements

Macroeconomic tightening is required because a credit crisis is, as the word *credit* itself suggests, a crisis of confidence. When the ability to service the debt has been demonstrated, confidence returns and credit becomes available again. How long the demonstration takes—that is, how long the debtor countries have to show a current account surplus or at least go without a deficit—nobody can say at the moment. But we can say with some confidence that the domestic effects of the macroeconomic tightening necessary for the demonstration will depend on the extent of the simultaneous microeconomic liberalization. In particular, the level of unemployment prevailing during the austerity period will be inversely related to the extent of liberalization.

Politically speaking, spontaneous liberalization on the part of the debtor countries is nowhere in sight. This is an unpropitious time to preach unilateral *aperatura* policies to Latin America. They were tried and, despite considerable initial success, ended badly—sunk, so to speak, in the exchange rate waves made by the large countries. But it is too late for sermons for other reasons as well.

When international trade discipline collapses, and almost any industry in any country can obtain additional protection practically for the asking, producing for export becomes singularly unattractive. An instance of getting protection for the asking was the widely publicized cave-in of the Reagan administration before the textile lobby.[2]

[2]See Pine (1983a, 1983b, 1983c, and 1984) for a discussion of changes in U.S. textile policy.

The industry obtained more than it had even dared to hope for, and is now on its way to realizing its old dream: a guaranteed share of the national market. This is just the most recent example—an all too typical Washington confrontation, with all the drama of a resistible force meeting a movable object.

Under these conditions, uncertainty itself becomes a highly effective trade restraint, even in markets that are technically still open. It obviously takes a much greater degree of macroeconomic pressure to push exports in such a situation than under conditions of guaranteed market access. Let us not forget, either, that the private sector is now the minority sector in all the most indebted economies (which goes a long way toward explaining their debt problem), and that the public sector is notorious for its capacity to evade macroeconomic cutbacks. The private sector thus has to bear the brunt of the monetary and financial tightening and, notwithstanding what I have said about its capacity to take a beating, there are limits to everything.

Finally, consider the purely political effects of the contrast between the policies demanded of the debtor and those in force in the creditor countries. Preaching free trade to unresponsive listeners, I am reduced to envy thinking of the vast and impassioned audiences that the Marxist preachers of all kinds of financial conspiracy theories are enjoying in the debtor countries—whose governments are being urged to liberalize while their creditors are increasing protection! Politically this means that the creditor governments are not alone in thinking along mercantilist lines. The debtors think that way too, only more so.

If there is to be a liberalization of import as well as domestic economic policies, to provide the dynamic impulses capable of offsetting the employment effects of the unavoidable austerity, the creditor must meet the debtor countries half way. This would do more than merely help the latter to service their debt because, apart from the outstanding IOUs, the economic-political problem is much the same on both sides. The creditor countries, too, face the necessity of fiscal and monetary restraint—and they, too, are looking for ways to offset the temporary effects of the tightening. Basically they know already that the only way to stabilize their own economies is to allow the market to play a larger role, to restore the international price system, and to shrink the public sector relative to the private sector. Their only problem is how to do it, how to get there.

The governments of all Western democracies know that the conception of economic policy, of the government's role in the economy, that guided them through the 1960s and a good part of the 1970s is dead. Under that conception, unemployment was considered worse than inflation; the government viewed itself as the vanguard of progress, leading the private society into the future; and consumers, businessmen, and financial agents were regarded as a pack of Pavlov's dogs duly salivating and otherwise appropriately reacting to the signals of the scientific policymaker at the center.

Economics as a professional discipline has been recovering from this intellectual blight for some two decades. It is now becoming generally accepted in the profession that the only policies whose consequences an economist can hope to predict are policies generated by relatively permanent and widely understood rules. On what may result from policy improvisation that changes from quarter to quarter, the economist can speak with no more authority than the average chatty drinker in your neighborhood bar.

For governments, abandoning long-held fallacies is difficult even when they have been perceived as such. Governments embody social authority and whatever they do is a precedent, binding or at least influencing their future actions. Involved as they have become in the impossible responsiblity of guiding large, complex and still largely free economies into the future, they can only zigzag. Can one be surprised if, forced to zigzag, they also try to cut corners? As international economic policy conflicts multiply, their settlements are improvised under pressure and often in ways that raise legal doubts. It is no exaggeration to say that the increasingly conflictual nature of international economic relations has begun to erode the integrity of national legal systems.

It is on the background of these developments that the need for a serious trade liberalization may be fully understood. A speedy agreement on trade liberalization can be achieved only among a limited number of countries. Why not among the major creditor and debtor countries who have the most at stake here? The results of their agreement could then be generalized to all other countries by the unconditional most-favored-nation clause, and additional countries could join the negotiation later. A reduction of obstacles to trade and a more rapid expansion of international exchanges, of course, would contribute to financial stabilization. Yet even at this stage these financial effects must be considered only secondary benefits. On the face of it, trade restrictions protect particular industries and interest groups. In the last respect, however, they protect a particular conception of economic policy, of the government's role in the economy, and a particular form of politics, all of which are at variance with constitutional prescriptions.

## The Threat to Democratic Constitutions

We can no longer overlook the threat to democratic constitutions from an excess of government's "responsibility" for the economy of its people. Democracy is, after all, only a political method of accommodating change without a revolution. It must therefore rely mainly on procedural rules and have only a minimum of substantive and discretionary content. When the state comes to be so involved in the processes of society that it becomes the necessary support of the existing economic and social structures, it has become identified with the *status quo*. Then, of course, the basic function of democracy—change without upheaval—has become undischargeable.

## References

David, François. *Le commerce mondial à la dérive*. Paris: Calman-Levy, 1983.

Hauser, Heinz. "Preface." In *Protectionism and Structural Adjustment*, pp. 7–8. Grusch: Verlag Ruegger for the Swiss Institute for Research into International Economic Relations, Economic Structures, and Regional Science, 1986.

Page, Sheila A. B. "The Revival of Protectionism and Its Consequences for Europe." *Journal of Common Market Studies*, September 1981.

Pine, Art. "U.S. Delays Decision on Penalty Duties on Chinese Textile Imports until December 16." *Wall Street Journal*, 7 December 1983a, p. 8.

Pine, Art. "U.S. May Halt Textile Imports of Some Nations." *Wall Street Journal*, 14 December 1983b, p. 2.

Pine, Art. "U.S. Crackdown on Textile Imports Seen as Uneasy Truce with Domestic Producers." *Wall Street Journal*, 19 December 1983c, p. 2.

Pine, Art. "Behind the Scenes: How President Came to Favor Concessions for U.S. Textile Makers." *Wall Street Journal*, 6 January 1984, p. 1.

Simons, Henry C. *Economic Policy for a Free Society*. Chicago: University of Chicago Press, 1948.

# Index

# About the Editors

James A. Dorn received his Ph.D in Economics from the University of Virginia. He is Editor of the *Cato Journal* and Professor of Economics at Towson State University. He is also a Research Fellow of the Institute for Humane Studies at George Mason University and a member of the White House Commission on Presidential Scholars. He is coeditor with Anna J. Schwartz of *The Search for Stable Money* and directs the Cato Institute's annual monetary conferences.

William A. Niskanen received his Ph.D in Economics from the University of Chicago. He is Chairman of the Cato Institute. From 1981 to 1985 he was a member of the Council of Economic Advisers, serving as acting chairman for nine months. Niskanen was the Director of Economics at the Ford Motor Company from 1975 to 1980 and was Assistant Director of the Office of Management and Budget from 1970 to 1972. He has held professorships at the University of California at Berkeley and UCLA. His recent book, *Reaganomics: An Insider's Account of the Policies and the People,* was chosen as one of the ten best books of 1988 by *Business Week.*

MIX
Papier aus verantwortungsvollen Quellen
Paper from responsible sources
FSC® C105338

If you have any concerns about our products,
you can contact us on
**ProductSafety@springernature.com**

In case Publisher is established outside the EU,
the EU authorized representative is:
**Springer Nature Customer Service Center GmbH**
**Europaplatz 3, 69115 Heidelberg, Germany**

Printed by Libri Plureos GmbH
in Hamburg, Germany